EVER WONDERED?

Who are the Metis? How and where did they originate? What are their virtues? How did they serve the fur trade? Why did they become fugitives? Where did they find refuge? What replaced buffalo as their staff of life? How did they live before mechanization? What did Metis mothers use instead of diapers for infant hygiene? What do we know about the genealogy of the Kelly Lake Metis?

Why did a 20-year-old schoolmaster choose the remote Metis Outpost at Kelly Lake? How did he teach the "three R's" to beginners who knew only Cree? What were the alternatives to "a bed teacher" for learning Cree himself? Why did his scholars advance most rapidly in Arithmetic?

Why was liquor smuggled from BC into northern Alberta in the early 1920s? How did White pioneers cope with the Peace River wilderness? Was there hostility or friendship between them and the Metis?

Why did Gerry and his companions take packhorses through the Rockies via Pine Pass in Summer, 1924? How did they find their way without a guide? How did they make bannock on the trail without a mixing bowl? Why is the sound of a horsebell the packer's lullaby? Why were they out of grub when they reached McLeod Lake Post? Why did the Sekani children there think the party were riding "funny moose"? Who perished in Pine Pass six years later?

Why did Gerry return to Kelly Lake for a second year? How did he converse with the blind 110-year-old matriarch who spoke no English? What did she tell him? Why was she buried in his white flannel pyjamas? What were and are Gerry's "Alphabetic Jewels"? What was a token of gratitude for his services as "Doctor"? Why were Kelly Lake children reputed to speak the best English in the region after less than two years' schooling?

Why was their Metis guide on the packtrip to Jasper in 1925 affectionately nicknamed "Neestou"? How could grilled moosehorn be a gourmand's delight? What was Barkerville like when they entered by its backdoor on horseback 60 years ago?

What did Gerry find on his trips to the Peace River country in later years? How did his early experiences there affect a long and colorful life with friendships and other benefits which money could not measure?

****

These and other questions are answered between the covers of this book.

THE FIRST KELLY LAKE SCHOOL (1923) WITH THE 12 ORIGINAL PUPILS

Inside the door, centre, a partition divided the building, with the schoolroom to the right and Jim Young's store with living quarters to the left. A separate entrance to the store was around the far left corner. The small building, far left, was an unheated cache. The flag indicates a southeasterly breeze. Figure 1, opposite page, is the floor-plan. Pupils are identified in Photo 6, page 58.

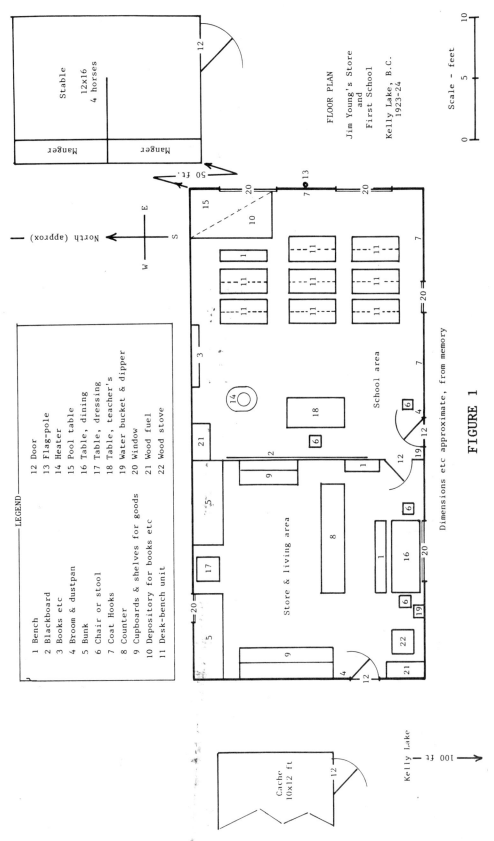

LEGEND

1 Bench	12 Door
2 Blackboard	13 Flag-pole
3 Books etc	14 Heater
4 Broom & dustpan	15 Pool table
5 Bunk	16 Table, dining
6 Chair or stool	17 Table, dressing
7 Coat Hooks	18 Table, teacher's
8 Counter	19 Water bucket & dipper
9 Cupboards & shelves for goods	20 Window
10 Depository for books etc	21 Wood fuel
11 Desk-bench unit	22 Wood stove

Stable
12x16
4 horses

Manger

Manger

FLOOR PLAN
Jim Young's Store
and
First School
Kelly Lake, B.C.
1923-24

Scale - feet
0   5   10

North (approx)

N
W   E
S

50 ft.

School area

Store & living area

Dimensions etc approximate, from memory

FIGURE 1

Cache
10x12 ft

Kelly Lake

100 ft

iii

TO THE PIONEERS

of whatever

Race
Color
Origin
Creed
Skills
or
Estate

1: St Boniface Cathedral 1980. Only its beautiful facade survives the disastrous fire of 1968. Gone are "the turrets twain" whose bells called "To the boatman on the river, To the hunter on the plain", immortalized by Whittier (1859). Established in 1818 by Bishop Joseph-Norbert Provencher, St Boniface was the mother church for the original Red River Metis. My birth and childhood were within ear-shot of its sweet Vespers. (GSA #6841)

METIS OUTPOST

by

Gerry Andrews

Memoirs of the First Schoolmaster
at the Metis Settlement of Kelly Lake, BC
1923-1925

Victoria, British Columbia
CANADA
1985

Canadian Cataloguing in Publication Data

Andrews, G.S. (Gerry), 1903-
    Metis outpost

Includes index.
Bibliography: p.
ISBN 0-9692169-0-4

1. Andrews, Gerald Smedley, 1903-
2. Teachers - British Columbia - Kelly Lake - Biography.
3. Kelly Lake (B.C.) - Biography.
4. Metis - British Columbia - Kelly Lake.*
I. Title.
FC3849.K44Z49 1985   971.1'1   C85-091389-6
F1089.5.K44A52 1985

48,010

Typeset by Effective Information Processing Ltd., Victoria, Canada.
Printing by Amity Press & Screen Printing Inc., Victoria, Canada.
Editorial consultant, John Stuart, Victoria, Canada.
Published by the author.
Marketing by Pencrest Publications, 1011 Fort Street, Victoria,
    BC, V8V 3K5, Canada.

Gratefully acknowledged is a grant from the **British Columbia Heritage Trust** which covered almost one-tenth of production costs.

FOREWORD

In the fall of 1923 young Gerry Andrews travelled to the little community of Kelly Lake to be its first school teacher. When he arrived he discovered that there was no school house, no classroom furniture, no supplies (other than a few things he had brought with him), and that only one of his dozen pupils, all beginners, had even a smattering of English.

It was obvious that the usual rules and routines would have to go out the window, and the narrative that follows reveals the extraordinary patience, intelligence and understanding with which Gerry tackled his problems. Gifted with an unusual ability to offer and attract friendship, the rapport that grew up between his pupils, the community and himself was such that he stayed on at his post for a second year. Nor was this the end; his contacts with the community have continued until the present day. Kelly Lake came to mean a great deal to its first teacher, and I suspect that in retrospect he still regards it as one of the most interesting and rewarding experiences in his long and distinguished career.

It was long the custom to regard local and even regional history as being of relatively little importance. But of late it has been recognized that if the generalizations that properly characterize broader studies are to be valid, they must often be based upon local sources that are frequently the only record of past events, changed conditions and vanished life-styles. The great number of local and regional studies now being published will result eventually in a much better and more perceptive general history of British Columbia, and, indeed, of Western Canada.

Metis Outpost is a prime example of such a source. Only its author could have preserved it for posterity. It is a little jewel in the treasure house of history.

W. Kaye Lamb
Former Dominion Archivist and
National Librarian of Canada

vii

AUTHOR'S PREFACE

Perhaps this should be labelled "Apology", under which heading some early writers placated their readers. This book's conception was innocent and plausible but its gestation may have produced unforeseen monstrosities, like the six formidable appendices, which just "grew like Topsy". They embody laborious research and compilation which serious readers may appreciate. Others may ignore them.

The design, construction and mechanics of a book, like those for a home, should aim at comfort and convenience as well as spiritual enjoyment. Convention may govern but should not dictate. My longtime friend and colleague, Bert Ralfs used to say "Rules are for wise men to observe and for fools to obey". English has been enriched by its piracy of other languages, like the buccaneers of old bringing booty to the Royal coffers (for which they received estates and titles). Must every foreign "mot" be italicized? My orthography is from the Concise Oxford Dictionary with some Canadian and American usage. Mavericks like "teepee" and "pack-horse" must stand on their own merits. My Cree words may be questioned by Kelly Lake friends but I know they will forgive me.

A weakness for detail is offset partly by the habit of brevity from my professional and military background. Abbreviations and some austerity in punctuation do conserve space. I avoid false modesty by referring to myself in the first person.

Footnotes are a necessary evil for non-fiction. They confirm or amplify a statement and reduce the author's onus for it. To minimize annoyance, mine are numbered in one sequence throughout the text, and appear together after the appendices. Each reference is identified by its code, also to save space and verbiage.

An objective review of this book as now structured may raise a few doubts. Some items in Appendix 3 might have been omitted. Most of them contain primary history and many have ingenuous human interest with sparkles of humor. The John Bennett tragedy, while relevant, is not part of my story, so it appears as an appendix. The Epilogue may interest my Peace River friends more than it does others.

Hopefully what has been done will merit the consensus of my readers, who surely will endorse the aim to encompass a good measure of material at modest outlay.

CONTENTS

Photographs are in numbered sequence throughout the text.

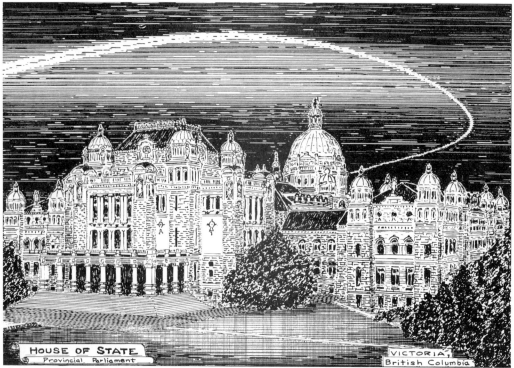

HOUSE OF STATE
Provincial Parliament

VICTORIA,
British Columbia

2: South face, Provincial Parliament Buildings, Victoria, BC. It
was here during the summer of 1923 that J.L. Watson, Registrar of
Teachers, arranged my appointment to the Kelly Lake school. Later,
during my career with the Department of Lands, Forests and Water
Resources, 1930-1968, my offices were located mostly in this beautiful building. When this sketch was done in 1961, vapour trails
from jet aircraft were still a novelty.

3: Fred Haggman, with whom I cut firewood in the summer of 1922.
My apprenticeship was on the other end of the nine-foot saw. Fred
and his wife, Catherine, were like foster parents, whose influence
— physical and spiritual — helped me to meet the challenge, later,
at the Metis outpost, Kelly Lake.

INTRODUCTION

This is my story of two youthful years in the small and remote Metis community at Kelly Lake, British Columbia, some 60 years ago (1923-25), as its first schoolmaster. In addition to experiences and friendships garnered in that vast and rustic region, it includes journals of two packhorse trips through the Rocky Mountain wilderness to the west. Because I write about real people, dates, events and places, due care has been taken to record these as accurately as memory and surviving records permit. Of four lakes officially so named in British Columbia, the Kelly Lake of this story is about 35 miles due south of Dawson Creek, BC, and 25 miles west of Beaverlodge, Alberta. These distances were longer by primitive and circuitous wagon trails. With the exception of Jim Young, the fur buyer, and myself, all Kelly Lake residents were Metis who had begun to settle there about 1910, most having come directly from Flyingshot Lake Settlement near Grande Prairie, Alta. Kelly Lake was thus the end of a long fugitive trail of Metis migrations north and west from their origin in the Red River Valley of what is now Manitoba and neighboring parts of the USA. This exodus spanned about a century, at least three generations and a thousand miles.

There is now a sizeable bookshelf of scholarly and interesting literature about the Metis people. Much of it centres on their self-styled Messiah Louis "David" Riel (1844-1885), who first identified the "Metis Nation" which he tried to establish under British sovereignty in the then Canadian Northwest. The pros and cons of Riel's conviction of treason and tragic execution at Regina 16 November, 1885 are not part of my story. We can certainly thank him for the creation of Manitoba as the fifth province of Canada in 1870 and for safeguarding the Canadian West from militant American expansion north of the 49th Parallel at that time. In following paragraphs I outline briefly the history of the Metis people.

They are mostly of Cree (maternal) and French (paternal) ancestry, with some infusions of other paternal blood, such as Scotch and Iroquois. Census data for them remain obscure. The first for Manitoba, presumably 1870, listed 5,757 Metis, 4,083 "English Halfbreeds", 1,565 Whites and only 558 Indians.[1] This was before Manitoba had been twice expanded. Another estimate for 1879 totalled some 33,000 Metis, more than half of whom were in Minnesota, Michigan and Wisconsin, 2,500 in Dakota and Montana and the balance, some 13,000, in Manitoba and the (then) Northwest Territories.[2] During the early 1920s in both the Cariboo and Peace River district of British Columbia, I remember only the term "halfbreeds" being used – or simply "breeds". In the Cariboo their ancestry was generally Shuswap (Interior Salish) maternally, and quite varied paternally, from fur traders and miners. In the Peace River country, the term was identified more closely with the original Metis concept of French-Cree.

The Metis legacy of European and American "Red Indian" ancestry reflects the dominant characteristics of each. Authorities like George Catlin eulogized "the noble Red Man" in his pristine state for many virtues – physical prowess, endurance, courage, discipline, stoicism, honesty, dignity, generosity, skills in woodcraft, as well as morality within their established codes.[3] In contrast, his vices were deplored – lust for human blood (especially of enemies), cruelty and improvidence. The Red Man is not alone in such anomalous extremes. No race, creed or color has a monopoly on either vice or virtue, which display themselves according to war, peace, want or plenty. Indians of absolutely pure blood are probably rare today and it would be surprising how many so-called White people have at least a trace of Indian blood, of which they are not aware. In my own ancestry through eight generations of record, it is a matter of regret to find no incidence of Indian blood. My wife, a beautiful blue-eyed blonde, is one eighth Iroquois! This becomes evident on rare but exciting occasions when she chases me around the menage with a tomahawk. At least our children share this enviable heritage.

Evils imposed on aborigines of the New World by the White man are well-known – slaughter, dispossession, disease, liquor and immorality. Benefits were few – the horse, firearms, the wheel and metal hardware.

It is ironic that the Genus Equus (the horse) evolved in the Americas to spread and thrive in Eurasia and Africa, and then, mysteriously, became extinct in the Western Hemisphere. When Spanish Conquistadores arrived in the 16th century, their horses of Arabian (Moorish) stock found a benign environment in which to multiply, escape and survive as wild mustangs far to the north into Canada. In the 1920s I had the privilege of seeing, owning and using some of their wild diminutive, but tough and sure-footed progeny. Catlin gave a fascinating account of wild horses and the superb horsemanship of the Camanchees (sic) in what is now Northwest Texas in 1834.[4] On the prairie the Blackfeet were famous for their use of and skill with these animals which gave them a distinct advantage in hunting and warfare, as well as transport. The Cree word for horse is "mestatim" (big dog). Without the wheel, their device for transport on the plains was the "travois".[5] The small ends of two slender poles were fastened to the dog's shoulders. The large ends dragged on the ground behind, spread apart by cross-braces which supported a hide receptacle for the load. In larger dimension, the travois was readily adapted to the horse.

Maps showing boundaries between Indian tribes and nations were valid only for the dates specified because such boundaries were ambient, according to the relative power of neighbors they separated. The Jenness Map of 1932 [6] divides Canada on the 85th Meridian near Sault Ste Marie. East of this his tribal boundaries are as of 1525, before European penetration. To the west he shows boundaries as of 1725, before significant explorations there. Since those dates such boundaries have changed more or less according to the fur trade, ravages of disease, and more recently, the inexorable tide of settlement and exploitation of natural resources. The Crees obtained firearms before the Blackfeet, which enabled them to spread into the latter's territory. When the Blackfeet got them, they in turn dominated the Kootenays. When the fur trade circumvented the Blackfeet through Athabasca Pass, it restored a measure of parity to the Kootenays. Tribal boundaries reflected such changes in the balance of power as indeed international boundaries do in world politics. Apropos current agitation for aboriginal land and other "rights", we may well ask how these "rights" originated. Were there no prior claimants? Indeed, there were. Were their "rights" recognized? No. The age-old law that "might is right" applied. The predecessors were massacred, enslaved and otherwise dispersed. Justice with mercy is the valid approach to "aboriginal rights". Their legality is minimal.

When New France was formally ceded to Britain in 1763, exploration and incipient fur trade had already pushed westward as far as the Rocky Mountain foothills. The British came from Hudson Bay (Kelsey, 1690-92; Henday, 1754-55) and the French came from the St. Lawrence via the Great Lakes (La Verendrye et fils 1731 et seq). French free-traders were already defying monopolies and royalities imposed by their autocratic governors. After 1759, the early French fur trade structure was soon appropriated mainly by Scotch entrepreneurs in Montreal. They quickly enlisted the willing and expert services of seasoned French-Canadian and Iroquois "voyageurs" – remarkable canoemen and hunters. By 1783 these Montrealers had combined into the North West Company with stature and vigor to challenge the Hudson's

Bay Company on even terms. They reached far beyond the Red River depots to the Arctic and the Pacific coasts (Mackenzie, 1789, 1793; Thompson, 1807-12; Fraser, 1805 et seq). For the HBC, Hearne had reached the Arctic Coppermine (1771-72). Meanwhile, British navigators – Cook (1778-79) and Vancouver (1792-94) – had charted the west coast of America from California north to pack-ice at 70° North Latitude. These explorations shattered the illusion of a "Northwest Passage to Cathay" but they confirmed the potential riches of fur trade in Northwest America.

Lord Selkirk's "Red River Settlement" begun in 1812 aggravated a vicious rivalry between the HBC and the NWCo, which ended with their amalgamation under the name of the older company in 1821. This union brought stability, new vigor and efficiency, combining the talents and resources of each. Whisky and other evils were brought under control and the company exercised a paternal monopoly in trade, and a degree of law and order over the vast territory not yet under colonial administration. The most remote outpost was Fort Yukon (1847-67), well into Russian Alaska. Access from the Pacific was well established (1825-26) at Fort Vancouver on the Columbia River and at Fort Victoria (1843) on Vancouver's Island. The intrepid HBC governor (Sir) George Simpson (1792-1860), in his "Character Book" of 1832 listed 25 Chief Factors and the same number of Chief Traders. Some were former NWCo men.[7] Many "servants", mainly Scotch, Orkney men, French and their mixed-blood progeny, were eligible for promotion "on merit". E.B. Osler wrote to good effect in 1961:[8]

> Northward, westward across mighty Lake Superior... through the Lake of the Woods...along the Saskatchewan, the Slave, and the Mackenzie rivers, down the Thompson and the Fraser...to the Pacific shore they probed seeking profit and adventure. Trading forts were re-opened at the strategic locations or sprang up for the first time. French-speaking white men occupied them ... and,

in the natural course of events, took unto themselves
Indian wives. Many of these unions were happy and permanent ... almost all of them were fruitful. ... Gradually a distinct race of half-breed people emerged, a
race of "people of the plains" who called themselves
"metis".

Pembina on the Red River, the cradle of the western Metis,
was founded about 1780 by French free-traders, and became an
important NWCo depot in 1793. The HBC arrived there in 1801.
After the 49th Parallel was designated on paper as the
International Boundary (1818) Pembina was correctly alleged to be
in American territory, so in 1823, having absorbed the NWCo, the
HBC moved its main depot 60 miles north to Fort Garry (now
Winnipeg) at the forks of the Red and Assiniboine rivers. The
invisible boundary, as yet unsurveyed or marked, practically bi-
sected Lord Selkirk's grant of Assiniboia for his Red River
settlers. It was a prize example of remote diplomats imposing a
partition of territory in complete ignorance of local geography. It
was an annoyance to local people, mostly Metis, and an embarrassment to authorities on both sides.

Before Riel's Insurrection of 1869-70, the Metis flourished in
the Red River Valley and on the plains in the west. It was ideal
for their free and nomadic life. They occupied narrow riparian
homesites fronting on the rivers. There were enough trees for log
cabins, fuel, and fence rails for vegetable gardens and hay. They
enjoyed grazing rights on the open prairie behind. The Metis
filled a vital economic role in the fur trade whose depots and
brigades were not self-sufficient for food. They were the primary
source of pemmican and hides, obtained on semi-annual buffalo
hunts. Between times they served as freighters with their crude
home-made two-wheeled carts on routes more or less directly
across the plains between the ubiquitous fur depots. This was
more efficient than the old circuitous canoe routes. Metis enclaves
were also located at St. Joseph, 20 miles west of Pembina in

Dakota, and near Fort Garry at St. Boniface, St. Norbert, St. Vital and other places. As Osler remarked, Metis communities also appeared at depots all along the trade routes.

The West, especially along the North Saskatchewan River where prairie yields to the northern forest belt, was well-suited to Metis tastes and needs. Buffalo on the plain to the south supplied meat and hides. Many lakes abounded in fish and fowl. There were logs for cabins and fuel. Slender Lodgepole Pine provided shafts, teepee poles and fence rails. Their Red River carts were made entirely of local woods. Edible berries, medicinal herbs and roots were in abundance. Birch was favored for toboggans and snow-shoes. The strong trade tobacco in ½-lb plugs was "diluted" with Indian tobacco ("mikwapemigwa") from the Red Willow (Cornus stolonifera). On the plains, buffalo "chips" supplied fuel and smoke for drying meat. A tasty Spring tonic was the sweet pulpy inner bark of the Jackpine. The forest belt was habitat for moose, a vital alternative to the dwindling herds of buffalo, and furred animals whose pelts were valid currency in trade. Tough Indian ponies for cart, saddle and pack thrived on the prairie with a minimum of husbandry.

From the French the Metis inherited gaiety, sociability, "poli-tesse" and adaptability. Some Indian instincts were an aversion to agriculture, indifference to private property, skills in woodcraft and preference for the nomadic life. Some have criticized their improvidence which may be due to over-confidence in their skills to survive, faith that the Almighty will provide and a fatalistic acceptance of adversity with endurance and stoicism. Most were illiterate and their mother tongue was Cree. In religion they were mostly Roman Catholic with some pagan overtones. An old saying that "when a Frenchman marries an Indian he becomes an Indian" meant that he adapted fully and happily to the Indian way of life. The Scotch of the HBC were different: "Once a Scot always a Scot." They encouraged their native wives to conform to the European lifestyle. In either case these unions provided contentment far from home (the women performed vital domestic services) while fostering good relations and trade with the Indians.

Joseph Howard, under the heading "Big Business on the Plains"[9] gives a vivid description of the June buffalo hunt, c1840 from Pembina. Mobilization and organization there was a festive occasion where relatives and friends could socialize, with romantic scope for Romeos and Juliettes. The logistics were quasi-military. A "commandant of the hunt" of repute was elected with "captains" for every 10 hunters. Duties were assigned in detail and discipline was strict. This particular hunt comprised 620 hunters, 650 women and 360 children. There were 1,220 carts with draft animals and 403 prize hunting ponies. In addition to harness and camp gear, there were 740 guns, 150 gallons of gunpowder and 1,300 pounds of lead balls. Instead of pagan buffalo dances to supplicate the spirits, a priest went along to solicit divine blessings each day, and the Sabbath was religiously observed.

When scouts located the herds, near or far, utmost restraint was enforced until the "moment crucial" when the chief signals the attack. Then, in the mad melee of excitement it is every man for himself – clouds of dust, stampeding beasts bellowing and snorting, shouting, superb horsemanship and gunfire on the gallop. Within the hour, shot and powder expended, the dust settles and the hunters return on their tracks to claim their quarry without dispute, and return to camp. The women then go out to skin, butcher and haul in the bounty. Feasting on the delicacies is spiced with gossip of the fray and the process of drying the meat begins. Wolves feast on scraps and surplus left in the field overnight. The routine is repeated until the carts are overloaded with the bounty of meat and hides, and the homeward trek begins. There the dried meat is processed with tallow and dried berries into pemmican and compacted into hide containers ready to trade for cash or against debts. Two celebrated "commandants of the hunt" were Cuthbert Grant (1793-c1880) a Scotch halfbreed, and Gabriel Dumont (1838-1906), Riel's military tactician both in 1869-70 and 1885.

The Metis "golden age" spanned at least two generations between 1810 and 1870 and their core homeland extended from the Red River valley west on both sides of the unmarked 49th Parallel. The blend of their dual blood heritage proved virile and prolific such that they soon assumed their unique Metis identity, quite distinct from either of their primary ancestral origins. Their "advance guards" reached all remote extremities of the fur trade routes – north via the Mackenzie drainage to the Arctic tundra, west via the Peace, Yellowhead and Athabasca passes to New Caledonia and southwest via the upper Missouri to Oregon Territory and the Pacific Ocean. They were among the "freemen" of Peter Skene Ogden's Snake River Journals, 1824-26.[10] Catlin's faithful and cheerful servant "Ba'tiste" on the upper Missouri (1832) was surely a Metis.[11]

Several factors combined to erode and undermine the Metis "utopia" some of which were incipient before 1870. Exploitation of the tremendous agricultural potential of the Canadian West was inevitable, and began as early as 1812 with Selkirk's settlers. After initial troubles from the hand of Nature, insects, drought, floods and frost, and hostility of the fur trade, it survived to inundate the West, especially after the transfer of HBC lands to the juvenile Dominion of Canada in 1870. Steam power, first for navigation on rivers in the '70s and then by rail in the '80s, ended the Metis monopoly on freighting with their crude squeaky carts. A knock-out blow was the sudden disappearance of the buffalo soon after 1870, which pauperized both Indians and Metis. Political lethargy at Ottawa and bigotry of Ontario Protestants aggravated Metis distress to the point of insurrection under Riel 1869-70 on the Red River. The Manitoba Act was, in effect, a truce and activated Metis migrations west and north with concentrations on the Saskatchewan River near the confluence of its branches at Batoche, Prince Albert, Battleford and farther west at St. Albert and Lac Ste Anne. Another refuge was around Fort Benton, Montana where Riel found asylum c1876-1884. This area was exposed to the worst depravities of American traders, especially whisky. The propitious formation of the North West Mounted Police (1873) gave a significant measure of protection to Indians, Metis and Whites from such lawlessness north of the 49th Parallel, which was surveyed and marked during 1872-76.[12]   There were smaller sporadic Metis enclaves between the Boundary and the North Saskatchewan – Qu'Appelle, File Hills, Moosomin, Cypress Hills, MacLeod, Pincher Creek, Lethbridge and others. With the lesson of 1870 at Red River unheeded, the desperate distress of Metis and Indians sparked the second confrontation at Batoche in 1885. This was the final coup de grace for Riel's "Metis Nation". Thereafter the Metis became fugitives from civilization. Their vitality and adaptability was once more directed to the untamed wilderness – out and beyond.

As early as 1842 at Lac du Diable, about 40 miles west of Edmonton, the Reverend Father Jean-Baptiste Thibault (1810-1879) found enough Metis settled to establish a mission which he more appropriately named Lac Ste Anne.[13]   Most of the original Kelly Lake Metis were born there c1850-c1890. They still make an annual quasi-religious pilgrimage to Lac St. Anne in late July. Instead of days and weeks by wagon, they now make the trip in a matter of hours. In 1890, a special survey of the Lac Ste Anne Settlement was made by Phidyme R.A. Belanger, DLS, under instructions from Ottawa (see Chapter 5).

A continued line of retreat from Lac St. Anne was into the fabled Peace River country. An early route was via Athabasca River to Lesser Slave Lake thence to Sturgeon Lake and finally to Flyingshot Lake near "the Grande Prairie". MacGregor mentions a "well used trail from Lac St. Anne ... to Sturgeon Lake before 1879".[14]   When the Grand Trunk Pacific railway reached Edson, 120 miles west of Edmonton, in 1911, a wagon road was slashed out directly north to Sturgeon Lake and on west to Grande Prairie.

This "Edson Trail", notorious for mud and flies during summer, was used by White and Metis settlers for five years until 1916 when the Edmonton, Dunvegan and British Columbia Railway reached Grande Prairie, Alta via Spirit River. The "end of steel" remained at Grande Prairie until 1924 when it was extended 12 miles to Wembley. It reached Hythe, Alta in 1929 and Dawson Creek, BC in 1930. Finally, in 1958, the long-awaited rail connection to the Pacific coast was made by the (then) Pacific Great Eastern Railway, via Pine Pass.

About 1894 Adam Calliou (1854-1948) with his brothers Esau and William journeyed by packhorse from Lac Ste Anne via Grouard and Sturgeon Lake to Grande Prairie. Louis and St. Pierre Gauthier with Alfred Gladu followed before 1905. Others followed them.[15] They chose to settle around Flyingshot Lake, two miles southwest of Grande Prairie. Here again a special survey was made of their Metis settlement in 1907.[16] Their stay there was short-lived due to the flood of settlers coming to Grande Prairie by rail 1916 et seq.

A final destination for many of these Metis was Kelly Lake, some 60 miles due west from Grande Prairie, which they passed en route to their traplines in the foothills and mountains further west. It offered good water, wild hay, logs for cabins and fuel. The surrounding bush was well stocked with moose and smaller game. Earlier, this had been Beaver Indian country but disease had decimated them, and they had a superstitious taboo about a "windigo" in the lake. For the Metis, its isolation was an attraction and it was not too far from supplies at Beaverlodge. The first-comers were Narcisse Belcourt (1876-1953) and St. Pierre Gauthier (c1860-1930) who squatted there about 1910. Other families followed – Calliou, Campbell, Gladu, Gray, Hamelin, Letendre and Supernat. Most were originally from Lac Ste Anne.

Three Kelly Lake families claim Iroquois paternal ancestry – Calliou, L'Hirondelle and Thomas. They were the intrepid voyageurs and hunters of the old NWCo, from the St Lawrence River.

After the union with the HBC, many of them stayed in the West as "freemen" trapping and trading. Dr. (Sir) James Hector of the Palliser Expedition, ascending the Athabasca River toward Jasper House, recorded for 30 January, 1859.[17]

> ... found a camp, four tents of Iroquois half-breeds ...
> These ... were originally trappers in the service of the
> N.W. Company, and on the junction of that company with
> the Hudson Bay Company [1821] they turned "freemen" ...
> they all talk the Cree language besides their own, and
> have latterly intermarried a good deal with the Cree
> half-breeds of Lac St Ann's [sic].

This remark could certainly be pertinent to the Kelly Lake families mentioned, and now this Iroquois blood is shared by most of the younger generations there.

Professional bias influences me to note that the first recorded references to Kelly Lake were made by early surveyors in their field-notes and official reports. Surveyors were often the first competent observers to assess and report on unknown country, thus making a primary contribution to enlightened administration of undeveloped territory prior to settlement. In 1909, my old friend Guy H. Blanchet, DLS, BCLS, FRGS (1884-1966) surveyed the 16th and 17th Baselines south of Grande Prairie from the 6th Meridian (118°W Long) 78 miles west to the (then) unsurveyed Alberta-BC Boundary (120°W Long). He spoke highly of Celestin Gladu (c1860-c1940) whom he employed as guide and packer. Celestin, originally from Lac Ste Anne and later from Flyingshot Lake was a respected elder at Kelly Lake and grandfather of several of the first pupils of the school in 1923. Blanchet also referred to the McFarlane brothers who surveyed the DLS townships and sections west of Grande Prairie in 1909.[18]

R.W. Cautley, DLS, BCLS, ALS (1873-1953) surveyed the Alberta-BC boundary on the 120th Meridian south from Pouce Coupe in 1920 and 1922. This boundary passed Kelly Lake about a mile to the east, placing the lake just inside BC. He named the lake "Fritton" after Fritton Mere near Ipswich, Suffolk. This was a misnomer as the name Kelly was well in use then, but it was not officially recognized until 1952. The following quote from Cautley's official report is interesting:[19]

> A few Halfbreed families have their houses on the north shore of Fritton [Kelly] Lake, and regard the location as their headquarters. The men, of whom three were on the party in 1920, are particularly good trappers and hunters, who work in the summer times on the farms in the settlements or at whatever other employment they can get, but it is amazing how improvident they are. For instance, there is excellent soil all around their village where the women and unemployed men loaf away the hot summer, and do not even grow potatoes. They have horses, but put up just enough hay to bring them through a mild winter. Rather than put up a few extra tons — with hay going to waste all around them — they take a chance on losing their horses which they very much need to provision their traplines, pack in meat etc. ....

I hope this will not offend my Kelly Lake friends who may read it. It is a matter of record. My personal views have been expressed.

In 1921, A.R.M. Barrow, BCLS (1867-1953) surveyed seven district lots, Numbers 308-314, at Kelly Lake (see Map 4). All were half a mile square (160 acres less water area). Numbers 308, 309 and 314 fronted on the north side of the lake. Narcisse Belcourt occupied No. 313 on the south side of Gauthier Lake. His daughter, Mary (Mrs. Billy Gladu), still lives there with her family. In addition to Belcourt, Barrow's field-notes mention three Callious (J., P. and W.) and three Gladus (A., J. and S).[20] He also notes a fur trader "Abdool" (reputed to be a Syrian). Abdool's store was on Lot 314 at the northwest corner of the lake. Most residents were averse to formalities of filing on homesteads and paying the taxes implied. Jim Young from Ontario bought out Abdool in 1922 and got approval to establish the first school at Kelly Lake in 1923. In 1927 he closed his store in Kelly Lake and located at Rose Prairie, north of Fort St. John. Since then Kelly

Lake has been without a store of any account but the school, now a modern four-room structure, has had continuous operation and expansion under a succession of creditable teachers. The nearest store and post office now are at Goodfare, Alta, 12 miles east by a gravelled road which continues another 12 miles east to join No. 2 Highway between Dawson Creek, BC and Grande Prairie, Alta (see Map 3).

The tiny Metis "Shangri-La" at Kelly Lake has thus endured for over 70 years and more than two generations with some inevitable changes in lifestyle. There is now better access and electric power. Moose and other game continue to supply food, raiment and pelts for trade. Lakes still yield fish and fowl. Berry-picking safaris are one-day jaunts by pickup truck instead of week-long treks with horses. The Metis still enjoy their fun and sociability. Some young folk have sought a way of life far from Kelly Lake but a vigorous and happy core remains. Nearly all the original pioneers have passed on but their children, now elders, survive to cherish the lore and traditions of the past.

Metis migrations from the old homeland on the Red River through more than 1,000 miles and five generations, with pauses en route at Batoche, Lac Ste Anne and Flyingshot Lake to the ultimate spearhead at Kelly Lake are like the biblical Exodus with Riel in the role of a Moses. Now, there is no avenue of further retreat from Kelly Lake.

Mountain passes to the west offer no incentive. In their bowels, those mountains have gestated a formidable "windigo" in the form of coal. It waited long ages for the economic stimulus and the engineering obstetrics to give it birth. Delivery is now in progress and the maternity ward is Tumbler Ridge. This infant giant spells "No Exit" from Kelly Lake, and, indeed, threatens to blight the delicate flower of serenity there.

Concern about "aboriginal rights" engendered by the Berger Commission has encouraged the large corporations to make socio-environmental impact studies for their mega-projects, to minimize adverse effects. The Coal Division of Petro Canada at Calgary in programming its Monkman Pass Coal Project, south of Tumbler Ridge, has made creditable studies of the Kelly Lake community, whose trapping grounds will be affected. After more than two years' field studies by competent and sympathetic experts, this company has formulated realistic and acceptable compensation for the Kelly Lake people concerned, and is providing practical safe-guards for the environment.[21]

Aims of the Kelly Lake School, activated 60 years ago by fur trader Jim Young, were to teach the Cree-speaking children enough English to communicate in their widening environment, enough of the "Three Rs" to protect them in simple business and enough social sciences for better perspective in the big wide world opening up for them. Thanks to a long succession of dedicated teachers these aims have been achieved. There is much to support the hope that Kelly Lake young folk will adapt happily to major changes which seem imminent now.

I have tried to outline the background of the people I found at Kelly Lake so long ago, and of which I was then quite ignorant. My birth and childhood in Winnipeg were within earshot of "The bells of St. Boniface". My memory of St. Norbert is of the full-flavored cheese made by the Trappist monks there. I cried as a little fellow when my mother spoke in a strange language (French) to a Metis laundress who came to help on Mondays.

It remains to note some physical specifics about Kelly Lake (see Maps 3 and 4). It is circular, about a mile across, fairly deep with gravel bottom. It is fed from the west by Steeprock Creek and smaller streams draining a shallow basin of some 70 square miles. The outflow continues in Steeprock Creek eastward to join the Beaverlodge River near Hythe, Alta. The water divide to the west is with Kiskatinaw ("Cutbank") River, to the south with Redwillow River and to the north with upper Beaverlodge River. Its basin contains smaller lakes, hay meadows, muskeg with Tamarack and Black Spruce, and higher ground with Jackpine,

White Spruce, Aspen and some White Birch. There has been the usual incidence of forest fires. The lake's elevation is 2,810 feet. As the surveyor Cautley remarked, there is some quite good arable land. The Rocky Mountains to the west are not visible from the lake. The climate is continental: temperatures average 0° Fahrenheit in January, 60° F in July; with extremes from -50° F to +87° F. Annual precipitation is about 18 inches. Snowfall aggregates about 81 inches. Bright sunshine totals about 2,000 hours annually. One or more "Chinook" winds are an important winter feature. Strong, warm and dry, they can greatly reduce the snow-pack especially on southwest exposures. This can impede sleighing with heavy loads. On the other hand, they give wildlife and domestic stock a welcome "break" to move around to find vital forage.

There is no clear consensus about the origin of the lake's name. Francis Belcourt insists it was for a White trapper, Kelly, from Pouce Coupe who operated around the lake before 1910. Some think it is a corruption of Calliou, the prominent Metis family. S. Prescott Fay in his diary "Jasper to Hudson's Hope", Boston, 1914, mentions staying overnight, 1-2 November, 1914 at "Kelley's" near Hythe. This could identify George J. ("Kelly") Sunderman, first settler at Hythe, 1909 – a well-known guide and outfitter.

CHAPTER 1

THE FIRST KELLY LAKE SCHOOL YEAR: 1923-1924

These memoirs are supported by enough evidence, preserved, recovered and, indeed, discovered to raise them to the level of non-fiction. Now, some 60 years later they continue to give rewarding color and flavor to my life. Before the curtain rises for Act I of this drama a prelude of some personal background will set the desired perspective.

After writing Junior Matriculation at Calgary, 1920, age 16, I got a ranch job at Empress, Alta which lasted until after harvest, late October. This experience with hard work and horses augmented what I had obtained on a Manitoba farm, 1918, and as "bull cook": in the Yoho Valley, 1919. With most of my ranch pay intact, I was grudgingly admitted to first year Arts at the University of British Columbia, Vancouver. The penalty for "late registration" was that I could not write their final examinations in April. The session was thus abortive for academic credits, but it was certainly worthwhile for Dr. G.G. Sedgewick's inspiration in English literature. I recovered this lost scholastic year later as will be told. It was a prerequisite for admission to Forestry, Engineering or Medicine.

A summer job as horse-wrangler with the Brewsters at Field, BC, in 1921, helped to finance a teacher's diploma from the Vancouver Normal School in May, 1922. While cutting firewood with Fred Haggman that summer (Photo 3), scrutiny of "Want Ads for Teachers" (at remote schools which I preferred) resulted in my teaching the one-room log school at Big Bar Creek, northwest of Clinton until the summer vacation in June, 1923. As this school was to close for lack of pupils, I returned to Burnaby, again in the market for a frontier school. Having arranged an appointment with Mr. J.L. Watson, Registrar of Teachers in Victoria, a chum, Bert Masterson, and I got accommodation at the old YMCA, Blanshard Street, for $1.50 per night.

Ushered into Mr. Watson's office, third floor, west wing of the Parliament Buildings, I was much impressed to hear him recite my previous record in some detail — my full name, origin, age, one year's teaching at Big Bar, with satisfactory Inspector's report, mail order courses for Senior Matriculation, etc. I realize now that, prior to the interview, he had perused my personal file. A kindly discussion followed, in which I expressed my preference for remote frontier schools.

He said "How would you like a school in the Peace River country?"

"That would be great!".

"I have two openings there, one at Tupper (Swan Lake) on the Grande Prairie-Pouce Coupe Road, a White community, possibly 10 pupils, and the school has been in operation for some time. The other school is at Kelly Lake, an isolated backwoods community of Cree-speaking halfbreeds possibly 20 pupils, few if any can speak English and it will be their first school. You would have to bach, probably with the fur trader, Mr. J.S. Young, the only other White person there. The people live by trapping and hunting. Which would you prefer, Tupper or Kelly Lake?"

My choice was Kelly Lake, definitely.

Mr. Watson said he would convey my application to the Kelly Lake trustees from whom I should hear in due course, and he wished me "good luck". I then returned to a job at Fraser Mills near Coquitlam, staying with Fred and Catherine Haggman in New Westminster who had always treated me like a son. Seven years later, my office with the BC Forest Service was in the basement, four floors below that of Mr. Watson. I still regret that shyness prevented me from seeing him again to pay my respects and to thank him heartily.

In those days, both Big Bar and Kelly Lake were "Assisted Schools", one-room affairs in remote places. The teacher was wholly paid by the Education Department from Victoria while the community provided school premises and maintenance. Annual pay in 10 monthly instalments was $1,120 at Big Bar and $1,320 at Kelly Lake.

As September drew near I anxiously waited confirmation from Kelly Lake. After Labor Day, a letter came from Jim Young, dated 8 September at Leighmore, Alta describing the Kelly Lake setup and offering the job. I accepted by telegram at once. Mr. Watson also wrote from Victoria, 11 September, confirming my appointment but saying that the school would not open until 1 October and advising how to contact Mr. Young. It was a jolt to miss the first month's pay. I wired Jim Young at Beaverlodge as follows:

> Leaving New Westminster 18th for Edmonton/Will arrive Grande Prairie 21 September 4:45 pm thence will proceed to Pouce Coupe/Wire me here if not correct route for Kelly Lake School.

Later, Young advised me to meet him at Beaverlodge, 30 miles by horse stage from Grande Prairie, the end of steel. Meanwhile, I did some shopping in Vancouver for anticipated needs of a brand new school: chalk, pencils, crayons, copybooks, etc – and by divine inspiration, several yards of rolled blackboard cloth. These with personal effects were squeezed into a large trunk to be sent as baggage by rail to Grande Prairie.

I boarded the CNR train at Vancouver in balmy fall weather to find Edmonton the next day smothered in eight inches of equinoctial snow. Alas, my woollies were in my trunk, checked through to Grande Prairie. I think the ED & BC Railway train left Edmonton that evening to arrive in Grande Prairie next afternoon. By this time the snow, left behind in Edmonton, was followed by superb fall weather. I had bought brown bread, butter and anchovy paste for snacks en route. There was a lunch stop at

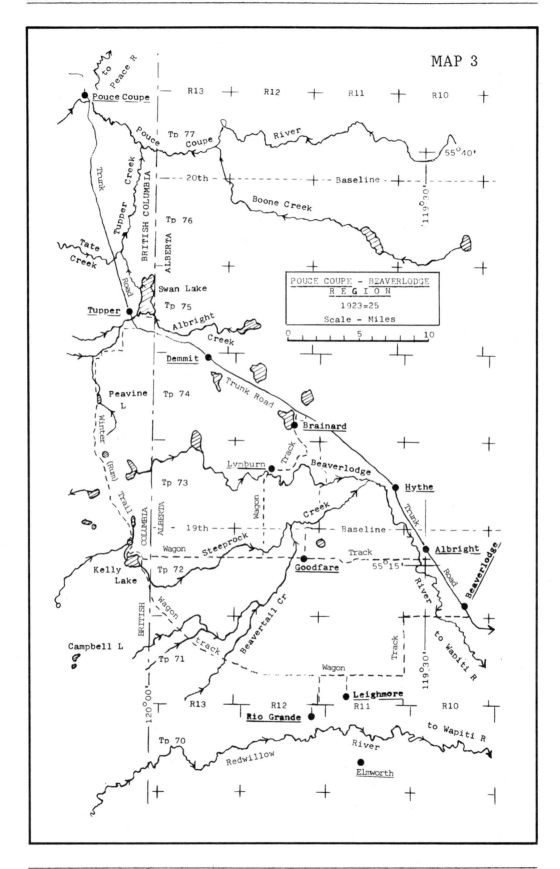

MAP 3

POUCE COUPE - BEAVERLODGE
R E G I O N
1923=25
Scale - Miles

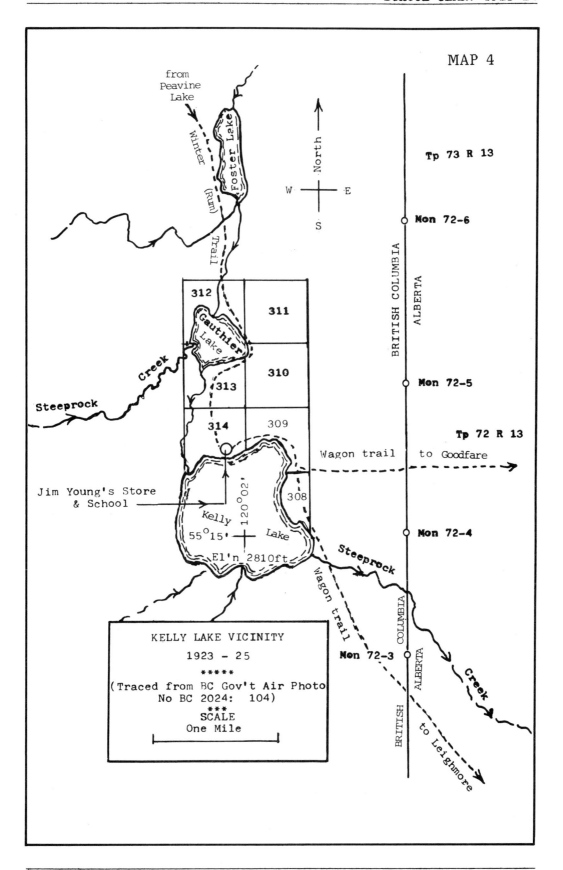

MAP 4

KELLY LAKE VICINITY
1923 - 25
*****
(Traced from BC Gov't Air Photo
No BC 2024: 104)
***
SCALE
One Mile

McLennan, Alta where all on board walked to a nearby restaurant, with an eye on the crew for when to rush back to the train. Passengers, displaying northern sociability, included a clergyman with his family returning from a holiday "outside". When he learned I was bound for Kelly Lake he was mortified – "a cesspool of iniquity, booze, gambling and immorality"...no place for the innocent young man which he presumed I was. In Grande Prairie I got supper and a room at the Donald Hotel, and next morning, with baggage, took a place on the horse stage for Beaverlodge. We arrived in time for supper and a room in Gaudin's store. They said Jim Young would likely be along in the morning. Mr. Gaudin was a member of the famous "Bull Gang" which had trekked in from Ontario with oxen in 1909.[22]

Sunday morning 23 September, Mr. Young appeared with team and wagon (Photo 4). We loaded up and headed southwest for the Redwillow district, to overnight with George and Sarah Beadle who ran the Leighmore post office. This was to be my mail address for the next two years. Perhaps I was the only teacher in British Columbia whose pay cheques were sent to an Alberta post office (see Map 3). It took all next day to reach Kelly Lake on the most primitive wagon track with neither culverts nor bridges, bumping over roots and stumps, avoiding or cutting out windfalls. Jim quoted a local character who said the best way to negotiate the worst places was to close your eyes, whip up the horses and crash right through. About a mile from Kelly Lake we crossed a conspicuous north-south cutline slashed through the bush. This was the Alberta-BC boundary on the 120th Meridian which R.W. Cautley, DLS had surveyed and marked just the year before, as mentioned.

This daylong trip provided my first impressions of Jim Young who was to be my baching partner, fellow traveller and mentor for the next two years and thereafter a lifelong friend. He was then unmarried, 20 years my senior, of medium stature, wiry, tough, dark-haired, clean-shaven, quiet but alert, and kept a low profile in dress and manner. He smoked a pipe. I was to learn that he was a superb horseman and a born trader with a quick eye for appraising horseflesh, fur or real estate. I was also to learn by experience and from others of his self-effacing generosity. Some highlights of Jim's career up to this time are from piecemeal fragments told to me and from a fine article by Georgina Keddell in the "Alaska Highway News", 12 September, 1963 on the occasion of his 80th birthday. The "JS" of his signature on cheques which were valid anywhere for any amount, stood for James Sutherland. He was born 6 September 1883, second child of James Young, farmer near Sarnia, Ontario. He first came west to Manitoba as a harvester, age 17, and returned the next year to stay. An early job was for Jake Grauer, pioneer farmer on Sea Island near Vancouver, moving and butchering cattle from Alberta. He told me that "Dal" Grauer, age 5, and "Little Jake", age 3, loved to ride with him on the wagon behind the team. Afterwards, he homesteaded at Red Deer, Alta until 1913, and evidently did well in real estate there. He then freighted on the old Edson Trail and hauled grain on the Rolla-Spirit River trail. His stories of the latter were epics of endurance and determination as he drove more than one outfit, tandem, alone in sub-zero weather. He homesteaded again at Halcourt, south of Beaverlodge. This was good country for fur buyers so it was quite natural that a man of Jim's talents and tastes would soon get involved in this type of business. In 1922 he bought out the interests and store of the Syrian trader named Abdool (or Abdul?) at Kelly Lake. Evidently Abdool had operated on a "double-take" basis, paying enticing prices for fur and then getting some or most of his money back by playing poker with his clients — a painless form of extortion. Part of his commodious store at Kelly Lake had been used as a games area for cards and even had a small pool table in it. This may have been the basis for the clergyman's lurid allegations of "gambling, booze and immorality" at Kelly Lake. Jim Young's use of this area for a new school, and the fact that in the two years I spent with him he never supplied even a smell of liquor to his Kelly Lake clientele, confirm the wholesome character of his business there. This introduction of Jim to my readers sets the stage for his leading role in my narrative to follow. If my story needs a hero, Jim Young is it!

Approaching Jim's store in a sunny clearing on the northwest side of Kelly Lake (Map 4), we passed several log cabins, homes of my pupils-to-be. The village seemed to be deserted, except for a tiny ancient blind lady seated on the ground in the after-noon sun beside a smouldering camp fire, and attended by a child. Jim said she was over 100 years old, and the great-grandma of most of my prospective pupils. We learned that the rest of the community was away on a berry-picking safari. This explained the month's delay in the school's opening.

Before dark we had time to open up the store, unload, settle in and get supper. With most of the people away it was quiet and I had a chance to size up my surroundings. The store was a large, well built log structure, about 20 x 40 feet. A long side, with a door in the middle faced south toward the lake. A second door was in the west end. There were ample windows. It had the typical sod roof – poles and straw, topped with several inches of clay. The west half of the building was laid out for store and living quarters. The east half had been the games area, including a small pool table with bead counters strung on wires overhead.

It was Jim's plan to use this games area for the school. So next day we put up a dividing partition, head-height, of "shiplap" lumber, with a door through for inside access. The outside door to the south served the school area, and the one in the west end of the building served the store area (see Figure 1). The partition offered the only flat wall for a blackboard, the others being of round logs. The blackboard cloth I had bought in Vancouver was tacked on at appropriate height. It turned out that the cracks underneath between the boards served as useful guides for drawing straight horizontal lines with chalk. There was a large "airtight" heater in the school area with its own chimney. We shoved the pool table into a back corner, handy for layouts and stores, instead of a cupboard. Out back behind the store was a snug log stable for four horses and to the west was a cache for outdoor storage, safe from countless ravenous dogs.

As yet there were no desks for the school. Jim had made a deal with the trustees at Tupper to get their old homemade units which had been replaced by factory made furniture. We had time for a quick trip to get these before the weekend. I think Jim would have contrived to have at least one meal at "Ma" Brainard's en route. By Saturday, the new school in Jim Young's store was as ready as could be for operation; meanwhile, the people had returned from their berry picking trek. By good luck a Swede trapper fluent in Cree ("Joker" Sanderson) came to the store. He cheerfully made the rounds of Kelly Lake families to tell them that school would open "next Monday morning, 1st October, at 9 o'clock".

Jim habitually hauled all his goods for the store from the "end of steel" at Grande Prairie, nearly a week's round trip via Leighmore and way points. Early that memorable Sunday morning he started back to comparative civilization, wisely leaving me to face and cope with the unprecedented challenge of starting the school quite alone. "A watched kettle never boils." No doubt on this lonely trip Jim speculated on what success the school would have. He had done his part to get it started, the officials in Victoria had been persuaded to sanction it; he had its premises reasonably ready and furnished, and now the new young teacher was "on location". If successful the school would be a wholesome reform from Abdool's former "double-take" tactics and it would be a stabilizing force in the community. Neither Jim nor I was a poker addict and we held out as celibates - whatever the temptations. As for me, would I succeed or fail? Time only would tell.

Monday dawned a lovely Indian Summer's morning. Up early completing my domestics, a bit after seven, I looked out the window to see little brown faces furtively peering at the premises from cover behind surrounding trees. These were my pupils arriving already! Few families had or needed clocks. They timed their days by the sun and their tummies. If I waited to open school at the statutory 9 am, the kids might lose heart and vanish - God knows where. So, before 8 o'clock I stepped outside, properly dressed, (tie and jacket), hoisted the large Union Jack to the top of the flagpole, and vigorously rang the old brass handbell which Jim had found somewhere. The children, one by one, cautiously emerged from cover into the clearing. Smiling, I beckoned them to approach, arranged them in line, girls first, smallest in front, ushered them inside and assigned them to their seats in the same general order (Photo 6).

There were about a dozen, nine boys and three girls. Ages ranged from about six to the oldest, Henry Belcourt, a handsome lad of 14 and taller than his teacher. They were shy, but bright and responsive. They were good-looking too – most with rosy cheeks under warm-brown skin, black eyes, hair and beautiful teeth. They were clean and neatly dressed. All wore moosehide moccasins. I never had occasion to suspect lice. (Photo 7).

With one exception, they knew only Cree. The exception, by the grace of God, was a bright 11-year-old, Colin Gladu, who had been exposed briefly to English in school, probably at Flyingshot Lake. Colin did crucial service as interpreter, especially at first. But I learned to be careful that he really understood me, and I, him. It is hard to remember just what we did in those first unprecedented hours and days. I doled out pencils, scribblers, erasers, rulers, etc. It was psychologically sound for them to receive something concrete, ab initio, as tokens of other benefits to follow.

With Colin's help. I asked each name, starting with the older children so the younger ones could benefit from example. I wrote these in block letters on the blackboard, then asked each to copy his name on the cover of his scribbler. I had to show some of the smaller ones how to hold a pencil, but all were naturally adept with their hands. Several became better penmen than their teacher! I alternated oral sessions with copy work, so they would not tire and become bored. I think the alphabet in block letters remained along the top of the blackboard for the whole of the first year.

I had Colin explain that our primary aim was for them to learn English as quickly as possible. All progress depended on that. I should also like them to teach me Cree — a two-way deal. But there being 12 of them and I only one, their learning English was 12 times more important than my learning Cree. It was necessary to explain the school routine: hours nine to four, Mondays through Fridays; a lunch hour; morning and afternoon recess. They were to stay within sight of the school - no wandering off. Drinking water was kept in a bucket by the door, also a wash basin, soap and towel, with a dipper hanging alongside. For the call of Nature, pupils were to raise the right hand with two fingers erect. There were no proper toilets, but they were accustomed to the seclusion of the surrounding bush.

A basic vocabulary (nouns) came first: — pointing to objects, I would say "window ... door ... floor ... roof ... desk ... table ... stove ... book ... pencil ... pail ... boy ... girl ... These words they would repeat in unison then individually, the older ones first. Each new word was written on the blackboard in block letters, then they would copy it. Endless repetition, review and testing. Next came auxiliary words: "this window ... that window ... this girl ... that girl ... my desk ... your desk ... his desk ... her desk ..." plurals: "one, two, three girls ... three windows ... one stove ... one roof ... four walls"... Simple verbs: "I stand ... I sit ... Mary stands ... Alec walks ... Adolphus writes".

Soon we got to questions and answers: "What is that? ... That is a lamp ... Where is the door? ... The door is there." I trained them to answer in complete sentences: "What is your name? ... My name is Alec Gladu ... Where do you live? ... I live in that house ... Who are you? ... I am Henry Belcourt ... Who is your father? ... My father is Milton Campbell ... How are you? ... I am quite well thank you". They learned the names and order of letters in the alphabet and numbers up to about 20. Phonetics were incidental at first, but later systematically learned. At the beginning I did not attempt to sort the children into grades. This would follow soon, according to age and ability.

About the third day a significant incident occurred. The children had just got settled inside from afternoon recess when Urbain Gladu, father of Colin and two younger pupils, entered without knocking. He sat down on a chair near the door with his hat on – in a truculent mood, I sensed. (He may have had a drink.) I confronted him, asked him to remove his hat, and told him he should have knocked and waited outside until admitted. No one is allowed to interrupt the school in session. He then complained that I had not placed his son, Colin, in a higher grade. Impulsively I grabbed his collar and shoved him out the door, saying I would grade the children in due course. If he had further complaints or wanted trouble, he could return after school when we could settle matters in any way he wished. I closed the door and resumed the routine without further interruption.

Urbain returned early that evening, but very contrite and full of apologies. I explained things more fully and assured him that Colin was a vital help in getting the school started and that he would be adequately graded very soon. Thereafter Urbain was almost too friendly, helping me a lot with Cree and regaling me with many stories of interesting local color. (Photo 8). Jim Young returned the following weekend with a load from Grande Prairie. When I told him about the episode with Urbain Gladu, he said, simply, "You will be OK here."

The Edmonton snowstorm that fall presaged a long and glorious Indian Summer — clear crisp sunny days, frosty nights and magnificent Autumnal colors. Orange-golds of Aspen and Tamarack with splashes of Redwillow contrasted delightfully with the sombre greens of Spruce and Pine. I located some large Aspen about a hundred yards west of the store. These were felled, limbed and hauled in with a horse. I bucked and split them for our cookstove. Dry Jackpine provided kindling and a hot fire for baking. I relished this exercise and fresh air, antidotes for confinement in school. I had previously acquired some skill with the axe and crosscut saw, so our woodpile grew handsomely as winter approached. Jim was agreeably impressed. This feature endured throughout my sojourn at Kelly Lake. I insisted that the fathers supply ample wood for heating the school, and allocated the responsibility among them in rotation. Our domestic water from the lake was clear and potable. At times it had to be strained to remove tiny shrimp-like larvae. I have wondered since whether, if boiled, they might have made a nourishing and palatable soup!

I gradually settled in to the school and domestic routines, but was quite lonely. Jim, my only real companion was away a lot on his trips to Grande Prairie. My year at Big Bar had familiarized me with the school curriculum and basic teaching methods. Preparations for my classes here were flavored by the language problem, with which we seemed to make good progress. I also had my own studies for Senior Matric, so had plenty to occupy my free time. Gradually I assumed responsibility for Jim's store during his absences, after school hours and weekends.

Much of the store business was by barter. One dollar was standard value for certain items — a pair of plain moosehide moccasins and muskrat pelts in exchange for 4-lb tins of jam or lard, a ½-lb plug of "T&B" tobacco or a pound of tea. Other staples at various prices were sugar in 10-lb or 20-lb sacks, flour in 50-lb bags, salt, raisins, rice, baking powder, matches, candles, kerosene, naptha gas (for Coleman lamps), etc. Dry goods were blue denim by the yard, woollens, socks, toques, shirts, underwear and mitts. A steady demand for soap was reflected in the clean decor of the children at school. Candy bars were popular and a temptation for me, not yet having acquired a taste for tobacco or alcohol. One trader (perhaps Abdool, not Jim) was alleged to sell candy bars for 5¢ each, 2 for 15¢ and 3 for 35¢. His customers invariably said, "Gimme three." The locals used lard for butter, which to me seemed revolting, but considering their diet and lifestyle was quite logical. Trade in the more valuable furs I left entirely to Jim, in cases of urgent need granting only a token credit (or "jawbone").

For our own use, Jim would bring local produce picked up from settlers: fresh eggs, butter, a joint of beef or pork and sometimes fresh fruit. We shared cooking and cleaning up, but Jim disliked dish-washing, so this was a good exercise for me in deference to an older friend with so many fine qualities. I learned to make sourdough bread with wholewheat flour from a local grist mill (not in Kelly Lake). I baked every two or three weeks, stockpiling loaves, frozen, in our cache outside. We didn't bother with fancy pastry, making dessert of bread and jam, and sometimes a rice pudding with lots of raisins. A favorite was stewed dried Loganberries which I have not seen on the market for many years. Habitually we obtained choice quarters of moosemeat from the locals at 5¢ per pound. This was kept frozen in the cache. Sometimes they would offer caribou, which we relished for a change, but they used it only for dog food, unless hungry. Jim always topped up his loads with oat sheaves. The surplus was thrown up on the roof of the stable, safe from local animals.

Jim and I had no formal agreement about my board and keep, or my little services for him. I think I insisted on paying him about $10 per month for my consumption of groceries. No doubt he appreciated my companionship, my sharing in the chores and looking after the store. The success of the school was certainly good for his business.

The superb fall weather continued. There was hardly enough snow for sleighing until nearly Christmas. About mid-October, Jim had accumulated enough fur to warrant a trip to the Government Agent in Pouce Coupe to pay the "royalties", a necessary formality before the fur could be sold on the open market. The fur was a bulky load, but light. We chose Thanksgiving weekend for the trip so I could go along for a welcome break. We took the wagon trail east and north to get on to the main trunk road near Brainard's (see Map 3), stopping for sociability with some of Jim's friends en route. The usual invitations for lunch or overnight had to be diplomatically declined – one from Pete Stuart, a bachelor.[23] The McClements' eligible daughter, Maggie, was a special attraction.[24] Her father was an authority on Carlyle's "French Revolution". A "must" stop for a meal was Ma Brainard's. She was the celebrated cook for miles around.[25]

We probably stayed overnight with the Taylors at Swan Lake. Martin B. Taylor was known as "Boone" to his friends, and as "Long-haired Taylor" to others due to his tonsorial style. Boone was a wedge-shaped giant of remarkable physical and mental agility. He had been a youthful gymnast with an itinerant circus in the USA. He was an entertaining raconteur and was highly regarded by the Metis for his prowess with the gun and at the poker table. His wife, Mary, was a diminutive doll, hardy and capable. They had (then) four sweet daughters, ages 13, 10, 6 and 2. The Taylors had located at Swan Lake in 1916 after coming over the Edson Trail by covered wagon two years earlier. With little more than the clothes they wore, they had toughed it out – practically living off the country. True pioneers!

I learned that Boone had bid successfully for the mail contract between Beaverlodge and Pouce Coupe. For performance, he badly needed a good team and set of harness. With neither cash nor credit, this posed a dilemma. Just in time, as if by magic, a team with brand new harness was delivered to his homestead, fully "PREPAID". The anonymous benefactor was, of course, Jim Young.

It is possible they had first met on the Edson Trail, but I am not sure.

The trunk road to Pouce Coupe from Grande Prairie was still quite primitive. It was graded, had culverts and bridges but was not well gravelled, and during spring breakup all traffic stopped until the gumbo dried and hardened. With dry weather on this trip, we made good time. I remember vividly the big Gundy ranch near Tate Creek. A bumper wheat crop (60+ bushels per acre) had been harvested and stacked in sheaves waiting to be threshed. The huge stacks seemed as thick as stooks in harvests I remembered elsewhere. The vast fields of stubble, crowded with these stacks, dropped from view in hollows to reappear in the distance on higher ground – a grand unforgettable perspective of abundance, confirming the rich potential claimed for this great Peace River country.

In Pouce Coupe the first business was at the Government Agent's to pay the fur royalties and have the pelts stamped. Then, after a quick lunch, Jim wheeled around to visit George Hart,[26] the Government Liquor Vendor, to load up with cases of hard liquor. We then headed back south without delay. At this time BC had legalized liquor sales by government vendors but northern Alberta was still "bone dry". When we arrived back at Swan Lake, instead of retracing our route on the main road into Alberta, Jim turned off to follow a wagon track south up Tupper Creek. In about nine miles, this brought us to Peavine Lake where an old Scotch trapper, Alec Anderson, had his cabin.[27] Here we stopped for the night. Jim and Alec were old friends. An appetizer for supper and a "nightcap" were provided from Jim's "stock", but he did not pressure me to break my youthful code of abstinence. This was typical of Jim.

Next day we had about 15 miles on Jim's "winter rum trail" angling southerly back to Kelly Lake. He attempted it with a wagon only because of the unusually dry weather. With the contraband cargo, we would encounter no traffic whatever. Privately, in thought, I was scandalized that I was now an accessory to "rum-running". However, the exigencies of the awful trail — bumping over roots and stumps, avoiding bottomless bog holes, cutting and heaving aside windfalls — were effective antidotes for any morbid self-recrimination. The weather was still glorious and although some leaves had fallen, the colors were magnificent. The Sphagnum moss in the muskegs was like "Joseph's coat of many colors". Subsequently I got to know this trail well, on foot, on snowshoes and by sleigh. Old Alec at Peavine Lake was one of my nearest White neighbors and was to become a staunch friend (see his letters Appendix 3).

We were glad to reach "home" at Kelly Lake about dusk, after such a strenuous but interesting trip. We unloaded and stowed everything inside the store. I noticed that Jim locked the doors securely at bedtime. Early next morning we reloaded and Jim left for Leighmore and Grande Prairie. I resumed the school routine much refreshed and with a better knowledge of local geography and people. The consignee for Jim's illicit load from Pouce Coupe was William Nathan ("Bud") Lay, who ran a gambling joint (for men only) in Grande Prairie.[28]

A memorable feature of that Pouce Coupe trip was rabbits. It was a "rabbit year". In cycles of about 11 years (like sunspots), these animals have a population explosion followed by heavy decimation. We saw literally hundreds of rabbits on the trip. They had already changed color from summer brown to winter white, and the snow had not yet come. They were ludicrously conspicuous and actually seemed embarrassed. This rabbit phenomenon is followed by a sympathetic increase in their predators, which portends good trapping.

Good progress in the school continued. Attendance was practically 100 per cent. It was evident the parents appreciated the opportunity for their children to learn English, to read, to write and to reckon — advantages most of themselves had been denied.

As colder weather approached, I called a meeting of the fathers to program the wood supply for school heating. Much of their discussion was in Cree and quite over my head. It was evident they relished and were skilled in oratory. Their gestures and intonations were expressive and dramatic. I had begun to appreciate the natural dignity and courtesy of these wholesome people. However, I had to take the initiative and exert some authority with them, much as I did in school. I also sensed that (too much) "familiarity breeds contempt" and endeavored to act accordingly.

In school the language program gained momentum in a sort of compound progression. The more they learned the faster they learned. Phonetic values of the alphabet helped them to reason out for themselves both spelling and pronounciation. I gave them copious doses of simple phrases and sentences. These led to easy stories and rhymes from their readers. We soon got started in arithmetic in which they made rapid progress. It perhaps depends least on language than any subject. (Ten years later, I studied integral calculus in German!) Most were good poker players before starting school, so had already the concepts of counting, addition and subtraction. The parents, being illiterate, spent long evenings playing cards, especially whist. Children are natural imitators. The bead counters strung on overhead wires for the old pool games, proved a useful teaching aid for checking addition, subtraction and counting. Every 5th bead was black, and each 10th one had a pendant marked with 10, 20, 30, etc.

I adopted the routine of taking the last hour or so each Friday for the whole school to coach the teacher in Cree. This we all enjoyed and it contributed to a warm rapport. They told me legends from their ancestral folk lore. I suspect some of these originated in early mission schools and not entirely in pagan mythology. Some Cree expressions are quite euphonious and expressive. They knew their teacher came from "far away across the Rocky mountains". In Cree this sounded like "wahayoo kwaskayee asinē oochē". We also started on a program in English anticipating a Christmas concert, to which the whole community would be invited.

My spare time left no room for boredom. I was preparing for five papers in the forthcoming Senior Matric exams: Trigonometry, and two papers each in English and French. This would leave three more for the following year. Senior Matric was required for university entrance to Engineering, Forestry or Medicine. One evening each week was given to coaching four adult men in the three Rs. All could speak English. I remember the names of only two, both married, Johnny Calliou and Isidore Gladu. We enjoyed these sessions. Looking after Jim's store was never onerous. It provided interesting contacts with the people and their mannerisms. They would come in at any time, except during school hours, without knocking or any formal greeting. Usually they would sit on a bench in silence for a moment to collect their thoughts, and then took the indirect approach to the real purpose of their visit. When ready, they would leave in the same way, without a word. It seemed our conventions of "hello" and "goodbye" were just not part of their ingrained etiquette. I asked what they said when they met a friend or stranger in the woods. They said a smile would suffice.

Over the counter in the store, I picked up quite a bit of Cree. Women who spoke no English rarely came, but one or two others helped with my vocabulary, and we often had fun with it. A local saying was, "The best teacher is a bed teacher." In this case, the first expression to learn sounded like "Wenstra pona ponorsa", which is literally "Get out of bed, light the fire, make breakfast". Need it be affirmed that I forewent this intimate form of instruction? With their French background, one had to be careful. Adolphus Gladu, one of my nine-year-olds was playing nearby one Saturday. I picked up a nail and asked him in Cree, "Tanisee eetuwan ee nayhēoek ēoko" – literally "How do we say in Cree this?". Smiling, he quickly replied "le clou". I then asked if he had another word for it. He said after considerable thought "peeopskwapōpoo" – at least that's how it sounded to me.

Further caution was advisable. One morning, after a heavy overnight snowfall, I ventured to observe to a lady in the store, "Timēo kwona anōts" (deep snow today). Later, one of the men cautioned that my accentuation of this expression gave it an obscene meaning. The lady, kindly, had only smiled.

Trying to learn Cree with neither dictionary nor grammar was uphill work. With so many preoccupations, to my regret, I never did get "on top" of it. Now, too late, I have Watkin's dictionary of 1865 and its revision of 1934. I have Father Lacombe's French-Cree dictionary (1874), and grammars by Horden (1871) and Hives (1948). I have also the excellent commentaries on Cree by R.A. Logan, DLS (c1958). The basic Cree (Algonkian) extends from the Rocky Mountains east, right across Canada into Labrador. The name "Mistassini" for the large lake north of Montreal is pure Cree for "Big Stone". In 1927, east of Lake Winnipeg, with my very rudimentary Kelly Lake Cree, I got a non-English-speaking Indian band to show us an obscure portage between the headwaters of the Berens and Poplar rivers. This saved us days of trial-and-error searching, and no doubt a lot of laborious portaging. At Minaki, Ontario, I noticed the Indians' word for pork was "kōkoos", the same word I learned at Kelly Lake. "Mississippi" is, of course, Cree for "Big River". (See my "Cree Commentary" in Appendix 5.)

With rabbits so abundant that winter, someone suggested I make a rabbit robe. A local lady showed me how. Four strong spikes are driven into a wall at corners of the desired format. For my purpose this was about 72 inches square. Lynx cord (like a light sash cord) is fastened and stretched around the four spikes. This serves as the four edges. The rabbit is skinned by removing legs and head, and cutting across the nether parts only. The hide is then peeled off by pulling it inside out over the head, like a sock. With flesh carefully removed, this tube is cut spirally into a ribbon about three-quarters of an inch wide, and perhaps six feet long. These are tied to a long pole and hoisted up outside in the sun and wind to cure and dry. The flesh side curls inwards, making a thick furry thong. Starting at the top left corner, on the wall, the first thong is fastened at one end there. The free end is looped along the top cord, in half hitches about an inch apart. Succeeding thongs are lapped in near the ends of those preceding. When the right-hand edge is reached, the thong is looped around the lynx cord there and then back toward the left edge, looping it through the loops above. Finally the bottom cord is reached and the thongs looped along it as at the top, and fastened. My robe used between 150 and 200 skins. Finished, it was like a furry blanket, about two inches thick. A finger could be poked through the loops anywhere.

The same lady (I think it was Annie Gladu, Isidore's wife) lined my robe with flannel and made the outside cover of canvas, with flaps, and moosehide tie-strings. It folded into a wonderful sleeping bag. It was almost like a furnace, and I used it outdoors on the coldest nights. It weighed about 20 pounds, too heavy and bulky for backpack, but OK on a sleigh. In summer it was too hot as a bag, but could serve as a mattress for two people. I paid my Kelly Lake school boys 5¢ per skin, processed into thongs. It was a bonanza for them.

On the subject of robes, I may remark here that an elegant and unique handicraft of the Kelly Lake women was the "lynx-paw robe". Lynx pelts were marketed with the forepaws removed. The women save and tan the skins of these, until about 200 are accumulated, enough for a warm, durable and beautiful robe. Thick soft fur on the lynx's large paws enables it to walk on soft snow. The color is light silver-grey, with dark longitudinal stripes on top. The little pelts are roughly wedge-shaped. They are assembled alternately "left-right" into a rectangular format of sufficient size and sewn with sinew fibre called "ustigut". Usually the robe is bordered with a dark contrasting fur. Their elegance would grace regal drawing rooms in palaces anywhere in the world. One of these robes was given me a few years ago by Guy H. Blanchet, DLS, BCLS, and later I donated it to the BC Provincial Museum in Victoria. Blanchet had obtained this robe in 1909 from Celestin Gladu whose wife had made it.[29]

My first Kelly Lake acquaintance, the diminutive blind great-great-grandmother, proved to be an interesting and, indeed, historic person, which I did not appreciate then as fully as I do now. However, I paid her occasional courtesy calls, in deference to her great age and importance in the community, taking modest gifts like fresh eggs or fruit as tokens of respect. She lived nearby with her daughter Marguerite (nee Calliou) and son-in-law, Celestin Gladu, who themselves were elderly grand-parents. Although blind and over 100 years old, she was responsive and coherent. Our medium of communication was French, hers being much better than my high school brand. Among other things which now sadly elude my memory, she told me about "la chasse aux bisons sur les grandes prairies – jadis – il y a longtemps longtemps!" I have more to say about this venerable matriarch in a following chapter.

I can confirm the early surveyors' remarks that the Kelly Lake men were expert hunters and trappers. Moose was the principal quarry and usually plentiful. It provided both meat and raiment. The meat – fresh, frozen or dried ("jerked") – and sometimes processed into "pemmican", was the chief source of protein. The hides were expertly tanned and handicrafted by the women into moccasins, gloves, jackets, bags, cord etc. The best work was sewn with "ustigut".[30] Rabbits, wildfowl and fish supplemented moosemeat when the large animals were scarce. Bear, beaver and lynx were also eaten as occasion offered or required. Other native elements of diet, berries, roots and the like were gathered by the women. Trade items, flour, tea, salt, lard, sugar, as well as clothing, hardware, etc. were obtained in exchange for the harvest of their traplines, and such handicrafts.

With the first permanent snow of winter, the men would organize their outfits and head out to their trapping grounds. The Kelly Lake trapping grounds included watersheds of the Kiskatinaw, Redwillow, Murray, Sukunka and Wapiti rivers - much of which now is in prominence for its coal resources. Transport was mainly with narrow birchwood toboggans, drawn by dogs "in line". These required narrower trails than packhorses, and in winter dog food was less a problem than horse fodder. Dogs were sometimes packed, running loose. This required a minimum of trail-making. A strong animal could carry up to 50 pounds, divided and balanced on each side in special bags. For trapping, snares, deadfalls and leg-hold steel traps were used. A book could be written on the art of trapping. I was interested to learn that various scents were used as lures. The trappers remained "out" all Winter, except for a light trip home for a short "break" at Christmas and New Year.

As I remember, in the early 1920s, the annual harvest of a good trapper could gross about $1,000 - adequate for the trade needs of his family, and for re-outfitting his trapline next season. A perennial problem for fur buyers like Jim Young was the granting of credit or "jawbone" as it was called. The effects of this balanced out as a form of communal welfare insurance. The yield of the more efficient, industrious and honest ones covered the shortcomings of less capable individuals. In those days there were no forms of public welfare.

My recollection of the kinds of fur and the approximate prices is as under:

	$		$		$
muskrat & weasel	1	cross fox	35	martin	?
coyote	10-15	black fox	50	mink	?
wolf	15-20	silver fox	80	otter	?
bear (black)	15	lynx	45-50	fisher	100
red fox	20-30	beaver	45-50		

(The values were "in trade" at the Kelly Lake store).

All pelts except bear and beaver were "cured" in tubular form inside out, stretched on thin wooden frames, but were turned fur side out again for the market. Bear and beaver were cut along the belly to open out flat, and were stretched in surrounding wooden frames.

The Kelly Lake people showed little inclination for agriculture, either field crops or livestock. They seemed instinctively oriented to hunting. One or two families had a few horses for packing, the saddle or wagon. These animals were left to "rustle" through most of the winter on their own. I remember no dairy cattle or domestic fowl in the settlement. However, dogs were too much in evidence. On the other hand, the "halfbreeds" at Big Bar in the Cariboo district, largely of Teutonic-Shuswap ancestry, followed their paternal instincts with horses, cattle and irrigated field crops. While good hunters, they were by no means as dedicated to trapping as were the French-Cree at Kelly Lake.

In addition to activities already mentioned, the Kelly Lake women snared small animals locally, for example rabbits, weasels, and muskrat. Some of the children did this, too. A specialty of the women was beautiful fancy-work in silk embroidery or beads on moose and caribou hide. "Fancy" moccasins, gauntlets, jackets, etc. brought premium prices in trade. Their silk embroidery in gay colors and floral designs excel any other such work I have seen. For small articles, caribou hide is sometimes favored, due to its finer texture, compared to moose. For larger items like jackets, caribou hide is rather hard and stiff, and often blemished with the scars of the bot fly, a parasite to which the moose seem to be immune.

Married women at Kelly Lake were often referred to as "Mrs. Alfred" or "Mrs. Johnny", instead of by the husband's surname. Most spoke only Cree, and with few exceptions, remained in the background. During my second winter in the community, indirectly I was offered a "high school course" in sex. This was declined as diplomatically as possible. I hasten to emphasize that this was an isolated case and in no way characteristic of local femininity. In fact, I was a bit offended, being sure I could do a doctoral thesis on the subject — purely from imagination, if not from experience.

Jim and I were invited to occasional local dances. Everyone turned out in their best finery. In addition to the ubiquitous square dances, they had some native routines, which seemed like adaptations from "old country" reels. One was the "wapoosaywin" or "rabbit dance". There was ample local talent with the violin for lively music like the "Red River jig". When we got home after one of these parties, I said to Jim, "Didn't young Marceline look cute tonight!" His gruff reply was, "You should go around and see her in the wigwam in the morning!"

Kelly Lake homes blessed with a new member of the family, not yet house-broken, were earmarked, not by a clothesline laden daily with white diapers, but by a pole rack outside, where a good supply of Sphagnum moss was spread out to dry in the sun and wind. Possessing remarkable absorbent and sterile properties, this moss was used for medical dressings during World War I. It was in abundant supply at Kelly Lake from nearby muskegs and was traditionally used for infant hygiene. Being disposable, it saved Mama the daily grind over the laundry tub. It was at Kelly Lake, too, that I first noticed little toddlers cavorting around in summer without pants, a practical and sensible custom I have since observed in some exotic parts of the world.

Once in a while the men had gambling sessions which could continue more than one night. These were the ubiquitous guessing contests with small tokens passed from hand to hand, hidden under a blanket between opposite rows of players. Invariably they were accompanied by beating a drum and a vocal chant. The monotony was interrupted briefly while the guessing took place. I suspect these sessions coincided with a temporary supply of liquor, either legitimate or "moonshine", a deadly home-distilled "rotgut". Probably this was why Jim and I were never invited to these. We could hear the muffled drum and chanting all through the night, or until Morpheus dropped his sound-proof curtain.

Winter snow did not begin to accumulate until early December that year (1923). Before this, clear cold weather, prior to the snow, had allowed the frost to penetrate deeply and harden the ground. The late snow delayed the men's departure for their traplines, so their return for the holiday break was also delayed. Our anticipated school concert was, therefore, postponed until after the New Year. School closed for the holidays on schedule, at noon on Friday, 21 December.

On that day, after a quick lunch, Jim and I started out with a sleighload of fur for Pouce Coupe. I took my new rabbit-robe sleeping bag, eager to test it. Our route this time followed Jim's winter trail to Peavine Lake. The ground being hard and smoothed with snow, it made for good going. Jim always had a strong, high spirited, fast-walking but gentle team, and Roanie and Kate admirably filled these requirements. In many trips with Jim, they won my esteem and affection. The weather continued clear and very cold. Darkness had overtaken us as we reached the top of a low hill overlooking Peavine Lake to the north, about 200 feet below. We could see the lighted window of Anderson's cabin shining like a mariner's beacon at the far end of the lake, near its outlet into Peavine Creek. It was less than two miles distant, a cheering prospect.

Descending to the lake we found it frozen over with a few inches of snow on top. Weather having been so cold, Jim decided to go out on the ice for smooth going and a more direct route than by the summer trail around the west edge of the lake. We made good time. As we approached the shore, less than 100 yards from Alec's cabin, suddenly the ice broke under the horses, but held firm otherwise. The "nigh" (left) horse found bottom without being completely submerged. The "off" (right) horse, in more depth, had difficulty aggravated by the sleigh's tongue on its landward side. With surprising agility, Jim unhitched both horses, without getting wet himself, and the nigh horse scrambled ashore. With a stout rope (always kept handy) fastened to the head of the off horse in the water, and to the other horse on shore, we were able to haul the struggling animal out, quite uninjured. Then, with both horses ashore and the rope fastened to the rear of the sleigh, we made them haul it slowly backwards on to firm ground, where we re-assembled the outfit and proceeded on shore to the cabin. No damage, no losses, nothing even wet – except the horses which were steaming from their exertions. All this happened within half an hour. Meanwhile, old Alec sat cozily in his cabin, quite unaware of the exciting drama so near outside.

Luckily Alec had a snug little stable for the team, which we unharnessed and covered with blankets to allow them to cool off and dry slowly. After this, we satisfied their thirst with buckets of tepid water. They got extra rations of sheaves and oats for their well-earned supper. The reward for us was a hot supper and an evening's sociability with Alec. At bedtime Jim and Alec indulged in a double nightcap, and I crawled snugly into my rabbit robe on the floor.

Early next morning we left "Peavine Castle", Alec's name for his abode, stopping only briefly at Swan Lake to greet the Taylors and "Ma" Fynn (Mrs. Jane Fynn?). The latter had taken over the Ellis Borden ranch there.[31]   Her son, Jack, roughly my age, had a livery stable at Pouce Coupe about this time. Later, "Ma" joined him and died there.[32]   At Pouce Coupe, we quickly repeated the routine of our previous visit, and headed back to Peavine Lake. In those days, government offices were open Saturday mornings. The whole of Pouce Coupe's "business district" comprised the Government Agent's office, the Provincial Police barracks, Frank Haskins' store,[33]   the liquor store operated by George Hart, and a pool room. Dawson Creek was then only a ranch post office, where I think meals could be obtained. It had been a long day when we got back to Alec's for the night at Peavine Lake.

Sunday morning we made good time on Jim's winter trail, taking no risks on lake ice with the heavier load and pausing at Kelly Lake just for lunch and to rest the team. We got to Leighmore that evening in time to pick up our mail and a warm invitation to return there for Christmas dinner with the Beadle family if we could get back from Grande Prairie in time for the festivities. We then spent the night with the Finn brothers, Tim and Bill, bachelors who lived not far away and who always made Jim welcome.[34]

Next morning (Christmas Eve) Jim was re-organizing his load, and temporarily set an open case of imported brandy out on the ground, the bottles of which were wrapped in straw jackets. A tall, raw-boned gelding, belonging to Jim, called "The Grey", happened to be loose in the barnyard. He seized one of the bottles with his teeth, and surprised at its weight, gave it a vigorous shake. The bottle dropped out on the snow, luckily without breaking, and the horse ran off munching the straw jacket. This discriminating animal was to become my saddle horse, on loan from Jim. He served me well over many trail miles, including the trip through Pine Pass next summer (1924). Perhaps we should have renamed him "Cognac".

It was a long haul that day to Grande Prairie via Beaverlodge. Arriving after dusk, Jim turned into a back lane, paralleling the one and only main street of town. About halfway along the lane, he opened a gate in a high board fence, to enter the back yard of Bud Lay's poker emporium. In this seclusion, we transferred Jim's cargo from Pouce Coupe into the rear of Bud's premises. He was obviously gratified that his holiday inventory would be in good shape, thanks to Jim. We were more than welcome to stay there overnight, but did not linger next morning, Christmas Day. After a long and bitterly cold trip, we got to Leighmore in time for Christmas dinner in the evening with the Beadles. The Finn boys had lots of room, so we went there again to bed down.

After five days' hard travel and with school holidays still in effect, Jim and I spent a few days socializing in the Leighmore neighbourhood. Our base of operations was at the Finns', thanks to their unfailing hospitality and their commodious quarters. For a bed, my rabbit robe served well, even on the floor, if necessary. I enjoyed this opportunity to become acquainted with Jim's coterie of Leighmore friends, most of them bachelors.

Lars Quittem (Kvittem?), from Sweden of course, concocted a vitriolic distillate from potatoes and other occult ingredients. When we drove into his yard, he would rush out shouting "By Yeezus, here iss Yimmy und Yerry! – Yump right out boyss, you iss just in time" (for lunch or supper).[35] Another Scandinavian was old Ed Quass whose moonshine enjoyed top repute. He used home-grown barley malt, sprouted on trays overhead in the warm air of his cabin.[36]

John McCormack was an old Klondiker. He lived with his cat, a dog, a milk cow, a couple of horses and enough chickens for a few eggs. He said the cow was "the mother" of them all. Perhaps Mac's "Klondike Story" should follow here instead of in the Appendices.

McCormack and about eight "greenhorn" companions from the East, left Athabasca Landing in May, 1897 and reached Dawson City in June, 1898, after 13 months on the trail. They lost everything but their lives in the first rapids but re-outfitted as well as possible at the nearest Hudson's Bay Company post, "by appropriation". Company managers were forbidden to sell to miners, as their inventories were barely sufficient for the fur trade. The HBC could however claim reimbursement through a federal "Miners' Relief Fund" for survival supplies "demanded" by desperate Klondikers.

After freeze-up on the Liard River, the McCormack party hauled their outfit on toboggans. They developed a routine whereby each of the party did his chores, according to ability, in complete silence – getting firewood, water, cooking and making a huge communal bed in which they all slept together for warmth. They took turns sleeping progressively from one side to the other.

At Pelly Banks, just over the Liard-Pelly divide, they camped to build boats with whipsawn lumber. These were to go down the Pelly River as soon as the ice went out. Here they all got scurvy, but survived by drinking tea brewed from spruce needles. The one exception being "Mac's" particular chum, who refused the bitter brew. He is still there in the lonely grave his pals made for him. In the Yukon they found no bonanza. Mac took a job on a river steamer until he could afford the trip "out".

After surviving so long on the trail outdoors, old Mac was surely wise in the ways of the wilderness, and in the real values of life. His ability to predict weather was uncanny. One balmy evening, under a beautiful "dapple" sky, he stepped outside and said, "Every indication of a storm". Next day the storm broke with a vengeance. Old Mac died alone on his homestead. He was found by his friend and neighbor Albin Ringstrom.[37]

After a couple of days' rest, Jim and I were quite ready to start back for Kelly Lake to be there in good time for New Year's Day; and with our festive dinner in mind, we bought a plump young turkey, nicely plucked and dressed, from one of the homesteads.

A few miles from Leighmore on the Kelly Lake trail were some large hay meadows. They were leased by Frank Bedier, a homesteader at Rio Grande.[38] He had a cabin on the lease and bached there when haying in the summer or when feeding stock in winter. Jim always stopped there to say "hello" or leave an order of supplies if Frank were there. Bedier liked to tease by calling me "Professor", but I sensed with just a bit of sarcasm. I disliked even being called "teacher" and encouraged my pupils (not too successfully) to address me as "Mr. Andrews". Being young, I probably could not fully conceal my dislike of Frank's insinuations.

On a later occasion, travelling alone, light, on horseback, it was expedient to stop overnight with Bedier. He dispensed the traditional hospitality of supper and breakfast, but let me sleep fully dressed on a canvas cot, with only an old worn out fur robe for top cover. It was bitterly cold. After the fire died down, I got a good taste of what freezing to death must be like. Thoughts of my cozy rabbit robe only increased my misery. It was a lesson that to keep warm one needs as much insulation under as over. Bedier probably thought of me as a tenderfoot "city slicker" needing some toughening up. The lesson for me was to take a bit of kidding in good humor. Frank probably had both objects in mind.

The significance of one memory from my travels with Jim Young is better appreciated now, having survived a war and seen some of its cemeteries in Europe. Along the lonely miles of Jim's backwoods wagon trails we occasionally passed an empty cabin in its clearing – evidence of bygone Hope and Courage, but now derelict with surrounding Nature reclaiming what had been briefly borrowed from her. In reply to "Who lived there?", Jim would name a 1914-18 war volunteer who had not returned. My mind paraphrases the lines from Bret Harte's "Dickens in Camp":

> Lost is that camp and wasted all its fire:
> And he who wrought that spell?
> Ah! towering pine and stately Flemish spire
> Ye have one tale to tell --
> And on that grave in Flanders' fields ...

It came time to prepare our New Year's dinner. Jim rather liked basic cooking, so this was a joint effort. We went "all out" on the turkey. For the traditional stuffing we assembled the usual ingredients, breadcrust, onions, raisins and spices – but we had no sage, as such. However, when leaving Big Bar the previous July, I had gathered some Blue Sage (Artemesia tridentata) to put in my trunk for moth deterrent and because I loved its pungent aroma. So a liberal portion of this was chopped up and added to the mix. The well-stuffed bird went into the oven to roast gently and long. Finally the feast was ready, and our appetites razor sharp. Jim carved the roast, emitting its aromatic vapors, and we loaded our plates. Horror of horrors! The turkey was inedible, as though it had been stewed in turpentine. It was a sad case of too much of a good thing. A tiny pinch of the Big Bar sage would have sufficed.

Soon after school resumed early in January and before the fathers returned to their traplines, we staged the long-anticipated Christmas concert. We had a day or two to freshen up the repertoire, which had been practically ready before the holiday. These were simple items appropriate for each age group, to show off their scholastic accomplishments: short recitations, a group song or two and some simple dramatics. The schoolroom was packed, with barely enough space for the performers. Furniture backed along the walls provided seats for the elderly and squatting on the floor was no hardship for the rest. Winter wraps and one or two somnolent infants were stowed in Jim's store area.

My father, a druggist in Elgin, Manitoba, had just sent me an ingenious little portable gramophone with some records, including one or two Christmas numbers. He suggested I might stage a surprise with it (Appendix 3, No 7). Our concert was the opportunity. I hid it in a corner behind a large wall map, all set to go. At the end of the kids' program and just before refreshments, I sneaked behind the map and triggered the machine. Suddenly, the hymn "Joy to the World ... the Lord is come!" boomed out in rousing volume, almost lifting the sod roof. Eyes opened like saucers and jaws dropped down on chests. It was a smashing finale to our program. More gramophone selections were played during refreshments. Candy, biscuits, etc. from Jim's store were dished out with lots of hot sweet tea. They had brought their own mugs. The first-ever Kelly Lake school concert was a signal success.

On the succeeding winter evenings the little "Deccaphone" as it was called provided some casual music for the clientele of Jim's store, but without becoming a nuisance. I also used it in school, my Haggman friends in New Westminster having sent me a fine selection of classical records, including the vigorous "Sextette" from Donizetti's "Lucia di Lammermoor". This became a favorite of old St Pierre Gauthier. He would listen to it in rapt delight, and after the crashing finale would exclaim "Gee! one hell big drunk, eh?" St Pierre was reputed an expert trail locator with a skilled eye for topography. He was with Alex Monkman when they found the Monkman Pass. It is alleged that St Pierre himself had discovered the pass, and led Monkman to it. In view of the prominence of Monkman Pass in connection with the coal resources in that area, it is appropriate that a mountain near the pass has been named Mt Gauthier. About 1930, he succumbed to injuries from burning his feet by an open campfire in cold winter weather.[39]

After the New Year, I felt it was time to insist that the children speak only English at school, indoors and outdoors, before and after school, at recess and during the noon hour. To monitor this, I contrived to play with them outside as much as possible. This really helped. They had the universal ability of children to acquire a language other than their mother tongue quickly − in play. I got some welcome fresh air and exercise, and learned one or two of their native games. Attendance continued at practically 100 per cent. No sickness and punctuality was good too. Those having farthest to come were the Campbells, Sarah, 14 and Alfred, 9. They lived about a mile across the lake ice, and a little farther in summer by the shore route.

I religiously raised the large and elegant Union Jack on the flagpole every morning at 8 o'clock, as a time signal. It was always lowered at sunset, in the best tradition. The flag symbolized order and authority and its bright colors against the grey winter sky gladdened my heart. Once or twice, a large owl would alight on top of the pole and remain for some time to survey his surroundings. His neck must have been completely swivel-jointed. He would follow me with his intent stare, without ever unwinding while I walked completely around the building. If he did unwind, he was too fast for detection.

In February, the days began to lengthen, a welcome trend. By this time Jim had a good stockpile of horsefeed (oat sheaves) on top of the stable, so he brought a saddle horse for my use at Kelly Lake. It was The Grey gelding which had displayed his taste for imported brandy in straw jackets at Leighmore. Jim also provided a good saddle, which I bought from him later (at cost). The Grey was gentle enough but having been running loose outside, was a bit skittish, until we got used to each other. I enjoyed exercising him and myself, and otherwise looking after him.

One Saturday I decided to ride to Goodfare, about 13 miles east in Alberta, with some outgoing mail. For his own reasons, Jim never went there. I tied the mail and a lunch in a sack behind the saddle, evidently not very securely. When we had gone about half a mile beyond the fork where the Leighmore road branched off to the right heading south (see Map 3), my mail sack came loose on one side and flopped down on the other, hitting the horse on the flank. Reacting instantly and vigorously, he threw me off. I was unhurt, but lost hold of the reins. Before I could rally, the horse had started back on the trail and evaded my attempts to catch him or head him off.

I concluded that when he reached the fork he would likely turn south on the Leighmore trail and head for "home" on it. The dragging reins would slow his pace somewhat. My one chance was to cut across through the woods as quickly as possible to the other trail, hoping to intercept him. Luckily I got there in time to meet him face to face. He was surprised and taken aback. With this advantage, I gently, but quickly approached him and got hold of the reins. The situation was under control. After this incident he seemed to acknowledge that I was the boss, and we got along well, with better understanding and mutual respect.

The School Inspector's visit finally materialized about the end of February. School inspection was a feature of BC's educational policy. Well-qualified inspectors reported annually on school premises, attendance, and teacher performance. The Peace River District was then served by Mr. G.H. Gower, based at Prince George. He had an enormous territory to cover, much of it by primitive and arduous travel. He arrived at Kelly Lake late one afternoon quite unexpectedly, having come in a light cutter with a driver via Swan Lake and Brainard's. Bed and board for them were no problem. Jim was away, so his cot was vacant. Mr. Gower spent most of the next day in the school and then left for Swan Lake in the evening, probably having late supper at Mrs. Brainard's.

He was friendly, sympathetic and helpful, and the evening gave us a chance to get acquainted. In the morning he had me go through my usual routines with younger and older age groups both separately and together. After lunch he took over with his own questions and routines. Asked to describe the action of putting out the light, one boy responded, "Kill the light." This amused Mr. Gower, who thought it entirely logical.

I sensed that the Inspector's reactions were favorable. I re-marked to him that, at the beginning, I had thought of writing to the Normal School in Vancouver for advice. "Forget it," he replied, "you already know how to handle this situation better than anyone there". He also expressed admiration for my whole-some way of life – baching, getting firewood, water, caring for and exercising my saddle horse, my evening classes for adults, pinch-hitting in Jim's store and my Senior Matric studies. He strongly urged me to return for a second school year, so our good start would not be in vain. I was encouraged and gratified. I had won a fine and helpful friend.[40]

During the short winter days, the sun would appear about 9 am, just east of south. It would sneak low across the sky and drop feebly below the treeline about 3 in the afternoon. There was barely enough daylight for the school children to come and go. Lengthening days in March gave promise, but winter maintained its frigid grip on our world. Spring break-up with thawing ground and water rampant, discouraged all travel.

Summer seemed to arrive overnight. Birds of all kinds flocked back, leaves exploded into soft fresh greenery, myriads of mosquitoes filled the air. New life was vibrant. For about a week, copious dog droppings, accumulated in cold storage all winter, suddenly thawed and vaporized odoriferously. But they soon dried and dissipated below the mantel of new grass, and the stench was forgotten for another year. The last token of winter was the ice clearing from the lake. The lake ice normally measured a thickness of about two feet. Open water appeared first near the shore. Here the earliest aquatic birds had to congregate — at obvious risk. Nothing like roast duck to relieve the monotony of moosemeat!

During my winter firewood operations I had noticed how hungry rabbits chewed off all the bark from green aspen cuttings, including felled logs. Anticipating next winter's requirements, I felled an extra dozen or more choice trees before the snow cleared, leaving them prone on the ground. The rabbits voraciously co-operated, so these barked logs lay drying all summer. They were well-seasoned by fall, making excellent fuel for cooking and heating.

I must have become infected with the Metis aversion to gardening; either that or was too busy. However, Nature provided a welcome crop of early greens from an unexpected source. On the "sod" roof of Jim's stable, where oat sheaves were stockpiled, an early and bounteous crop of common Lambs' Quarters (Chenoposium allum?) or "Pigweed" (Amaranthus retroflexis?) flourished, favored by convectional heat and ammonia-rich vapors from the animals below. This succulent crop, high on the stable roof and therefore, safe from corruption by countless dogs at large, was fully exploited.

Records indicate that the Kelly Lake School officially terminated its first year's operations on Thursday, 19 June, 1924. This was a day early due to the premises being requisitioned for a polling booth on the Friday. I promoted all scholars, roughly according to age and accomplishment: Colin Gladu, Sarah Campbell and Henry Belcourt to Grade 3; the rest to Grade 2. This left Grade 1 clear for beginners expected in the fall. Arithmetic had been the best subject, the oldest getting well into Grade 5 level. Most excelled in penmanship and drawing. Spelling, reading and vocabulary were favored by virtue of their keen memory and faculties of observation. Grammar and syntax proved more difficult because Cree is so different from English in these elements.[41] In general all scholars were in good shape to resume studies after summer holidays, when the curriculum would broaden to include geography, history and more advanced English. I probably had all pupils write neatly on clean paper, in large letters, "KELLY LAKE SCHOOL WILL OPEN AGAIN AT 9 O'CLOCK, TUESDAY MORNING, 2nd SEPTEMBER, 1924". This was to be pinned on the wall in their homes.

The school premises in Jim Young's store had served well enough for the first year. Occasionally audible business in the store behind the partition was a distraction, and the unseen audience there could sometimes embarrass our school routine. Some increase in enrolment could be expected and there was little room for expansion in Jim's store building. A commodious cabin within 200 feet from the store had been vacated by William Calliou who had moved with his family farther west to Jackfish Lake vicinity (near Moberly Lake). In anticipation of moving the school to this cabin, Jim started negotiations for it — with the advantage that Calliou was in debt to Jim for a sizable amount of "jawbone".

The provincial general election, on Friday, 20 June, 1924, brought Kelly Lake into momentary importance as a polling centre, like Hugo's atom fraternizing with the hurricane ("Les Miserables", Part IV, Book 11). The politicians must have been really scraping the bottom of the barrel for votes. The issue was between the incumbent Liberals led by "Honest John" Oliver and the Conservative opposition under William John Bowser. Coincident was a referendum pro or con beer by the glass. The Metis people at Kelly Lake enjoyed the franchise to vote as well as all other rights of citizenship. The settlement was in no way a reserve under the federal Indian Affairs administration.

As mentioned, the school room in Jim Young's store was designated a polling booth. It was a "first" for Kelly Lake. The scholars got an extra holiday and their teacher, still too young to vote himself, was free to savor the political goings-on. Jim was a scrutineer as well as landlord. Dry weather having facilitated travel, all kinds of unusual people showed up. One party made it in a Model T Ford car, which also must have been a "first" for Kelly Lake. Another novelty was the arrival of a string of pack donkeys, allegedly loaded with persuasive beverages, (although I remember no overt rowdyism). This strange pack outfit was owned and operated by Fred Callison with his attractive little wife, Dora, as "assistant" packer. It was rumored they had been hired by the Pouce Coupe merchant, Frank Haskins, whose political leanings were (and still are) unknown to me. They had used the surveyors' trail along Alberta-BC Boundary south from Swan Lake. The donkeys' tiny hooves must have been quite unsuited to any boggy muskeg terrain along that route.

The Voters' List totalled 38.[42] Some were complete strangers – recruited from God knows where. Among these was a venerable, dignified and colorful Metis called Batisse[43] who like many others was illiterate. It was necessary to explain the ballots in front of opposing scrutineers – all of which, with the beer option, was a bit too complicated for Batisse. Finally, at the end of his patience, the Returning Officer asked "Do you want Bill Bowser or John Oliver?" Batisse, with emphatic finality replied, "I like him George Hart." Thus he had succinctly indicated both his politics and his preference for beer by the glass. George Hart was not on the ballot, but having been appointed a liquor vendor, was probably a good Liberal, and beer was part of his stock in trade. Batisse likely thought George Hart was the most important man in the country.

The School Inspector, Mr. Gower, had written from Prince George in late March, advising me to apply formally to Victoria to write five papers of the forthcoming Senior Matric exams in early summer. I did this at once, yet when school officially closed 19 June, no instructions for the exams had arrived. With the elections finished on a Friday, Jim and I drove to Leighmore the next day, among other things, to get any mail. Still no word about the exams. But, first thing Sunday morning a delayed telegram arrived at Leighmore from the Registrar in Victoria instructing me to report at Rolla, 9 am Monday, 23 June. This was "tomorrow" and more than 80 miles distant by trail.

I saddled up at once, heading back for Kelly Lake on The Grey, the rangy four-year-old with a weakness for cognac in straw jackets. Arriving there mid-afternoon, I fed, watered and rested the horse and myself until about suppertime. We then took the old surveyors' trail along the Alberta-BC Boundary to Swan Lake. This was more direct than via Peavine Lake, and I had hiked part of it before.

It was practically the longest day of the year and our direction was due north. We sleuthed our way along the faint trail, detouring for the odd muskeg and windfall, dropping into and climbing out of occasional ravines. I could verify our whereabouts by the prominent boundary monuments at intervals of about a mile.[44] It was nearly 11 pm when the sun finally dipped below the horizon, just west of north. Then its twilight glow moved slowly to the right across our path ahead. The horse seemed to share my sense of urgency. He behaved willingly and well. As the twilight darkened we stumbled along without too many blunders. Horse and rider felt the magic of the semi-darkness, when bush, trees and boulders assumed weird and occult forms. Only our own sounds broke the mysterious silence. Gently the sun re-appeared ahead to right, promising another beautiful day.

About 3 am from a commanding hill we could see Swan Lake about three miles ahead, and 500 feet below, reflecting the full glory of the dawn. I soon reached Ma Flynn's, where all was dead quiet. I stabled and attended the horse, removing the saddle to air his back, then crept into the house to find a spot to lie down. Ma roused to ask "Who's that?" and told me to find a bed until breakfast time – which came all too soon. I then saddled up again.

We stopped briefly at Pouce Coupe to refresh ourselves, and arrived at Rolla early afternoon. By this time both horse and rider were getting a bit groggy. However, I reported immediately to the presiding teacher at the school and explained the circumstances of my late arrival.

I had already missed the first exam. But as I was the only candidate for Senior Matric, she said I could write it next morning and the other exams immediately following, instead of taking the whole of the week as per schedule – provided I would go right back to the hotel and to bed. May God bless her soul, sensible and kind. Having forgotten her name hangs heavily on my conscience now. She was very likely Miss Mabel M. Morrow who is officially recorded as having taught at Rolla that year and for several years following.[45] My debt of gratitude to her has compounded mightily over so many succeeding years, and its acquittal must now be postponed until the Hereafter, as I learned only recently of her decease c1980. She became Mrs. Everett Miller and was survived by her husband.

I still have Certificate No. 4929, dated July, 1924, signed by A. Sullivan, Secretary, Board of Examiners, Victoria, BC, confirming that I got a "Pass" in all five papers. (I should confess that percentage grades were mediocre: English Composition 72, English Literature 65, French Literature 40, French Grammar 59 and Trigonometry 40.)

I had no reason to linger in Rolla after the exams, so I set out for Kelly Lake at the earliest opportunity. My return trip was relaxed.

My first school year at Kelly Lake was now at an end. It had been most worthwhile in all respects and I was quite ready to follow Mr. Gower's advice and return there for another year.

4: Beaverlodge, Alta, 2 November 1914. This photo could well be entitled "Jim Young, with his outfit, meets Gerry Andrews on his first arrival here, 23 September 1923". (Courtesy S. Prescott Fay)

5: Kelly Lake, 1923. Jim Young with Kate and Roanie.

6: First pupils, Kelly Lake, 1923: L to R, back, Henry Belcourt, Billy Gladu, George Hamelin, Colin Gladu, Adolphus Gladu, Alec Gladu, Sarah Campbell; front, David Gray, Alfred Campbell, Jimmie Letendre, Mary Belcourt, Josephine Gladu.

7: Playtime at Kelly Lake School, December 1923. They balance on my firewood log, near Jim Young's store. Johnny Supernat's cabin behind.

8: Urbain Gladu at his cabin, Kelly Lake, autumn, 1923. His gun looks like a muzzle-loader, and slung from his shoulders may be a powder horn and a bag of shot. He wore moosehide moccasins winter and summer.

9: Airview, East Pine, BC, 1947. Murray R (silt-laden from glaciers) enters top right, from south; Pine R, lower right from west is clear (no glaciers in Pine Pass); Hart Highway, not yet completed to Pine Pass, crosses below forks. In 1924, wagon track from Pouce Coupe ended at Palmer's place on flat beyond the sandbar. After crossing rivers separately we found the packtrail and camped on near side of Pine R. (GSA #118)

10: Up Pine R to Hart Highway bridge at East Pine, August 1953. PGE Ry bridge here not yet built. In 1924, we camped below grassy slopes in right background. A.R.C. Selwyn also camped there 9 August 1875. Before backtracking downstream to Fort St John he climbed Mt Wartenbe (4003ft), the skyline mesa. (GSA #1104)

60

CHAPTER 2

PACKERS' PROGRESS THROUGH PINE PASS: 1924

Long months of confinement in store and school at Kelly Lake having sharpened our appetites for some action and adventure, Jim Young and I planned a packhorse trip over Pine Pass for the up-coming school vacation (July and August, 1924). Jim was interested in rumors of good livestock country west of Prince George and was optimistic about selling his horses there after the trip. I had been exposed to some packhorse travel with Brewsters at Field, BC in 1921 and had made a trip alone from Big Bar Creek via Lillooet to Pemberton in 1923 with my own two-horse outfit, but was not checked out on the professional packer's criterion of the "diamond hitch" (more on this later in the chapter).

My small-scale, one-sheet government map of BC, (1923; 1 inch=31½ miles) showed a wagon track from Pouce Coupe west to East Pine (see Map 2) and from there a packtrail following up the Pine River to its source in Pine Pass. About 20 miles beyond, down the Misinchinka River, the trail forked. The left branch headed southerly via the Parsnip and Crooked rivers to Summit Lake, which was connected by a wagon track to Giscome Portage and Prince George. The right branch continued southwest across the Parsnip River to McLeod Lake (the historic fur post) and on farther to Fort St James on Stuart Lake, which was connected by a wagon track southerly to Vanderhoof on the CNR. The map scale was too small for much detail but the situation as outlined looked inviting.

I was unaware then of the "BC Pre-emptor's Map" series (1 inch = 3-4 miles). They showed as much detail as then known and many blank areas were garnished with interesting notes about topography, soil, game, timber, grazing and minerals. However, the tiny map we did have was a treasured item of my personal kit and it proved sufficient to guide us to our chosen destination.

We decided on a party of three, which has the virtue of social stability. Important questions can be decided two votes against one, if not unanimously. Jim's teacher friend, Fred Barber, bachelor from near Beaverlodge, agreed to join us.[46] Both were 20 years my senior, which was also my age that summer. I think Jim originally had Barber in mind for the Kelly Lake school but he (Barber) could not get the necessary permit to teach in BC so I got the job. There was never even a hint of resentment about this. We decided on six horses − three to ride, two for packs and one spare − and to assemble and outfit at Kelly Lake in late June, 1924. Barber's two canine retainers (Tip and her son, Jerry) were also included.

On my tiny map the sinuosities of the route from Pouce Coupe to McLeod Lake, our last and first points of supply, stretched out to about five inches or 150 miles. If we could average 15 miles a day, a minimum of 10 days' rations was indicated. We allowed for 20 days. Information about the Pine Pass route was meagre and certainly not up to date. An oldtimer in Pouce Coupe recalled having come that way about 20 years earlier. All he could say was that "the Devil's Club was awful"! A hardy Scot made the trip alone on foot living solely on oatmeal. A forest ranger claimed to have gone as far as the pass where he found evidence of a trapper from Prince George. Some highlights of Pine Pass history, unknown to us then, may be noted here.

In 1872, Charles Horetzky, exploring for a CPR route with Professor John Macoun, up the Peace River route, reported rumors of "a low timbered pass at the headwaters of the Pine River used by the Indians". In 1875, Dr A.R.C. Selwyn, again with Professor Macoun, attempted to find this pass from both eastern and western approaches, without success, due to an inadequate canoe and unwilling guides. Finally, in 1877, (Sir)

Sandford Fleming, chief engineer for the CPR, issued specific instructions to the civil engineer Joseph Hunter, another of his exploratory surveyors, to investigate the elusive Pine Pass. Hunter approached the job from the west, via Quesnel, Fort George and McLeod Lake in June. The only informant he could find was an old Sekani lady at McLeod Lake who sketched the route from there in the sand by the shore: descend Pack River to the Parsnip, travel upstream on it to the Misinchinka and up the latter to the pass in which he would find a small lake (Azouzetta). Hunter ascended the Misinchinka some 50 miles to its source in a cul de sac of high peaks with no hope of a "low pass" there. Returning downstream about halfway, where the large valley took a sharp bend from northwest to southwest, he camped with his party for the night (see Map 6). After supper in the tranquility of the long June evening, smoking his pipe and cogitating what to do next, he heard the plaintive call of loons up a small tributary valley to the north. Could they be on the lake mentioned by the old lady at McLeod? Hunter retired with the decision to investigate that clue in the morning. Sure enough, following up the creek (Atunatche) about three miles they found the lake and the pass, at the low elevation of 2,850 feet (now the lowest railway crossing of the Rocky Mountains in Canada). Hunter and his party then followed down the Pine River to its confluence with the Peace and duly arrived at old Fort St John nearby.[47]

SOME PINE PASS HIGHLIGHTS

Prehistoric route of Sekani and Beaver Indians.

1877:   Joseph Hunter, CE, LS, eastbound.[47]

1879:   Dr GM Dawson with 100 horses & mules, eastbound.[48]

1893:   Henry Somers Somerset & his partner Pollen, westbound[49] (Father Morice's map of 1907 shows Azouzetta Lake as "Pollen Lake").

1898:   Hector Tremblay, et al, eastbound.[50]

1905:	James McCreight, westbound.
1911:	GB Milligan, BCLS, eastbound with horses from Fort St James.[51]
1914:	James Dixon, eastbound.[52]
1915 et seq:	disbanded GTP Ry workers used the route, eastbound, and others to evade conscription in World War I.
1922:	BC "Pre-emptor's Map 3E" shows detail "Location of projected PGE Railway".
1924:	J.S. Young, F.W. Barber & G.S. Andrews, westbound with six horses.
1929-30:	First air photo cover for "PGE Resources Survey".[53]
1930:	John N.P. Bennett, alone westbound, succumbed from exhaustion and exposure vic Azouzetta Lake (see Appendix 2).
1952:	Hart Highway (No 97) completed.
1957:	Natural Gas Pipeline completed.
1958:	PGE Railway extension completed to Dawson Creek and Fort St John. Microwave communication system completed through pass about this time.
1961:	Crude oil Pipeline completed.
1968:	BC Hydro's power transmission line from Bennett Dam in operation.

Today Pine Pass accommodates the highway, the railway, two pipelines, the hydro transmission, and a microwave communicating system – all vindicating Sandford Fleming's optimism more than a century ago and in vivid contrast to the pristine wilderness we found there in 1924!

The six horses we took with us belonged to Jim and were rounded up from various pastures in the Redwillow district. They had to get acquainted with each other and acknowledge a leader which turned out to be a stocky and wise little mare named Elsie. Appropriately, I rode The Grey which had already served me so well. Each of us had his own saddle and accessories. I then had a sturdy pair of furry goatskin chaps which I found too hot and heavy so Jim wore them with implications which became evident later. Packsaddles, boxes, covers, lashropes, halters, hobbles and related gear were in good supply in those days and, as with our provisions, the costs were shared equally. Wooden "coal oil crates" were commonly used for packboxes, one on each side of the horse. They were plentiful, as kerosene and naptha gasoline for lamps were imported in 4-gallon rectangular cans, shipped two per crate. They were fairly strong, made of ½-inch boards and 3/4-inch ends. Inside dimensions were roughly 10 x 12 x 20 inches. These boxes had many other uses in pioneer life for stools, cupboards, and whatever as containers. Handles at each end were improvised with half-inch rope inserted through two holes and knotted inside. They were not shatter-proof against striking trees along the trail on an inexperienced, clumsy or excited horse. We shod the horses in front only, with "never-slip" studded shoes. Worn studs were preferred, being not too sharp.

Our camp outfit was minimal. With no tent we could, if necessary, contrive shelter under a large canvas pack cover, which could also serve as a groundsheet. Personal bedding was supplemented with saddle blankets, powerfully fragrant, but there was ample fresh air. Lashropes for packing had other uses. They were 3/4-inch Manila about 45 feet long. They bound the whole load on the horse, on top of the pack covers, in the configuration of the celebrated "diamond hitch". For this, one end was attached to the ring end of a broad canvas cinch by a bowline knot, secure but easily undone when rope was required to tether a horse, support a tarp for shelter, or to bind logs for a raft. Cooking would be on open fires. Our kitchen box contained two iron frypans, three nesting kettles, plates, mugs and bowls (mostly of aluminum) and cutlery of stainless steel. A 1½-lb "Hudson Bay" axe was both adequate and light, and the butt could be used to drive in stakes or pickets. We took my 30-30 Winchester carbine and .22 rifles, which like the axe, could be slung on the saddle, ready for use. Barber brought his fishing tackle which he loved to use and I had my "No 2 Folding Brownie

Kodak" with some film. My rabbit robe was too hot, heavy and bulky for this trip. My companions took a good supply of T&B plug pipe tobacco and a 40-ounce bottle of overproof rum.

Our food was mainly dry staples – no need to carry water in any form. Our trip was to cross, not a desert, but countless clear, cold and sparkling mountain streams. For the horses we took a sack of oats, not as food but to entice them to camp to be caught. A block of rock salt was taken for the same purpose. As mentioned, we rationed for three men for three weeks. The total weight of supplies and gear did not exceed 300 pounds, a modest load for two pack animals on mountain trails. For this trip, none of us had mastered the "diamond hitch" but there are other equally important elements of horse-packing which I had learned, such as re-tightening cinches. The horses soon learn the trick of expanding their lungs on the first cinching.

Packs must be carefully balanced on each side of the animal and the centre of gravity should be kept low, near that of the horse itself. Otherwise the pendulum motion in travel tends to loosen things and cause saddle sores. Earmarks of a good packer include the delivery of his loads intact, at the right place at the right time, with a string of horses reasonably well-fed, free from saddle sores and other injuries of the trail. Man's art of packing animals, especially donkeys, is very ancient. The practice, as I found it in the mountains of BC, reflected evolutionary adaptations from mining and travel in Spanish America, the western USA, the Cariboo, the Cassiar and the Yukon. In contrast to some bizarre loads in the legends of packing, such as mining machinery, lumber and even pianos, our outfit was very simple. A strong horse can carry more than 200 pounds but for long trips on mountain trails where feed is sometimes scarce; 150 pounds is a better limit. Breast and breech straps help to stabilize loads on steep trails but we managed without them.

A couple of days were spent at Kelly Lake, assembling and organizing the outfit. Most of our staple provisions were from stock in Jim's store (at cost). We could get residual wants and a few luxuries to start out with — fresh eggs, fruit and vegetables — at Haskin's store in Pouce Coupe.

The following narrative of our trip is derived from the diary I kept (during most of it) which happily survives. Approximate mileages were logged for most days and, where missing, an estimate is inserted. The diary entries are quoted with minimal editing, with comments added from my present point of view and to carry aggregate mileages.

PACKERS PROGRESS

Kelly Lake (Peace River District) to Fort George,
Summer, 1924

Jim Young, F. Barber, Gerry Andrews

Elsie, Marguerite, The Grey, Roanie,
Bill Bowser, Sherman - horses

Tip, Jerry - hounds

DAY 1

1 July - Tuesday: 25 miles

Left Kelly Lake about 8 am. Weather fine. Arrived Pete Stuart's for lunch. Jim operated on one of Pete's mares. Got to Maggie's for supper. After tarrying long we finally got started for Swan Lake; made it about mid-night. Camped outside Fynn's barn.

We must have had an early breakfast and the horses were on good behavior for such an early start. Maggie's charms at the McClements' have been mentioned. This was the season of long days.

Aggregate: 25 miles

DAY 2

2 July - Wednesday: 0 miles

Stopped at Swan Lake all day. Made two rawhide panniers. Moved to Taylors for the night.

At Fynn's there were a couple of good, well-bleached raw beef hides hanging over a corral fence – a common feature of pioneer ranches. These were obtained from "Ma" for a token payment or gratis, and immediately put in water to soak. When dry, they are stiff as a board, but after soaking they may be cut, shaped over a form, in this case the coal oil crates, and stitched with rawhide lace, into elegant panniers for sidepacks. The fur was left outside and they had flap covers on top. They are light, capacious and unbreakable, but must be kept dry. I had learned to make these and other useful rawhide gear the previous summer, from a fine old Big Bar pioneer, Neil ("Pa") Adler, and had used them on my pack trip then. With the help of my partners, two good panniers were made that afternoon, and were sufficiently dry by evening. This operation attracted an admiring audience, which was a bit flattering for a young fellow.

Aggregate: 25 miles

DAY 3

3 July - Thursday: 18 miles

Had a good fish breakfast at Taylors'. Made Pouce Coupe for lunch. After considerable beer, the party turned in at Fynn's Feed Stable.

Some sociability at Pouce Coupe was to be expected – our last taste of "bright lights". We completed our shopping list and put up the horses in Fynn's stable for a modest fee. They could hardly be turned loose in the village.

Aggregate: 43 miles

DAY 4

4 July - Friday: 20 miles

Dawson Creek for lunch, Cutbank for supper. Stopped with old Mark [Devereaux] and his partner Art Young. Mark says to look up Shorty Hoff when we get to Prince George. Mark's favorite expression "God damn it boy!"

The sun was high in the sky when we finally got away from Pouce Coupe. In packing up there is always some initial confusion until the best routine becomes habitual. An interested audience was in attendance, mostly trying to be helpful. Our lack of experience must have been very obvious. Advice from spectators flowed freely, including various ways to "throw the diamond hitch". When we finally got away our conception of it was a fearful tangle of cinches, lash ropes, straps and tarpaulins, with odd bits of equine anatomy sticking out from a nucleus of confusion. Good-natured farewells were exchanged, and there was a twinkle of humor in more than one pair of eyes left behind. There was frank admiration, too, for our tackling what was reputed to be a tough trip, also one or two sarcastic predictions that we would be back in a couple of weeks, out of grub and beaten! We were glad when we got on our way, at last, each leading a pack-horse, and heading into the challenge of the Unknown ahead. At this time, Dawson Creek was little more than a post office.

Aggregate: 63 miles

DAY 5

5 July - Saturday: 18 miles
Made Stuart Flats [vic Groundbirch]. A good road but poor water. Flies are bad.

Devereaux and Art Young at Cutbank had given us a royal welcome. Horses were fed and housed in their barn, and ourselves likewise in their large log cabin. Old Mark was a real cook. Supper was tender moose steaks, an inch thick, smothered in gravy with onions. Mark had lived in Prince George and assured us that if we contacted "Shorty" Hoff, as his friends, the town would be at our command. While Mark was cooking breakfast, inspired by a good chaw of snoose (a lethal form of chewing tobacco), I watched with apprehension the dribbles running down his chin, hoping they would fall to sizzle on the stove and not into the eggs he was frying. Years later, I heard lurid accounts of his entertaining His Excellency Baron Tweedsmuir on the viceregal tour (c1937).

Aggregate: 81 miles

DAY 6

6 July - Sunday: 11 miles

Crossed the rivers at East Pine just after lunch. Made a good camp on the north side, on a bench. Splendid feed and good water.

Dropping down the long hill, we got to east Pine about 11 am. Here the Murray River from the south joins the main Pine flowing from the west. A friendly old-timer, Jim Daniels advised us to cross the two rivers separately, above the forks, to reach the main trail up the Pine on its left (north) bank. Below the forks, banks were too steep for landings, and the current was strong. A squatter at East Pine, named L.C. Palmer,[54] helped us make the crossing with his dugout canoe, for $3, which saved making a raft. The horses swam both rivers. Palmer gave us good advice for a camp on the far side and showed us his simple "diamond hitch" which we used thereafter to good effect. Dr A.R.C. Selwyn also camped here, 3 August, 1875.[55]

Aggregate: 92 miles

DAY 7

7 July - Monday: 25 miles

Horses got a good feed at East Pine. Rolled out at 5 am. No fish on Barber's line. Packed up and hit trail at 7 sharp. Trail follows north bank and follows northwest to Sundance Lake [vic Wabi, BCR]. Took left fork here, dropping down to river benches [again]. Stopped 11 am for lunch at small creek. Reached [vic] Middle Pine Forks [Sukunka] about 3 pm. Appears to be a good ranch there. Kept going to Centurion Creek, about 6 miles farther. Camped here in spite of poor feed. Had to tie some horses. We are hitting the hay early so as to get a good start in the morning. Will have to stop for feed at first opportunity. Vegetation: Jackpine & Cottonwood abundant; Spruce & Tamarack plenty; Fir (Balsam), Birch & Alder some. Lots of Peavine and fair grass in spots; Fireweed, Yarrow, Indian Paint Brush, lots of Liliaceae, Roses.

The trail from East Pine probably followed the present Hart Highway (97) to the vicinity of Wabi Station (BCR). It then dropped southwesterly toward the Pine River, but cut westerly across Twidwell Bend, below Mt Wabi to the mouth of Centurion Creek, about a mile south of the present town of Chetwynd.

Aggregate: 117 miles

DAY 8

8 July - Tuesday: 15 miles

Jim had a fire going at 2:45 am. Rest of us rolled out about 3. Hit trail at 5 sharp. Horses hungry. At 7 am struck a fine meadow [vic Dokie on BCR] and a cabin. Unpacked and fed, pulling out again at 11 am. Made camp one mile above Goodrich's [Goodrich Creek, vic DL: 1123]. Jack King was there. Feed is good but bushy. Rained nearly all night. Jim and Barber slept under canvas, Gerry under a tree. All beds dry in morning. Before reaching Goodrich's we [had] passed Middle Pine [Sukunka] Forks. One, Treadwell has a place there.

Our stop at Centurion Creek exemplified that priorities for an overnight camp are: (1) horsefeed, (2) water, (3) fuel and (4) a convenient campsite. In strange country, without a guide, grazing opportunities cannot be anticipated, so the best use of daylight so essential for following an unknown trail, cannot always be made. Good feed may occur too early in the day for an overnight stop, and no more may be found before darkness obscures all. The horses must then be tied up hungry and travel resumed next morning at first light, until feed is encountered. There, a two- or three-hour stop for the animals to fill up must be made at the price of wasting precious daylight. (For Geo Goodrich see Footnote 56).

Aggregate: 132 miles

DAY 9

9 July - Wednesday: 18 miles

A clear cold morning, grass and bushes soaking wet; later our clothes. Pulled out 8 am. Got to [Philip B] Esswein's at noon. He seems to be Swiss. Has a great place; nice little flat; good buildings. A trail from Hudson Hope joins the Pine Pass trail here — a 3-day trip. Made good camp at meadow 6 miles above Esswein's. Splendid feed, but bushy. Weather looks like rain. Noticed "Hushum" berries [Shepherdia canadensis] for first time on trip. Quite a lot of Horsetail [Equisetum]. Good timber near Peavine Flats. Esswein and Neaves say another 25 miles of good going, then 35 miles of bad trail to summit; 10 miles from camp is first good feed, then 20 miles to the next. Sulphur springs about 35 miles from Peavine Flats. Before coming to Callazon Creek, the trail crosses the Pine. Camp there and then follow up to the summit. They say it is a week's pull from Esswein's to the summit.

Esswein's was probably in the vicinity of DL 370, about three miles west of the present settlement of Pine Valley.[57] Neaves was a trapper who had several cabins along our trail ahead. Although Esswein was friendly and helpful with advice, he did not encourage us to linger. His 10-year-old son was quickly sent to open the far gate for us to pass through without delay. This was understandable, if not typical of the country. All his supplies had to be packed in from Hudson Hope, and our six hungry horses could soon gobble up the forage on his small place. "Peavine Flats" was probably the local name for Esswein's locality (Photos 11 & 12).

Esswein was the last person to see John Bennett alive in October, 1930 (see Appendix 2). Our camp this date was likely opposite DL 380, above Willow Creek.

Aggregate: 150 miles

DAY 10

10 July - Thursday: 26 miles

Up at 5 am and got under way at 6:30. Went 10 miles to the next feed and made lunch camp. Started again at 1 pm; kept going. Took wrong trail into Neaves' cabin; back-tracked about a mile and took left fork. Some bad places; thick timber; no feed. Finally made camp on a sidehill at 9:30 pm. No feed; horses restless; everybody tired.

The location of this camp was probably near LeMoray Creek, where a steep sidehill crowds close to the river. Below, where we had travelled, the valley floor is flat and poorly drained. It was a long frustrating day. My estimate of mileage, includes back-tracking, and may be high.

Aggregate: 176 miles

DAY 11

11 July - Friday: 4 miles

In the morning, no horses. Jim went back several miles for them. Got started at noon. Trail bad so crossed river and advanced on a sand bar, then recrossed to a small flat. Found hidden slough mentioned by Neaves, about 50 yards to right of trail, just after the old trail crossed a little bridge. Made camp on the trail. A good place but not much room. Nearly half the rum still left. Barber says it must be finished before the summit. Mountains getting higher and closing in. Barber saw a moose in meadow where we have the horses. They seem satisfied. First Devil's Club [Fatsia horrida] seen. Jim found a large horse bell in the slough. It will be a boon.

The horses had now become a mutually compatible social group, with more tendency to stay together. Elsie was the acknowledged leader, so she wore the bell which Jim had luckily found. Seasoned packers would never be without at least one horsebell, to help locate the herd, especially in bush country such as we were in. It is a packer's joy to wake in the night and hear the bell's soft resonance, assurance that the horses are nearby. At times, there is an ominous silence. The animals fill up in the evening, then may stand still in digestive somnolence until ready to feed again in the earliest morning hours. Suddenly, the bell mare shakes her head. The silence is broken and the packer can blissfully relax in his blankets for a little more "shut-eye". The Devils Club indicated that we were entering a moister eco-system, more typical of the western slopes.

Aggregate: 180 miles

DAY 12

12 July - Saturday: 8 miles

Pulled out from the good camp at 7 sharp. Trail quite good in places but hard to find. Came to [the] Sulphur

Creek at noon. Stopped for lunch in a parsnip glade
which seemed to have a blade or two of grass. In afternoon crossed the Pine several times, finally reaching
Neaves' cabin at Callazon forks. Camped here. Feed not
abundant. Trail seems to continue on the other side [of
the Pine]. We think it is still 20 miles to the summit.
Flies a burden, especially "no-see-ums".

When there was good feed at noon stops, we usually unpacked
to allow the horses more freedom and their backs to air and dry.
When flies are bad, the horses tend to mill round in circles, too
distraught to feed, so our halt would then be brief, without unpacking more than needed for a kettle of tea and some bannock.
The volume of the Pine River was progressively diminished each
time we passed a fair-sized tributary, so crossings became easier.

Aggregate: 188 miles

DAY 13

13 July - Sunday: 5 miles

Horses went back on the trail about 4:30 am. Got up
about 5:30. Jim (as usual) went back for them. Beans for
breakfast (short of meat). All think they are OK. Barber
lost his pipe. Left camp about 7:30. Crossed Pine and
Callazon to trail on opposite bank. Lost two or three
hours searching the trail. Recrossed the river and
camped for lunch in a parsnip glade. Away again at 1:30.
Crossed Gold Creek [Garbitt?] about 3 pm; made camp. A
good little meadow here. Rained hard from 5 to 6. Retire
early for an early start. Jim thinks we should made
summit tomorrow.

Our progress was now minimal due to weather and trail
troubles. My mileage estimates include a lot of trial and error
travel. While realistic in terms of time and energy spent, they
must be discounted for distance "made good". Like the horses,
the human trio had settled down to a simple and harmonious
routine. Responsibility and chores were cheerfully shared according to talent. Jim, of course, was best with the horses. Barber
had little chance to fish, except for his night lines which were
disappointing. I probably headed up the firewood department. Dry

willow was preferred for cooking. Various odd chunks served for warmth and drying out. Each washed his own dishes in the creek. Bannock-making offered good-natured rivalry. Our beds were mostly kept dry. Clothes, often sodden, would dry from body heat between showers. It was a healthy life – no ills, not even colds.

Aggregate: 193 miles

DAY 14

14 July - Monday: 7 miles

Got away from Gold [Garbitt?] Creek 7:30 am. Trail fairly good till noon; crosses another creek [John Bennett?] also a muskeg. We then crossed Pine to Neaves' cabin. Valley seems to swing to the south here. Lost trail badly after leaving cabin, but located it again after hours of wet scrambling in heavy shower. Made camp at 6 pm; poor feed, but some. Seem to be on the right trail, so are in hopes of a good day tomorrow. Weather looks bad. All got a good soaking today, but Jim could not wait for the rain, so fell into the creek at noon.

This camp was probably near Wolf Creek, and only about 10 miles, direct, to the pass. With such an obscure trail, where a major tributary joined, it was not obvious which valley to select. My little map was religiously studied, and although lacking in detail, it proved infallible. I studied it like a Bible in camp and on all occasions of doubt. In camp Barber liked to tease by intently studying a cigarette paper and mumbling for all to hear, "Now – Callazon Creek joins here – and the Pine takes a big swing – we must be just about there – mmm – only about 500 miles to the summit now boys!"

Aggregate: 200 miles

DAY 15

15 July - Tuesday: 5 miles

Rain – rain – rain – all night, all morning, all after-noon. Sat around a big fire all morning, but after lunch, packed up in the rain and pulled out. Pushed along for about 5 miles till we came to a trapper's cabin. Stopped here for the night. Weather looks like clearing.

This cabin was about halfway from the last camp to the summit. Trappers usually have a string of small overnight cabins along their "line", with a commodious and well-equipped HQ cabin in a strategic location. We preferred to camp in the open, but here we were glad of this shelter although gloomy and crowded.

Aggregate: 205 miles

DAY 16

16 July - Wednesday: 0 miles

Still raining today, but had a good night in the cabin. Spent the morning scouting for the trail. After lunch Jim and Gerry went ahead to clear out the trail for a mile or so. It is very indefinite and bad. Weather looks like changing. The old sun came out for a few minutes at 6 pm. Creek is high and murky due to heavy rains. The mountains take on a more severe aspect here. A pretty cascade plunges over a rocky ridge into the river below. We are cheerful and hope to make the summit tomorrow. It cannot be far away now. The valley seems to run to the northwest, and we move upstream to the southeast. Made good use of the trapper's cabin to dry our wet clothing. Sugar is practically gone, also bacon and ham. Lots of flour, beans and rice, should be enough to see us to McLeod. Enjoyed a good feed of hushum berries today. Having a bad time with the axe. The handle keeps coming off, in spite of Barber's efforts to wedge it.

We certainly should have had a spare axe. Our supplies were beginning to run out. We saw practically no game and were too preoccupied with trail problems to hunt. Bannock had become our staff of life. Frills like butter, jam, syrup, and even sugar were becoming memories. Ever since this trip, I have preferred tea clear without sugar. While the bacon lasted, we took turns swabbing out the fry pan for the grease, with a piece of bannock. We used the old prospectors' method of mixing bannock dough right in the flour sack. Dry items, salt and baking powder are mixed first in a hollow, on top. Then a little lard, if any, is worked in by hand. Water is gradually added and mixed till the dough is "right", then the whole is lifted by hand into the frypan and the flour sack is tied up. This saves carrying and cleaning a mixing bowl. We were soon to learn that the dough can be cooked in the frypan without grease. A little dry flour in the pan prevents the dough sticking. In those days there was no aluminum foil, with its magic for baking at an open fire.

I think it was at this camp that my companions used up the last of the rum. They insisted I participate in this final toast to our success and survival. They decanted my modest portion into a mug, offering hot water for mixer, which I declined, affirming that if I had to drink rum, I would have it "straight". Choking violently, I wasted most of the precious nectar coughing and sneezing, to the dismay of my generous "hosts". We identified this place appropriately as "Wetass Camp".

Aggregate: 205 miles

DAY 17

17 July - Thursday: 6 miles

Left the cabin about 8 am. Scrambled over some soft places and slippery declivities for about 3 miles. Trail then goes left [east] and up over a rocky ledge and continues for a couple of miles on a little plateau. Struck the Pine again here. Camped for lunch and scouted around for the trail which seems to disappear. Found it up on the mountain side to the left. Following this for a couple of miles through thick timber [at long last!] we came on to Summit Lake [Azouzetta]. Found good camping and feed at the south end. Slept in a well-built trapper's cabin. On the roof were some pretty pansies in full bloom.

Summit Lake is about 2 miles long, north and south; width varies from 30 yards to ½ mile. Three or four small islands covered with dense Spruce occur in the middle. Water is clear and cold. Bottom can be seen 20 feet down. Good slough grass at the lower [south] end. The Murray Range runs north and south on the east side. Old Friend Mountain on the west side. The west shore has the form of a rocky ledge some 100 feet above the lake. A small waterfall plunges over this cliff.

Aggregate: 211 miles

DAY 18

18 July - Friday: 0 miles

Rained a little during the night, but no rain today. Barber caught 24 dandy little rainbow trout; used raft belonging to the trapper. Everybody shaved and changed underwear. Spent most of the day resting and cleaning up. A little dark for taking pictures. Weather looks better tonight. Plan to hit the trail for McLeod in the morning. Trapper who built the cabin is Axel Rosene from Prince George.

Arrival at Summit Lake (Azouzetta) in the pass was the high point of our trip, both topographically and spiritually (Photo 16). We were lucky to find feed and a congenial camp. Men and animals were more than ready for a day's rest. The horses were now more reconciled to the travel habit and were becoming weaned from the nostalgic urge to head back toward "home". They showed a growing dependence on and faith in their masters and began to regard each successive camp as home. Token "goodies" like rock salt, and occasional handful of oats or a nibble of bannock, with attentions like rubbing itchy spots all helped to engender this desirable attitude.

Barber's fish were a Godsend, especially as our diet was becoming protein deficient (Photos 17 &18). They were carefully filleted and salted — over 30 pounds of extra provisions at a critical time. Rosene's cabin was beautifully built of peeled logs and looked quite new. The sod roof was a mass of floral color, and thanks to our arrival, the pansies had not been "born to blush unseen". The trapper must have scattered the seed up there when he left in late spring or early summer. They had been well watered by the recent weather. His name and origin ("Prince George") were inscribed in bold letters above the door. It cheered us to think that Mr. Rosene had travelled the route we were now to take. It was also reassuring to know that we would now be following downstream drainage — no more doubts as to which branch to ascend at each fork.

I have a 1961 photo taken from the highway, across the lake in which the cabin roof is discernable (Photo 14), and in 1964 I stayed overnight in Pine Pass with time to walk around the lake, as far as Rosene's cabin which I found caved in and nearly over-grown with brush.

Aggregate: 211 miles

DAY 19

19 July - Saturday: 3 miles

All up early and got under way by 6:15. Followed a well-blazed trail south-ward along side of the mountain, till we descended down to the Misinchinka. Here is another small cabin of Rosene's. Trail very hard to find on other side. Jim found some old blazes, very ancient. While looking around, Sherman took a notion to buck off his pack. Followed Jim's blazes down river till 1:30. Very dense growth of Alder, Willow and Devil's Club, along with soft spots, made the going very bad. Trail led on to a sand bar in the river. Camped for lunch. From here failed to locate any trail whatever. After searching for a couple of hours, we doubled back to the crossing. Then I tried [what seemed to be] an old trail going up the mountain, but it was lost in heavy timber and windfall. At last we returned to the crossing and made camp. Hope to find some kind of trail in morning. Flies very bad and no feed for horses.

From Azouzetta Lake we had followed down Atunatche Creek (then known as Tillicum Creek), about three miles to its junction with Misinchinka River. The latter was a good-sized stream in a large valley, which, at this point, took a huge L-turn from flowing northwest to southwest (see Map 6). This is where Joseph Hunter had camped in June, 1877 when he heard the loons, so I now refer our camp nearby as "Hunter's Camp". About a mile up Atunatche Creek is where John Bennett's remains were found, 24 May, 1931 (see Appendix 2).

On the trail down from the lake, we noticed with interest that the more recent blazes were all 12 feet or more above ground on the trees. This implied they had been made in winter on top of at least eight feet of snow! It confirmed that recent travel had been on snowshoes with no need for a summer horse trail. I logged three miles for this day, with a note that we had travelled at least 10.

Aggregate: 214 miles

DAY 20

20 July - Sunday: 0 miles

In the morning, Jim and Barber went down yesterday's trail on foot, but no luck. In the afternoon, Barber and I took another scout up the mountain — again no luck. At supper, we held "council of war", debating [the obvious] question. Finally decided to go down in the morning where we turned round yesterday, try crossing the river for a trail on the other side. This was "the last straw". Grub enough to reach Cutbank should we turn around, and probably enough to reach McLeod if we have half-decent luck. Figure it is not more than 40 miles to McLeod. Our grub should last 7 days more. If we find a good trail, we are OK.

Here we were at the moral "summit" of our trip — the point of no return. All were loathe to admit defeat and face the humility of returning beaten to our Pouce Coupe friends. It was probably near here, too, that poor John Bennett must have turned back in despair. Jim Young's determination and guts tipped the scales for going ahead, no matter what. With typical generosity, he said we could butcher one of his horses if we got to such extremity.

Aggregate: 214 miles

DAY 21

21 July - Monday: 7 miles

Left camp at 8:10, got down to the crossing and had lunch there at 11:30. On our way down, lost the horse bell, but luckily found it some distance back. Found a cabin and a trail on the other side [the right, or west bank]. Followed down river in pm. Trail very indefinite, over-grown with Alder and Willow. Beaver dams are a great hindrance. Camped on a sand bar for the night. Jim found the trail on the right bank. Indications show a great quantity of beaver. Feed is scarce and flies are bad.

The weather must have improved, as my diary references to flies implied that it was hot and dry. This camp must have been near Hungry Moose Creek on today's maps, about a mile below beautiful Bijou Falls Park. The Misinchinka flows quite rapidly here, and exposed numerous sand bars in its channel. On these we were duly impressed by numerous and enormous grizzly bear tracks. We had no desire whatever to encounter one of these monsters, so the bell on Elsie was left unmuffled to clank loudly to announce our coming, well in advance, for Mr. Bear to vacate the trail with his accustomed dignity. This raucous noise had the same effect on lesser game which might have augmented our larder.

Our frequent use of sand bars in the river to avoid beaver dams and other frustrations provided excitement to break any monotony. Emerging from the bush in the heat and flies, onto the soft dry sand, the horses had a compulsion to get down and roll, with dire effects on their loads. In momentary pandemonium men gallop ahead to prod a horse on bended knees, only to see another behind in the same stance or already down. The silent solitudes were shattered with profane and blasphemous shouting until order was restored. This part of the valley must have been a trappers' paradise for beaver. Their engineering works made a labyrinthine mess of the valley floor. For this reason the trail, when we could find it, tended to stay on the sidehill. The cabin mentioned in this day's diary entry was likely Frank Horn's where John Bennett had taken shelter and left his last pathetic note, dated 15 November, 1930, when he finally turned back (see Appendix 2).

Aggregate: 221 miles

DAY 22

22 July - Tuesday: 6 miles

Left camp on the bar and forded to the right bank, following Jim's trail to a large cabin. Valley seems to swing to the southwest here. Had the usual trouble picking up the trail beyond the cabin, but finally came to some good grass on a willow flat. Camped here. River is [now] quite wide and meanders considerably.

This camp was probably near Honeymoon Creek on today's maps. The large cabin mentioned earlier was likely opposite Old Friend Creek, on the river, with no nearby feed. We noticed there a large 45-gallon drum and other evidence that it was a trapper's headquarters at the head of river navigation from McLeod Lake. This implied that horses were not used for transport, certainly in recent years, and explained our trail troubles. Winter travel on snowshoes over deep snow is not impeded by soft ground, water or underbrush.

Aggregate: 227 miles

DAY 23

23 July - Wednesday: 12 miles

Left camp at 7:30. Had more difficulty with beaver dams. Later, trail improves. Made night camp beside a mica creek. Some fair feed, but flies worry horses to misery.

This camp was at a small unnamed creek about a mile above Trappers Creek. Along this part of the original Hart Highway mica schist (rock) was formerly conspicuous, but seems less in evidence now with more sophisticated highway engineering.

Aggregate: 239 miles

DAY 24

24 July - Thursday: 17 miles

Trail quite good till noon, when we crossed the Misinchinka and found an old trail heading southwest, leaving the river. Followed this, with several searches till we arrived at the Parsnip River. Could see no apparent ford so camped on the east bank — good feed. Made a raft and got everything ready for the morning. Hope to make McLeod tomorrow. Parsnip quite wide, about 200 yards; current is swift. Three old camps on this side, one old [dilapidated] cabin. Valley seems very wide here. Colbourne Creek, clear and cold runs in from the East.

The Misinchinka was not too deep to ford and the current was comparatively slack. The trail beyond crossed a classic, broad, fairly level "Jackpine flat", well-drained gravel, solid and relatively free of underbrush, a pleasant change from the swampy jungle of the Misinchinka. We had now entered the huge valley of the Rocky Mountain Trench. It was good to see so much sky.

The chaos of horses rolling on sand bars is rivalled or surpassed by another hazard of packhorse travel. In warm weather, after the mid-day stop with nothing to disturb the drowsy monotony of horses and men plodding along the trail, the lead horse suddenly disturbs a wasp nest, and may continue with impunity. No 2 horse and his followers arrive in turn to receive full attention from the irate insects. With loud detonations from both ends, the animals stampede, like shrapnel in all directions, regardless of trees, windfall, underbrush or whatever. To re-assemble horses and hopefully, scattered parts of their loads, can take more than an hour, after which the whole outfit is thoroughly awake.

Our camp was pleasant, at the mouth of Colbourne Creek [58] [59] and facing west across the big river. We added our names with date to many others inscribed on the unattended "guest book" on the walls of the old cabin. It was cheering to find so much evidence of humanity after all the lonely days since Esswein's. This location had the indications of a crossing point and tallied with my map. At low water it was likely a ford, but now the river was running too high from glaciers melting in the mid-summer heat. We were on a historic river route of explorers, prospectors, surveyors, trappers et al. That pleasant evening, looking across the Parsnip, reflecting the glory of the evening sky, I was thrilled to think that, here, just in front of us, Alexander Mackenzie and his voyageurs had passed in their ascent and descent of this river 131 years before. Maybe they had also camped just here! Mackenzie's journal for 6-7 June, 1793, ascending the Parsnip River, places him very close to where we crossed it at Colbourne Creek.[60]

Aggregate: 256 miles

DAY 25

25 July - Friday: 8 miles

Everybody shaved this morning. Crossed the river, swimming the horses and rafting the stuff. Packed up on the west bank and hit up an old trail at 10:45. Trail leads up over a low ridge, winding among dense, dry hard windfall. Very slow going and flies are bad. Came on a patch of fine blueberries, everybody snatched a filling. Did not unpack until 5:30 pm. Camped in a little gulch. Should be halfway to McLeod [from the Parsnip].

There was plenty of dry driftwood along the river edge for our raft, to carry two men and all the gear in one trip. We had lots of rope to bind the logs together. Looks did not matter as it would be a one-time conveyance. With the strong current we had to allow for both raft and horses drifting downstream some distance. Exposed gravel banks on both sides offered ample room for departure and landing. I was elected to ride the lead horse across, being the only one to admit he could swim. Actually, I felt better about swimming on a horse than riding on the rickety awkward raft. When all was ready, I mounted The Grey and, leading Elsie, we plunged in. Just as my horse began to swim, I realized the saddle cinch had broken — not so good! Luckily we got turned round and regained the shore. The cinch was soon repaired, but I also realized that The Grey was not a good swimmer. Too lanky and raw-boned for buoyancy, he would be at a disadvantage with me on his back. We transferred the saddle to Elsie, shaped like a canal barge. This time, leading The Grey, we started in again, Jim and Barber chasing the other horses to follow, loose and without loads. All went well. Elsie swam high and I got wet only to the waist. It was a relief to feel her feet strike bottom on the far side, about a quarter mile downstream. I was then able to catch and tie the other horses as they emerged. After that, it was my turn to be spectator as the others crossed on the raft, working frantically with clumsy improvised paddles. The crossing was a success — nothing lost and nothing wet that mattered. It could have been otherwise.

From the Parsnip at about 2,250 ft elevation, our trail, which was quite definite when we could see it, continued southwesterly, and "switch-backed" steadily up to a ridge about 1,000 feet above the river. About a mile southeast of the trail, this ridge is dominated by Mt Chingee at 4,220 ft elevation. Chopping our way through the heavy windfall took a lot of time and work. The burn was too extensive to bypass. At the summit, it was a relief to get back into green timber, and drop down a few hundred feet into a nice little gulch where there was feed and water for camp.

Our rations were practically exhausted. While Jim and I set up camp, Barber wandered off with the .22 and soon returned with a porcupine, skinned and nicely dressed, ready for the pot. I suspect it was a grandfather. With no grease for frying we boiled it. Broiling might have been better. In spite of sharp appetites, I did not relish it, tough as rubber and strong as billygoat. All we had for breakfast, after this repast, was a handful of flour for a tiny bannock and a pinch of tea for a weak brew. Good thing we had filled up on the blueberries earlier. That evening, my little map confirmed we were "on course" and not far from McLeod. Our optimism was tempered, however, by the horrible apprehension that McLeod might now be derelict, as some old HBC posts were by this time. Barber teased that I get getting "that lean and hungry look". We all were.

Aggregate: 264 miles

DAY 26

26 July - Saturday: 9 miles

We made McLeod at 2 pm. It was surely a pleasure to see, first the water shining through the trees, then a house or two, a church steeple with a cross on it, and finally the large white building with HBC painted on the roof in large characters. McIntyre, the factor proved a good fellow. The lake is about 16 miles long and ½ to 3 miles wide, surrounded with low wooded hills. About 15 Indian families. These are Sekanis, full blood. Everybody uses canoes or dugouts with kickers on them. The children had never seen a horse.

McIntyre gave us a generous bunch of delicious lettuce and a loaf of excellent bread, his own baking. He also took us out for a ride in his boat, up and down the lake. Made a good camp. Turned in about 11 pm. We are all pleased with McLeod. It is a pretty little place. Sugar, butter, jam, milk [canned] etc. make a grand change from tea and bannock.

The trail from our camp down to McLeod Lake continued through green timber and was evidently an old one. We made good time. Although we could not see the lake until practically on its shore, there was a noticeable illumination in the sky which presaged its proximity. I have observed this phenomenon elsewhere and others have remarked on it. A large lake surface reflects the sky's light upward again. Living outdoors as we had been, the senses became more acute to subtleties of this kind (Photo 23).

When our outfit broke out of the timber on the lake shore, near the outflow down Pack River, a flotilla of native canoes crossed at once from the little settlement opposite, to greet us with obvious surprise and curiosity. "Where you come from?" they shouted. We countered with, "Where can we cross with the horses to get to the store?" They indicated an easy ford across the Pack River nearby. We soon drew up beside the HBC depot and dismounted amid great local clamor, especially from the children. I asked one friendly old man, who spoke a little Cree, why the kids were making such a fuss. He replied "Him never see him horse, him think you ride him funny moose!" This added to so much other evidence that certainly, recent travel in this region was entirely by water in summer and with dogs and snowshoes in winter. In earlier days, especially before the advent of the outboard motor, horses had been in greater use, as witnessed by intermittent fragments of the well-worn old packtrail we had found.

The HBC manager, Justin E. McIntyre, proved a great character. I got to know him well in later years. We entered the store at once, having nothing whatever with which to make our lunch. "Mac" looked out the window at our outfit and repeated the Indians' question. When we mentioned the Pine Pass trail from Pouce Coupe, he said, "You've had a tough trip!" – and disappeared through a door behind the counter. He returned with four glasses and a bottle of rum, poured a hefty slug in each glass and said, "Your health, gentlemen!" He explained he had worked on the PGE railway extension survey up the Misinchinka River a few years earlier. He insisted there was now no feasible route for horses directly to Prince George, but we should have no trouble on the old trail to Fort St. James, which had been a main thoroughfare for horses in earlier days. I met McIntyre again in 1948 and often thereafter. By then he had set up his own store on the lake's east side, accessible from Hart Highway. He was a great favorite with all survey crews using this route to and from the North. I have a letter of his dated 1953,[61] and think he died about 10 years later.

McLeod Lake was discovered by James McDougall of the NWCo in 1805 and was first called Trout Lake. The depot established here under authority of Simon Fraser, the same year, was later known as McLeod Lake Post, named after Archibald Norman McLeod, a senior partner of the NWCo. It was the first trade depot established in BC west of the Rocky Mountains.[62]

Aggregate: 273 miles

DAY 27

27 July - Sunday: 18 miles
Barber and Gerry attended the 8 o'clock mass at the
native Catholic church. Some scows of freight arrived
from Summit Lake [near Prince George] in the morning.
Pulled out for Fort St James at 10:30. Trail is good.

It was Barber's idea that we attend mass, pretending he was a good Catholic, which I doubted. There was no priest. A native elder led the service, prayers, hymns, etc. in their native tongue, Sekani. It was evidently a devout band, reflecting the enduring influence of Father Morice, some 20 years after his retirement from Fort St James Mission. The congregation squatted on the floor or stood at the back, women and infants on the left, men and boys on the right. The service lasted about half an hour.

The arrival of scows from Summit Lake via the Crooked River confirmed we were crossing the main water route from Prince George to points north, Finlay Forks, Fort Grahame and Ware.

This was likely before R.F. ("Dick") Corless became the celebrated river freighter on this route. In 1939, I was in charge of airphoto flying along the Rocky Mountain Trench from Finlay Forks to the Yukon Boundary, so got to know some of the people and places, and had a unique look at this whole region from the air. That year, Corless delivered all our supplies and aviation fuel to Finlay Forks and Ware.

We must have camped near War Lake, where McIntyre said we could find lots of arrowheads, evidence of tribal fighting there. At this time I do not remember that we noticed the beautiful falls below War Lake on the McLeod River.

Aggregate: 291 miles

DAY 28

28 July - Monday: 21 miles

Passed Carp Lake and proceeded toward Muskeg River. Later crossed a small swampy river with a bridge across. Think it must be Muskeg River. Trail is splendid, very old.

The trail from McLeod Lake obviously had been well-travelled in former days, if not recently. After what we had experienced as far as McLeod, it seemed like a highway. It was well-cleared and blazed, with no trees near the path for a careless horse to bump his load against. We followed along the northwest shore of Carp Lake and cut across the narrow, shallow and sandy entrance to Sekani Bay (see NTS 93J/14). This was a pretty spot and the map now shows a small Indian Reserve there. Evidently we crossed the Muskeg River near its headwaters. It is aptly named. Soft spots on the old trail had been corduroyed, which, the logs having rotted, were treacherous footing for the horses. We took due care and had no trouble. Our camp was in nondescript country a mile or two past Muskeg River. James McDougall, mentioned above, was the first White man to follow our present route, early in 1806, which led him to discover Stuart Lake about which he reported favorably to his chief, Simon Fraser.[62]

Aggregate: 312 miles

DAY 29

29 July - Tuesday: 23 miles

Going continues very good, heading to the southwest almost without deviation, till we got to Carrier Lake. This is a pretty sheet of water, with a mountain rising in the background to the west [Mount Pope, 4828 ft, on Stuart Lake]. Camped just a mile or two past the lake.

When all goes well, as it did for this part of our trip, pack-horse travel offers its unique delights. High in the saddle, one commands a wide overview without having to concentrate on the trail, which your horse follows by habit. The pace is slow and quiet enough to savor the passing scene in full — topography, flora and fauna, as well as Nature's symphony of sounds, unmuffled by man's raucous engines. In the morning freshness, a distant mountain ahead, in miniature perspective, gradually zooms to awesome proportions. By midday, near its base, the lofty summit dominates the skyline. In the drowsy afternoon, slowly it falls behind to resume a minor key in the total scene. At sunset, the shadow relief reveals added charms of its anatomy. Finally, at camp, when old Sol has dropped below your horizon, his warm radiance lingers on that distant summit, reluctant to yield the stage to night's gently falling curtain.

Somewhere along this part of the trail we came upon a tiny lonely grave in a peaceful little glade. It was marked by a crude wooden cross, mute for name and date but eloquent of grief and affection. Years later, in the final scene of Constantin-Weyer's "Un Homme se penche sur son Passe", the grave of little Lucy Monge vividly revived my memory of this touching scene in the remote Nechako wilderness. It is easy to imagine Lucy's name inscribed on that simple hand-hewn cross there.

Another virtue of this old trail was the abundance of horse-feed. There were many wild hay meadows, especially between

Carrier and the Great Beaver lakes, with evidence of hay-making, probably by people from Fort St James, not far away now.

Aggregate: 335 miles

DAY 30

30 July - Wednesday: 18 miles

Arrived at Fort St James about noon. Camping facilities are poor [scant horse feed]. There are two real stores at this place. Jim traded off Bill Bowser for a 30-30 rifle and some cash. Chances of selling more horses [here] seem slim.

Before entry to Fort St James with the full outfit, we stopped a couple of miles out for Jim and Barber to go ahead and buy me a new pair of pants and scout for a campsite. My old pants were in shreds, approaching indecency. This was the price of lending my chaps to Jim. Nearing the settlement the trail widened to a wagon track and descended a gentle slope, from the top of which the prospect was pleasing, as it must have been to McDougall more than a century before. Prominent for us, was the graceful spire of the mission church, behind which spread the big lake, with the bulk of Mount Pope on the right.

I was to appreciate the historic importance of Fort St James more fully the following winter after reading Father A.G. Morice's "History of the Northern Interior of British Columbia". His like named map at scale 10 miles per inch, published by the BC Government (1907), shows the entire pack trail we had used, from Esswein's place on the Pine River, with only minor deviations. Some of his names are now obsolescent. Simon Fraser reached Stuart Lake 26 July, 1806, by the longer canoe route on the Parsnip, Fraser, Nechako and Stuart rivers. The HBC governor, (Sir) George Simpson, arrived at Fort St James with typical "pomp and circumstance" 17 September, 1828, but having had to walk from McLeod Lake on the same trail we had used. He recorded " ... that it was "a very fatiguing part of our journey". It took him five days compared to less than four days for us.[63]

Our arrival in St James caused less interest among the locals than had been the case at McLeod. The store in competition with the HBC was probably operated by a Mr. Dickinson, whom I met in 1936 when there on field work for the BC Forest Service.

Aggregate: 353 miles

DAY 31

31 July - Thursday: 10 miles

Had considerable difficulty rounding up the cayuses, but Jim finally found them about 5 pm. Anxious to get away, we packed up and made about 10 miles toward Vanderhoof.

We suspected that local boys had deliberately chased our horses away, because one or two came later, offering to round them up for $10, which was declined, without too much prejudice. Each of us then searched in different directions. I crossed the bridge over the Stuart River, about two miles from camp, and followed a track westward along the south shore of the lake. Approaching an Indian's place, several husky dogs raised a clamor, but seeing chains attached to them, I proceeded with confidence to make enquiries. The chains were attached only to the dogs, and I was at once surrounded by a vicious pack. Fortunately the owner came to my rescue. He had seen no horses. We followed the old wagon road toward Vanderhoof, and probably camped near DL 1603.

Aggregate: 363 miles

DAY 32

1 August - Friday: 24 miles

Going seems slow, but we plugged along till we came to some feed.

This camp was probably in Section 30 Tp 11, on East Murray Creek, about 6 miles from Vanderhoof.

Aggregate: 387 miles

DAY 33

2 August - Saturday   6 miles

Arrived Vanderhoof at 8 am. About 3 miles from the town we saw a deer and two fawns. Found fair grazing at Vanderhoof. No demand for horses.

It was ironic that these deer, within three miles of civilization, and one moose spotted 11 July, were the only large game seen on the whole trip, some 390 miles through wilderness. This was mostly in thick bush, and we had other preoccupations.

Aggregate: 393 miles

DAY 34

3 August - Sunday: 0 miles

Put in a slow day.

Aggregate: 393 miles

DAY 35

4 August - Monday: 40 miles

Jim traded off his outfit for a Ford car and we started for Prince George in it. Barber had already gone ahead by train. The road is fine, all but a short stretch. Camped about 20 miles from Prince George.

The Ford was a 1921 Model T touring car, a five seater with folding canvas top. We kept our riding saddles, guns and camp outfit, which were somehow stowed aboard, leaving seats in front for two, and one behind. Some articles were tied on the running boards. The engine had to be started with a hand crank. They advised us not to go on the old "Blackwater Trail", along the telegraph line direct to Quesnel, reputed impassable even for wagons. There was a fair road directly to Prince George, and a new road was under construction from there to Quesnel, on the east side of the Fraser River, on which we could get through. Jim and I probably camped just east of Isle Pierre that night.

DAY 36

5 August - Tuesday: 20 miles

Got to Prince George at 8 am. Found Barber and decided to go down to Vancouver "a la tin Lizzie".

Barber was easily located in Prince George, and we probably found Shorty Hoff to convey salaams from his old pal Mark Devereaux, back at Cutbank. Now, when I skirt Prince George on its bypass and look nervously toward its "city centre" and in any other direction, I relish my memory of that tiny, sleepy hamlet in 1924. My narrative "Packers' Progress through Pine Pass: 1924" can be terminated here with the following summary:

Statistical Summary

PACK HORSE TRIP: KELLY LAKE to VANDERHOOF, via PINE PASS

By: JS Young, F Barber & GS Andrews with 6 Horses

1 July – 2 August 1924

* ** *** ** *

Date	Days Agg-reg-ate	Camps:	Route Miles .Agg.		Date	Days Agg-reg-ate	Camps:	Route Miles .Agg.
		KELLY LAKE			18	18	PINE PASS	0 211
1	1		25*		19	19		3
2	2	Swan Lake	25		20	20	Hunter's Camp	0 214
3	3		18*		21	21		7
		Pouce Coupe	43				H Moose Cr	221
4	4		20*		22	22		6
		Cut Bank	63				Honeymoon Cr	227
5	5		18*		23	23		12
		Stewart Flats	81				Trappers Cr	239.
6	6		11*		24	24		17
		EAST PINE	92				Parsnip X-ing	256
7	7		25		25	25		8
		Centurion Cr	117				Chingee Gulch	264
8	8		15		26	26		9
		Goodrich Cr	132				McLEOD LAKE	273
9	9		18		27	27		18
		Esswein's + 6	150				War Lake	291
10	10		26		28	28		21
		Le Moray Cr	176				Muskeg River	312
11	11		4		29	29		23*
		Le Moray Cr +	180				Carrier Lake +	335
12	12		8		30	30		18*
		Callazon Cr	.188.				Ft St JAMES	353
13	13		5		31	31		10
		Garbitt Cr	193				DL 1063	363
14	14		7		1	32		24*
		Wolf Creek	200				E Murray Cr	387
15	15		5		2	33		6*
16	16	"Wetass" Camp	0 205		3	34	VANDERHOOF	393
17	17		6		4	35		40*
18	18	PINE PASS	0 211				Isle Pierre	40
		(see Column 2)			5	36		20
							PRINCE GEORGE	60

By wagon trail:	Route miles	Days enroute	Av mileage per diem
Kelly Lake to East Pine	92- 0 = 92	6-0 = 6	92/6 = 15.3
Fort St James to Vanderhoof	393-353 = 40	33-30 = 3	40/3 = 13.3
Totals & overall average	132	9	132/9 = 14.7
By pack trail:			
East Pine to Pine Pass	211- 92 = 119	18- 6 = 12	119/12 = 9.9
Pine Pass to McLeod	273-211 = 62	26-18 = 8	62/ 8 = 7.8
McLeod to Fort St James	353-273 = 80	30-26 = 4	80/ 4 = 20.0
Totals & overall average	261	24	10.9
Grand totals & average	393	33	393/33 = 11.9

(* Estimated, when daily mileage not recorded in diary).

Before our trip we had estimated the route distance between Pouce Coupe to McLeod at 150 miles. It logged 230, a factor of 1½. On this same stretch we averaged 10 miles per day instead of our forecast of 15, again a factor of 1½. It took us 23 days, more than double the optimistic 10 days' estimate. On this stretch, we had three days without progress: "Wetass Camp", Pine Pass, and at "Hunter's Camp". These are included in the reckonings, as they were necessary, roughly one day in seven, thus endorsing the biblical admonition: "Six days shalt thou labour, and on the seventh shalt thou rest, that thy ox and thy ass also rest" (Exodus 23:12).

The mileages logged, if high, were realistic in terms of time and energy used. Detours around windfalls, bog-holes and up and down hills on switch-backs add significantly to map distances. Sometimes the trail would suddenly vanish at an abrupt dropoff, where the river 20 feet or more below had washed out a steep cutbank. Searching for and regaining the trail beyond, added miles and hours to the aggregates.

Jim's trade of his horses for the car at Vanderhoof had only brief mention in my diary. This sudden and unforeseen change in our situation demanded immediate reorganization and planning. However, parting with our equine friends, if brief and sudden, was not without some feeling. They had served us well on a long and arduous trip. They had often gone hungry when we had sufficient. They had suffered viciously from flies. They had adroitly negotiated many miles of difficult and hazardous travel without injuring themselves or us. They had afforded us both interest and amusement. Like humans, each had displayed indivuality and character. It was with affectionate regret that I bade farewell to The Grey, my companion who had shared so many experiences and miles with me, since that December morn in Finns' barnyard at Leighmore, when he made off with the straw jacket of the brandy bottle. He still holds his special place in my crowded album of memories.

From Prince George, the faster pace and the new mode of travel proved too much for diary-keeping, so I now make a brief synopsis from memory. The new road to Quesnel was rough going. In spite of the old Ford's high clearance, the engine casing got a couple of bangs against stumps. From Quesnel we used the old Cariboo Road via Soda Creek, Williams Lake, and Clinton to Cache Creek, thence to Kamloops and down through the Okanagan to Osoyoos. From there we had to go via Wenatchee and Everett, because the historic road down the Fraser Canyon was then derelict. I was the most experienced driver, but Jim and Barber soon gained skill and confidence. We camped along the road, if possible on the brow of a hill, with a rock wedged against a wheel. In the morning, when all was ready, we kicked out the rock, to free-wheel down grade, switching on the ignition and engaging the clutch near the bottom, hoping the engine would fire up to continue under power. Climbing the long hill from Soda Creek, the clutch spindle burned out, possibly from hitting a stump north of Quesnel. We got a tow into Williams Lake for repairs. We stopped a day at Oliver with a Peace River friend of Jim's, and filled up on his luscious fresh cantaloupe.

At Oroville, the US Customs looked with disdain at our uncouth outfit across the road, and contemptuously waved us through. We could have been loaded with contraband. We stopped two or three days at Tonasket to replace a broken crankshaft, and stayed at the quaint old hotel there, with little to do but loaf. At 10 each morning, a venerable gentleman in a black frock coat and broad-brimmed hat would emerge from the hotel and sit in the shade of a giant Balm of Gilead tree, in front. Snow-white curls fell to his shoulders. With plenty of time, I greeted him respectfully, and engaged in conversation. He was very deaf, so I let him do most of the talking. His age was then 104. He had walked across the Panama for the "49" gold rush in California and then had followed north for the Cariboo "rush" in BC. His "stake" allowed him to stay at this hotel, near a favorite camp of days gone by, until it would be time to go prospecting once more through the Pearly Gates, now not far away. Leaving Tonasket, Jim said the old man told him he had "talked more to that young fellow than to anyone for a long time". About 20 years ago, I stopped again at Tonasket, long enough to enquire about this remarkable gentleman, but could find no one whose memory went back more than 10 years. If there is a local history of Tonasket, it might satisfy my curiosity about the old man's identity and no doubt other interesting details about him.

It was after mid-August when at last, we arrived in Vancouver. There, we settled mutual accounts, and each went his own way, I to the Haggmans' in New Westminster for a short holiday, before heading north again to rejoin Jim Young at Kelly Lake and to get organized for another school year there.

Memories of that epic trip by car, now 60 years ago, are happily refreshed each time I intercept its long traverse. In those days, the country was so delightfully empty, almost devoid of man's presence and clutter. The road, single track, unsurfaced and crooked, dictated a slow pace, with ample time to contemplate and react to the varied and charming surroundings. The incidence of man was then so rare as to be interesting and reassuring. How different today!

Our Pine Pass trip had been a success after all, thanks to the efforts of man and beast, and a providential measure of good luck. The Pouce Coupe skeptics had been wrong in their forecast of failure. For me it had been an ideal vacation, even if a bit more expensive in time and dollars than I had planned, due partly to my share in repairs to the old Ford car at Williams Lake and Tonasket. I had enjoyed the companionship of two very fine senior friends in an exciting and arduous adventure. There had never been a moment of discord among us. I had been the target of some good-natured teasing, especially from Barber, but I know now that this was a genuine expression of regard. For me, both geographically and historically the trip had opened wide and wonderful vistas. That summer, in Vancouver, I bought for $5 a secondhand 1904 edition of Father Morice's classic, and soon after acquired his wonderful map, already mentioned. These were the beginnings of my fine library of like literature and maps which has afforded pleasure and interest through many, many years and has been helpful in giving substance and truth to these pages.

11: At Phil Esswein's 9 July 1924. Mounted are Jim Young (left) and Fred Barber. Neaves, standing, holds my horse.

12: Jim Young left and Phil Esswein at his new barn, 9 July 1924.

13: Typical cache — Neaves' trapline on Pine R near Callazon Cr, 12 July 1924.

14: Azouzetta Lake, BC, June 1961. View East from Hart Highway. Rosene's clearing on far shore centre; PGE Ry behind follows old packtrail of 1924. Murray Range in background. (GSA #2289)

15: Rosene's cabin, Azouzetta Lake, 1947, 23 years after our camp there. In 1964, the roof had caved in. Hart Highway built along far shore in 1952. (Courtesy Frank A. Clapp)

16: Horses get welcome feed at Azouzetta Lake in Pine Pass, 18 July 1924.

17: Azouzetta Lake, 18 July 1924. Jim Young cooks Fred Barber's trout while his "long-johns" dry in sun.

18: At Rosene's cabin, Azouzetta Lake, 18 July 1924, Fred Barber
collects scraps for Tip, whose table manners were the best. Canvas
water bucket, lower right, was excellent for this trip.

19: Airview NW'ly along Rocky Mountains divide, 1962, from vic
Sentinel Pk (c8,000 ft). Foreground Anzac River, left; Sukunka R
drainages, right; Pine Pass, beyond top right. (Courtesy A.H. Ralfs)

20: Airview S'ly over Azouzetta L, 1957. Rosene cabin on left shore, far end; PGE Ry, left; Hart Highway, middle; gas pipeline, right; Old Friend Mt (6,133 ft) centre skyline. (GSA #1663)

21: Downstream to Hart Highway bridge over Parsnip R, August 1953. Typical freighting boats as built and used on these waters by Dick Corless. Our 1924 crossing was three miles upstream. (GSA #1111)

22: W'ly across Pack River at outlet McLeod Lake, August 1982. In 1924, we forded on riffles extreme right and left to reach the HBC store on far side, view, to the left. (GSA #7209)

23: McLeod Lake Indian village 26 July 1924. Next morning Fred Barber and I attended mass at the church. Both the HBC depot and our camp were out of view, to the right.

24: McLeod Lake, BC, July 1950: View west from McIntyre's float to the old HBC buildings. (GSA #681)

25: McLeod Lake, BC, July 1950: Airview NW'ly to Sekani Indian Village and old HBC post. (GSA #679)

26: SW at Carp Lake from BC Gov't wharf August 1982. In 1924, the old brigade packtrail followed the NW shore, right. (GSA #7219)

27: WNW'ly over Stuart Lake, September 1939. Mt Pope (4,828 ft), left foreground, is prominent feature from Fort St James, five miles away. (GSA #0095)

28: Fort St James, September 1960. Our Lady of Good Hope Mission, established in 1873 by N. Blanchet, OMI. The round spire does not appear in a photo by A.G. Morice, OMI, about 1899. Mt Pope (4,828 ft), left skyline. (GSA #2183)

29: Airview S'ly over Fort St James and outlet Stuart Lake, September 1960. Vanderhoof near left skyline approximately 35 miles away. In 1924, I met husky dogs behind island, middle right. (GSA #2195)

30: Airview N'ly up Fraser R, July 1950. Nechako R enters from left, above CNR bridge. South Fort George in foreground. (GSA #700)

31: Kelly Lake silhouettes, winter, 1924-25. L to R, Homer Wright, unidentified, Silvertip Campbell, Jim Young.

32: Kelly Lake School, 2nd Year, Autumn 1924, in the old Wm Calliou cabin: L to R, Sarah Campbell*, Delphine Gladu*, Florence Gladu*, Mary Belcourt*, Annie Belcourt*, Josephine Gladu*, Delphine Calliou or Nora Napoleon, Jimmie St Arnaud, Leo Campbell, Alec Gladu, Jimmie Letendre, Alfred Campbell, David Gray, Adolphus Gladu*, George Hamelin, Joe Gladu*, Colin Gladu. Gerry Andrews*, schoolmaster, far right. Asterisked names are ones I am reasonably certain of; others are speculative. Billie Gladu and Henry Belcourt absent.

CHAPTER 3

THE SECOND KELLY LAKE SCHOOL YEAR: 1924-1925

When Barber, Young and I disbanded in Vancouver mid-August, 1924, it was already time to think about getting back to work. We had trekked nearly 400 miles across the mountains with horses and almost 1,000 miles by car. Jim sold the car in Vancouver and returned north by rail. I enjoyed being "home" with the Haggman family in New Westminster for about a week. In addition to some respectable clothes, I bought a neat little Remington portable typewriter with a teach-yourself kit for "the touch system", which has paid off handsomely, although I overwork the correction key in a later model now in use.

With Jim's connivance I was able to buy a "harvester's" rail ticket right to Grande Prairie for only $10. It was restricted to day coach but that was no hardship. In Edmonton I had time to look at the University of Alberta and to enquire about its requirements for admission to Medicine. I had been thinking about that as an alternative to Forestry, my original choice inspired by a fine old science teacher at high school in Calgary. Jim met me in Beaverlodge and we got to Kelly Lake a good week ahead of statutory school opening, Tuesday 2 September, 1924.

Part of the deal Jim had completed for accommodating the school in William Calliou's vacant cabin was his taking possession of an elegant McClary's Kootenay cookstove which Calliou had left there, probably against "jawbone" still owing to Jim. The Calliou house needed only minor reconditioning, roof, doors, windows and floor being in good shape. We replaced the big cookstove with a capacious Camp Comfort barrel heater which accepted four-foot logs. The school furniture was easily accommodated with room to spare. We covered part of one wall with enough flat lumber to support the cloth blackboard which had served so well. I also installed the poolroom bead counters strung on wire overhead, which were so useful for teaching "numbers", especially to beginners. The flagpole was erected at one end of the building, an important item in my scale of values.

With the school ready for business, we turned our attention to the space it had vacated in Jim's building, converting that to more commodious living quarters, with the partition there giving us a modicum of privacy. The "new" cookstove was the prize feature with its large firebox and oven, a hooded warming rack above and a hot water reservoir. It shared the chimney with the airtight heater which was retained for slow burning overnight fires in winter. The tiny old cookstove was left in place. The extra space in the store, being rid of our domestic clutter, was an improvement there, too.

School in the new premises got off to a good start on schedule with an effective enrolment of 18, including all 12 from the previous session. The six beginners comprised ages up to 12 and none could speak English nor had been to school before. Three of these were children of Alfred Gladu and his wife, Marceline, nee Gauthier, who had moved to Kelly Lake during the summer, possibly attracted by the new school. Alfred was a big man, progressive and responsible. They were welcome additions to the community. His children were bright, well brought up and good-looking.

The beginners had the advantage of my improved teaching experience and their schoolmates' command and use of English. My "English only" rule at school continued rigorously, and with good effect. I resumed my evening "tutorial" sessions for the four adults. The School Inspector, Mr. Gower, was rumored to be coming in late September, but he did not appear during the whole school year, Kelly Lake being still quite inaccessible. He probably assumed we would maintain the standards he found to his liking on his previous visit. This was a compliment, but I was disappointed nevertheless.

Soon after school started, Jim took an extended business trip back to the Red Deer country in Alberta, where I think he still had real estate interests. I missed him sorely, even with my waking hours so fully occupied – the school, the store, winter firewood to cut, the evening classes and my self-instruction and practice on the new typewriter. I rather neglected my Senior Matric studies until later that winter. By Thanksgiving weekend (early October) I was ready for a break and some sociability.

Being temporarily without a saddle horse, I decided to hike over Jim's winter rum trail, about 15 miles to visit Alec Anderson at Peavine lake. The weather had been fine, with fall colors in full glory. I took only a snack for lunch, knowing that Alec would provide food and a bed. I had not heard from him since early summer and was eager to see him and get caught up with his news. Days were shortening, but I reached the hill overlooking Peavine lake about sundown. Not until then did I entertain misgivings that Alec might not have returned from his summer jobs. However, from the hilltop I was reassured to see Alec, in the distance, standing beside his cabin in a bright red shirt, which I thought a bit odd. My trail then dropped down through the woods, obscuring the view till with warm anticipation, I arrived at the cabin.

All was quiet – no smoke from the chimney and the door was padlocked. I then noticed a large red lard pail set on a stout fence post near the cabin. This explained Alec's bright red shirt! It was a case of "the wish being father to the thought". I had deluded myself. Hunger, fatigue and loneliness accentuated my disappointment. It was getting dark so I decided to carry on another nine miles by wagon track to Swan Lake. I knew the road and it was easy to follow, even in the dark. Arriving at Fynn's about 10 pm, I was welcomed, fed and put to bed. They did not run a hotel, but catered to casual travellers. Next morning,

Sunday, I found Alec at Frank Ward's cabin on the lake, near the Taylor place. Ward had a trapline around the lake. He and Alec had been working on the harvest. Alec was ready to return to his cabin at Peavine, so we went back there together that afternoon. I stayed overnight with him and hiked back to Kelly Lake on the Monday (Thanksgiving Day).

On this trip, at Ward's cabin, I saw the first radio I can remember. Frank had a little "Peanut tube" crystal receiver with earphones, and powered by a single dry-cell battery. It performed best at night. Its "magic" was exciting. It was unbelievable that he could remark "They had snow in Edmonton yesterday" when such news normally took a week or more to come by mail. Radios began to appear that year sporadically among enthusiasts like Ward. It was at Frank Ward's, on this occasion that a "Trappers' Christmas" at his cabin was proposed. It was to include Alec, Jim Young, Al Millar and myself. The "ante" for each was to be a bottle of rum, except for Frank who would provide the eats and accommodation. I was flattered to be included.

One aspect of the new school premises was that the old homemade desk units, in addition to being crude and uncomfortable, especially for smaller pupils, were inadequate for the larger enrolment. This meant crowding some of the smaller ones three to a unit instead of two. While Jim was away on his trip to Red Deer, I decided to remedy this problem. He still had some one-inch dressed lumber, plenty of nails and basic tools. I planned on three desk units, a little higher than coffee table height, with simple benches to match, especially for the smaller people. The desk tops, a shelf underneath, the bench tops and cross-braces would be of lumber and the legs would be round sections of pine poles selected from the woods nearby.

Lodgepole Pine (Pinus banksiana) in dense young stands grows tall, slender, with little taper and is self-pruning in the shade below the crown. From time immemorial these have been used by the Indians for teepee poles (hence the name "Lodgepole"). Their occurence, still standing in naked teepee form, or leaning against a larger tree for preservation, always indicates a good campsite, mutely endorsing the wise choice of former occupants, long since departed.

I spent some evening hours designing the desks and benches to match – on paper. Simplicity, strength and light weight were aims. Some simple mathematics provided for the round legs to spread slightly on the floor for stability. I worked out a uniform cutting list for all pieces and then assembled them on a mass production basis. Manual training at high school in Winnipeg and Calgary paid off in this operation. It was done in Jim's store, all completed and tidied up before his return. The three desks with matching benches were then installed in the school, relieving the congestion there and winning the delight and admiration of my scholars, both young and older.

That fall I began to smoke a pipe. I loved the piquant aroma which emanated from my friends' smoking in their snug cabins after long days outdoors on the trail, and I hungered for the solace it seemed to impart. I began with T&B tobacco, which, in half-pound plugs was a universal trade item at $1 each. The "technique" of its use was almost a ritual. A few thin shavings are sliced from the plug with a sharp pocketknife. These are crumbled by rubbing between the palms, and then packed not too tightly in the pipe bowl. Jim used to say, "The finer you cut it and the more you rub it, the better it smokes". The T&B brand was full strength, to put it mildly. For me, a novice, one pipe in the evening sufficed. It never made me sick.

My Cree friends used "store" tobacco ("staimow") sparingly, by mixing it with their own "mikwapemigwa". This was the inner bark (cambium) of Red Willow (Cornus stolonifera). It was usually prepared by a dutiful daughter. The red outer bark is scraped off and discarded. Then the soft inside cambium layer is carefully stripped down the slender stem and may be left attached in spirals at the end. These are then dried or toasted by sticking the stems in the ground or snow around a campfire, or they may be dried in an oven.

Most of the Cree men carried a "fire bag" ("kuskipitakun") of moosehide, often embellished with embroidery or beads. It was either attached to the belt or hung on a shoulder cord. In the bag would be a "heel" of T&B, a good supply of the Red Willow product, and matches. In the old days it would also contain a flint, steel and tinder. Best for lighting a pipe is a glowing ember from the campfire. A splinter may be used, igniting it from the fire or a lamp. I liked the fragrance of the Cree blend, and occasionally prepared my own Red Willow "mixer" to dilute the strong T&B. The dried leaves of Kinnikinnick or Bear Berry (Arctostaphylos uva-ursi) are an alternative to Red Willow. It is more easily gathered and prepared but to my taste it is rather too sweet and bland, lacking the piquance of Red Willow.

As I have remarked, the art of smoking plug tobacco in a pipe is almost a ritual. If suddenly faced with a difficult question or decision, one could deliberately take out his pipe and place it in his teeth. Next come the tobacco and the pocketknife. A few shavings are carefully sliced, the knife and plug are put back in pocket. The tobacco is rubbed out, and carefully loaded in the pipe. It is then ignited, and a couple of satisfying puffs drawn. All of this in silence, when the smoker is collecting his thoughts and framing his reply or proposal. Meanwhile, the other party has become so engrossed by this strange procedure that he is distracted from his original line of thought, and may have quite forgotten his question. I sometimes used this strategem in World War II, with people who had never seen or heard of plug tobacco. The Kelly Lake men used this "preoccupation", perhaps subconsciously, when entering the store. It allowed all concerned to adjust to their presence.

Jim Young returned about mid-October with his usual load from Grande Prairie. He seemed pleased with what had transpired in his absence. He went over his inventory and checked the accumulation of muskrat pelts and moccasins and cash which I had taken in trade at the usual prices. He also checked the more valuable furs which I had accepted on his behalf, granting only token credit against their full value. For these he would make final settlement with the owners in due course.

As with men, Jim had a "way" with animals. He always got full response from his horses, even though they were high-spirited. Habitually he had a dog which had attached itself to and worshipped him. One of these, Poker, a mixedbred collie, he left with me at Kelly Lake for company. We became good pals. Poker had an uncanny sixth sense for anticipating Jim's arrival from his long trips. Often, hours before Jim appeared, Poker would get restless and start fussing. I got to know from this that Jim was surely on his way from Leighmore or Peavine Lake. How the dog knew was a mystery, as scent could hardly carry over so many miles when Poker would begin his symptoms.

Unlike the previous year, permanent snow came early and copiously in the fall of 1924. Under this early snow, it took longer for frost to penetrate and harden the ground beneath. First time over a trail, one had to be careful for hidden soft spots. Once the trail was broken, the frost could go down and do its good work. Winter imposed his stern discipline on our world. In real cold snaps with temperatures down to minus 50° F or lower, invariably the air would be clear and deathly still, with smoke rising straight up from chimneys in a dense thin vertical column. Minute ice crystals in the air sometimes gave rainbow effects, duplicating the sun's feeble image in ghostlike color echoes, left and right. We called them sundogs. In the night sky, Aurora Borealis made spectacular displays. Some claimed it made hissing sounds but I could never hear them.

During such deep freeze spells, all life is immobilized, taking refuge from winter's tyranny beneath the snow, in thick bush, in camp or cabin. If one is caught out on the trail, care must be taken against over-exertion, because breathing the incisive air too fast could freeze the respiratory membranes with dire effects on horses, dogs or humans. We were so caught once between Peavine and Kelly lakes. Jim slowed his team to a snail's pace with frequent rests and our own exertions were minimal. Trees exploded like gun shot with the frost, and lake ice roared like cannon fire. If rum were carried for emergency it was placed inside one's shirt next the body. Otherwise the frigid liquid could freeze mouth and throat.

There was a measure of irony in returning to our dark cold cabin in winter from a day or more away, especially alone. Fatigue, cold and hunger in the final hour of travel engendered keen anticipation of imminent shelter, warmth and food. With fires kindled, liquid water fetched from the lake and lamps lit, preparations for a big meal would begin. Meanwhile, the cold sterile air of the cabin would moderate with fragrant vapors from the cook stove. Finally, with the table set and the hot meal ready the anticlimax would be complete and sudden loss of appetite, with most of the food put away uneaten. In these circumstances, eventually I learned to keep it simple – a bowl of hot porridge, coffee and to bed – with a hearty breakfast in the morning. There was a psychological factor, too, because if I had company like Jim it made a difference.

One bizarre aspect of very cold weather was not anticipated. The previous summer I had bought an army trench coat of rugged khaki material, with belt, high collar, large lapels and pockets – very military and masculine. It had two button-in removable linings, one a light waterproof oilskin and the other of heavy wool. It seemed like a good all-weather deal, if somewhat cumbersome, The first time I wore it in extreme cold weather, when hitching up the horses, the oilskin lining, rendered stiff by the cold, made sharp crackling sounds. The team took fright and nearly bolted.

At the store, I took pleasure and pride in maintaining a good supply of choice firewood. At bedtime our big airtight heater would be topped up with a couple of large chunks of green birch with draft and damper closed. In the morning there would be a good bed of hot embers to start a quick fire to warm things up. On leaving our premises for more than 24 hours, a routine was to empty all containers of water. Otherwise buckets and kettles would be misshapen by the expanding ice. A bucket with a bulging bottom is an abomination. We always left a supply of shavings and dry kindling ready for a quick fire on our return, cold, tired and hungry. In the North, if one took shelter in a cabin during the owner's absence it was standard etiquette to tidy up and leave a supply of dry wood and kindling for the next-comer.

During winter, before breakfast, it was my habit to go across to the school and fire up the big heater so that as the kids arrived, they could enter and get warm. By 9 o'clock the building would be sufficiently comfortable to start lessons. We lost only a couple of days from extreme cold. On these, the poorly insulated building was just too frigid, in spite of a roaring fire. On the first such morning, all showed up as usual. I let them warm up around the big heater with informal chatter in English. When the sun was high enough to radiate its feeble cheer, they ate their lunch, bundled up and went home. I had to tell them not to come next day, if the intense cold continued. These children were naturally stoical and never complained or whimpered from dis-comfort or pain. Those crossing the lake ice sometimes got their feet wet from water pressured up from below the ice and spreading under the snow. Their cold little feet would clonk on the floor like blocks of ice. We would dry their socks and moccasins as best we could over the heater while they stood barefoot on an old rug. These experiences together engendered a warm esprit de corps among us. They were great kids!

For outdoor recreation in winter, in addition to working on my wood-pile, I often hiked around the area on snowshoes. These were of the "Lac Ste Anne" pattern, locally made. They were long and narrow for bush travel, in contrast to the broad "bear paw" type used on open prairie. I acquired the habit of wearing plain moccasins, winter and summer. They were cheap, well-made and allowed full blood circulation. With thick socks and insoles, they were warm in the dry cold. Mrs. Isidore Gladu made me a wonderful moosehide jacket decorated with fringes only. I didn't want beads or embroidery. She used the hides of twin calves. The jacket was soft and fine-textured like chamois. It was light and windproof. Over a heavy wool sweater it was ideal for riding or hiking. I also wore gauntlet mitts of moosehide over woollen gloves. They were suspended on a cord around the neck.

On long winter hikes, alone, I always carried matches in a waterproof container, and a short length of candle. To make a fire en route, fuel, dry twigs and a curl of birchbark if handy, were gathered with mitts on. Then, when all was ready, in a sheltered spot, mitts were removed as quickly as possible, the candle ignited, matches then put away and mitts replaced. The lighted candle could tolerate more wind than a match and would burn longer. With it, the tinder could be lit, then the kindling, and soon a blazing fire. Without the candle, one's fingers could quickly become so numb that they could not hold a match, let alone strike it. It might be impossible to button up again and one could be in serious trouble.

For weaponry I had acquired, as mentioned previously, a dandy little Winchester carbine 30-30 repeating rifle. These were popular, and ammunition was easy to obtain anywhere. They were handy for saddle or on foot and were powerful enough for any local game one should aim at. Some claimed this rifle was inadequate for grizzly bear whose habitat was confined mostly to the mountains, to the west. Against these monsters I had no unfriendly intentions whatever. I also had a neat little 20-gauge shotgun, single-shot, but good for birds. My non-repeater .22-calibre rifle completed the arsenal. I was a fair shot in those days, but except for the pot, I was never an ardent Nimrod. I am ashamed now for rare instances of slaughter "for sport".

I vividly remember the utter delight of those northern woods on a clear bright winter day without wind. The silence was absolute. One's own tread in the soft virgin snow was soundless. Rabbits, in perfect white camouflage, moved in the snow like ghosts. Only occasionally was the silence broken by the cheery chirps of saucy, acrobatic chickadees. An owl's muted flight could almost brush one's ear without sound, startling and mysterious. Colors were iridescent in purity and brilliance: deep blue sky, varied greens of Pine and Spruce, white bark of Aspen and occasional Birch, purple hue of snow in shadows, and brilliant patches of sunlit snow mushroomed on conifer boughs. These, with a dendritic filigree of naked branches all combined in exquisite compositions of form and color to delight an artist's soul.

Kelly Lake was in the zone of Chinook winds which characterize the eastern foothills of the Rockies from Montana well into northern BC. They were presaged by the "Chinook arch", a broad arc of clear sky over the mountains in the southwest, with a blanket of cloud overhead. Following a cold spell they brought welcome relief from its severity. They were strong, balmy and dry, thawing and absorbing snow on exposed slopes. Often they arrived suddenly, overnight.

The store's clay roof was quite impervious to ordinary rain but was not fully proof against melting snow. Drops during the night were sometimes the first evidence of a Chinook's arrival, waking us to get up and place receptacles under the worst leaks. Snow falling through the atmosphere absorbes carbon dioxide gas and traces of ammonia. These gases are held in cold storage until the snow melts and remaining in solution, reduce the water's surface tension, allowing it to percolate through the clay. This also explains accelerated plant growth after heavy snowfall.

Plans for our "Trappers' Christmas" at Swan Lake with Frank Ward began to "gel". Jim had made a recent trip that way to confirm that I would join Alec Anderson at his cabin Christmas Eve and we would hike to Frank's next morning for the big meal at noon. Jim had to beg out due to commitments in other directions. School closed for the holiday Friday, 19 December. I had lots of time to tidy up and get ready at Kelly Lake. Jim had left my rabbit robe at Ward's (it weighed at least 20 pounds). Alec had ample bedding at "Peavine Castle".

On Wednesday the 24th I hiked over the winter trail to Peavine, travelling light, with only a snack for lunch and of course my matches and bit of candle. (Jim had left my "ante" in bottle form at Ward's.) My hike was pleasant, and without incident, and there was Jim's sleigh track to follow. I arrived in good time for supper and a pleasant evening with Alec – more cheery than my earlier visit that fall. Christmas morning Alec and I set out on foot nine miles to Swan lake, arriving at Frank's with sharp appetites for the big feast at noon. We were four, Frank, Alec, Al Miller and myself. Frank had a beautiful goose, well-cooked with all the trimmings (but no Big Bar sage!). I was initiated to a "nuclear" concoction of hot rum, honey and fresh cream.

After cleaning up the dishes, rather drowsily, we took turns going out to Frank's fishing hole on the lake ice. His lure was a strip of bacon fat, slit in two except at the end, which was impaled on the hook. This was lowered on a handline through the hole and activated gently. Presto! in no time we hauled out a three- to five-pound jackfish. These are a variety of pike, poor eating in summer, but in winter were firm and tasty. The catch was thrown up on the roof of Frank's cabin to freeze. We would then duck inside to warm up with another round of "rhum à la creme". And so passed a pleasant afternoon.

The Boone Taylors had invited us all for another Christmas dinner with them in the evening. So, at dusk we headed over there, feeling no pain. My appetite hardly did justice to a second feast, but it was great to be with the family. Four cute daughters round the table and helping "Mom", with the baby (a girl) in the crib. Boone had recently acquired a luxurious "superheterodyne" radio with lots of power, loud speaker, dials, and knobs for tuning, tone and volume. It brought in Christmas music from far-away places, including the choir from the Young Street Methodist Church in Winnipeg, where, as a child, I had attended services and Sunday school. It was a warm emotional experience, reviving memories of childhood Christmases with my family in the fond embrace of our dear mother. Finally, at a late hour, we returned to Ward's cabin and to bed – after a wonderful day in all respects. Next morning I noticed that our tracks in the snow had meandered rather widely from a direct line to the Taylors'.

Sadly, after such a dramatic introduction, the big radio at the Taylors' was to become a vexation. Instead of being addressed by Boone's entertaining personality, as of old, we saw only his broad back while he fiddled with knobs on the machine. Squeaks and squawks with disjointed broadcast fragments were baneful substitutes for his own varied and colorful anecdotes. When Taylor was buying fur for Revillon Freres, he used an effective ploy. Going into places like Kelly Lake he would meet other itinerant buyers coming out who warned that "there is no fur to buy there". He knew that trappers withheld their fur when they suspected buyers were looking for bargains. On arrival he would affirm that it was a purely social visit, and would then start playing poker with our friends. After letting them win for a while, Boone would start taking most of the "pots", until his clients ran out of cash. He would then, "reluctantly" accept their furs at bargain prices to cover their bets, knowing they would stay in the game at any price.

The weekly "Northwest Farmer" published a picture of photogenic Martin B. Taylor standing with his plough and horses. In the background the freshly turned furrow led off into the distance as straight as though laid out by a land surveyor. The caption identified Boone and remarked on the skill and industry of the Peace River pioneers. The neighbors alleged that the ploughing had not been done by Boone at all, but by his dimunitive wife, Mary.

Not having to hurry back to Kelly Lake, Boone had suggested that I go on up to Pouce Coupe with him the next day. After breakfast with the family, and before leaving, Boone sat in a chair by the stove while Mary combed out his long black hair, braided it in two pigtails and fastened them around the back and sides of his head. He wore a big "ten gallon" hat, with no protection for his ears. Mine would have been frozen. He cut quite a glamorous figure around Pouce Coupe, especially among his Cree friends. In the poolroom, there was a set of platform scales. Boone got them betting on his weight. With all bets "in", he dramatically mounted the platform. When all eyes were concentrated on the scale bar, Boone covertly edged his elbow on the solid stand, to make the balance indicate his own bet.

From Pouce Coupe we went on to Rolla for a dance which I did not enjoy, being among mostly strangers. I was glad to meet Ralph Hull, principal of the school there, with whom I had attended Normal School in Vancouver. I remember the Henderson brothers, prominent pioneer farmers at Rolla. Instead of hauling their grain the long miles to Grande Prairie or Spirit River, they fed it to hogs which they marketed with less cost for transport.

In Pouce Coupe, during winter, there was a "round-the-clock" poker game. Local and other participants could "sit in" for as long as they wished or until their luck and cash ran out. Late winter, before the trapping harvest came in, money was scarce so the bets would be covered in kind rather than in cash – saddles, guns, or whatever. One morning Frank Haskins stepped out of his store to sniff the weather. Seeing George Hart across the street, he shouted "How did the game go after I left last night?". Hart shouted back, "Pete with a straight raised with his bull calf. So Joe with a full house called with his red sow." It was said that Chief Calhazon (Callazon?), of an Indian or Metis band in the headwaters of the Pine River, would bring in a fur harvest for his band valued at $30,000 each spring. Indirectly some of this was a welcome infusion for the Pouce Coupe poker circle.[64] Calhazon was too smart to let the locals "take him for a ride".

The Taylor family tell an amusing story of their father, Boone, arriving home from Pouce Coupe late on a winter day, when he drove into the home yard at Swan Lake calling for his wife to please come to unhitch the horses. This unusual request was explained by his need of both hands to hold up a blanket wrapped around his middle. In the notorious Pouce Coupe poker game he had lost not his shirt, but his pants! (I learned these stories from the Taylors when in the Dawson Creek area in August, 1982).

In some of Boone Taylor's notes which his daughters lent me recently, he confirmed my reference in Chapter 1 to Jim Young providing the team and harness for Boone's mail contract. It is quite likely that he and Jim first met on the old Edson Trail in 1914. Referring to the awful boggy stretches on that trail, where people detoured around them by different routes, Boone mentioned a blazed tree at one of them inscribed boldly with the notice, "It doesn't matter which trail you choose, you'll wish you had taken the other one!"

Another anecdote relates that Boone was unexpectedly delayed overnight while tending his trapline out from Swan Lake. He found a thick patch of dried Saskatoon berries on which he filled up, and also stuffed his pockets full of them. Then he found a spot to bed down in a hollow under an overturned tree. It was well-lined with dried grass and surprisingly cosy. His bedfellow was a hibernating bear! Whenever the drowsy animal roused, Boone would stuff its mouth with the dried berries which seemed to have the desired soporific effect. Boone did not linger when daybreak came next morning.

An oldtimer who lived down in the valley of Pouce Coupe River, below the town, was reputedly the dirtiest bachelor in the country. I have conveniently forgotten his name. He placed his spent wads of chewing tobacco progressively along the crevice of a log wall inside his cabin, then filled his pipe with the trailing end of dried-out wads. Jim Young introduced me to him, but I never was inside his cabin to verify his notoriety.

My return to Kelly Lake during the 1924 Christmas holidays, featured an overnight with Alec Anderson at Peavine Lake. Frank Ward had given me a liberal supply of fishhooks and line to try my luck with his technique when I got back. My early enquiries about fishing at Kelly Lake had been answered with "namoya meeosin" (no good). They said a few were trapped in spring when the fish went up the small streams to spawn. I lost no time in trying out Ward's tactics through the ice. With axe, shovel, hooks, bait and line, I walked out on the ice about 200 feet in front of Jim's store. I cleared away the snow and chopped a hole. I could feel all eyes in the village focused on my strange actions. I got a "strike" almost at once – a 7-lb. beauty. I threw it well clear on the ice and tried again, this time a nice 4-pounder. The third was another big one, about eight pounds. With such spectacular success and not to crowd my luck, I then gathered up kit and catch to return triumphantly to the store, very conscious of my unseen audience around the lake. I cleaned the fish before they froze, put the big ones in our cache to freeze and kept the small one for supper.

Bright and early next morning old Celestin Gladu came in the store. After the appropriate interlude of silence, when I greeted him, he said, "You catch um fish." I fetched the big one from the cache as a present for him because I liked and admired the old man. He wanted to buy some hooks, which Jim did not stock, so I gave him some of mine, and explained the baiting details. Then after a brief smoke, he left. Before sundown that day there were several fishing holes in operation on the lake, with apparent success. This continued for several days until the community had a good stock of frozen fish to vary and supplement its diet of moose and rabbits in the hungry season. It was ironic that these people, so skilled in woodcraft, took this little lesson from their young "greenhorn" teacher.

Our second annual concert must have been staged soon after school re-opened in January, 1925. My memory is quite blank on details now, except one amusing incident. During refreshments, when passing a large plate of candy, I first offered it to one of the older scholars who happened to be nearest. He grabbed the whole plateful, thinking it was his ration. Embarrassment was avoided by treating it as a joke.

By this time the school curriculum became more comprehensive. A quote at Normal School had been, "If you wish to know a thing – teach it". Another was, "The teacher must know 10 times as much as he hopes to teach." My own education certainly bene-fited significantly. The basic Three Rs in all grades continued to be drilled in by endless review. The new subjects, geography and history leavened the others. For geography the starting point was HERE, and for history it was NOW.

The children already knew quite a bit about local trails and places, with distances and time of travel between. Together we made rough maps in the scope and style of maps 3 and 4. These were first done on the blackboard and then copied in their scrib-blers. We listed the names of friends and relatives who lived in these nearby places. In our English lessons we described what they did and interesting things about them. They had heard their elders speak of farther places, Grand Prairie and Flyingshot Lake – and still farther, Lac Ste Anne and Edmonton. Our maps broadened accordingly. I explained the significance of the cleared-out Boundary Line, just a mile away, between British Columbia and Alberta. This led to a full map of the two provinces, with their salient features including the prairie, the Rocky Mountains and the Pacific Ocean. Progressively we then looked at all of Canada, the USA, the continent, the oceans and the other continents. Lacking a proper globe, we improvised with our round football.

Their fathers knew about the mountains to the west (not visible from Kelly Lake) where they trapped and hunted. What was beyond the mountains? As already mentioned, I liked the Cree for "far away across the Rocky Mountains". It sounded like "wahayoo kwaskayee asine ooche". Their teacher had come from there. We discussed what people did, in those far away places, and how. They knew about farming from hearsay if not example. Flour, oatmeal and cornmeal were made by grinding the grains into a powder. This could be done at home with a stone mortar and pestle, but better in a mill with huge grindstones and power. All this could be described and shown in pictures. Their parents could tell them more.

The source and manufacture of other trade goods, familiar to them, was a comprehensive topic. We all enjoyed these expanding horizons. We learned about other climates and ways of life different to ours. They were intrigued with the concept of the tropics, without snow, ice or winter, or even the need of clothes, except for decency. We looked at simple quantitative geography, latitude, longitude, equator, tropics, temperate and polar regions. The Earth's rotation, day and night, time and seasons began to fall into place easily in their logical and observant minds. Exotic flora and especially fauna intrigued them: elephants, giraffes, rhinos, hippos, lions, tigers and whales.

In History we used the same approach, starting with the familiar. The spread of their own ages was itself a unit of history. The older ones could remember when their juniors were born, and so on. Who came first to Kelly Lake, and when? Their parents could tell them, and they could then tell me. Was anyone here before that? This led to the concept of aboriginal people. Kelly Lake is in what was originally Beaver Indian country of the Athapaskan nation (now to the west and north). Their Cree ancestors were Algonkian, from far to the east. Who were the first

White men, where were they from, and why did they come? By what routes? The children were of course, receptive to lore of the fur trade. Life in the old lands of Europe where their French ancestors originated was something new. They were aware of English and French people. Their parents knew about others, like Scandinavian and German. This led to a simplified "look" at Europe and its story.

We dramatized explorers like Alexander Mackenzie and David Thompson. We discussed the materials and construction of their canoes, paddles and related equipment. Other topics were their provisions, navigation, hazards and skills. These children were more familiar with transport by dogs and horses, but it was all quite realistic. They knew something about living off the country. I gave them highlights from the explorer's journals. My recent trip through the Pine Pass provided some anecdotes which they easily understood and enjoyed. Geography and History were specifically for the upper grades and ages but I let the younger ones listen in, to stimulate their curiosity and incentive to learn English.

My life-long interest in the history of the Great Northwest began in this manner and about this time. My treasured copy of Father Morice's "History of the Northern Interior ...", Briggs, Toronto, 1904 is inscribed with my name and "Kelly Lake, BC, 1924". In it the original inscription was "JB Hobson, Bullion, BC". Another useful reference was "The Conquest of the Great Northwest" by Agnes C. Laut. This book was from my father's library. Miss Laut had attended university in Winnipeg. Her life-span coincided exactly with my father's, 1871-1936. Father said she had taught him how to dance. There may have been a hint of romance in this, before he married Emma Harris (Smedley), my mother, in 1896. I have been able to collect half a dozen of Miss Laut's works, for their own merit as well as sentiment. She made history "live".

In late February, 1925, Milton Campbell, father of Sarah, Alfred and Leo in the school, was brought in from the traplines sick, on a toboggan. Milton was one of the hardiest and best trappers. His friends came to the store saying gravely, "Milton — he home sick." I did not pay too much attention at first, as they often came with minor complaints for first aid, sympathy and sociability. When they came again to repeat "Milton — he awful sick — can't eat — can't drink — can't talk", I realized it must be serious. The symptoms suggested quinsy, a painful abscess inside the throat. My oldest sister had been subject to it, to the point of delirium. The abscess finally bursts, with immediate relief and quick recovery. My father, a pharmacist, had sent me quite a comprehensive first aid kit, which included hydrogen peroxide, a throat atomizer and camphorated oil. I selected these items for Milton — he could not swallow pills. I asked his friends to tell him I would come to see him that evening.

After an early supper I went across the lake on the ice, guided by the light from Milton's cabin and leaving a lamp in my window for a return beacon. I found several adults there playing whist and the children were still up. Milton, in his best clothes, lay on the floor with his head on a pillow against the wall. After a general greeting, I approached Milton, who smiled wanly. I said I was sorry to find him sick and would do what I could for him. I asked him to keep his mouth open wide. Then, with the atomizer I sprayed a liberal dose of undiluted hydrogen peroxide down as far as possible. I then massaged his throat and neck outside vigorously with the camphorated oil. Finally a wool sock was wrapped around and fastened with a safety pin. I said it was all I could do, and hoped it would help. By this time, I was nearly suffocated, the air being thick with so many people, and minimal ventilation to keep out the cold. I took my leave, glad to get out into the cold clear air and head back home across the lake ice.

Early next morning old Celestin, Milton's father-in-law came to the store and without the usual protocol of silence, exclaimed "By

God!" repeating it several times. When I asked what was up, he replied "By God — one hour after you leave last night Milton he's alright-by God!". Evidently my diagnosis had been correct, and accelerated by my treatment, the abcess had collapsed. My reputation as a "muskekeaweno" (doctor) hit an all-time high. Pointing to his stomach, Celestin then said, "Mebee you help old man." Evidently he had a mild case of intestinal parasites. The best remedy I could think of was phenolphthalein tablets, a drastic purgative. I warned him to be ready to run — and fast!

Milton Campbell made a quick recovery and soon returned to his trapline. Later, in early summer, his pretty eldest daugher, Eva (Mrs Johnny Calliou), came to the store, placed a neat package, sewn up in clean flour sacking, on the counter and said shyly, "That for you — from my father!" With her consent I opened it at once. It was a beautiful cartridge belt for my 30-30 Winchester rifle shells. It had a moosehide base and was faced with caribou hide and embellished with a full length floral wreath in colored beads. With sincere admiration I complimented her on the beautiful work. This was Milton's and his family's "thank you" for the quinsy cure. The belt is still a cherished possession.

Jim and I were glad to dispense the traditional hospitality to casual visitors, which we enjoyed so fully in our travels. Our fare was simple as were their needs and tastes. Most had their own bedding and a pad or cot could be improvised. There was always plenty of staple food in the store. One interesting visitor was Jack Blanchard who ranched in the Goodfare area.[65] He arrived in cold weather, just before Christmas with horses, guiding two, hardy and well-to-do (British) ranchers from the hinterland of Argentina. Hardy types, they wanted to see and hunt in our northern Rockies in winter. They were interesting but stayed only one night in order to spend Christmas in the mountains. Instead of a conventional A-tent with stove and chimney, Jack carried a large canvas teepee. For it he could find or cut poles on site. With the circumference outside banked with snow and a small open fire in the centre inside, they could be quite comfortable. Later Jack went placer mining on the Finlay River where he became well-known. A creek and a mountain are now named for him in that area. Jack was also a juror for the John Bennett inquest (see Appendix 2).

Other visitors were itinerant fur buyers who ranged rapidly over wide areas. They paid cash for furs which should have come to the local store in payment for "jawbone". However, there was little if any hard feeling and they would frequently drop in to say "hello". One of these was old ("Silvertip") John Malcolm Campbell. He had come from Saskatchewan (Prince Albert and Kinistino) in 1910, and later had a store near Hythe on the Beaverlodge River. He was spry for his 70-odd years, and wore a long white beard. Hence his nickname.[66]

Thanks to these roving fur buyers, my Kelly Lake Cree scholars got the reputation of speaking the best English anywhere in the country, including White settlements. The reasons are not surprising. These children heard me speak only the best English I knew, and they were not normally exposed to bad English. At home only Cree was spoken. I trained them to speak politely, grammatically, in complete sentences and with clear articulation. "White" children do not always have these advantages, and are certainly exposed to bad English at every turn, except perhaps at home.

Living in remote isolation, far from medical services, we simply had to be healthy and were, with rare exceptions. Just prior to Easter holidays, 1925, I contracted an abscessed molar which at times was nagging torture. A wad soaked with oil of cloves might dull the pain temporarily. By coincidence, a rumor filtered through that a dentist, on tour from Grande Prairie, would be in Pouce Coupe for a few days at Easter.[67] This was vague, but not to be ignored. The holidays were from Saturday, 11 April to Sunday, 19 April inclusive. Jim was away in the Grande Prairie direction so I decided to hike to Pouce Coupe hoping to intercept the dentist, there. Spring breakup was just beginning, when road traffic would be minimal. I had to walk most of the way to Pouce Coupe. When I arrived there, Sunday evening, 12 April or the next day, to my dismay, the dentist had already departed for Grande Prairie. He was in a hurry to avoid worsening road conditions. I had little choice but to follow on foot, stopping for food and bed wherever, and happy to pay for it as necessary. I would have contrived at least one meal at Mrs. Brainard's. I remember walking 30 miles one day, and probably got a lift the last few miles into Grande Prairie. I think it was Thursday when I got into the dentist's chair. He was sympathetic and did a good job quickly, but scolded me for smoking a pipe – "a filthy habit". The weekend allowed sufficient time to get back to Kelly Lake via Leighmore in time for school opening on Monday 20 April. My complete "dental circuit" would have logged about 180 miles, more than half of which was done on foot.

After the ice had cleared from the lake, early morning mists often hid ducks chattering noisily near the shore. By sneaking down to the water's edge with my shot gun, it was easy to get a bird as the fog lifted. But retrieval without getting wet was a problem. It was strange that no one seemed to have a boat on the lake. I decided a raft might be a good idea. I found enough dry Spruce logs (for buoyancy) and snaked them down to the lake near the store with my saddle horse. For better handling, I made it long and narrow. Amidships I built supports port and starboard for oarlocks and contrived a low seat between. Oars were hewn, also from Spruce, it being light and stiff. I was familiar with canoe and rowboat from boyhood summers at Gimli and Minaki. With this critical background, I found my raft was hopelessly heavy, awkward and tippy – a disappointment. However, it was not a complete write-off. Stabilized with stakes driven into the lake bottom, it served as a jetty for getting cleaner water from its deep end.

Jim Young was remarkably thoughtful and generous on my behalf. His quick eye for bargains on his wide travels was cheerfully shared with me at no markup. In this way I acquired my array of guns, a good riding saddle and other items at very modest cost. By this time Jim had replaced his sleigh with a wagon. One day he arrived at Kelly Lake with a 12-ft flat-bottom dinghy on the running gear in place of the usual wagon box. He had contrived a temporary wagon seat. He had bought the boat for $2.50 from a homesteader. After unloading, we lifted the dinghy into the lake and, with my rough oars shortened a bit, it was ready for use. For his trip back to Leighmore with no load, Jim improvized a temporary driver's platform on the bare running gear. I had lots of fun with the dinghy which was great for retrieving ducks. My respect for wind and waves was also revived.

Somewhere Jim had acquired a heavy steel bear trap so we decided to try our luck with it. A small creek entered the southwest corner of the lake, where nobody lived. We took the beartrap there in the dinghy and set it a short distance up the creek in what seemed a good place. The trap was secured to a heavy log with a length of strong chain. Our Cree friends would have been amused, but this was our own private little project. I was to monitor the trap after school or in evenings. The days were long and it was pleasant exercise rowing across the lake. I took my 30-30 rifle and an axe. Leaving the boat tied on shore, I would sneak cautiously up the creek, rifle at the ready and very alert. Each time, I was profoundly relieved to find the trap – empty. We had not thought about finding an enraged powerful bear in it. Thankfully Mr. Bear never did appear. We soon "lifted" the trap and called it quits. The trap could be a hazard for anyone not aware of its gaping and powerful jaws.

Homer Wright was one of Jim's friends in Beaverlodge.[68] Not much older than I, he was an ardent sportsman and owned a beautiful black quarter-horse team. On the long weekend of 24 May, he and I decided to run Jim's dinghy downstream from Kelly

Lake to Beaverlodge on the spring freshet, the only time of year when there would be enough water for navigation. After some initial trouble with windfall across Steeprock Creek, we had good going, paddling only enough to control the boat. Around many sharp bends we approached silently to surprise and shoot ducks of all kinds. We arrived in the vicinity of Beaverlodge before dark with a nice bag of birds, which Homer shared with his friends in town. Somehow I managed to get myself and the boat back to Kelly Lake in time for duty. It had been a delightful weekend and a chance to get acquainted with Wright, who was to join us on our trip to Jasper later in the summer.

I have mentioned Jim's favorite team, Roanie and Kate. They were strong, fast walkers, high-spirited, but gentle. Most of the time he supplied me with a saddle horse. It was fed with green-cut oat sheaves stockpiled on the roof of the stable. It was a pleasant chore to feed, water, exercise and otherwise care for the horse. There was a good corral near the store where horses could move about loose for sun and air. Jim was a good "paramedic" veterinarian. He often "altered" colts and bull calves for his friends. The previous summer en route to Pine Pass, we had stopped at Pete Stuart's, where one of his mares had a huge carbuncle, like a grapefruit, on its leg. We threw the mare and stabilized its hind legs in rope slings. Then Jim deftly cut away the carbuncle, seared and dressed the wound. The mare recovered.

One day Jim arrived at Kelly Lake leading a fine but sick mare (not Kate). I think he said she had "blackwater fever". He left her in the corral to recover or die, and continued his journey, after which I looked after the mare. She took some water, but ate little. I noticed there were no droppings, evidently she was constipated. My first aid kit included a syringe, bag, tube, and hard rubber nozzle. So I decided to give the mare an enema. I knew how to throw a horse with its hind legs in slings, as mentioned above. One could do this alone if necessary. I took a large pailful of warm, soapy water, my syringe outfit and rope. I got the mare down and stabilized, and injected the enema – all of it. Holding the syringe bag high created enough pressure, and I refilled it as necessary. The whole "works" stayed "in". I then removed the ropes and let the mare take her own time to get up. Next day her bowel movements were evident and continued; also her appetite picked up. When Jim returned she was quite recovered. He gave me full marks for this and said he would never have thought of my novel treatment.

Another first aid emergency occurred that summer. A family of visiting relatives had come in a wagon. They set up a teepee near Celestin Gladu's cabin. I had noticed their arrival, soon after which, someone came running to the store, saying that a 15-year-old girl had cut her leg badly. Jumping down from the wagon the calf of her leg was torn by a sharp square plate of rusty steel which had been improvised to hold a wheel on its spindle. I found her sitting on a blanket in the teepee. Fortunately the artery had not been severed and the bleeding had subsided, but a deep gash obviously needed some stitches. Disinfecting my hands, the wound, needle and black linen thread (all I had), I grimly put in half a dozen stitches to close the wound sufficiently, but not too tightly. It was then bound up gently with some sterile dressing. Meanwhile, the poor girl had shown no visible reaction whatever. That was it. I went back a couple of times to change the dressing and remove the stitches. Evidently the wound healed and if the girl is still alive, she would be nearly my age and her name? I wish I knew.

The end of my second school year at Kelly Lake was now imminent. I was reasonably satisfied with what had been accomplished. The aims had been, not to make white-collar professionals of the pupils but rather to give them enough English to acquit themselves creditably in the surrounding settlements where they might circulate. They should have enough arithmetic to protect them in elementary business and to meet other quantitative needs. They should be able to write simple communications and read letters, newspapers, periodicals and books, and they should have some perspective of their local environment in its broader setting, timewise and spacewise.

In school there had been few, if any problems of behavior. Like their parents, the children were by nature courteous and gentle. There may have been one, or perhaps two cases of corporal punishment (legal in those days). Had I been smarter, these could have been avoided. One incident was a lesson for me. One sunny day, when playing outside at recess or noon, two 12-year-old boys began to fight. They were evenly matched for size and strength. So, with my YMCA background in boxing, rules and all that, I let them go to it, but stood by to referee fair play and prevent any real damage. The father of one of the boys happened to see this, ran up and made them stop. He then told me if there was any more fighting he would take his children out of school. I realized at once he was dead right and assured him there would be no further cause to complain. What he knew, and what I had not fully appreciated, was that these normally peaceful people, if roused, were capable of extreme violence. Boxing as a sport was just not part of their code.

In only two confrontations with parents, one at the beginning and this one near the end of my Kelly Lake sojourn, I had the moral advantage in the first with conviction and effect. In the second, the father was right. The score was even.

One bright Saturday morning in early June, some older women came to the store to announce that Old Granny Calliou, our centenarian, had just died. They wanted some white sheeting for a shroud. Jim stocked only colored denims – "Too bad, too bad!" I told them, "Wait just a minute." (Almost any situation is the better for a little fun.) Deep down in my trunk along with the Big Bar sage, was a pair of new white flannel pyjamas I had never used. These I exhumed and re-entering the store held up the pants high in display, and asked how these would do.

"Meeosin, tapooi meeosin!" (Good – very good!). They had called my bluff, but I was glad to donate my elegant pyjamas for such a worthy cause. Later, old Celestin Gladu led a delegation of men to ask if I would officiate at the burial the next day. Kelly Lake was too remote for a priest to be notified or to come, and at this season interment could not be delayed. I assured them I should be glad to do my best. The time would be 11 o'clock "tomorrow" at the local cemetery in a sunny clearing on the east side of Kelly Lake, about half-a-mile from Jim's store.

That evening, thinking about what I should do and say next day, and having no prayer book, I perused my treasured little Bible, inscribed to me by my mother only two months before her death. Tucked in it, I also kept a tiny leather-bound memo book containing 23 scriptural quotations, alphabetically arranged. At the end, after "W" is the note: "This little book is copied by father from the one prepared by your dear mother during her last illness." At the beginning is the inscription "A few Jewels for my darling Gerald. – Mother – Sep 6 – 1913". She died a week later. Knowing these pretty well by heart, I decided to use them the next day, instead of searching through the Bible for others. For the record, here are mother's alphabetic "Jewels":

A little child shall lead them. (Isaiah 11.6).

Blessed are the pure in heart for they shall see God. (Matthew 5.8).

Come unto me and I will give you rest. (Matthew 11.28).

Dear children be ye therefore followers of God. (Ephesians 5.1).

Even a child is known by its doings whether it be pure and whether it be right. (Proverbs 20.11).

Fear not, I will help thee. (Isaiah 41.13).

God is Love. (I John 4.8).

Happy is he that has mercy on the poor. (Proverbs 14.21).

In Thee do I put my trust. (Psalm 7.1).

Jesus said, "Suffer little children to come unto me, for of such is the kingdom of Heaven. (Matthew 19.14).

Keep thy heart with all diligence, for out of it are the issues of life. (Proverbs 4.23).

Let not mercy and trust forsake thee: Bind them about thy neck; write them upon the table of thine heart. (Proverbs 3.3).

Mark the perfect man and behold the upright, for the end of that man is peace. (Psalm 37.37).

None of us liveth unto himself and no man dieth to himself. (Romans 24.7)

Oppress not the widow nor the fatherless, the stranger nor the poor, and let none of you imagine evil against his brother in your heart. (Zechariah 7.10).

Pride goeth before destruction and a haughty spirit before a fall. (Proverbs 16.18).

Quicken Thou me in Thy way. (Psalm 119.37).

Remember now thy Creator in the days of thy youth. (Ecclesiastes 12.1).

Shew me Thy ways O Lord; teach me Thy paths. (Psalm 25.4).

Thy word is a lamp unto my feet and a light unto my path. (Psalm 119.105).

Uphold me with Thy free spirit. Restore unto me the joy of Thy salvation. (Psalm 51.12).

Vengeance is mine; I will repay, saith the Lord. (Romans 12.19).

Wait on the Lord, and be of good courage; and He shall strengthen thine heart. Wait I say on the Lord. (Psalm 24.14).

Mother had not the strength to complete the alphabet.

Sunday dawned clear and peaceful. Properly dressed, I arrived at the cemetery a few minutes early to find the whole community there assembled, also in their best attire. The home-made coffin and the grave were ready, and hardly bigger than for a child. After a moment of silence, and with the attention of all, I solemnly removed my hat. The men followed my example; it was not their first funeral. Holding my Bible open, with Mother's little verses tucked ready inside, I said it was an honor for me to act now on their behalf. I emphasized the remarkable longevity of the deceased and that so many present were her descendants. At least 18 of Marie's great-grandchildren here had learned their alphabet at school – the basis for all knowledge. "I shall now read a sacred alphabet from the Holy Bible." I did this in good voice, clearly and slowly, omitting the references. It took only about ten minutes. I grasped a handful of earth, sprinkled it on the coffin, and indicated it could be lowered into the grave.... This done, I shook hands with some of the elders and patted one or two of my younger pupils on the head. If all had not understood my words, they were impressed with their dignity and beauty. I have re- marked in Chapter 1 that these people relish a bit of oratory for its own sake. My black leather Bible was a symbol of divine authority which they well understood. Their silent attention had been reverent and sincere. They seemed satisfied.

As I walked meditatively back to the store alone, I could not help thinking how cute dear old Marie would look in Heaven, wearing my jaunty white pyjamas instead of the conventional nighty! My duties at Kelly Lake, in addition to those of teacher ("ōkiskan-hamagayō"), doctor ("muskeekee-aweenō") and veteri- nary, had now included those of priest ("amahay-aweenō") – a challenge and a privilege. I did not have to solemnize a wedding, like Guy Lawrence did for the young (Taku) Indian couple, using, for lack of a prayer book, a recipe from his mother's cookbook (see "40 Years in the Yukon Telegraph", 1965). Surely Mother would be pleased that her Jewels had served her "little son" so well in this unforeseen situation, as surely they have also done in other ways, throughout his, now, long and full life.

My Senior Matric studies during this year had boiled down to just two subjects; Algebra and History. These filled many even- ings and were a challenge intellectually, a good antidote for the tendency of some teachers to let their minds descend to the level of their pupils', and stay there. At Normal School they kept saying, '"Get down to your pupils' level". They should have added: "but bounce back to adult level". I have just discovered in an old note book my reading list for 1924-25, viz:

> Shakespeare: 3 tragedies; 3 comedies; Chaucer: "The Knight's Tale"; Thomas More: "Utopia"; Bacon's Essays; Dickens: "Great Expectations", "Curiosity Shop", "Little Nell"; Marlow: "Doctor Faustus"; Begg: "History of BC"; Morice: "History of Northern BC"; Savin, Editor: "Canadian Poets"; "Astronomy"; Haliburton: "Sam Slick"; Haggard: "King Solomon's Mines"; Scott: "Quentin Durward"; Hugo: "Hunchback of Notre Dame"; Cooper: "Last of the Mohicans"; Zane Grey: "Heritage of the Desert"; London: "Star Rover"; Minerals and Rocks; and Political Economy.

This was not a bad menu for a young fellow in the wilderness. I remember reading some of the list, but probably did not get through all of it.

My time at Kelly Lake was coming to an end. Full and varied as it had been I began to think it was time for a change. Friends at Big Bar had written that my old school there was to be re-activated with an anticipated influx of new scholars. They invited me to return, and I accepted, so the balance of my time at Kelly Lake was conditioned by this outlook. Meanwhile, Jim and I were making plans for the summer. These were flavored by our trip over the Pine Pass with horses in 1924. This time a larger party with more horses was planned.

On our Pine Pass trip we had not fully mastered the art of "throwing the diamond hitch", the traditional method of lashing a load on a horse to hold securely against the varied and formidable vicissitudes of the trail. Now, we were fortunate to get checked out on the "diamond" by a renowned expert in the person of Denny Cornock. He was Homestead Inspector for BC provincial Crown lands in the South Peace River District. Cornock's homesteads were first at Rolla and later at Swan lake, on the main road, next to the boundary with Alberta, on the BC side.[69] His cheery visits at Kelly Lake were always welcome.

On his wide-ranging duties, Cornock travelled alone, with saddle horse and pack horse over long and obscure trails. He had this down to a fine art, and his horses were like pets. He rode a well-broken, sure-footed mare. His packhorse, Bozo, a docile gelding, followed the mare like a colt, running quite loose and free behind to nibble choice bits of forage along the trail. Occasionally Bozo would lag back out of sight. To break the monotony, and for a bit of fun, Denny would sometimes wheel his mare quickly off the trail and hide behind a bush to wait for Bozo galloping past to catch up, anxious to rejoin the mare. Denny would then follow to meet poor Bozo sheepishly back-tracking.

Approaching a lake one time; with Bozo behind as usual, Denny noticed a huge wasp nest hanging from a limb over the trail ahead. Thinking to liven Bozo up a bit, Denny grasped a dead limb from a nearby tree, and as he passed the nest, gave it blow, and spurred his mare to escape the results. Poor Bozo arrived to get full attention from the angry wasps. He galloped ahead and crowded tight against the mare, as animals do when in panic. The whole outfit had to take refuge deep in the lake until the wasps dispersed. So they all got a ducking in addition to stings. This time, Denny's joke on Bozo had backfired.

Cornock's coaching in the "diamond hitch" had practical application on our long trip to Jasper when we, too, became experts. I can still "throw" it and take more pride in this qualification than in others confirmed impressively on framed parchments now hanging on the walls of my study.

The Kelly Lake School's second year of operation ended on the statutory date, Friday, 19 June, 1925. The nominal roll of its "charter" pupils as tabulated below is the best I can do from memory and old notes. Efforts to retrieve the original registers and related records of the school for this period, both in Victoria and at School District 59 offices in Dawson Creek have been abortive and frustrating, to say the least.

KELLY LAKE SCHOOL

First Pupils, 1923 - 1925

No.	Names	Attendances 1923-24	Attendances 1924-25	Approx Ages (June, 1925)	Genealogical Codes (Appendix 4)
1	Belcourt, Annie	x		8	C14425
2	Belcourt, Henry	x	x	16	C14422
3	Belcourt, Mary	x	x	9	C14424
4	Campbell, Alfred	x	x	11	C14453
5	Campbell, Leo		x	7	C14454
6	Campbell, Sarah	x	x	16	C14452
7	Gladu, Adolphus	x	x	11	C14332
8	Gladu, Alec	x	x	10	G...x2
9	Gladu, Billy (Wm)	x	x	16	C14331
10	Gladu, Colin	x	x	13	G...x1
11	Gladu, Delphine		x	12	G...x2
12	Gladu, Florence		x	10	G...x3
13	Gladu, Joe		x	13	G...x1
14	Gladu, Josephine	x	x	8	G...x3
15	Gray, David	x	x	9	C14411
16	Hamelin (Hambler) George	x	x	13	C14462
17	Letendre (LaTente) Jimmie	x	x	8	L....x
18	St Arnaud, Jimmie	___	x	7	S...14
	Total Enrolments	12	18		
		==	==		

Relationships No's	Parents
1, 2 & 3	Narcisse Belcourt & Emily (nee Gladu)
4, 5 & 6	Milton Campbell & Annie (nee Gladu)
7 & 9	Marceline Gladu (nee Calliou)
8, 10 & 14	Urbain Gladu & wife (nee Breland)
11, 12 & 13	Alfred Gladu & Madeline (nee Gauthier)
15	Joseph Gray & Louise (nee Gladu)
16	Francis Hamelin & Caroline (nee Gladu)
17	parents unknown
18	Dan St Arnaud & Florence (nee Ferguson)

My old notes include also Delphine Calliou and Nora Napoleon, beginners in the second year, 1924-25 but they attended only a few days and then left with their families for parts unknown, so were, in army parlance, "struck off strength".

Terminal promotions for the second year were, evidently two to Grade 4, four to Grade 3 and the balance to Grade 2. As in the preceding year, this left Grade 1 clear for beginners anticipated in the fall of 1925. The older scholars were actually doing more advanced work, especially in arithmetic, but I was reluctant to over-grade any pupil in deference to the teacher (unknown) who might succeed me for the 1925-26 school year.

Both official and personal records are vulnerable to errors for committing aural information to paper. This is especially so with illiterate informants. In the initial school register I recorded George Hamelin's surname as "Emmila", which I realize now reflected my phonetic interpretation of the French for Hamelin. I had then no literate adult to help with such names. George's father was Francis Hamelin, which appeared on the Flyingshot Lake petition of 1906 (see Appendix 3) as "Francois Hamlin". Later George's surname was again corrupted to "Hambler", which spelling got into the official records for his old-age pension and medicare benefits. He said it was just too much trouble to rectify this "as long as the cheques came" and were negotiable. In the Kelly Lake Cemetery, 1981, George's brother and sister-in-law are identified as "Joseph Hamelin, 1906-1980" and "Delphine Hamelin, 1914-1980". Presumably these were verified by the officiating priest. George's descendants and relatives have good reason to be proud of their true ancestral surname. Father Morice, in his "Dictionaire Historique ...." (A38) lists three Hamelins, all of high repute. Baptiste Hamelin, a devout Catholic, defied Riel's religious persecution at Batoche in 1885. Louis Hamelin was a comrade-in-arms of Charles de Langlade (1729-1800), prominent in French-Canadian history. The Hon Salomon Hamelin was one of seven members of the "Council of Manitoba" in 1871. In Morice's words, Salomon Hamelin "était Métis, et a laissé une nombreuse descendance". The Kelly Lake Hamelins could well be among these. In a like manner, I registered Jimmie Letendre as "LaTente". Such aliases must be nightmares for genealogists!

When Kelly Lake School closed for summer holidays, 1925, my next concern was to write the Senior Matric exams, again at Rolla, during the week 22-26 June. My good patron, G.H. Gower, School Inspector, again made the official arrangements on my behalf. Details quite escape my memory now. Likely I went on horseback from Kelly Lake, but under less duress than during my trip the previous year. I attempted only two subjects, getting passing percentages in each: History, 55 and Algebra 82. This left only Geometry to write as opportune, when and where. My return to join Jim Young at Kelly Lake was unhurried, with warm farewells to the good friends at Swan and Peavine lakes. At the Taylors', I facetiously suggested to Boone that if he would cut his hair short, he might sire a little brother for the five girls. Later I heard that he must have acted on this, and the next child was, indeed, a boy! They named the poor little fellow "Gerald". I was both flattered and upgraded. Previously friends had used my name (Gerry or Jerry) for calves and colts.

33: The Gladu Family, Kelly Lake, about 1928. Back, Joe, Madeline (nee Gauthier); front, Madeline, Alfred, Jean, Florence, Delphine. The three older children attended Kelly Lake School, 1924-25. (Courtesy: Mrs. Lena Toole, Delphine's daughter).

34: Alec Anderson and "Tiny", near Swan Lake, Christmas Day 1924.

35: Gerry Andrews, near Swan lake, Christmas Day 1924.

36: At Jim Young's store, winter 1924-25. L to R, Jim Young, Johnny Calliou, Isidore Gladu.

37: Kelly Lake, February 1925. Milton Campbell leaves for his trapline after recovery from quinsy.

38: Vicinity Beaverlodge Lake, BC, winter 1924-25. Typical trapper's cabin with Jim Young's sleigh in foreground.

Martin B. Taylor, Pouce Coupe, B.C., with three silver fox skins. Mr. Taylor is a fur buyer and trader at this point, which is about one hundred miles from Grande Prairie, and the nearest railway.

39: Clipping from "Northwest Farmer", 1925.

40: On summit of Nose Mountain Trail, 2 July 1925. Sam "Neestou" Wilson, left, and George White.

41: Near summit, Nose Mountain Trail, 2 July 1925. L to R, George White, Jim Young and Homer Wright; "Mike" left background; "Maxis" right foreground.

CHAPTER 4

TO JASPER AND BEYOND WITH PACKHORSES: 1925

Survival from our Pine Pass trip in 1924 inspired plans for another such trip in 1925. Jim Young's friend, George White, an ardent horseman, had his homestead about two miles west of Rio Grande in the Redwillow area.[70]   He proposed a trip to Jasper by the Nose Mountain trail which headed southeasterly from the Wapiti River to link up with others from Grande Cache on the Smoky River, to Entrance (near Hinton, Alta) on the Athabasca River. There, an old wagon road followed up the valley from Edson to Jasper. These were trappers' trails to trade at the places mentioned. They crossed streams and ridges aligned northeasterly from the main Rocky Mountain Range to the west. George had heard that there was a good market for horses to ride and pack with the big outfitters at Jasper – Fred Brewster and Donald ("Curly") Phillips. His friend, Sam Wilson, a Metis member of the Chatelaine (Shetler) band, based at Shetler Flats on lower Nose Creek, agreed to accompany us as guide. Sam had made the trip to Entrance as a boy with his elders. His mother was Madeline, nee Wanyandie, who later married Peter Chatelaine, the hereditary chief of the band. Sam's father was reputed to have been a "Captain Wilson". Sam was about 30 years old, handsome, quite dark complected, athletic and quiet in manner. We all developed a high regard for him so he was appropriately nicknamed "Neestou" (Cree for cousin or kinsman).[71]

Our party comprised the following:

MEN		HORSES	DOGS
Jim Young	with	2	Maxis
George White	"	6	
Sam Wilson	"	2	
Homer Wright	"	2	Mike
Gerry Andrews	"	2	
Totals:		5 men 14 horses	2 dogs

Each of us had his own saddle with accessories. I must have worn my furry chaps because I had them later at Big Bar. Some one supplied an A-tent big enough for the whole party. We pooled pack equipment and supplies for four horse-loads which left five spares. Wright had his fine quarter-horse driving team and White's horses included four fine heavy draft animals. Some were broncos from the open range, which would have to be broken to ride and pack on the trip. Mine were bought from Jim for less than $25 each. I kept a diary for most of the trip, which is the basis for the following journal:

DAY 1

27 June - Saturday: 25 miles

After closing the store at Kelly Lake, Jim and I proceeded to Beaverlodge, probably with most of the provisions from Jim's stock. We stayed with Homer Wright at Beaverlodge.

Aggregate: 25 miles

DAY 2

28 June - Sunday: 20 miles

Spent day fixing up outfit. Wright made panniers of caribou hide. In pm saddled up Wright's horse and Gerry's mare. Both took it like oldtimers. After supper packed up Judie, and she is OK. Don tore around for a while with one bag hanging on the saddle, dropping occasional loaf of bread. Reached George White's about 10 pm.

Before leaving Kelly Lake, I had made a batch of wholewheat bread. Having used empty lard pails for baking tins, the loaves were almost spherical in shape. As they spilled out from Don's bucking spasm, they rolled far and wide, but were all retrieved, quite intact. They were unbreakable, but nourishing.

Aggregate: 45 miles

DAY 3

29 June - Monday: 20 miles

"Started off via Rio Grande. Everything OK. Loaded up [at Rio Grande store] with chocolate bars & tobacco. Did not unpack till we got down to Wapiti. River is about 120 yards [wide] and swift. Lies in a deep abrupt valley about 200 ft below upper benches. Sidehills heavily timbered. Too deep for fording, so got a raft. Took six hours to get horses to swim. Flies bad. Camped on south bank.

I may have assumed my previous role of swimming on the lead horse across the river. I preferred this to the trip on the crowded and tippy raft.

Aggregate: 65 miles

DAY 4

30 June - Tuesday: 15 miles

Made Nose Creek tonight about 5:30. Camped at Pierre Shelter's cabins [72]. Good feed and good water. Quite a few bog holes on trail, but no bad luck. Weather looks like rain so put up tent tonight. Holds all five. Diamond hitches are proving OK, no repacking at all.

Aggregate: 80 miles

DAY 5

1 July - Wednesday: 18 miles

Reached the foot of Nose Mountain tonight at a small creek. Good water and feed. Got here about 3 pm, so camped. A little rain. Neestou and Gerry go hunting moose. Lots of tracks.

Aggregate: 98 miles

DAY 6

2 July - Thursday: 22 miles

Climbed hill. Just as we reached top, both dogs plunged
into a porcupine. Maxis covered all over head & mouth.
Thought we would have to shoot him, but at noon Jim and
Neestou pulled all quills with pliers. They were an hour
on this job. A great view from top of ridge. Saw one
deer looking down at us. In pm tried to reach Chicken
Creek, but stopped at a meadow 3 miles short of it.
Slough feed only fair. Trail follows top of ridge all
day. Great view to Rockies to West.

Maxis, a large Airedale, was Jim's dog. It was his first encounter with a porcupine – and his last. A few days later he just
disappeared, probably the victim of quills working their way into
his vitals. Photos 40 and 41 were taken on Nose Mt.

Aggregate: 120 miles

DAY 7

3 July - Friday: 14 miles

My horses and Jim's were all missing this am. I went
back about 3 miles to round up the culprits. Saw 3
moose. Got away at 7:45. Just after leaving camp, a bear
with 2 cubs stampeded George's horses. Swung down to
Chicken Creek and over another ridge to Porcupine
(Kakwa) River. Lovely valley with peavine feed.

A string of 14 horses can stretch out more than half a mile
along the trail. On this trip Sam Wilson habitually took the lead
and one of us, in turn brought up the rear, with the others at
intervals between, each keeping an eye on the animals nearest.
The bear and her cubs must have crossed in a lengthy gap. Her
scent would have alarmed the horses following. Sam had not been
over this trail since boyhood, but in all cases of doubt he chose
the proper lead.

My diary entry of "Porcupine" for Kakwa River reflected local
usage at that time. The 1930 edition of the "Geographical Gazetteer of British Columbia" lists "Kakwa River (not Porcupine)". I
notice also that the Key Map for the Alberta-BC boundary atlas,
(Part III, 1925) labels this river "Porcupine", but the detail sheet

No 39, shows it as "Kakwa" which is the Cree word for porcupine.

Our crossing of Kakwa River (approximately 54°15' - 119°20') must have been quite close to where Edward W. Jarvis and party left this valley to head southeast for Jasper House along the route which we also would follow closely. During the winter of 1874-75, like Joseph Hunter two years later, Jarvis received instructions from Sandford Fleming to explore "the Smoky River Pass through the Rocky Mountains". With Charles F. Hanington, as assistant engineer, Alex Macdonald in charge of the dog teams, five Indians and initially 24 dogs, the party left Fort George 14 January, 1875 ascending the Fraser and McGregor rivers. Finding no likely pass at the head of Herrick Creek they retracked to follow-up the McGregor by which route they reached Jarvis Pass at 5,300 feet elevation on 25 February. Thinking they were on the BC-NWT Boundary, they blazed a tree with a notice to this effect adding their names and the date.[74] The actual boundary as surveyed in 1924, is six miles farther east, on the 120th Meridian.[73] From there the party, now reduced to the three White men, two Indians and one dog team (the others had been sent back to save rations), continued eastward aiming for Edmonton and eventually Winnipeg. They soon discovered that all streams draining the eastern slopes of the Rocky Mountains flowed in a northeast direction toward the Peace and Mackenzie rivers. Being critically short of food, they elected to head southeasterly across successive valleys and ridges aiming for Jasper House on the Athabasca River, where they expected to replenish supples. Arriving there about mid-March after dire privations and on the point of starvation, their dismay was acute on finding the depot abandoned. Providentially a small band of Indians nearby was able to revive them with some rabbit stew and provide what food they could spare for the 200-mile trip to Lac Ste Ann where they arrived at the end of March, again on the verge of starvation and exhausted. Here and beyond, they received generous and effective help from the HBC managers along their route to Winnipeg where they arrived 21 May, 1875.

On the Kakwa River, above where they left it to head south-easterly, Jarvis made this interesting comment for 28 February, 1875:

> The next day we saw marks of Indian chopping, and camps, apparently of last summer; and here, for a distance of twenty miles we noticed the almost total absence of snow, a phenomenon said to occur all along the eastern base of the mountains. At one of our camps there was not more than two inches of snow anywhere in the vicinity. Our rate of travelling improved in consequence, and we made one big drive; but next day the old state of things returned, and the snow soon reached its average depth of two and a half feet, making the walking terribly heavy.[75]

The Kelly Lake people have remarked on several localities of very light snow in the foothills, west of Kelly Lake, where their packhorses can winter without extra feed, viz: Monkman Cabins (54°48'-120°43'), Five Cabins (54°48'-120°58'), Callazon Flats (54°56'-120°45') and Rhubarb Flats (Poona-tik-sipi) (55°00'-120°47').[76]

Jarvis's vivid narrative of that epic journey, as recorded in Sandford Fleming's official report for 1877 (p 145-161), should be prescribed reading for all Canadian high schools, along with better-known classics such as the journals of Alexander Mackenzie (1798-93), Simon Fraser (1808), David Thompson (1784-1812) and Paul Kane (1845-48).

Aggregate: 134 miles

DAY 8

4 July - Saturday: 24 miles

> Got up early and were on the trail at 7:30. Trail goes through some bad windfalls, hills, and over many soft places. Reached Prairie Creek about 1:30, stopped for lunch. Very cold coming over a long high ridge this am. Splendid view of the Rockies — a sweep of a hundred miles of snow peaks in a grand panorama. Got away after lunch at 3:45, worked up Prairie Creek some miles, cros-

sing half a dozen times. About 6 pm we started to go down, and before us the valleys of Sheep Creek and Smoky River came into view. They are deep and wide, in generous proportions. Dropped quickly and came out on a large river flat. Hay is rather short. Some buildings here, also about 20 head of horses and same number of cattle. The latter are rolling fat. Pretty tiger lilies growing in poplar benches. Some huge steers, must be six years old and weigh 1,500 to 1,600 lbs. Camped about 7:30 pm.

Our descent into lower Sheep Creek must have been just east of Cutpick Hill on today's maps, vic Tp59 R8 W6.

Aggregate: 158 miles

DAY 9

5 July, Sunday: 7 miles

Moved down river 7 miles to crossing. A halfbreed, Davis, is squatting here [we did not see him]. A splendid flat, lots of grass. Got logs ready for raft before lunch. Made a good raft. Crossed river, horses swam with little trouble. Great feed on this side, peavine and long grass, although a little bushy and rough. Camped. Smoky is about the same width as the Wapiti here, but swifter. Valley is wider and deeper. Neestou killed a young bull moose in evening.

Again, I had the dubious privilege of crossing the big river on the lead horse, without wetting my camera as my photos of the others following on the raft confirm (Photos 42 & 43). The horses were less nervous about swimming the Smoky no doubt due to the confidence they had gained from crossing the Wapiti which they had been reluctant to attempt. Horses are always more trouble during the initial days of a trip when they must learn to adjust to the routine of travel, to each other and to the authority of their masters, and also to overcome a nostalgia for their home pastures. After a few days, especially if there is good feed and water and no major grief, they settle down to a more relaxed cooperative attitude.

After the Smoky crossing, it looked like rain so we put up the tent. Meanwhile, Neestou went off with his rifle and soon returned with the nose and liver of a young bull moose which were a welcome "special" for our supper menu. He also brought in the moosehorns which at this season were "in the velvet". Our curiosity about this was satisfied later, when after supper he placed them in the embers of the fire, and occasionally turned them over. Just before bedtime he pulled them out and showed us how to chip off the charred velvet to expose the soft, tender and delicious meat inside. This was a tasty late evening snack washed down with fresh sweet coffee. I had never before eaten grilled moosehorn nor have I since!

When building our raft for crossing the Smoky River, we found, tacked to a tree, a message in Cree syllabics, pencilled on paper, as illustrated, which I still have. Sam Wilson, our Cree-speaking companion, was not literate in this script. Earlier efforts to have the message decoded proved futile, due possibly to the script being faulty, or to a peculiarity of dialect. One scholar identified the writer as Samuel Nease, in the first line. In the 1920s there was indeed a Nease family in the South Wapiti area. By coincidence, not long after our 1925 trip, Sam Wilson married a widow Nease (nee Desjarlais) who had sons, Harvey and Joe, from her earlier marriage.[77] These facts seemed to lend substance to a connotation with Samuel Nease, the alleged writer. However, just prior to these words going to press, my friend Mike Robinson was able to obtain a full translation of the message, quoted (without editing) under Figure 2. I assume the second word "MAY" refers to the calendar month and that the year was 1925 because the fragile message could hardly have withstood the ravages of weather for more than a year.

Aggregate: 165 miles

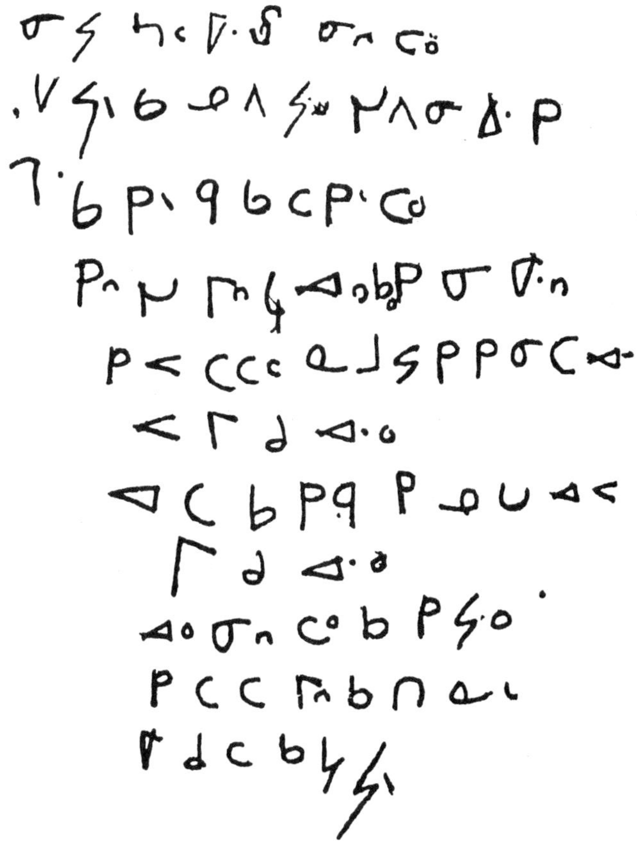

FIGURE 2

Message in Cree syllabic script found at Smoky River crossing seven miles below Sheep Creek, 5 July, 1925. Unedited translation, March, 1985, by Mr. Adolphus Ghostkeeper, age 92, of Paddle Prairie, Alberta reads:

THIS MAY SAM WESIS MY BROTHER-IN-LAW ONE DAY PASSED AWAY. YOUR BROTHER SUFFERED ALL SUMMER WITH FAINTING SPELLS. THERE WAS NOTHING THAT WE COULD DO FOR YOU ALL THIS TIME. MY BROTHER-IN-LAW WAS GOING TO SEE YOU. I SAY GOOD BYE TO ALL OF YOU.

DAY 10

6 July - Monday: 0 miles

Rained nearly all day, so camped and tried to eat up all the moose meat but there was lots left [to take with us, as long as it would keep].

Aggregate: 165 miles

DAY 11

7 July - Tuesday: 20 miles

Pulled up the hill and when near the top George's big horses all turned back and ran right to the bottom before they could be stopped. Muskegs occur nearly all day, bad windfall country too. Reached Muskeg River [well named] about 7 pm. Indian teepee here belonging to Dan Niande [sic].

The creek up which we followed, south from the Smoky is named "Wanyandie" on today's map (NTS 83L). The name "Niande" above perhaps should have been "Wanyandie". It has been remarked, too, that Sam Wilson's mother, Madeline was nee "Wanyandie". So our Sam and Dan at this camp could have been relatives.

Aggregate: 185 miles

DAY 12

8 July - Wednesday: 30 miles

Followed on the Forestry Trail from Mile 61 to Mile 35. Good feed at Mile 45 for noon. Warden's and trapper's cabins at Mile 35. Good trail. Flies bother a little.

This camp was on Berland River, tributary to the Athabasca, confirming we had crossed the height of land from the Smoky. Here my original diary is interrupted until 29 July, well beyond Jasper, on the Goat River. During this interval we were in comparative civilization. To fill the gap, daily entries are from memory and are reasonably close to reality.

Aggregate: 215 miles

DAY 13

9 July - Thursday (35 miles): Having made good time on the forestry trail we camped at Entrance. Here we met Ed Johnston

from Elmworth near Beaverlodge.[78]   He had come all the way alone
on the old Edson Trail with 10 horses assisted by his remarkable
dog to herd them. Ed was also bound for Jasper and points
beyond, and being acquainted with my companions, was invited to
join forces with us. While following up the big river from Edson,
some 70 miles, he had helplessly witnessed a tragedy. A man
going downstream on the far side by raft was upset in some tur-
bulence and disappeared – presumably drowned. This was a grim
reminder of our own good luck, so far, with the hazards of
wilderness travel. About 10 miles from Entrance our trail had
passed Jarvis Lake named for E.W. Jarvis,[79]   confirming that we
had closely followed his trail.

Aggregate: 250 miles

DAY 14

10 July - Friday (18 miles): With six men and 24 horses we now
formed quite a cavalcade. Evidently we did not cross the Athabasca River to Entrance station on the CNR and the wagon road
there. The 1934 Jasper Park Map (A36), shows only the railway
bridge there, which we may have used on foot to get groceries.
Instead we followed up the left (northwest) bank to camp on the
west side of Brule Lake. The park map shows some wagon trails
and a continuous packtrail which we must have used.

Aggregate: 268 miles

DAY 15

11 July - Saturday (23 miles): At the north end of Jasper Lake
we passed close to the old site of Jasper House, and near there
crossed the lower reaches of Snake Indian River (Photo 44). In
the late afternoon the stream was in full diurnal spate from
glaciers melting in the hot July weather. The milky waters spread
over a wide floodplain before joining the Athabasca. By following
riffles obliquely upstream we were able to ford without unpacking.
I happened to be in the lead and reached the far bank without
trouble. In the deepest channel there, the water just reached to
the horse's belly. A pack animal following close behind thought

she could make a shortcut across swift deep water to the near bank but was swept off her feet and carried downstream some distance where she eventually emerged safely, except that her pack was soaked. This was a good place and reason to camp, and dry things out. The only significant loss was a 20-lb sack of sugar which had completely dissolved – no doubt sweetening the palates of fish downstream. This was before the appearance of waterproof plastic bags. A sack of flour will seal itself against a brief wetting, preserving most of the contents intact. Being in the lead, I got a couple of good photos of the outfit strung over the wide crossing, with the bulk of Bedson Ridge (mountain) in the background.

Aggregate: 291 miles

DAY 16

12 July - Sunday (12 miles): We arrived at Jasper about midday and found a good campsite down by the river at a bridge where the road to Jasper Lodge crossed. This was far enough from town for privacy, beyond the range of curious idlers. We arranged to keep the horses at Brewsters' corrals in town, where baled hay and water were available. One horse was retained for packing supplies to camp including the odd case of beer. Weather was fine and warm.

Aggregate: 303 miles

DAYS 17-24 incl.

13-20 July incl.: About a week was quite agreeably spent in Jasper selling off most of the horses to Fred Brewster and "Curly" Phillips. The dealing was friendly and prices were satisfactory, judging by my own case (I got about $50 each for mine). Our routine was to walk up to the corrals each morning, leading the packhorse. Most of the time was spent showing off and tending to the horses (Photo 45). About mid-afternoon we would return to camp, have a few beers and make supper. Neestou habitually preferred to remain in camp. One morning we left a large kettle of white beans simmering on the fire, to be well cooked for supper. On our return, we found the beans upset and scattered, and some of the grub packs missing – ravages of an uninvited bear. Meanwhile, Neestou had been fast asleep in the tent! He soon recovered the packs, where the bear had hidden them nearby. The losses, including the beans, were not serious.

Our presence in town was a matter of some interest. I remember the police checked on us, in a friendly way. We certainly were not hobos. By 20 July most of the horses had been sold, and plans for dispersal of our happy little company began to clarify. Jim Young and Homer Wright planned to go south by rail. Eventually George White returned home with Wright's dog, by train, and I think Sam Wilson went home by the trail, with one or two horses, including Wright's "Don", which, it seems, Jim had bought from him. Ed Johnston kept three horses and persuaded me to accompany him through the Yellowhead Pass to points beyond. This suited me as I was heading for Big Bar, and Ed was interested in the country west of Vanderhoof. I kept my riding saddle, rifle, etc. for this trip. We had a horse each to ride and only one to pack, for which Ed had equipment. He was ready to start, so left on 21 July, with the plan that I would catch up to him by train at Red Pass Junction in a couple of days.

Aggregate: 303 miles

DAY 25

21 July - Tuesday (21 miles): Ed probably camped at Yellowhead Lake, just west of the pass.

Aggregate: 324 miles

DAY 26

22 July - Wednesday (20 miles): I caught up with Ed at Red Pass Junction, where we camped at the outlet of Moose Lake. He had no trouble getting that far alone. Ed was nearing 50 in age, of Irish descent, and was good with animals, including me, so we got along well.

Aggregate: 344 miles

DAY 27

23 July - Thursday (21 miles): We followed down the right (north) bank of the Fraser River on the old railway construction tote-roads. A dense crop of timothy hay had seeded itself along them, probably from hauling baled hay in the old days. This was a Godsend for our horses, as otherwise it was heavily timbered country with little feed. The old roads meandered and divided so it was necessary to go ahead to scout the route through. I did most of this, leaving Ed with the horses to feed. At one place, I was a bit long returning to them, and poor old Ed had worried that I had abandoned him! At Tete Jaune we had a friendly welcome from Mrs. Chapin and her partner Switzer. They operated a large chicken farm (some 1,500 purebred White Leghorns (Photo 46). Practically all their eggs and fryers were shipped to the lodge at Jasper on the CNR. They advised us to cross the Fraser River here, and to follow on the CNR (formerly the GTP Ry) down to McBride and Goat River. From there a trail led over to the summit to Isaac and Bowron lakes and to Barkerville, whence the old Cariboo Road would take us to Quesnel.

Aggregate: 365 miles

DAY 28

24 July - Friday (0 miles): We spent the morning visiting and inspecting the chicken ranch. After lunch Switzer helped us cross the Fraser with his dugout canoe. We led the horses across without any trouble and found a good place to camp near the crossing.

Aggregate: 365 miles

DAY 29

25 July - Saturday (21 miles): We followed along the CNR grade to Dunster. This took some getting used to. Mostly there was enough shoulder on either side for footing so we didn't have to "walk the ties", which is bad enough for humans, let alone horses. At a couple of small streams we dropped down to ford them rather than

attempt using the railway bridges, which were certainly not designed for horses. Evidently, on this stretch we met and accompanied Leo Allgeier, returning home on horseback to Dunster. Details are now vague. I took a photo of him and Ed at his cabin, and later had a letter from him.[80]

Aggregate: 386 miles

DAY 30

26 July - Sunday (20 miles): We reached McBride in time to make camp on its outskirts which were not that far from "city centre". Raush River was too deep to ford, so we had to cross on the railway bridge, not a pleasant operation with horses, but it can be done with care as I had learned on Anderson Lake in 1923. Trains were not frequent and we were aware of their approach in time to drop down off the grade to safety. Their passing was a bit terrifying, but we had only three horses to control.

Aggregate: 406 miles

DAY 31

27 July - Monday (2 miles): By the time we had taken in the sights of McBride and made a few purchases to fill our "wants list", the Liquor Vendor had opened at 10 am, so Ed had to make a purchase there, too. This resulted in spending most of the day in McBride. I remember poor Ed sitting under a wagon in the shade, feeling no pain and contriving all kinds of reasons why we were in no hurry to move on. Finally, at about 5 pm I persuaded him to pack up and move to a "Hudson's Bay Camp", just far enough along the trail that it was too far to walk back for "another one".

Aggregate: 408 miles

DAY 32

28 July - Tuesday (23 miles): We arrived at Goat River without incident. There the Forest Ranger Jack Jowsey and his wife were most kind and gave us valuable advice about the Goat River trail to Barkerville. My diary was re-activated on the morrow (Photo 50).

Aggregate: 431 miles

DAY 33

29 July - Wednesday: 10 miles

Left the railroad on east side of Goat River, at bridge.
Fire warden, Jack Jowsey, and wife there very decent.
Camped for lunch at Boulder [Bounding] Creek, no feed.
In pm passed two men working on a cut, using ditched
water from above [Diggins Creek?]. Crossed Milk River
and camped on upper side of the forks. No feed.

The miners were typical of their breed. When asked how they
were making out, their reply was, "The gold is just there –
ahead a bit!" Photo 51 shows miners working.

Aggregate: 441 miles

DAY 34

30 July - Thursday: 2 miles

Pulled out at 5:30 am. Went about 2 miles and found
feed, so stopped for the day. Snow on both sides of
river, probably from a slide. Goat River is beautifully
clear and green, about 20 yards wide, rapid, with stony
bottom. In am washed about four pans of gravel but no
colors. A frypan is miserably small for this work. In
pm walked up trail about 2 miles. Tracks of Barkerville
fellows quite plain in places.

Either the Jowseys or the miners must have told us that a
party from Barkerville had come down the trail recently. This
was reassuring.

Aggregate: 443 miles

DAY 35

31 July - Friday: 12 miles

Pulled out at 7:30. Grass wet. Crossed river about 4
miles above camp. Found fair trail up NW side of Goat
River. Camped for lunch at McLeod Creek. Moved on at 3
pm for 4 or 5 miles. Water is green and cold. River is
smaller. Underbrush is awful, Devil's Club, Parsnip,
brush, lilies and ferns. Camped for night in a small
sidehill meadow. Good feed. Figure it is about 4 miles
to summit.

A few years after our trip up this river, Cliff Kopas and his
bride took this same route on their epic ride to settle at Bella

Coola.[81]   It was with some relish that I read his lurid account of the horrors of the Goat River trail.

Aggregate: 455 miles

DAY 36

1 August - Saturday: 15 miles

Followed up river about 2 miles, then crossed and re-crossed to get around cutbank. Later trail runs into beaver pond. Lost it there for an hour. Crossed summit over a low timbered valley. High flat-topped mountain to SW [Wolverine Mountain, 6,747 ft]. Hit Wolverine Creek running west about noon. Good feed, so stopped for 3 hours. Trail hard to find. Climbs hill on right bank of stream, going down and continues on steep side-hill above Isaac Lake. Followed till dark, no feed, so tied up. Windfalls bad and Devil's Club thicker than hell. Isaac Lake beautiful, surrounded by high Mts on all sides, gravel bottom, water clear and green. Fish jumping like squirrels in evening. No room for beds, so rolled up in the trail, makes a good bunk!

Our lunch stop was in beautiful alpine country near the summit. Luckily the horses had a good feed there. Before finding the trail as described, we followed a well-beaten game trail on the left bank of Wolverine River, right down to lake level, where it vanished in heavy timber. We then had to climb all the way back up to recover the right trail. The beauty of the scene that night from our sidehill bivouac high above the lake is still vivid. The moon, above Mount Peever (7,500 ft) was reflected in the lake far below.

Aggregate: 470 miles

DAY 37

2 August - Sunday: 16 miles

Moved on at 5 am. Trail bad in spots, windfall. Found small patch of feed on a point. At 9 am reached end of lake and stopped in meadow there. Good cabin with many names from Barkerville direction. Pulled out from meadow at 2 pm and reached west end of Indian Point Lake. Here McKabe was building a large log house. His wife gave us some nice lettuce and onions. They gave us information about trail to Bear [Bowron] Lake. Reached Bear Lake about 7 pm, camped on shore, good grass for horses. Ed sick tonight.

Between the lakes, Isaac, Indian Point, Kibbee and Bowron, the trail served as a portage, so was well-cleared, and heavily trodden by game and humans. We had most trouble going round the lakes, with windfall and little evidence of travel. It was along Indian Point Lake that we met a lone traveller heading in the opposite direction and driving a fine rangy horse ahead with bridle and reins. A voluminous pack was fastened on a riding saddle. When asked why he didn't lead the horse, he replied, "You couldn't lead that so-and-so with a tractor and logging chain!" He said he was bound for the Peace River country — "or bust!" It cheered him to learn that we had just come from there, and had chopped out a few windfalls for him. McKabe had cleared out the trail from Indian Point Lake to Bowron, so we made good time.

Aggregate: 486 miles

DAY 38

3 August - Monday: 12 miles

Left for Barkerville in pm. Reached Little Valley Mines. Good feed and cabins.

Aggregate: 498 miles

Photo 53 was taken at Little Valley Mines.

DAY 39

4 August - Tuesday: 5 miles

Inspected the mine, deep shaft. Much good machinery apparently abandoned. Got into Barkerville at 11:30 am. Put horses into livery stable. Town a roadway, lined on both sides with unpainted buildings of ancient vintage. All structures including sidewalks are built up on stilts. A creek used to run down through the town. The Masonic Hall stands out prominently, the date on it 1869. They say the level of the town is 27 feet higher than the original, due to build up of tailings from hydraulic operations on Williams Creek.

Barkerville is now quite dead, depending solely upon two operating mines, the Antler Creek Dredge and the Lougheed Hydraulic operation. Quite a few old prospectors in the vicinity. Some old boys 80 years mellow, but still hardworking hopeful gold seekers. Chinese make up a large part of the population. Hay is $55 to

$65 per ton. Freight from Quesnel is 2¢ per pound. Got all horses shod in evening.

The privilege of seeing Barkerville when it was still a viable town, running on its own steam – even if slowing down, and not a "showcase" exhibit, – is more fully appreciated now. In 1925, a few venerable miners of the early days were still around. Some had never returned "outside" since their arrival. When Ed and I checked out, the bill for the horses at the livery stable was more than that for us at the hotel.

Aggregate: 503 miles

DAY 40

5 August - Wednesday: 22 miles

Left Barkerville at 8:15 am for Quesnel 60 miles by road. Camped at Jackpine Flats. Good grass. Road is dry and hard."

Aggregate: 525 miles

DAY 41

6 August - Thursday: 25 miles

Moved on to 13-Mile House and camped. Met an old Ontario man with team going to Barkerville.

Aggregate: 550 miles

DAY 42

7 August - Friday: 13 miles

Made Quesnel today at noon. Moved down to Camping Ground.

Aggregate: 563 miles

This was my second arrival in Quesnel. It was a year before, almost to the day, that Jim Young, Fred Barber and I had arrived here in the old Ford car from Vanderhoof and Prince George. I had thus "closed" a complete loop from Kelly Lake – some 450 miles via Pine Pass in 1924 and 563 miles via Jasper in 1925, for a total of practically 1,000 miles (see Map 2). Ed and I enjoyed a couple of days at Quesnel in a pleasant camp, and the townfolk were friendly. The time had come to settle our accounts and each go his separate way. Ed had proved a good companion.

He headed out alone with his three horses and faithful dog on Blackwater Trail for Vanderhoof and points west. A letter from him dated 4 November, 1925 was from Dewey, near Sinclair Mills, where he had taken a job as Mill Engineer. The Burns Lake country did not appeal to him.[82] I shipped my saddle and a few odds to Clinton by rail express, to be picked up there later, and with minimal kit, took the PGE train for Williams Lake.

The account of our Pine Pass trip of 1924 in (Chapter 2) stressed the importance of my tiny map. In spite of the small scale and lack of detail, its basic features served to guide us safely to our destination through many miles of wild, rough and uninhabited country. For our 1925 trip, the first 300 miles, from Beaverlodge to Yellowhead Pass, were all in Alberta, for which at that time I had no map at all. Instead, we were fortunate in having a remarkable guide in the person of Sam Wilson.

I cannot remember now what map Ed Johnston and I used, if any, for the trip from Jasper to Quesnel. Possibly I had the same small-scale map of BC which we had used the year before. It would likewise show the basic features now of concern to us. There were 1923 editions of the BC pre-emptor's maps covering the country between Yellowhead Pass and Quesnel (maps 3G, 3H and the southeast corner of 3A). These, at 3 miles per inch, showed quite good detail along the larger rivers and travelled routes, but still had large blank areas between. I may not have known about the pre-emptor's maps in 1925, but did so after. Air photo mapping did not come into effective use until the late 1930s. After six years' slowdown by war, it was revived with greatly enhanced tempo and efficiency. Thanks to air photography, all of British Columbia now is covered with accurate and detailed maps at various scales (the National Topographic Series). With these I have plotted the routes of both our 1924 and 1925 trips in detail and have been able to pinpoint each of our campsites closely. In 1925 between Jasper and Quesnel, the only comparative wilderness on our trip was about 60 miles up the Goat River, over the summit and down to Bowron Lake.

A statistical summary of our complete 1925 trip is tabulated as follows:

Statistical Summary

PACK-HORSE TRIP: KELLY LAKE to QUESNEL via JASPER

27 June – 7 August 1925

Date	Agg-regate Days	Camps:	Route Miles	Agg	Date	Agg-regate Days	Camps	Route Miles	Agg
27 (June 1925)		KELLY LAKE	25	0	21 (July)	25	JASPER	21	303
28	2	Beaverlodge	20	25	22	26	Yellowhead Lake	20	324
29	3	Rio Grande	20	45	23	27	Red Pass Junction	21	344
30	4	Wapiti River	15	65	24	28	Tete Jaune	0	365
1 (July 1925)	5	Shetler Flats	18	80	25	29		21	
2	6	Nose Mountain	22	98	26	30	Dunster		386
3	7	Chicken Creek	14	120	27	31	McBride	2	408
4	8	Kakwa River	24	134	28	32		23	
5	9	Sheep Creek	7	158	29	33	Goat River	10	431
6	10	Smoky R Crossing	0	165	30	34	Milk River	2	441
7	11	Muskeg River	20	185	31	35	Milk River + 2	12	443
8	12	Mile 35	30	215	1 (August 1925)	36	McLeod Creek + 3	15	455
9	13	Entrance	35	250	2	37	Isaac Lake	16	470
10	14	Brule Lake	18	268	3	38	Bowron Lake	12	486
11	15	Snaring River	23	291	4	39	Little Valley M.	5	498
12	16	JASPER	12	303	5	40	Barkerville	22	503
					6	41	Jackpine Flats	25	525
					7	42	13-Mile House	13	550
							QUESNEL		563

By wagon trail:	Route miles	Days enroute	Av mileage per diem
Kelly Lake to Wapiti River	65– 0 = 65	3–0 = 3	65/3 = 21.7
Entrance to Jasper	303–250 = 53	16–13 = 3	53/3 = 17.7
Bowron L to Quesnel	563–486 = 77	42–37 = 5	77/5 = 15.4
Totals & averages	195	11	195/11 = 17.7
By Pack-trail:			
Wapiti River to Entrance	250–65 = 185	13– 3 =10	18.5
Jasper to Tete Jaune	365–303 = 62	27–24 = 3	62/3 = 20.7
Goat River to Bowron L	486–431 = 55	37–32 = 5	11.0
Totals & averages	302	18	302/18 = 16.8
On CNR Grade:			
Tete Jaune to Goat River	431–365 = 66	32–27 = 5	66/5 = 13.2
Grand Totals etc	563	34	16.6
Stop-over at Jasper		8	
		42	

COMPARISON – TRIPS 1924 & 1925

Kelly Lake to Quesnel	Wagon Trail			Pack Trail			Total		
	miles	days	mi/d	miles	days	mi/d	miles	days	mi/d
1924 via Pine Pass	132	9	14.7	261	24	10.9	393	33	11.9
1925 via Jasper	195	11	17.7	368	23	16.0	563	34	16.6
Totals etc:	327	20	16.4	629	47	13.4	956	67	14.3

The average daily mileage for the Jasper trip in 1925, was 16½ compared to 12 for the 1924 Pine Pass trip. The higher average was due to several advantages. Sam Wilson certainly saved us a lot of trail-searching; horsefeed was much better, and flies were not a problem, thanks to a prevailing wind from the high Rockies to the southwest. Beyond Jasper, Ed Johnston and I averaged about 14½ miles per day, still better than 12 for the Pine Pass trip. These differences also reflect the benefit of more experience.

From Williams Lake where I may have stayed overnight, I hiked the old wagon road via Springhouse, Alkali Lake, Dog and Canoe creeks to Big Bar Creek, carrying only a haversack with iron rations. The first night I was a paying guest with old Antonio Boitano at Springhouse. Next day I had lunch, probably gratis, at the Wynn-Johnson Alkali Lake ranch and bivouacked the second night on the old Meason place, then unoccupied, down near the Fraser River. The third night darkness overtook me in the little canyon halfway up Canoe Creek. There I had the eerie experience of being dive-bombed by swarms of bats, so as soon as I emerged from their unfriendly stronghold I bivouacked by the roadside. Breakfast next morning was with the Jim Riley's at OK Ranch on upper Big Bar Creek, later owned by Harry Marriott and featured in his classic book "Cariboo Cowboy" (1966). After confirming my arrival with the Big Bar Creek school trustees and arranging for accommodation, I got a ride to Clinton and Ashcroft, where I boarded the CPR train for New Westminster and a short visit with the Haggmans before returning to Big Bar Creek to start the 1925-26 school year. Meanwhile, my trunk shipped by old John McCormack from Grande Prairie, my saddle and other items from Quesnel all duly arrived at Clinton.

On return from Kelly Lake to the Big Bar community, my enhanced status was noticeable. The young greenhorn teacher they had known two years before had now become an adult with a measure of competence and self-confidence. My experience with horses was not ignored in a ranching community like Big Bar. My Kelly Lake trophies – the moosehide jacket, gloves and moccasins – were worn to practical advantage, and I must confess to some extent as status symbols. Dear little Mrs. Louise Coldwell at the Jesmond store and post office had her own pet nicknames for local characters. For me it became "Buckskin Gerry", but others did not adopt it. I did refrain from wearing my cartridge belt and chaps to school!

My sojourn at the Metis outpost – Kelly Lake – and the adventurous summer trips from there, were now behind me on Life's trail. On the balance sheet for those two years, assets heavily outweigh liabilities. Some items, on the credit side of the ledger, not necessarily in order of importance are: (1) becoming acquainted with the Metis people in their own unique environment and learning to appreciate their fine qualities and a little of their history; (2) the challenge of opening and teaching the first Kelly Lake school with some success, and an enduring affection for my pupils, whose offspring I now think of as (my) grandchildren; (3) exposure to the Cree language which widened my concepts of grammar, syntax and vocabulary; (4) the companionship of Jim Young, who was so generous and who taught me so much; (5) the friendship of pioneer individuals and families – Alec Anderson at Peavine Lake, the Taylors at Tupper, Denny Cornock, and the bachelor homesteaders in the Leighmore area; (6) practical experience in keeping myself reasonably fed, warm, clean and tidy, and of wilderness travel with horses. On the debit side of the ledger, there seems little to enter – perhaps a lifelong addiction to pipe tobacco and a modest taste for overproof rum. This shows a pretty good balance for the investment of two years of my young life. Some of the long-term dividends are described in the next chapter.

42: Crossing the "Big" Smoky River, 5 July 1925.

43: Big Smoky crossing, 5 July 1925. "Ship ahoy! Throw me a line!"

44: Fording Snake Indian R, 11 July 1925. L to R, Jim Young, George White, Ed Johnston, Sam Wilson. N'ly view to Bedson Ridge.

45: At Brewster's Corral, Jasper, 15 July 1925. George White with his big teams.

46: Tete Jaune, BC, 24 July 1925. Ed Johnston, Switzer and Mrs. Chapin.

174

47: Tete Jaune, 24 July 1925. Fraser R crossing.

48: Dunster, BC, 25 July 1925. Leo Allgeier and Ed Johnston.

49: NW'ly from Tete Jaune down Fraser River, 1948. Cariboo Mts left, Rocky Mts right. In the "Trench" are Dunster, mid distant & McBride, far distant. In 1925 we followed CNR grade along left bank of Fraser. Isaac Lake trough extreme left horizon. (BC Gov't Airphoto BC762:110).

50: Goat R, BC, 30 July 1925. Looking downstream; Ed Johnston and his remarkable dog.

51: Vic Goat R, BC, 29 July 1925.
Miners at Diggins Cr.

52: S'ly from Bowron Lake Park HQ, September 1972. Ed and I camped
here, 2 August 1925, then followed the wagon track around end of
lake, right, 18 miles to Barkerville. Mt Murray (6,577 ft) and
Sliding Mountain, right in distance. (GSA #4931)

53: At Little Valley Mine, vic Barkerville, 4 Aug 1925. "Gerry throws the diamond."

54: Outskirts of Barkerville, July 1950. The scene is unchanged from 25 years earlier when Ed Johnston and I arrived here on horseback from Bowron Lake. (GSA #0672)

55: Quesnel, BC, 8 August 1925. Historic dug-out canoe formerly
used on Fraser R between Soda Cr and Fort George.

56: The old Meason Cr ranch, Fraser River, 1 September 1965. I
bivouacked here about 12 August 1925. (GSA #3260)

57: View SW'ly across Fraser R to Gang Ranch, from old road vic Dog Cr, September 1959. This was the type of scenery I enjoyed on my hike in 1925, and countless times since. (GSA #2026)

58: Big Bar Cr, autumn 1925. Standing, L to R, Mrs. Millie Cover, Clarence Cover, Bernice Cover, Mrs. Adler, Pa Adler, Bert Drake (teacher at Jesmond), Dave Jones, Bessie Wilkinson; Sitting, Margaret Cover, Neil Darrough (teacher at Big Bar).

59: Near Field, BC, July 1919. L to R, back, Mr. Rice, YMCA Secretary, Kinnaird, unknown, G. Andrews; front: Herb Drake, his brother, others unknown.

60: Big Bar Cr, May 1926. Bert Drake, left, and Neil Darrough. They display my Kelly Lake trophies.

61: Coldwells' Ranch, Jesmond, BC, September 1977, originally "Mountain House". They operated a store and post office for many years. My school on Big Bar Cr was four miles away by road. (GSA #6320)

62: Vic Rose Prairie, BC, September 1947. Lynch Callison's homestead on Beatton R flats. (GSA #121)

CHAPTER 5

EPILOGUE

This chapter outlines how the Kelly Lake School survived and expanded after my two-year sojourn there, and it updates information on many of the people mentioned earlier, including the author. Because it is not fiction some research has been necessary to confirm identities, relationships, dates, places and events. Although interesting, this has been laborious, time-consuming and for me a learning process. I could have done it better and sooner had I known at first what I know now. As the Irishman said, "After I saw how it was, I could have told you how it was going to be." Such research seems endless. Each alluring lead proliferates into others – ad infinitum. A limit must be imposed, even though some questions persist. Hopefully gross errors and omissions are minimal and I apologize now for them. Some residual material has been relegated to the Appendices for those interested.

After Jim Young and I left for Beaverlodge that last Saturday of June, 1925, I was not to see Kelly Lake again for 28 years. Those years spanned the prime of life when I looked ahead and not behind. They were replete with challenge, action, effort and some providential success, especially in riches which money cannot measure. In 1925, Jim had proposed a partnership to raise beef on some wild hay meadows north of Swan Lake, but I held to my early ambition for a career in Forestry, which promised outdoor work using one's head rather than just a strong back. During my second stint in the Big Bar country (1925-26), I was among old friends and in an environment I loved. I suffered no acute nostalgia for Kelly Lake but my friends there were not forgotten, as the correspondence in Appendix 3 confirms. Contacts with them diminished as the years passed but happily some have survived and flourished to this day.

The extra year teaching at Big Bar Creek augmented my finances enough to register in Forestry at the University of Toronto in the autumn of 1926. Outstanding academic requirements for this were analytical geometry and an upgrading of my French. These were obtained at the University of Manitoba Summer School in Winnipeg, my birthplace, which I had not seen since 1918. Four years later I returned to my adopted British Columbia with the coveted Forestry degree, having had summer jobs in Manitoba, Quebec and the East Kootenays. The next 10 years with the Surveys Division of the BC Forest Branch were interrupted by 16 months' "depression leave without pay" (1933-34). These were spent on a postgraduate program in airphoto interpretation, then relatively new, at Oxford in Britain and Dresden in Germany. At a critical time near the end of this, I won a $500 bursary which was augmented in 1935 with another $1,000 for "travel and research" in this new science. The travels led to discovery of a "gold nugget" from Placer County, California which I imported into Canada duty-free by marrying her. We were soon blessed with Mary, the first of our family.

Rehabilitation from six years' war service, mostly overseas, placed me in the BC Surveys & Mapping Branch where I served until retirement in 1968. So many years of field-work in forestry and surveying took me to all parts of British Columbia and beyond. In 1939, my first-ever look at the mighty Peace River itself was where it began at Finlay Forks. It was 1947 when I first returned to the Peace River country and 1953 to Kelly Lake.

Statistics for the Kelly Lake School as tabulated below (1923-62), and visits there in 1973 and later, when I found a well-equipped, four-room school with gymnasium and teachers' residences and an enrolment approaching 100, confirm its record of continuous operation and expansion which happily endorsed Mr.

G.H. Gower's optimism when he urged me to return there for that second year of teaching (1924-25).

KELLY LAKE SCHOOL
(SD 59, Peace River South)

STATISTICAL RECORD

1923-1962

Data as published in Annual Reports, Department of Education, Victoria, BC.
Data from other sources are in brackets.

School-Year	Teachers Name:	Lic. Cl.	Sal-ary	Total Days	Enrolment Total	Boys	Girls	Attendance Daily Average	%	Top Grade
1923-24	Gerald S Andrews	2nd	1320	170	12*	9	4*	11.23	94	2
1924-25	do	"	"	184	18	10	8	15.21	84	3
1925-26	Mrs Katie E Easton	2nd	"	159	15	10	5	12.11	81	4
1926-27	do	"	"	187	17	10	7	11.23	66	5
1927-28	Joseph Lionel Marion	"	"	179	21	12	9	13.29	63	5
1928-29	Cephas Arthur Ward	1st	"	94	14	7	7	10.42	74	5
1929-30	do	"	"	195	26	12	14	18.12	70	6
1930-31	do (new bldg)	"	"	187	25	11	14	21.90	88	6
1931-32	do	"	1330	194	28	13	15	25.68	92	7
1932-33	do	"	1200	192	32	17	15	24.05	75	8
1933-34	do	"	800	192	28	14	14	19.01	68	6
1934-35	do	"	800	189	31	16	15	19.01	61	7
1935-36	do	"	850	182	24	14	10	14.31	60	6
1936-37	do	"	930	157	18	9	9	7.19	40	7
1937-38	do	"	930	174	19	8	11	8.61	45	6
1938-39	do	"	930	184	20	9	11	10.22	51	6
1939-40	do	"	930	184	19	10	9	9.10	48	6
1940-41	do	"	930	176	16	8	8	6.90	43	7
1941-42	do	"	950	174	14	6	8	6.34	45	6
1942-43	do	"	1000	175	16	6	10	7.90	49	6
1943-44	do	"	1050	172	17	3	14	8.59	51	5
1944-45	do	"	1140	178	18	7	11	8.70	48	5
1945-46	do	"	1240		26	11	15	14.32	55	6
1946-47	do	"	2000		24	9	15	15.96	66	4
1947-48	do	"	1800		25	9	16	17.43	70	5
1948-49	(do?)				39	18	21	22.81	58	6
1949-50	(do?)				33	15	18	23.48	71	6
1950-51					35	17	18	29.00	83	7
1951-52					47	20	27	38.76	82	7
1952-53	(Mr&Mrs Jules H Serans) (c1951-c1962) (2 rooms)				47	21	26	42.55	91	5
1953-54					51	22	29	39.64	78	6
1954-55					53	25	28	44.84	85	7
1955-56					54	27	27	43.62	81	8
1956-57					50	25	25	39.27	79	8
1957-58					50	23	27	42.76	86	8
1958-59					52	24	28	44.49	86	8
1959-60					39	20	19	36.44	93	8
1960-61					39	23	16	32.19	83	7
1961-62					38	20	18	31.39	83	7

(Left margin brackets: "Depression" spans 1930-31 to 1939-40; War II spans 1940-41 to 1944-45)

*The published Total for 1923-24 of "13" included one abortive enrolment.

Average daily attendances are more significant than total enrolments. In Figure 3, the peaks for 1931-32 and 1954-55 are noteworthy. The all-time low for 1941-42 was critical. These fluctuations also reflect the community's vitality. In the sequence of teachers as shown, my immediate successor (1925-27) instead of being an adventurous (or desperate) youth, was a middle-aged woman! – Mrs Katie E. ("Ma") Easton. Her epithet, shared with "Ma" Brainard and "Ma" Fynn, implied affectionate esteem. She had been the first teacher at Taylor ("Flat") in 1919-20,[83] taught at Swan Lake North (1923-25) and at Hudson Hope (1927-29), leaving when her husband died "outside".[84] They had been pioneer farmers at Fort St. John. She did well to survive two years' living and teaching in the old Calliou cabin at Kelly Lake. She baked bread for Jim Young and no doubt he brought her mail and supplies. She was generous, and popular with the Kelly Lake children. I am curious to know more about "Ma" Easton.

Joseph Lionel Marion (1906-1978) followed Mrs. Easton for just one year – 1927-28. It was his first school. He was a polio cripple with crutches. He and his sister, Odila (Mrs. Augustus Dumont), wrote a good story of the pioneer Marion family at Rolla.[85] Poor Lionel must have had a lonely year baching and teaching in the old Calliou house. In comparison how lucky I was! Marion's later postings were: Swan Lake North (1928-32), Dawson Creek (1932-34) and the Devereaux School near Arras (1934-45). He is mentioned in Alec Anderson's letters, Appendix 3.

Cephas Arthur Ward (c1890-?) taught at Kelly Lake for a record of more than 20 years, from 1928 to 1951. Anderson's letter of March, 1931 put Ward's age then at about 40 and noted that he had built a house at Kelly Lake and that there was a new school building. Denny Cornock also mentioned Ward and the new school. Ward's full name and that of his wife, Lillian B., were derived from the Kelly Lake Voters' List for 1933. (Appendix 3). They were English without children or relatives in the district. Mrs. Ward was generous with her skill as a trained nurse. His failing health influenced them to move to Edmonton where they owned an apartment house. Once Dave Gray contacted them there, and being invited for dinner, appeared at noon to find that it had been for the traditional English "dinner at eight". He was welcomed for lunch and dinner. The Wards could have told us much about the Kelly Lake school and community. The BC Department of Education Annual Report for 1936 contains a photo of "the old Kelly Lake School" which I recognize as the old Calliou house. Its dereliction is very evident in the photo.

After 1948, teachers were not identified in the departmental reports. The incumbency of Jules and Lucille Semans (1951-62)

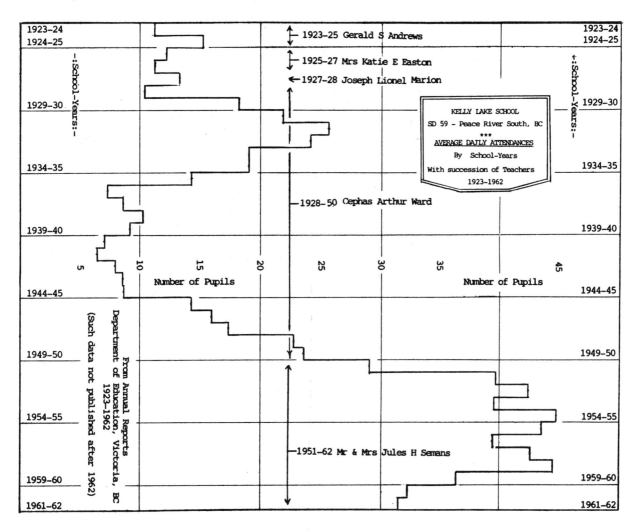

is derived from his 1953 letter and a Christmas note in 1962.[86] He mentioned a "2-room school", a "new RC church", the death of old Narcisse Belcourt at 87 under pathetic circumstances and of Alfred Gladu. With their children, Grant, born in 1942 and Betty Lew (1945), the Semans enjoyed their time at Kelly Lake, especially its tranquillity. Their leadership in music met with good results. Dorthea Calverley said the Kelly Lake School choir took top honors at the Dawson Creek musical festival. The children also made a fine impression in their immaculate white uniforms and with their good manners.[87] I was able to meet Lucille at Beaverlodge in 1981 and 1983, then having remarried – to George Beck. I was welcomed in their attractive home surrounded by lovely flowers and a model garden. I was sad to learn that Lucille had also been bereft of her son Grant. It was evident that her gentle charm had been a factor in the Semans' fine record of service to the Kelly Lake community.

A happy coincidence at Big Bar Creek in 1925-26 was renewing acquaintance with Herbert E. Drake, then teaching at Jesmond School only a few miles from mine (Photo 59). We had first met at Field (summer 1919). In the Big Bar country we enjoyed much in common. I must have done a good selling job for the Peace River region because the next year, 1926-27, Bert taught the Swan Lake school. His letters in Appendix 3 give interesting details about friends and events there. He filled a gap in old Alec Anderson's lonely life which I had vacated. He was several years in the Dawson Creek school where he became principal, and was active in community affairs. Bert's letters cover a time of interesting developments including the arrival of the railway from Grande Prairie. After some years in the Greater Vancouver area, he died in 1962, leaving his widow, Gladys; a son, Robert, and a daughter Lynne. I regret having lost touch with them.

Jim Young closed his store at Kelly Lake in 1927 and by the next year was settled on his Rose Prairie homestead about 20 miles north of Fort St John where he became postmaster and eventually a Justice of the Peace.[88] Likely Jim found it lonely at Kelly Lake without his young sidekick to keep the fires going and for company. In his letter of 23 January, 1931 Jim gave no hint of his impending marriage later that year to the pioneer Red Cross nurse, "Anne" Roberts. The Youngs became celebrities in their region. Good biographies for Jim's 80th and 89th birthdays by Mrs. Georgina Keddell appeared in the "Alaska Highway News"

(1963 and 1972), and a fine story of both by Cora Ventress is in "Peacemakers of the North Peace".[89]

My first reunion with Jim was in September, 1947 when I was involved in air photo mapping. As chief of the new BC Air Surveys Division, I had to make an appraisal of the airfields along the Alaska Highway as far as Teslin. Having arrived by air at Fort St John, without a car, Floyd Nelson, forest officer, kindly drove me out to Rose Prairie. I found Jim in good shape in his mid-60s and was well impressed with Mrs. Young, in her early 50s, and their children: Robert, 15; Mary, 14; and Dorothy 11. They had a substantial two-storey log home with the usual array of outbuildings and animals including some fine saddle horses. We had a lot to talk about, but as usual Jim let the rest of us do most of it. In the guest room upstairs I was snugly submerged in home-made feather mattress and quilts. I got to know that bed well.

In following years our survey operations were very active in Northeast BC. They included photo flying from Fort St John, Fort Nelson, Watson Lake and Whitehorse; right-of-way surveys of the Hart and Alaska highways; Crown Land alienations; provincial boundaries on the east and north; triangulation control for petroleum exploration and tenures; standard topographic mapping and detail surveys for the big hydro power scheme at Hudson Hope. As Surveyor General and Director of Mapping (1951-68), these activities took me to and through this huge area most field seasons. Much of my travel had to be alone with a four-wheel-drive vehicle. Whenever opportune, I contrived to visit the Youngs at Rose Prairie. Occasionally Jim would accompany me on shorter trips. His knowledge of local conditions and people provided valuable background for my official concern with policy, programming and public relations. Starting early after a good farm breakfast, Jim always brought a small paper bag which contained his sustaining "medicine" – used with his habitual moderation, and as of old, without urging me to share. My rule was total abstinence until the day's travel was finished, and I usually had my own supply, as a reward for virtue.

Jim Young's good rapport with the Metis people was certainly evident at Kelly Lake. It was the same with the Indians of the Blueberry, Beatton and Doig reserves generally to the north of Rose Prairie. In August, 1950, I accompanied my Chief, Norman Stewart, then Director of BC's Surveys and Mapping, to inspect various operations in the Peace River District, including Duncan Cran's camp in Tp88 R17 W6, north of Rose Prairie and across the Beatton River. I realize now that I was being groomed to succeed Stewart who was to retire the next year. We stayed with the Youngs overnight and discussed with Jim the best way to get in to Cran's camp. His advice was to drive to Petersen's Crossing of the Beatton River, about six miles north and to hire two saddle horses and a mounted guide from Chief Pooscapee's Indian band who were camped there. Next morning Jim went with us to negotiate on our behalf to good effect. I am sure that without Jim's help we would have gotten nowhere. It was gratifying that Mr. Stewart was highly impressed with my friend, Jim, and his family at Rose Prairie.

In August, 1954, I was heading south and home via the Hart Highway so persuaded Jim to come as far as Williams Lake whence he returned by bus. Much of this road closely followed our Pine Pass packtrail of 1924. We enjoyed being reminded of incidents long since forgotten. We stopped the first night at the survey camp of Tony McLaughlin, BCLS, one of my staff, at Bijoux Falls on the Misinchinka River. This was close to where we had almost turned back with the horses 30 years before. At McLeod Lake we lunched with our old friend J.E. McIntyre who by then had his own store near the highway. Mac took delight in showing us his privy, located precisely on our old packtrail from the Parsnip crossing. On the near side the trail was well-worn, but beyond the wilderness had reclaimed its own. From Williams Lake I was scheduled to visit one of our photo flying detachments then operating from the Puntzi airstrip. Instead of hours by road, the photo aircraft picked us up and returned us to Williams Lake in a matter of minutes. This was Jim's first airplane ride which he enjoyed with his usual equanimity. He was interested to see the ranching country in the Cariboo and the Chilcotin – so different from that in the Peace River country.

On some of our trips Jim and I were able to see old friends like Denny Cornock, Mary Taylor, Duncan Cran and Alwin Holland. On a run to Hudson Hope where I wanted to check our surveys for the Bennett Dam, Jim and Duncan Cran came along. They introduced me to local notables like the Gethings and Kyllos at "the Hope" and the Ardills at Farrell Creek. A surprise highlight at Hudson Hope was to find Bud Lay, still operating his poker den, but here much more comfortable than the one I remembered at Grande Prairie that cold Christmas Eve of 1923. No doubt Bud exploited the hefty Bennett Dam payroll to good effect. The Peace River valley, especially from Fort St John upstream into the Rocky Mountains is one of unforgettable beauty and grandeur. I have often enjoyed it by winding road, up and down, and from low-flying aircraft. The placid buffalo herds seen by Mackenzie on the grassy park-like slopes of the sunny north side are gone, but more elusive game and domestic stock survive there. The Ardill ranch down on the broad river flats with its fine home-bred horses is a scene of unusual beauty.

On our return to Fort St John, Jim wanted to stop at the Murray ranch, really to see the daughter Georgina, a special favorite like Maggie McClements of old, near Kelly Lake. There I met George Murray, Margaret ("Ma") and son, Dan, as well as Georgina. This initiated a long and warm friendship for me, especially with "Ma" Murray and Georgina, now Mrs. Keddell. Another stop just west of town was Knox McCusker's ranch where I met his charming widow, Gwen. McKusker who had died in 1955 was a celebrated land surveyor, guide and outfitter who helped locate the Northwest Staging Route of airfields and the Alaska

Highway. In earlier work east of Lake Winnipeg, he also knew the Cree people and their language which he humorously described in "All in a Day's Work".[90]   Sometimes from Rose Prairie I had to drive a couple of miles beyond to find Jim baching at his sheep camp with Adolf Dolstrum, an old friend from Halcourt in the Red willow area.   I suspect the sheep camp was a "retreat" from the goings on of Jim's busy family at home.   Under the bed there was always a jug of "tonic" to console their loneliness and for special guests.

I saw Jim for the last time in 1973. Early in June I was driving west alone, on Highway 16 through Edmonton.   Not having been to the Peace River country for a couple of years and not being in a hurry, I decided to take the loop by Highway 43 through Whitecourt, Valleyview, Grande Prairie, Dawson Creek and Fort St John, thence home over Pine Pass.   The first part of this route, as far as Grande Prairie, I had not seen before. At Dawson Creek I was easily persuaded to stop for dinner and a pleasant evening with Wendy and John Hooke, but I phoned Rose Prairie to announce that I planned to arrive there the next day. To my surprise Mary (Mrs Tom Mickey) answered, saying her mother had just died and urging me to come for the funeral in Fort St John on Monday, 4 June.   At Rose Prairie on Sunday, I found most of Jim's family and connections assembled.   Robert and Gerry-Ann who had taken over the farm were hosts.   Among the comings and goings were Mary's family (the Mickeys); Dorothy's (the Snippas), neighbors and other friends. Jim, in his 90th year, was calm and quiet, but I am sure I "got through" to him.   That night I was thankful for the privacy of my van and my own bed in it.

I was proud to be among the honorary pallbearers at the service next day in Fort St John where the large church was overflowing in tribute to the pioneer nurse who had devoted her energy, courage and talents to safeguard the beginning of life and the survival of mothers for many present.   After the service a long cortege proceeded by road to the little cemetery at Rose

Prairie. It was a beautiful Peace River June day. Interment was on the crest of a low hillock in sight of the old Young homestead across the road. For the commital, six stalwart pallbearers were outlined against the limpid blue sky, each having benefited at birth from Mrs. Young's devoted skill as midwife, and now a parent in his turn. I was grateful that providence had allowed me to be present at this moving and, indeed, historic occasion. I thought of how much we had enjoyed Mrs. Young as houseguest when she attended Women's Institute meetings in Victoria and how she had relished the comparative luxury of our bathtub.

Jim soon needed special care in a home for the elderly. This was found in the Hotel-Dieu, an auxiliary of the Sisters of St. Joseph at Whitelaw, near Grimshaw, Alta, about 100 miles east of Fort St John, close enough for family visits. He became their "oldest and best resident" and was quite happy until his turn came 25 January, 1976, in his 93rd year. I did not attend his funeral, my visit in 1973 having been our fond farewell. Descendants of Jim and Anne Young are tabulated in Appendix 4.

When Jim died, I told his family that my friendship with their father must now pass to them as a legacy from him; and, of course, mine from Jim has been theirs. Son Robert's short life was in sad contrast to his father's long one. "Rob" with his fine wife Gerry-Ann and their four children provided happiness and security for the parents in their later years. Rob's widow with help and support of relatives carries on courageously at Rose Prairie. Circumstance has allowed me to keep in closest touch with the Mickey family in Whitehorse where official duties took me frequently before retirement, and since then I have made many trips to my cabin in Atlin, close enough for easy visits to and from Whitehorse. Dorothy's family, the Snippas, are well-established in Fort St John, close to Rose Prairie to help as needed.

I have brought the reader up-to-date on Jim Young and his family at some length because he is the raison d'être for this book. He got official sanction to start the Kelly Lake School, he provided the first accomodation for it in his store, rent-free, and he sponsored, befriended and mentored its first young teacher. When he died, his daughter Mary appealed to me to write what I could about her father's earlier life before marriage which his family knew little about.

In 1953 I was returning from lengthy travels, clockwise, up the BC coast to Skagway, the Whitehorse area and down the Alaska Highway to Rose Prairie and Dawson Creek. At Tupper, I found Denny Cornock. The weather was fine and he offered to come and show me the best road in to Kelly Lake for just a quick visit. It happened to be a federal election day (10 August) and we found some people assembled at the local polling booth, including my old pupils Mary Belcourt (Mrs. Billy Gladu), George Hamelin and David Gray (see Photo 73).

When I asked Mary how many children she had the reply was "Eight"! Records now in hand show that George Hamelin also had as many. It was a happy if brief reunion. Joking, they alleged that in the old days, to make shy little Mary Belcourt hold her head up, I tied her braided pigtails to a rafter overhead with string. Such stories lose nothing in the telling – and who shall escape calumny? I may have threatened this remedy. Both Jim Young's store and the old Calliou school house had vanished but I got a photo of Alfred Gladu's old home. The Semans were away on holiday. I had then no idea whatever of writing these pages, so lost an opportunity to make invaluable notes. I had learned from Denny about Boone Taylor's death only a few months before, but was unable to see his family at this time.

My next visit at Kelly Lake was 20 years later, June, 1973, on the trip already mentioned. I had passed Beaverlodge in a "million dollar" rain and noticed the sign for the Goodfare road which looked well-gravelled so I ventured out on it, stopping at the Goodfare store to make enquiries. Learning that I was the original Kelly Lake teacher, they directed me to the nearby home of Mrs.

Mary Dupont (?) where I could purchase their recently published local history "Pioneer Roundup."(A47). She regretted that I had not been mentioned in the book. I was advised to keep right on the centre of the road to Kelly Lake and to go through to the gravelled school yard to turn round.

Being Saturday, there was no one at the school and I dared not attempt to visit the scattered homes on such voracious gumbo trails. I had passed one occupied cabin close to the road so decided to stop there before heading back through Goodfare, and by good luck found Isidore Gladu at home in it. He had been one of my best adult friends and was glad to see me. At the ripe age of 77 he was now a local patriarch, surrounded with delightful grandchildren – all speaking Cree. My curiosity about the identity of the ancient great-grandmother for whose burial I had officiated in 1925 was satisfied at last when Isidore said she was his grandmother, Mrs. Thomas Calliou, nee Marie Finlay 1820 or before. Isidore himself was then to live less than two years longer, and could have told me so much more. His taped interviews with Rick Belcourt and Lee Phillips about this time [91] are interesting and confirm much of what I have written. Isidore was born at Lac Ste Anne in 1895 and came to Flyingshot Lake with his parents in 1905, and to Kelly Lake about 1920. Mike Robinson's notes [92] relate that Isidore first met his wife Annie at her father's trapping camp on Rhubarb Flats (Poona-tik-sipi) when she was only 12 years old, a case of love at first sight. He asked her father, Napoleon Thomas, if he could return in two years and marry her – which he did. I have more to say about Annie later.

My daughter Kris flew up to Atlin early September, 1977 to accompany me homebound on the Alaska Highway and, weather permitting, for a quick look at Kelly Lake which she had heard so much about. We detoured on the Canol Road to Ross River, thence on the Campbell Highway to Pelly Banks and past Frances Lake back to the main road at Watson Lake. This loop, new to me, was of historical interest. My friend, Guy Blanchet, had located the Canol route in 1942 and old John McCormack had told me about wintering at Pelly Banks in 1897-98. I did not attempt to find the grave of Mac's pal who refused the spruce-needle antidote for scurvy. We contrived to have morning coffee with the Youngs at Rose Prairie, had lunch at the Kiskatinaw bridge and then visited the Dawson Creek Museum to make enquiries. There, Mrs. Glenn Ireland was interested in what I could tell her about our Pine Pass trip in 1924. I learned that George Hamelin was living in town, but his house was locked up. A neighbor said he was off on his fall moose hunt, a disappointment. We also heard about the new Heritage Highway south from Tupper, offering a more direct route to Kelly Lake. We had early supper at Pouce Coupe where I was glad to find the old Provincial Police barracks well preserved as an attractive motel. Before dark we had time to drive out on the new road from Tupper as far as Peavine Lake. It followed closely Jim Young's old winter "rum" trail. The evening and country were delightful. With evidence of some new settlement along the way, I wondered about frost on the higher levels. Instead of going on to Kelly Lake at a late hour and uncertain of the road, we back-tracked to Hythe where Kris could sleep in a nice little motel and Dad had the privacy of his van parked outside.

Next morning bright and early we took the Goodfare road to Kelly Lake. I stopped to show Kris where the Alberta-BC boundary crossed, then we continued on through the settlement to the school where all was quiet, it being the last Friday of summer vacation (9 September). With no one to interrupt, we looked around and had lunch there. It was a beautiful day with autumn colors beginning. I showed Kris where Jim Young's store and the old school had been, nearby, and inspected the new school premises. Pressed for time as always, we could not linger. Kris had to get back to work and I wanted her to see the Peace River Valley as far as Hudson Hope. Leaving Kelly Lake the way we had come, I stopped at Lective Campbell's where there seemed some evidence of life. Their welcome was typically warm. They all knew who I was, and were pleased to meet my sweet young daughter, but their identities were confusing to me, most being in a younger generation. My cryptic notes mention Lective, his wife Caroline (Isidore Gladu's daughter), her mother Annie, Gordon Belcourt (Milton Campbell's grandson) and Shirley Letendre. I was glad Kris had seen Kelly Lake in its quiet beauty and was able to meet at least some of the folk there.

From Atlin in 1978, I wrote George Hamelin to say that if he could be home in early September I would come south via Dawson Creek especially to see him, and enclosed an addressed reply envelope. This arrived promptly with a good letter in his own hand saying he would be there and glad to see me. I duly arrived in time to spend an evening with George and assorted members of his family, which seemed to fill the house. David Gray from Kelly Lake happened to be there too. I had brought prints of my early Kelly Lake photos to leave with George. These provided great interest and fun for all to see Grandpa George and his companions as school children so long ago. I was greatly taken with Mabel, George's wife, and told her that she looked young enough "to have 13 more children" to which she replied, "No way!" They treated me like a great grandfather which was just how I felt. Teachers are not supposed to have favorite pupils, but George had to be one. He was bright responsive and affectionate. His grandfather Celestin Gladu had told me that George was so cute at birth that he was nicknamed "muche napao" (bad man). When I mentioned this they were delighted and knew all about it. After a successful career as trapper and big-game guide at Kelly Lake, George had moved to Dawson Creek about 1969, suffering acutely from inflammatory arthritis – the penalty of exposure and hardships in the wilderness. I could not spoil the fun that evening by attempting to note vital statistics of George's large family, hoping for a future opportunity to do so. Before leaving Dawson Creek next morning, I called at the School District 59 offices to leave a nicely framed enlarged photo of "The First Kelly Lake School, 1923" to be conveyed to the school when opportune. Poor weather and lack of time precluded going to Kelly Lake on this trip.

In October, 1979, David Gray's son, Jarvis, wrote from Edmonton asking for copies of the Kelly Lake photos David had seen the year before, for his essay on Kelly Lake sponsored by the Metis Association of Alberta. These I gladly supplied. In response he sent me some early genealogical data about Kelly Lake families which I have incorporated in Appendix 4. Further contact with Jarvis has proved elusive.

On my return from China in June, 1981, there was a message to phone Michael Robinson with Petro Canada in Calgary. He had recently been in Kelly Lake in connection with his company's Monkman Coal Project which would encompass the Kelly Lake trap-lines. He had been advised to contact "Gerry Andrews who was here at the beginning" and could tell him all about it then. We agreed to meet in Dawson Creek Sunday evening, 9 August. For the trip north I enjoyed the company of "Axel" Kinnear, a friend and professional colleague of many years. Sunday morning before Axel had to fly home, we took a run north through Rolla as far as Doe River, across beautiful rolling prairie. Alas! my photos were all blanks on this trip! I was glad to see the old Rolla hotel and the school where I had written the Senior Matric exams in 1924, and 1925. The old school is now part of a larger modern complex.

During the next two days, Robinson and I interviewed Dorthea Calverley, George Hamelin and Gerry Clare in Dawson Creek and at Kelly Lake we saw Annie Gladu, Dave Gray, Alfred Campbell, Mary (nee Belcourt) and Billy Gladu, Eva Calliou, Caroline Campbell and others. We took the Heritage Highway from Tupper to Kelly Lake and I regaled my companion with anecdotes of rum-running and visits with Alec Anderson at Peavine Lake. We stopped first at the Kelly Lake school about midday where we found a group of children with Caroline Campbell and Eva Calliou.

I noticed how attractive, well-mannered and nicely dressed the children were, and that they spoke mostly English. We learned that Caroline taught Cree at the school. How times had changed! I was pleased that Eva Calliou remembered me. We must be close in age. In anticipation I had brought some Kelly Lake handicrafts from home, including the beaded cartridge belt which Eva had made. She was delighted to see it still in perfect condition, and its story was explained to the admiring group. Mike took a nice photo. I was pleased to see my framed photo of "The Kelly Lake School" hanging prominently in the school lobby.

After lunch we had a long visit with Annie Gladu in her old log cabin where she likes to be in daytime, although she sleeps mostly at her daughter's place nearby. A widow since Isidore's death in late 1974, Annie enjoys preserving the old native arts, crafts and herbal remedies. The Lac Ste Anne pilgrimages are still important to her. It was either Annie or her mother-in-law who showed me how to make my rabbit robe in 1923. Annie did make the beautiful moosehide jacket (pakhegan?) which I had brought to show her. It is still as soft and pliable as chamois and the sinew "ustigut" stitching is intact after nearly 60 years. Speaking of Red Willow Indian tobacco "mikwapemigwa", Annie promised to make some for me. A generous package arrived at Christmas time. I mix it sparingly with my usual blend and enjoy its aromatic piquance. I told Annie that when smoking it I could almost speak good Cree again. Mike recorded stories of some dramatic encounters with bears by Annie, Dave Gray and George Hamelin. Dave, who had joined us, and Annie, were able to identify some old Kelly Lake photos Mike Robinson had obtained, a nice selection of which he published later.[93]

Before supper Mike and I had time to visit Alfred Campbell on his father's old place, rather detached from the main settlement, fronting on the southeast sector of Kelly Lake. I learned that his father, Milton, had succumbed to pneumonia caught while fishing through the lake ice. I failed to note the date, but it could have been before 1933 because Milton's name is not on the Kelly Lake Voters' List for that year which does include Annie Campbell, his wife.[94] We then looked at the cemetery, in a secluded spot by the lake facing west. We could identify only about half a dozen names.[95] Then we decided to park nearby for supper and the night, enjoying a skinny dip and the beauty of the sunset reflected in the placid lake.

Next morning, on our way out to the Heritage Highway, we stopped to see Billy Gladu and his wife, Mary, nee Belcourt. We were agreeably impressed with their attractive home and garden on the old Belcourt homestead (DL 313). Mary still has the sweetness that won my heart when she was the shy little pupil with pigtails. Billy confided to Mike that, "Gerry Andrews was our best teacher, and taught me and Mary to speak English!" I was deeply touched.

My previous return visits to Kelly Lake had all been hurried and casual. This one with Mike was relaxed and comparatively in-depth. He is a skilled interviewer and obviously had won warm regard in the community. He made copious notes, an art I envy, and has generously shared them and his excellent photos. I got the impression that the Kelly Lake people still do a lot of trap-ping and hunting. They now move about more freely for visits and jobs, and the 12-miles-drive to a store and post office at Goodfare is no hardship. Access to their traplines is by pickup, instead of horses, and on their traplines they use skidoos instead of dogs. The chainsaw has replaced the old hand crosscut. They have electricity for light, cooking, refrigeration and power tools. Old log cabins are still in use but some new homes are of frame construction. A church, built about 1953 stands at the eastern edge of the settlement, without a resident priest. It was nice to see a few horses grazing contentedly around the settlement and to note the conspicuous absence of dogs. Big game outfitting conti-nues to be a specialty which explains the presence of horses. The population has probably doubled since 1925, but the homes are still quite scattered.

Returning to Dawson Creek for Mike Robinson's afternoon flight back to Calgary, we took time on the Heritage Highway to check out the site of Alec Anderson's old cabin at Peavine Lake. We found no visible trace of it or the little stable. In Dawson Creek we found George and Mabel Hamelin now living with Mabel's mother, Mrs. David Calliou who had recently become a widow. Mike had heard a lot about George from me and others and had met his younger brother, Albert, at Kelly Lake. One of George's bear stories was about out-staring a grizzly in the mountains with no rifle. He said, "The bear didnt know who I was, but I sure knew who he was!" We enjoyed this visit. I have the impression that older people like Mabel's mother, Annie Gladu, and Eva Calliou still communicate better in Cree than in English.

The time with Mike Robinson had been very enjoyable and worthwhile. After he left I spent a couple of days seeking more specifics for this book. I had thought of going home on the Forestry Trunk Road south from Bezanson to Hinton, but smoke haze restricted visibility and dust on gravel roads was bad. I have mentioned my visit with Lucille and George Beck in Beaverlodge. From there I drove as far as Rio Grande where I found ten pertinent names in the cemetery.[96] The Leighmore post office had closed in 1941.[97] I found no relatives of the Beadle, Bedier, Finn or George White families. At one stop the people knew less of local history than I did. I then returned to Kelly Lake to check out more fully the families of Alfred Campbell, Mary and Billy Gladu and Annie Gladu. Darkness and fatigue dictated a stop for the night near Demmitt.

At the Alberta-BC boundary next morning, Mrs. Joan Cornock was up early but Bruce, Denny's son, had already gone to work. I took the service road in to Tupper post office and store, re-joining the highway farther north. I was curious to see the old Taylor and Fynn properties but found developments there confusing. The area still had its lush charm. At morning coffee with Aubrey and Agnes Gunter in Pouce Coupe, Grandpa Seth Gunter joined us, remarkably bright for expecting his 94th birthday in a week. Seth and his first wife had been Alec Anderson's close friends and had acquired Alec's property at Peavine Lake. Mrs. Gunter had written in the early 1940s to advise me of Alec's death. It was good to learn that Alec had inherited a modest legacy from Scotland which eased his later years. Adolphus Gladu, my pupil was reputed living in the Pouce Coupe area but he had no phone listing, and I could not take time to seek him out.

I spent a couple of fruitless hours at School District 59 offices in Dawson Creek looking for the original school registers and related material for Kelly Lake. Similar searches at the Education Department in Victoria suggest they are buried or lost beyond retrieval.

A pleasant interlude was lunch with Iris and Hans Scholz where I got some news of the Boone Taylor family. Finally George and Mabel Hamelin patiently gave me details of their many and widely scattered children.[98] I notice in such interviews, the wives are much more specific about ages, names and marriages than are their husbands. A brief farewell with Mrs. Calverley concluded this 1981 trip. I took the usual route home through Pine Pass which never loses its appeal. I had obtained a good measure of information – but the more one gets the more he wants. As the French say, "L'appetit vient en mangeant."

Family matters monopolized my concern until the summer of 1982. Returning from Ontario in late April, I enjoyed a 24-hour stopover with Mike and Lynn Robinson in Calgary. At the Petro Canada offices I was brought up-to-date on their Kelly Lake studies now embodied in an array of reports[99] containing interesting background material which I need not duplicate here.

Some stubborn questions motivated yet another trip to Kelly Lake in August, 1982. For company I had Captain James Butterfield, who had survived the 1981 trip to China with me so was inured to my bad habits. As usual the price was rationed time. James had to be back on duty in 10 days. In Dawson Creek, where we saw Mrs. Calverley and George Hamelin, I bought the encyclopaedic tome "Lure of the South Peace", recently published.[100] At the Scholz home I was delighted to find Iris's oldest sister, "Girlie" (Leona), visiting from McLennan, Alta. I had not seen her since June, 1925, at their Tupper home when she was a 15-year-old. We accepted an impromptu invitation for supper with the family at the Scholz homestead near Peavine Lake. Another pleasant surprise there, was to find Bessie (nee Taylor) with her husband, Nick Albert, from Edmonton, who were holidaying on their own place nearby. Bessie was not yet 4 when I last saw her. She accused me of having greeted her then with, "Hello, Dirty Face!" My defence was that teasing is a most sincere expression of affection and that the temptation to tease her now was as strong as ever. Brother Jerry Taylor also arrived from Dawson Creek. There had been some good staff-work to assemble four Taylors and two husbands for their party. We were regaled with wonderful food, wine and conviviality. I took this opportunity to read excerpts from my manuscript relevant to the Taylor family, before Jerry and Iris were born, and they gave me some welcome addenda.

As we left to retire in the van, just out of sight of their cabin, Jerry Taylor confided to James that he now felt a little better about his namesake. With our thanks and goodbye we said that when they wakened in the morning we would be gone. Just as we were ready to start, Hans appeared with a large parcel from "Girlie" for my wife. He had driven all the way back to town for it – a beautiful black furry Teddy Bear which Girlie makes for special customers. It is a show-piece in our living room and a delight for old and young to cuddle. This reunion with so many of the Taylors, so near their old home, Alec Anderson's "Peavine Castle" and Jim Young's oft-travelled rum trail, was a nostalgic highlight.

Instead of turning left to Kelly Lake we continued on the Heritage Highway to Stony Lake, hoping to reach Kinuseo Falls, but were stopped by a derelict bridge near the Monkman Cabins. After about an hour's drive back to Kelly Lake, we stopped at the school to find Ray Irwin, one of the teachers and his wife, Gloria, a granddaughter of Eva Calliou. They were just leaving to fish on the Wapiti River but said they would be glad to see us on their return that evening. We then made the rounds to see Annie Gladu, Billy and Mary Gladu and Dave Gray. Alfred Campbell happened to be away. Francis Belcourt whom I had not met before, invited us to his home for tea. He is Mary Gladu's younger brother, and was too young to attend school in my time. On our return from Goodfare, where we had gone for fuel and some other needs, we stopped for a friendly chat with Lective Campbell. I had wanted to check my Cree vocabulary with his wife, Caroline, but she had taken their son, Dennis, to Vancouver for medical treatment. We returned to the schoolyard to make supper and park for the night and enjoyed a pleasant evening with the Irwins in the teacherage. Later Ray sent me helpful data about his wife's relatives for my Kelly Lake genealogies (see Appendix 4).

At Beaverlodge next morning I wanted to buy "Beaverlodge to the Rockies" (1974) and its "Supplement" (1976)[101] which are not generally available. For these I was directed to see Albert and Madelon Truax at their beautiful home a few miles east. My status as first teacher at Kelly Lake and the coincidence that Albert's uncle, Major A.J. Truax, MD, Medical Officer at Canadian Army HQ, overseas, had been a wartime friend and colleague, qualified me to buy the desired volumes. I learned there about the forth-coming album of Euphemia McNaught's paintings and gladly subscribed for it. This book arrived early 1983 and is a fine tribute to the artist and to her friends whom we can thank for its production. I was sorry to miss seeing Lucille and George Beck who were away. Homeward-bound, James was able to see the grand Peace River Valley and the Bennett Dam. From McLeod Lake we drove out to Carp Lake Provincial Park. The well-gravelled road must closely follow our old packtrail of 1924, when the picturesque falls on the McLeod River had escaped our notice.

At home in following months, I studied the array of local histories then in hand and other works listed in my Bibliography & References. For these, indexes which are so helpful, vary from nil to full. It was often necessary to sift through the whole text for pertinent material, like sluicing gravel for gold nuggets. I must admit that much of the "gravel" was interesting. The "home-spun" family stories are short and long, subjective and objective, naive and scholarly, vague and meticulous. Most are epics of pioneer life — adaptation to a strange and often hostile environment. They display courage, perseverence, ingenuity, humor, pathos, neighborly kindness, tolerance, tragedy and triumph. From them, a superb anthology of pioneer life could be selected and edited to take top rank in high school curricula and in public libraries. For my own convenience, selected items were indexed and listed alphabetically. For the benefit of others these are offered in Appendix 1.

Settlement of the great Peace River country which sweeps across the interprovincial boundary, about the turn of the century, included both White and Metis pioneers. The latter are featured in my Introduction. White settlers from more distant, varied and civilized origins sought homesteads to own and develop. Most were unaccustomed to the wilderness and travel in it. Instead of hostility between Whites and Metis, there was a measure of wholesome compatibility. Their interests were often complementary. The Whites wanted arable land, easily cleared, in compact communities for supplies, services, schools, mail and worship. The Metis were completely happy in the surrounding forests and beyond. There are many examples of friendship between White and Metis neighbors with helpful exchange of their respective skills and products, but always with a mutual underlying reserve. In ignorance, White settlers sometimes referred to the Metis as "Indians" which is understandable but quite wrong.

Thoughtfully, Mike Robinson phoned from Calgary in early February, 1983 to advise that George Hamelin had died in Dawson Creek on the 7th instant, less than a week after his 71st birthday. For poor George it was a release from long and painful affliction. My lifelong regard for George compelled me to prepare an obituary at once. Thanks to Dorthea Calverley to whom I sent it, and to the publishers, this appeared unabridged in the "Dawson Creek Mirror" for 16 March, 1983. It concluded with these words:

> George Hamelin was exemplary of the best in his European and North American ancestry. He will be remembered affectionately by his family as a devoted husband, father and grandfather and by others as a friend and gentleman in the finest Metis tradition.

In the history of the Kelly Lake people, the significance of Lac Ste Anne and Flyingshot Lake had now become more fully appreciated. I had not seen either, so they were put in my 1983 itinerary for a trip to Atlin. Northbound, I wore out two companions, Duff Wight as far as Dawson Creek and Bruce Chambers beyond. At McBride we found no oldtimers who remembered my 1925 friends at Goat River, Dunster or Tete Jaune. We were interested to see Edson, southern terminus of the historic trail (1911-16). When we found the Lac Ste Anne mission, near noon, there was an important funeral in session which seemed to involve all local people, several nuns and the priest. I was reluctant to intrude or to inspect the adjoining cemetery where I might have found some significant identities. The mission has a pleasant setting for the annual Metis pilgrimage, then due to begin in a couple of weeks. Open fields around the church and down to the lake looked ideal for campsites. We could not linger so returned to Hinton and stopped for the night near Grande Cache on the Forestry road leading north. It is well-gravelled and climbs over some high summits. It parallels our old Nose Mountain packtrail of 1925 but is too far east for commanding views of the Rocky Mountains which I remembered. Rains had cleared the air for good visibility. We saw mountain sheep, moose and deer on the higher levels.

I had already learned that a good place to get information, especially historical, is the local museum. Fortunately the one in Grande Prairie was open when we arrived on Sunday. At the reception desk Mrs. E. Dunkley was both knowledgeable and friendly. She showed me their recently published history "Along the Wapiti" (A3) which I bought at once and have used with much benefit since. She directed us to the Valin home on Lot 16 of the old Flyingshot Lake Settlement, the original occupant of which had been Johnny Gladu c1907. Had time allowed, Mrs. Valin, nee Edith Tissington, born in the area of English parents[102] could have told us much about my Kelly Lake friends who had lived there. To regain the Beaverlodge road we circled Flyingshot Lake. The area is flat and where not cleared is quite bushy. It had been famous for water fowl, often shot on the wing, hence the name Flyingshot.

Later in 1983, Mr. RF Baker, ALS, Director, Land Survey Branch, Edmonton, kindly sent copies of the original survey notes and plans for both the Lac Ste Anne and the Flyingshot Lake settlement. The former was surveyed in 1890 by Phidyme RA Belanger, DLS. His plan and notes identify the following "occupants":

*Belcourt, Benjamin
 SE35-54-3-W5
*Belcourt, Jean-Baptiste
 NW35-54-3-W5
*Belcourt, Narcisse
 NE35-54-3-W5
*Belcourt, "Widow" Lot 16
*Callot (Calliou?), "Widow" Lot 2
 Court-Oreille, Louis (?), Lot 18
 Cunningham, Albert "Squatter"

*Gladu, Benoit,
 NE24-54-4-W5
*Gladu, Celestin Lot 1
*Gladu, John Felix
 NE17-54-3-W5
*Letendre, Jean-Baptiste Lot 7
 Paquette, Antoine "Squatter"
 Plante (Laplante?), Abraham
 Lot 9
 Plante do, Xavier (?) Lot 17

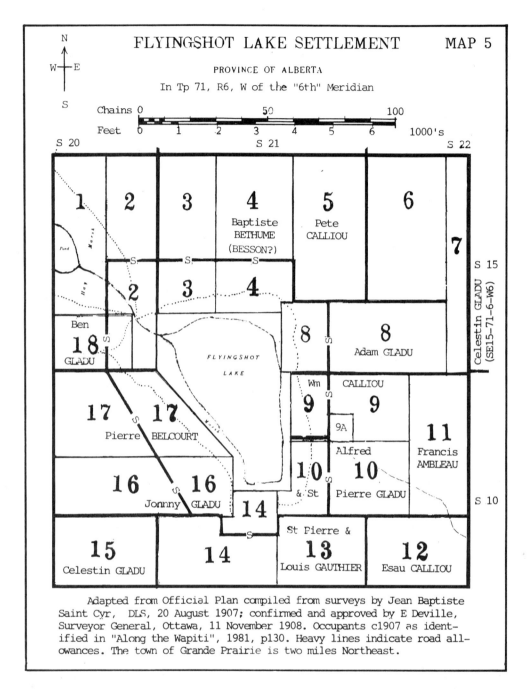

FLYINGSHOT LAKE SETTLEMENT   MAP 5

PROVINCE OF ALBERTA

In Tp 71, R6, W of the "6th" Meridian

Adapted from Official Plan compiled from surveys by Jean Baptiste Saint Cyr, DLS, 20 August 1907; confirmed and approved by E Deville, Surveyor General, Ottawa, 11 November 1908. Occupants c1907 as identified in "Along the Wapiti", 1981, p130. Heavy lines indicate road allowances. The town of Grande Prairie is two miles Northeast.

Several of these families (*) are later known at Kelly Lake. Was the Widow "Callot" Celestin Gladu's mother-in-law, old Mrs. Marie Calliou, nee Finlay? These people would have been age 21 or older, (ie born prior to 1870). A sketch of Belanger's large and complicated plan has not been attempted.

A petition to the Minister of the Interior, Ottawa, dated 18 July, 1906 to have the Flyingshot Lake Settlement surveyed, bore 19 names, of which 13 were illiterate ("X" his mark") and 15 were familiar Kelly Lake surnames.[103] Ottawa's response was prompt. The survey was completed 20 August, 1907 by J.B. Saint Cyr, DLS, whose plan is shown as Map 5. On his survey crew of 10, Henry Calliou, Milton Campbell and Adolphus Letendre are listed as "labourers" (axemen). Presumably these people were also age 21 or older (born 1886 or prior). Fifteen original occupants are identified on their respective lots, as shown on Map 5.[104] Within 20 years all the Metis had sold their lots to White settlers, in many cases for only token payment. Louis Gauthier, Lot 13, was the last to leave, about 1925.[104] I was gratified to identify Celestin Gladu and Narcisse Belcourt as early as 1890 at Lac Ste Anne.

At Beaverlodge, the Becks directed us to the home of Euphemia McNaught and her sister Mrs. Isabel Perry where we were served a delicious lunch as if by magic. Euphemia had studied Art in Toronto at the same time I was enrolled in Forestry there. Members of the Group of Seven occasionally spoke to us undergrads in Hart House, and their original paintings adorned the walls there. The strong dynamic land-forms of Lawren Harris have always appealed to me and I see this same quality in Euphemia's mountains in the Monkman Pass area. Her atmospheric perspectives in these are especially good in my opinion. I confessed my disappointment that her beautiful painting of Monkman Lake, reproduced in "The Beaver" (Summer, 1981) had not been included in her album of paintings, and learned that this original treasure had gone to England so was not then available. Our hostesses suggested local cemeteries of possible interest. Pipestone Park on the Wapiti River was so pleasant that we spent the night there. The adjoining Indian cemetery commemorates the Chatelaine family and others related to Sam Wilson.[105] There had been a ferry on the Wapiti here, but our crossing of 1925 was about 20 miles upstream. Next day we found Doug and Doris McFarlane at their attractive home on the east edge of Beaverlodge. Doug's uncles were the pioneer land surveyors who had done most of the original townships in this area. I was surprised to notice one or two of Owen Goward's paintings in their home, and pleased to learn that the Gowards of Victoria are mutual friends.

The next night at Kelly Lake some friends were away. Lective Campbell confirmed that he is a younger brother of Milton Campbell, about the same age as his nephew, Alfred Campbell. I had thought they were cousins. Lective's father was Alex C. Campbell from Eastern Canada, who married a Gauthier daughter of Lac Ste Anne, possibly St Pierre's sister.[106] I was glad to meet Albert Hamelin (Hambler), George's younger brother, for the first time. Next day in wet weather we drove to Tumbler Ridge via Stony Lake. It was a chaos of construction and mud but worth seeing. We thought it discreet to return the way we had come, but to Tupper instead of Kelly Lake. It was good to find Bruce Cornock at home for a change. The Gunter family provided their usual morning coffee at Pouce Coupe.

Duff flew home from Dawson Creek 14 July. This had been our first trip together, informally as friends. He knew parts of the country better than I, having supervised our control surveys of this area in 1956, when from his base camp at Stony Lake I had used his helicopter and float-plane facilities to see places like Bearhole and Kakwa lakes and beautiful Jarvis Pass from the air.

Before Bruce Chambers arrived at Dawson Creek on Saturday afternoon I saw some but not all the people on my list. At the library I searched the Calverley Archives without success for the reputed taped interviews with Isidore Gladu (1973). Thanks to Gerry and Nan Clare, copies of these came to hand later by mail. I was glad to learn from Mabel Hamelin that my obituary for George had not given offence (one never can be sure). She had sent copies to their more distant children. I was invited to supper with Mary and Austin Sones. His father, aunt and grandparents were old friends in Victoria and are related to Ray Irwin's mother. It is a small world! It was not reassuring to learn that Iris Scholz was soon to take Hans to Edmonton for specialists' attention. Early 1984 she phoned to tell me the sad news. I thanked Dorthea Calverley for her help with the Hamelin obituary but "The Mirror" office was closed for the weekend when I got there to thank the publishers, Marilyn and Paul Croutch.

The young people at Nawican Friendship Centre were certainly friendly and interested in my quest for Kelly Lake lore. Vincent Horsman tried to decode the message in Cree syllabics I had found on the Smoky River in 1925 (see Figure 2, Chapter 4). It proved too difficult, for various reasons, the script itself and perhaps the dialect. He thought the first line identified the writer as Samuel Nease, which seems valid because the Nease family were prominent in the area between the Wapiti and Smoky rivers.[107] Mary Olita at the Centre knows or is related to the Goodwin family in Atlin. Her name suggests that she may also be related to Harry Garbitt and his wife Martha, nee Desjarlais, of Moberly Lake, who had a daughter Mrs. Gertrude Olita.[108] Later I had a nice letter from Sandra Smith, program supervisor for the Nawican Alternate School. Five weeks of poor weather at my Atlin cabin, without phone, TV or daily paper, favored a more thorough and systematic study of the local histories bought and brought for the purpose. Then at home in the latter months of 1983, I had determined to forego further research and to finalize this book for better or for worse.

But "man proposes, God disposes". The arrival of Messrs. Sprague & Frye's newly published "Genealogy of the First Metis Nation"[109] suddenly put me in the role of Ali Baba with his "open sesame" to a treasure-house of data with tempting Kelly Lake connotations. Ensuing months passed all too quickly while I amplified and recompiled the Kelly Lake genealogies in Appendix 4. These now embody the sum total of data obtained from my verbal, manuscript and published sources. Emphasis was placed on the progeny of my original pupils, Mary Belcourt and her husband Billy Gladu, Alfred Campbell, Sarah Campbell (Mrs. Eugene Gauthier) and George Hamelin, which are relatively complete. Others must remain fragmentary. The vital statistics in Appendix 4 need not burden us here. To conclude this chapter and this book, I now add some further comment about selected members of my rather lengthy dramatis personae, beginning with my original pupils as listed at the end of Chapter 3.

Of the three Belcourt children, Mary has been mentioned several times. Her taped interview (1973) in the Calverley Achives[110] reflects her wholesome attitude to life and the benefit of schooling. Henry Belcourt, handsome but shy, did not marry. I was sorry not to see him before he died in 1978. I have no information about their younger sister Annie. Sarah Campbell married "Zen" (Eugene?) Gauthier late in 1925.[111] They had at least six children before Sarah's untimely death c1940.[112] Their son, Lorne, claimed his great-grandfather was St Pierre Gauthier.[113] Alfred Campbell's wife, Virginia, was nee Belcourt, but her relationship with the others is not clear. I understand that jolly little Leo Campbell did not survive childhood. Lective Campbell's relationship with this family is now clarified as mentioned. Billy Gladu has been updated in connection with his wife Mary, nee Belcourt. His younger brother Adolphus, married Adeline LeGlace of the Horse Lake Reserve and they had 12 or more children.[114] I was unable to find his alleged location in the Pouce Coupe area.

The children of Urbain Gladu, whose mother was a Breland, are said to be all deceased. Colin married and died under tragic circumstances which people seem reluctant to talk about. The mother of Alfred Gladu's children, nee Madeline Gauthier, died in 1930[115] and Alfred in 1953.[116] Good-looking Joe had one or more children before his divorce from Tootsie Halpenner. Delphine married Joe Hamelin, George's older brother. They died together with "Big Johnny" Supernat in a traffic accident (1980) and are buried in the Kelly Lake cemetery. Their daughter, Lena, married Vern Knott. Florence Gladu married David Capot and a younger sister, Jean, married David Gray, whose children are Della and Jarvis. An excellent photo of this Gladu family is in Photo 32 .

I need not amplify numerous references to George Hamelin and his family already made. Jimmy Letendre evidently married Galena Calliou, daughter of Eva, nee Campbell.[117] Jimmie St Arnaud, son of Dan and Florence, nee Ferguson, well known around Grande Prairie, was victim of "TB" in 1937. His older brother, John St Arnaud was the source of interesting material in Chapter 1 of "Along the Wapiti".[118] My genealogies, in Appendix 4, place the parents, aunts and uncles of the original Kelly Lake pupils in the "n+5" generation. Of them, to my knowledge only Annie Gladu and Lective Campbell survive at Kelly Lake, both being late arrivals in that generation. Eva Calliou in the "n+6" generation is older than her uncle Lective Campbell – a case of overlapping generations.

I have dealt at length with the Jim Young and Boone Taylor families. Their genealogies are added to Appendix 4. My first re-visit with Mary Taylor was in 1960 at Tupper when she was a widow in the old home, with the Scholz family for company. I saw her last in 1967 at Dawson Creek in her own house, having sold out her property at Tupper. Mary faithfully sent me Christmas greetings until her death in 1977 at age 90. (I might add here that Alec Anderson of Peavine Lake had worked in the mines in South Africa before coming to Canada. I think he was born in Perth, Scotland.) Fred William Barber, my teasing companion through the Pine Pass in 1924 was a popular teacher at Hillhead School near Wembley. In the early 1940s he continued teaching at Olds, Alta, where he married an old sweetheart, Veda. He wrote from there in 1952 to say he was not well enough to join Jim Young and me on a proposed trip over the then, new Hart Highway. He died some time later.[119]

A good account of Denny Cornock (1888-1975) and his wife, Anna, nee Paynter (?-1976) is in "Lure of the South Peace".[120] Of their six children I have seen only Bruce, the eldest, at Tupper. Justin Edgerton McIntyre at McLeod Lake died in November, 1963. We had exchanged Christmas greetings until near the end. His full name appears in the Voters' List for "Stuart Lake" (Fort St James) in 1920, as "Clerk" (with the HBC). Sam Wilson, our worthy "Neestou" in 1925, was killed on the road near Grovedale late in 1970. He was born in 1895. Interesting anecdotes about Sam may be found in A3p9, p15, p176, p307; A5p429, p543; and A6p238. He married the widow, Mrs. Nease. Their daughter Lena had a large family.

At rest in the Halcourt cemetery are: George Beadle (1887-1957), Sarah Beadle (1899-1931), George Samuel Cox White (1892-1980) and at Rio Grande are James Finn (?-1931) and William Finn (1872-1931). Tim Finn later moved to Calgary where he died.[121] References for more than 200 selected identities listed alphabetically are in Appendix 1.

Here at the end of this rather lengthy Epilogue, I must confess that, while preparing it there have been moments of doubt – about its content, how best to structure it and, indeed, whether it should have been attempted at all. Now that it is finished I hope it serves to emphasize how deeply my two youthful years at the Metis outpost of Kelly Lake, have influenced and enriched a long and full life since. The investment of that short segment of my early career has compounded through long years into an incalculable wealth of friendships, experiences and fond memories.

My mind now takes supersonic flight back through 60 years to an episode in Young's store at Kelly Lake when I was in midstream of my time there. It was probably a Saturday when I was free from the school and Jim was present doing his business. A young Metis came in to get a grubstake and supplies for his trapline. He was a stranger and perhaps only a year or two older than I. He was good-looking with a quiet but proud and dignified manner. Obviously he was a competent trapper and his credit with Jim was good. He was accompanied by his shy but attractive young wife carrying their bright-eyed and healthy infant. This young man was already a qualified professional, after teenage apprenticeship with his elders. He had a wife and the beginning of a family. I was consumed with envy. What a contrast to myself – still working to qualify in my chosen field, with long years of study still ahead and domestic bliss not even in sight! I realized that an elaborate parchment, embellished with seals and signatures, crests – and perhaps "cum laude's" – was not the only criterion of professional competence and status in life.

Finally, Mother's little list of alphabetic Jewels, used so appropriately for our farewell to old Granny Calliou in the Kelly Lake cemetery on that peaceful Sunday morning so long ago, has been carried with me always, well-protected in a soft pouch of Kelly Lake moosehide, expertly tanned by Annie Gladu when she, like myself, was on the threshold of a long and rewarding life. I am sure Annie believes, as I do, in a Guardian Angel and that she is thankful for hers as I am for mine.

63: George Hamelin with trophy grizzly, vic Monkman Pass, about 1950. (Courtesy: Francis Belcourt)

64: McLeod Lake, BC, July 1950. J.E. McIntyre's store; L to R, Bill McPhee, McIntyre, unidentified, unidentified, A.W. Bentley. (GSA #683)

216

65: McLeod Lake, BC, July 1950. View East to J.E. McIntyre's store;
BC Gov't "Beaver" CF-FHF. (GSA #682)

66: McLeod Lake, BC, July 1950. View from McIntyre's landing NW'ly
to source of Pack River; the old ford was near, to the right;
typical "Finlay River" freight boats. (GSA #680)

67: Vic "Peterson's" Beatton R crossing, BC; August 1950; N.C. Stewart and Jim Young at Chief Pooscapee's Camp. (GSA #741)

68: Vic Beatton R, BC, August 1950. Duncan Cran and Norman Stewart. (GSA #743)

69: Dawson Creek, BC, about 1953-54. Prize-winning Kelly Lake School Choir. (Courtesy Mrs. Lucille Beck, formerly Mrs. Jules H. Semans)

70: Duncan Cran, BCLS survey camp, Cache Creek, August 1953. (GSA #1088)

71: Rose Prairie, BC, August 1953. Jim and Anne Young with daughters Mary and Dorothy. (GSA #1100)

72: View NE'ly to farm land between Fort St John and Rose Prairie, August 1953. (GSA #1099)

220

73: Kelly Lake, BC, polling booth (federal election), 10 August 1953. L to R, Gerry Andrews, polling clerk, unidentified, Mrs. Mary Gladu (nee Belcourt), George Hamelin, unidentified, Denny Cornock, Dave Gray? (GSA #1102)

74: Puntzi Airstrip, BC, August 1954. BC Gov't Anson V photo-aircraft CF-EZI with, L to R, pilot "Speed" Norman, Jim Young and Bob McAra. (GSA #1150)

75: View SW at survey camp of A.D. Wight, BCLS, Stony Lake, BC,
September 1956. Bone Mountain (7,446 ft) centre skyline. (GSA #1606)

76: Bearhole Lake, BC, September 1956. Pilot, Glen Lamont, BC
Gov't Beaver Aircraft CF-FHF. (GSA #1612)

77: Airview to Jarvis Pass (c5,000 ft) and Mt Ida (10,000 ft),
September 1956. This is typical of the panoramas we enjoyed on the
Nose Mountain Trail, 1925. (GSA #1607)

78: Airview south over Kakwa Lake, BC, September 1956. Wishaw Mt
(c8,500 ft) left centre; McGregor Pass (c5000 ft) right centre.
(GSA #1609)

79: View W'ly up Peace River from Cache Creek hill, August 1957.
Jim Young stretches a leg. (GSA #1664)

80: Hudson's Hope, BC, August 1957. Jim Young attends St Peter's
Anglican Church — on Monday, not Sunday! (GSA #1665)

81: Tupper, BC, August 1960; Gerry visits the Taylors at their old home. L to R, Mrs. Iris Scholz (nee Taylor), Marie Ann Scholz and Mrs. Mary Taylor (nee Hoffman); Swan Lake in background. (GSA #2159)

82: Victoria, BC, September 1961. Anne Young (nee Roberts) at Andrews' home on Blenkinsop Road, with "Bingo" on guard. (GSA #2397)

83: Airview SW'ly over Cache Creek escarpments, vic Bear Flat, August 1964. Strata probably Lower Cretaceous. (GSA #3011)

84: Tupper, BC, July 1967. Denny Cornock, left and Jim Young. (GSA #3672)

REFERENCES FOR SELECTED IDENTITIES

The Genealogies in Appendix 4 required scrutiny of local histories and other works as listed in the "Bibliography", in some cases of which the Indexes were inadequate. Many identities had to be recovered by laborious search through the complete text. For the convenience of those interested these are tabulated below, alphabetically. In some cases the genetic "code" as explained in Appendix 4, is shown. Where these are preceded by "+", the code is that of the spouse.

Anderson, Alex: A32p593,698; A52-1920
Andrews, GS: A5p372,543; A43p293; A44
Ardill, John: A43p75+,H39
Austin, Alfred: A32p236; A47p39
Barber, Fred Wm: A3p225,334,386
Beadle, Geo J & Mrs(Sarah E): A5p375, 504,523,542; D1,2
Beaverlodge: A6p29,59
Bedier, Frank etc: A5p504,537; A6p195, 220, A47p67,83,93,159 / A15 XIp354
Belcourt, Adelaide(B..x) (Mrs John Glenn)/
Belcourt, Albert(B.....x): D4
Belcourt, Archie(B.....x):A47p431; D23
Belcourt, Clarence(B...x): A44p27
Belcourt, Dolphus(B....x):A44p27
Belcourt, Edward Chas(B.....x): D24
Belcourt, Evelyn(B....x): A5p391
Belcourt, Family: A6p338; A44p19/A47p100
Belcourt, Francis(C14426): A44p3,6,21,24/
Belcourt, Geo(B....x): A52-1933
Belcourt, Henry(C14422): A44p42; A52-1933
Belcourt, John(B....X): A44p22
Belcourt, Madeline(B.....x): A5p524
Belcourt, Mugler(B....x): A6p332
Belcourt, Narcisse(B1111): A3p162-3; A44p21,40,54; A52-1924,1928,1933
Belcourt, Pierre(B...x): A3p130
Belcourt, Roger(B.....x): D25
Besson, Baptiste(+C148): A6p257
Blanchard, Jack: A47p68
Borden, EP & Mrs(Mary E): A7p351; A32 p21; A47p26,233,451; A52-1920
Brainard, "Dad" & "Ma": A4p478; A6p66; A33p372; A47p180+,394
Buffalo: A3p17; A44p34
Callazon(Calihasen), Chas, Joe & Wabi: A32p202-4; A35p72/505-6; A6p211,257; D26
Calliou, Adam(C143): A3p130,158; A5p90/
Calliou, Adolphus(C14..x): A52-1933
Calliou, Alberta(C14516): A42p476
Calliou, Archie(C14341): A5p506
Calliou, Asleas, Mrs: A52-1924,1928
Calliou, Charlie(C144514): A44p57,62/p343
Calliou, Cliff(C144519): A44p2,7,57; A47/
Calliou, Dave(C1434): A3p159; A5p505; A47p70,104
Calliou, Ed(C14342): A5p506; A47p100
Calliou, Esau(C142): A3p130; A5p505
Calliou, Eva(C14451): A44p3,6,21,28,30
Calliou, Family: A3p86; A44p21,58
Calliou, Gibney(C1432): A3p159
Calliou, Henry(C1451): A42p476
Calliou, Joe(C14.x): A52-1924 /1928
Calliou, John(C14.x): A44p57; A52-1924/
Calliou, John(C14517): A42p476/A42p476
Calliou, Julia(C14512)(Mrs Ted Knott)/
Calliou, Kathrene(C14.x): A52-1924
Calliou, Lillian(C1435)(Mrs Lawrence?) A3p159 / A42p476
Calliou, Louis(C145): A14pix; A33p249/
Calliou, Louise(C14511): A42p476
Calliou, Malcolm(C14515): A42p476/Gladu?)
Calliou, Marceline(C1433): A3p159 (Mrs/
Calliou, Marie(+C14)nee Finlay: D5
Calliou, Mary(C14513): A42p476; A52-1924
Calliou, Melanie(C148): A6p257

Calliou, Pete(C146): A3p130; A52-1924
Calliou, Sam(C14.x): A52-1924
Calliou, Veronique(+C143): A3p158; D27/ 22
Calliou(Callihoo), Victoria(+C145): A14pix,
Calliou, Victoria(C1436): A3p158-9
Calliou, Virginia(C14514): A42p476
Calliou, Wm(C1431): A3p130,159; A5p505; A44p27,39; A52-1924, 1928
Callison, Fred C & Mrs(Dora Elton): A32p244, 267; A43p244; A52-1920
Calverley, Dorthea H: A32p7,9,241,244,267, 347,524,654,901,928; A44p2
Campbell, Alex C(C..x): A3p208,256; A5p90
Campbell, Alfred(C14453): A44p42
Campbell, Annie(C1445), nee Gladu: A52-1933
Campbell, Caroline(C14471) nee Gladu: A52-1933
Campbell, Ed(C..x5): A52-1924
Campbell, Family: A44p21
Campbell, Harry(C..x4): A52-1933
Campbell, JM "Silvertip": A3p17,140.171-2, 225,348; A5p264,307,338,421,515; A47p207
Campbell, Lecoff(C..x3): A52-1924
Campbell, Leo(C..x2): A52-1924
Campbell, Lester(C..x6): A3p261
Campbell, Louis(C..x.x): A52-1933
Campbell, Louise, Mrs: A52-1924
Campbell, Maggie, Mrs: A52-1924 /1928
Campbell, Milton(C..x1): A44p29,30; A52-1924/
Campbell, Pete(C..x8): A3p159; A5p90;A52-1924
Campbell, Ray(C..x7): A3p256,262
Campbell, Sarah(C14452): A44p42
Capot, Family: A44p21/p333; A44p21; A47p433
Chatelaine, Family: A3p11; A6p238-242; A38/
Cornock, Dennis L & (Mrs) Anna: A32p35
Cran, Duncan, BCLS: A43p392+,397
Desjarlais, Martha(Mrs Harry Garbitt):A43pH9
Desjarlais, (Mrs Sam): A47p431-3
Devereaux, Martha: A32p42,352,651 /p283
Dolstrum, Adolf: A5p332,379; A6p204; A43/
Drake, Herbert E: A32p650,707
Ducharme, Family: A44p21
Dunkley, Mrs Wm (nee Emma Solberg): A3p143
Easton. Mrs Katie E: A43p31,32,H2,H63
Esswein, Phil & Mrs (Edna): A32p124,353
Ferguson, Florence: A3p9,10.280 / 505
Ferguson. Leon & Mrs: A3p15,16; A5p168-9,/
Finn. Tim & Wm: A5p504; D32
Flyingshot Lake Settlement: A3p129,130
Fynn, Jack & Mrs: A32p130,241+,856 /171
Gaudin. Irving Esdale & Family: A5p164,168,/
Gauthier, Eugene (Zen?)(G.111): A52-1924,28,33
Gauthier, Family: A44p58
Gauthier, Louis(G.12): A3p130; A5p505
Gauthier, Madeline,Mrs(+G.11): A52-1924
Gauthier, Paul(G..x): A32p12,86
Gauthier, St Pierre(G.11):A3p130, A5p505; A44p21-2,39,54; A52-1924,1928
Gauthier, Wayne(G...x): A32p416,419
Gessler(Gizler), Frank: A32p350
Gladu, Adam(G..x): A3p130
Gladu, Adolphus(C14332): A44p42; A47p431
Gladu, Alex(G...x2): A44p42
Gladu, Alfred(G...x): A3p130; A5p505; A44 p45; A52-1924,1933
Gladu, Alvina, Mrs: A52-1933
Gladu, Annie,Mrs(+C1447): A44p6+; A52-1924,33
Gladu, Ben(G..x): A3p130

85: Dawson Creek, BC, July 1967. Jim Young and Mary Taylor; (GSA #3673)

86: Whitehorse, YT, September 1968. L to R, Jim Young's grandsons, Glenn, Michael and Jim; Kris Andrews, and Mary Mickey. (GSA #3901)

MAP 6

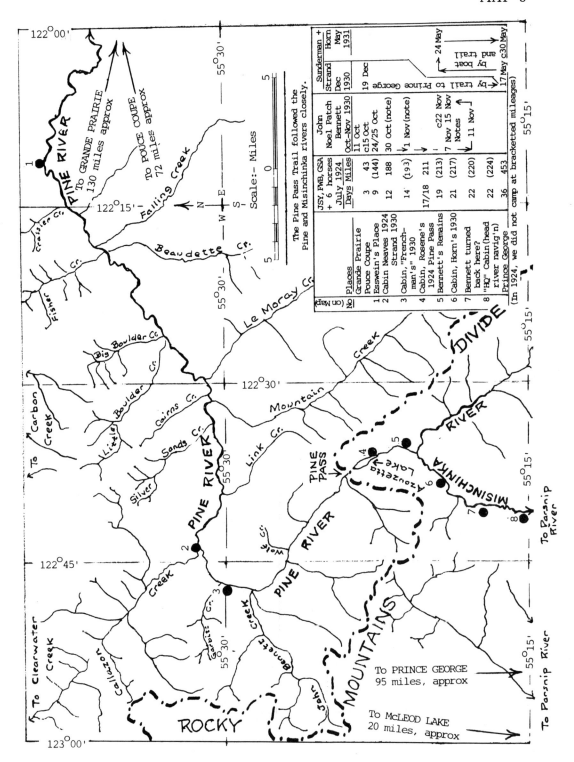

The Pine Pass Trail followed the Pine and Misinchinka rivers closely.

Scale:- Miles

No (on map)	Places	Days July 1924 JSY, FWB, GSA + 6 horses	Miles	John Noel Patch Bennett Oct–Nov 1930	Strand Dec 1930	Sunderman + Horn May 1931	Notes
	Grande Prairie						
	Pouce Coupe	3	43	11 Oct			
1	Esswein's Place	9	(144)	c15 Oct			
2	Cabin Neaves 1924	12	188	24/25 Oct			
	Strand 1930			30 Oct (note)			
3	Cabin, "Frenchman's" 1930	14	(193)	↓1 Nov (note)			1 Nov (note)
4	Cabin, Rosene's	17/18	211				
	1924 Pine Pass						
5	Bennett's Remains	19	(213)	–			c22 Nov
6	Cabin, Horn's 1930	21	(217)	7 Nov 15 Nov			11 Nov
7	Bennett turned back here?	22	(220)	↓			
8	"HQ" Cabin (head river navig'n)	22	(224)		19 Dec	by trail to Prince George	by boat and trail
	Prince George	36	453		17 May c30 May	24 May	

(In 1924, we did not camp at bracketted mileages)

APPENDIX 2

THE JOHN BENNETT TRAGEDY

Death by exposure and exhaustion of John Noel Patch Bennett, the adventurous 18-year-old lad from England, alone, in the vicinity of Pine Pass occurred a few days after 15 November, 1930. This was six years after our packtrip through the same area in 1924 (Chapter 2). The young man's difficulties with trail-finding, weather and short rations were very similar to our experience in this same locality – the tangled jungle of the Misinchinka valley, downstream from Atunatche ("Tillicum") Creek. Our troubles there were in the long warm days of midsummer. John Bennett's were in the dark, cold and stormy onset of winter. There were three of us, experienced in wilderness travel and incomparably better equipped. Even so, we very nearly gave up at this same place, to go back whence we had come. Poor John, a novice, ill-equipped and alone, in desperation turned back. He did not survive.

I am not aware of a full, clear and factual account of the John Bennett tragedy. Its close affinity with our experience, in place and circumstance, motivates me to attempt this synopsis from fragmentary and somewhat disorganized material in hand, viz:

1. REPORT by Cpl Wm B. Stewart, BC Police, 20 January, 1931 "Re: John Noel Patch Bennett, Missing. Refer Radiogram No 10 19 Jan/31." (Copy from Toponymy Office, Ministry of Environment, Victoria, BC, 17 August, 1984).

2. NEWSCLIP, probably late January, 1931 in Victoria Times or Daily Colonist "JNP BENNETT STILL MISSING NO TRACE FOUND", describes charter flight with Peace River Airways plane from Grande Prairie to Phil B. Esswein's place on the Pine River, by J.A.G. Clokie, Imperial Bank, Grande Prairie; pilot Art Craig; mechanic Harry Beamer to seek information about Bennett. (This item was put in my personal file during my first winter in Victoria with the BC Forest Service. Our Pine Pass trip of 1924 would be still fresh in mind. An early lesson in archival discipline, I neglected to note its date and source.)

3. INQUEST, Prince George, BC, 1 June, 1931 into death of John Noel Patch Bennett. (Photocopy from PABC "305/31"). Coroner: Dr. H.G. Trefry, MD; Jury: Chas VanSomer (foreman), Morton Teare, John Blanchard, O.R. Hughes, J.B. Turnbull, and Robt Fry; 1st Witness and BC Police representative: Insp Wm Spiller; 2nd Witness: "Kelly" Geo J. Sunderman, outfitter of Hythe, Alta; 3rd Witness: Chas A. Boyd, riverman, Isle Pierre, BC. After the formalities of swearing in, viewing the remains and effects of the

deceased, and hearing the evidence, the verdict was "that the deceased had met his death between 15th and 22nd November, 1930 on the trail between Misinchinka River and Azouzetta Lake, from exhaustion and exposure in extreme low temperatures through no fault of anyone or evidence of foul play attributed to anyone." (Of the jurors, I knew Jack Blanchard at Kelly Lake in 1924 and Mort Teare and Bob Fry at Finlay Forks in 1939, where I likely met VanSomer or his sons who were then rivermen for Dick Corless.)

4. NEWSCLIP: Vancouver Daily Province, 11 June, 1931, p2 (untitled transcript from PABC) reporting on results of the Inquest (No 3 above) and quoting notes and excerpts from Bennett's diary, found with his remains.

5. NEWSCLIP: Victoria Daily Colonist, 13 June, 1931, p2 (untitled transcript from PABC), similar report to No 4 above.

6. MEMO Re: "BENNETT, John Noel Patch – Missing" further to "previous reports" (including No 1 above) and to Inquest (No 3 above). Dated 2 June, 1940 by Insp Wm Spiller, BC Police. (Copy from Toponymy Office as for No 1 above.)

7. NEWSCLIP: Victoria Daily Colonist, 28 July, 1940, p1-2 entitled "COURAGE IS RECOGNIZED". This reports a decision of BC Lands Department officially to name a creek in the Pine Pass vicinity commemorating John Bennett, with a brief eulogy.

8. NEWSCLIP: Victoria Daily Colonist, 1 August, 1940, p4. This is an untitled transcript, similar to No 7 above.

Apparently press representatives were at the Inquest (No 3 above) and were allowed a quick look at Bennett's diary from which they quoted excerpts, not always fully documented for time and place. I shall first give a chronological account of John Bennett's movements and experiences, and then a summary of the searches for him, all from the above-listed sources, but without further references.

We should like to know much more about John Noel Patch Bennett than I can give here. We do know that he was a teenager who came to Canada alone with the idea of hiking from Pouce Coupe to Prince George via the Peace River or Pine Pass routes. What was his motive? Presumably he travelled by rail from an eastern port to Grande Prairie, where he got a horse and cashed a cheque or otherwise got funds. He did not carry a lot of money because later he could not afford to buy a pair of showshoes offered at $11. In addition to the diary, his packsack contained postmarked letters addressed to him at various points en route and, of all things, a small Latin-English dictionary! His notes left at trappers' cabins gave his home address as "Oakdeane, Manor Road, Coventry, England". Apparently his financial agent was the

Imperial Bank (of Canada) at Vancouver and Grande Prairie. What about his family? Was he an only child? What was his father's occupation? His effects were sent to "his mother" in England. Was she a widow? Reports suggest that his family was cultured and well-to-do, that John expected an inheritance on his majority, and planned to enter the diplomatic service. I assume that he had just completed his secondary education and was allowed to indulge in this adventure before returning home to university. His carrying a Latin dictionary suggests scholarly inclinations or perhaps he was weak in Latin. Other aspects of John's character will be evident from the narrative which follows of his movements and experiences, in chronological sequence. Map 6 is provided with eight numbered strategic locations to clarify the geography.

John Bennett's Trek over Pine Pass, October-November, 1930

c11 Oct: John left Grande Prairie with a packhorse, a .22 rifle and a week's rations, probably having arrived by rail, and contacting J.A.G. Clokie, manager of the Imperial Bank of Canada for money. Likely he bought his horse and rifle there also, at "top prices" which left him with little cash.

c15 Oct: At Pouce Coupe, he questioned Constables Wm. C. Murray and H.L. Norman of the BC Police about the Pine Pass trail. They warned him against attempting such a trip without a capable guide.

c19 Oct: Diary: "Snowshoes cost $11, I cant buy them. Two trappers told me that there was an awful journey ahead of me and tons of snow." This could have been at East Pine.

24-25 Oct: Overnight with Phil B. Esswein (No 1, Map 6), who warned it was highly dangerous to go through the pass at that late season and without a guide. He insisted on giving John two weeks' rations but his offer of stout boots was declined. John was wearing only moccasins. Esswein was the last person to see John Bennett alive.

c27 Oct: Diary: "Rain started." His bedding got wet and he was discouraged.

c28 Oct: Diary: "Horse fell in river – raining – lost trail – burst moccasin – Betty [horse] fell again – searched for trail most of day." He arrived at Ted Strand's cabin (No 2, Map 6) where he found and read a note left about two weeks earlier by one Geoffrey Wood who had come through Pine Pass eastbound and remarked on troubles with the trail. John added this note on the same sheet:

> Oct. 30th. Also on solo trip to McLeod. Glad to dry things after horse fell in river. 2 inches of snow here and storm coming. John Bennett, Oakdeane, Manor Road, Coventry, England.

Wood arrived at Fort St John on 2 November. He may have gone there on the trail from Esswein's to Hudson Hope, and thence by trail or river. He was also young. Kelly Sunderman later referred to him as "a boy named Wood".

c30 Oct: Diary: "Progress seems hopeless but since Providence has enabled me to travel this far, will doubtless get through alright – not worrying any more."

31 Oct: He arrived at "The Frenchman's" cabin (No 3, Map 6) and left this undated note:

> Was very grateful for 2 nights rest here after losing the trail and during a terrific rainstorm. It is still raining and doesn't look very much like clearing off at present. However I hope for the best. Am on a solo trip to Fort Mcleod with one packhorse. John NP Bennett.

2 Nov: Diary: Lost his horse, axe and gun. Spent day recovering them.

c4 Nov: Diary: "Raining – spent time drying blankets – pretty hopeless. Wandered most of day, trail-less. Burst one moccasin – still wearing what remains of it. Floundered hopelessly all day. Betty, the horse fell again."

c5 Nov: His horse fell but got it up again – no place to sleep at night. Wandered sleepless all next night – raining hard. He mentions neither the pass nor Rosene's cabin here. Perhaps he was too distraught to record them.

c6-8 Nov: He reached Frank Horn's cabin (No 6, Map 6) and left this note:

> To the owner: Am very grateful for 3 nights rest here during bad weather after a tough trip alone over the Pass. As my provisions are very low, I took the liberty of taking some of your food. Some moosemeat, a little flour and some rice. I hope you won't mind. I am afraid I have no money to pay you with unfortunately, else I would leave some, however I may be able to do you a good turn some day. I proceed on my way to McLeod now. John NP Bennett. November 8.

This note was found by Horn when he arrived at his cabin 8 December. Later he took it to McLeod Lake where Kelly Sunderman picked it up.

c8 Nov: Lost his axe, blankets wet, had but few matches.

c9 Nov: Diary: "Camped wet and without fire – matches wet. Poor Betty entirely without food."

10 Nov: Ate raw duck he shot, remaining food one tin of beans and a little flour.

11 Nov: Forgot rifle, recovered it and continued. Near dusk he decided to abandon horse and turn back (No 7, Map 6). Diary: "Ate plain flour, no fire but not bad, though feet frozen, terribly painful." He tied a note to the horse's bridle stating his condition. There is no record that this note or the horse was ever found.

c12 Nov: His matches wet, feet terribly raw and frozen. He crossed the Misinchinka barefoot in floating ice. Reached cabin at dusk. Kept fire going all night (No 6, Map 6).

15 Nov: At Horn's cabin. Diary: "Woke at intervals during night and ate macaroni and milk – and tea – quite good as milk provides flavor. Finished one tin milk, saving the other one." Here he added another unsigned note on the overleaf side of his previous note, viz:

November 15, 1930. Have failed to get through to McLeod, ran entirely out of food. The trip is useless for McLeod country so am going back. A list of supplies taken by me is here. If you write me c/o the Imperial Bank of Canada, Vancouver, BC, I will pay you back in full. Meantime your cabin and food have just about saved my life, and I am deeply grateful. I set out today back across the Pine [Pass]. My feet and fingertips are frostbitten. I have abandoned my horse. However I think I will make it. Sorry to have taken so much but it is very necessary. Following is a list of provisions taken:

½ lb bacon	½ lb prunes	3 candles
1½ lb flour	1 oz lard	1½ lb rice
1 lb macaroni	1½ lbs moosemeat	1 table knife
3 tins milk	½ lb tea	1 spoon
2 boxes matches	1 tin baking powder	

22 Nov or before: About a mile up the Atunatche Creek trail from the Misinchinka River (No 5, Map 6) in waning daylight, John's faltering footsteps halted. Having lost his axe, he painfully broke off some dry branches for a fire, but failed to ignite them. With his extremities frostbitten and pieces of burlap tied around his feet – he sank to the ground, soon to become unconscious – mercifully – and to dream of home and family in far away England. Beside him were his rifle and his securely tied packsack containing underwear and a little food. In the darkening gloom, falling snow covered John with its soft white quilt which before spring would thicken to a depth of eight feet or more.

There are some ironic "ifs". Instead of turning back, if John had gone about four miles farther to the large headquarters cabin (No 8, Map 6) he would have found shelter, comfort and some food, either to wait until Horn would appear, in early December, or to restore his strength to reach Parsnip River, where chances of encountering travellers would have been better. His timing was just too late to meet up with Geoffrey Wood, more experienced and fresh from the awful trail over the Pass, who might have persuaded John to go back with him to Esswein's place. Later, he could have met Strand or Horn. His full diary might reveal other significant aspects of his experiences and reactions.

Search for John N.P. Bennett-Missing

19 Nov/1930: The first official notice was on this day when J.A.G. Clokie, mentioned above, presumably on behalf of Bennett's family in England, notified Constable G.H. Greenwood, BC Police, Peace River District, that "a young man about eighteen years of age, named John Noel Patch Bennett from England was missing and that he had left Grande Prairie with the intention of going through either the Peace or Pine Pass to Vancouver". This was within a day or two of John's demise, just beyond Pine Pass.

19 Dec: Sunderman and Strand, engaged by Clokie on behalf of Bennett's family, left Pouce Coupe to follow Bennett's route through Pine Pass to McLeod Lake and Prince George, where they arrived shortly before 20 January, 1931. On 1 January, they found Bennett's notes at Strand's and "The Frenchman's" cabins (No's 2 & 3, Map 6). Later, at McLeod Lake, they picked up the notes left at Horn's cabin (No 6, Map 6). At Prince George, after reporting to Cpl Wm B. Stewart of the BC Police, they left 20 January by rail for the Peace River country. No doubt Sunderman also reported the results of this search to Clokie at Grande Prairie. They had been a month on this winter trip.

Late Jan 1931: After hearing from Sunderman, Clokie engaged the Peace River Airways cabin plane (on skis), CF-AOQ, pilot Art Craig and mechanic Harry Beamer, to fly him from Grande Prairie to land on the river ice at Esswein's place about noon (No 1, Map 6). They had to stay overnight while Esswein junior, then age 16, hiked up river to fetch his father from his trapline. Father and son returned in the dark, arriving home after midnight. This trip merely confirmed what was already known, or indeed, unknown!

17 May: Presumably as soon as river navigation was clear of ice, Sunderman, with Chas Boyd, riverman, of Isle Pierre, and Frank Horn, trapper on the Misinchinka River, left Prince George, by boat, to Mcleod Lake, down the Pack River, and up the Parsnip and Misinchinka rivers. They travelled on foot from the head of navigation. On Sunday, 24 May about a mile up the Atunatche Creek trail from the Misinchinka, they found John Bennett's remains and effects (No 5, Map 6). According to Sunderman's description at the inquest, the skeleton was "scattered in a radius of 40 feet", having been ravaged by wild animals. Torn clothing included khaki breeches, a green woollen scarf, a piece of navy-

blue overcoat, a fur cap with leather top. Animal tooth marks were on the stock of the .22 Remington rifle. John's packsack which was still intact, contained the items already mentioned. After taking photographs, and gathering up everything pertinent, they returned with them immediately to Prince George, arriving in time for the inquest, Monday 1 June, 1931. Bennett's remains and effects were held in Prince George after the inquest, pending instructions from the family in England. News reports as mentioned, followed on 11 and 13 June, and indicated that the remains were then en route to England by rail and sea.

The expense of these searches for John must have been considerable and were no doubt borne by his family. The Search and Rescue Service we enjoy today did not exist then. If it had, this might have been a different and happier story. This further ironic "if" may be added to those above mentioned.

Early in 1940, nearly 10 years after the fact, Major G.G. Aitken, then Chief Geographer, BC Surveys Branch in Victoria, made formal recommendation to the authorities in Ottawa, that a sizable creek entering the upper Pine River from the northwest, about 10 miles downstream from Pine Pass, be officially named for John Bennett. This creek had been previously known as Canyon Creek, one of more than 20 other creeks in BC, then so named! The new name was duly confirmed and appears on today's maps covering this area.

It might be appropriate for the BC Heritage Trust to place one of its attractive roadside plaques at a spot on the Hart Highway opposite the mouth of John Bennett Creek, only about 400 yards from the road (near No 3, Map 6). An alternative location might be opposite where Bennett died (No 5, Map 6) about 1,600 yards across the steep valley of Atunatche Creek from the highway and some 300 feet below.

Most of the accessible waterfrontage on beautiful Azouzetta Lake in Pine Pass has been alienated from the Crown. This would be an ideal location for a provincial campground, with the name "John Bennett Park". The nearest existing campsite is Moberly Lake Park, beyond Chetwynd. Bijoux Falls Park on the Misinchinka River has no camping facilities.

Few are still alive who had personal connection with John Bennett's case to confirm or refute what I have written here. Had he survived, John would now be in his early 70s. Are any of his family still living? Phil Esswein, Mort Teare, Bob Fry, Jack Blanchard, Charlie VanSomer, and Kelly Sunderman have all passed on. Lately Mrs. Edna Esswein was in a "home" in Kamloops. I am curious about her son.

Roy McDougall (1888-1984), trapper, postmaster and storekeeper at Finlay Forks, 1925-c1962, latterly living in Sidney, BC where I saw him when opportune, remembered hearing of Sunderman and Frank Horn, but did now know them. He knew Fry, Teare, Blanchard and VanSomer well and vaguely remembered the Bennett case. He explained that at Finlay Forks they got little news until they visited McLeod Lake or Prince George. A colleague in the BC Surveys and Mapping Branch, George New, BCLS, went into the Parsnip River area about 1931 and until the late 1940s, trapped on the Anzac River, parallel to and south of the Misinchinka. George vaguely remembered hearing of John Bennett and says that Frank Horn eventually died on his trapline.

This review of the John Bennett tragedy reminds me that just before Jim Young, Fred Barber and I left Kelly Lake on our Pine Pass trip in 1924, I had written to my sister Nora (later Mrs. John M. Sloane), telling her of our plans and imminent departure. When we got through to Vanderhoof, more than a month later, I never thought to write anyone of our safe arrival. When Nora eventually heard I was alive and well, she had been on the point of contacting the BC Police at Pouce Coupe to report that her dear brother was missing on a dangerous trip through the Rocky Mountains! Thankfully no search party had to look for us.

During several war years in Britain, because of military and other preoccupations, I missed the opportunity to seek out John Bennett's family at Coventry, to learn more about him and them, and perhaps to be allowed to see his diary. At the risk of hurting tender memories, I could have told them much about the scene of poor John's valiant but fateful demise.

87: Rose Prairie, BC, October 1970. Jim Young's grandchildren "off to school", L to R, Darla (8), Kevin (10), Sheri-Lynn (6) Grandpa Jim can be seen behind, through windows. (GSA #4383)

88: View up Pelly River vic Houle River, YT, September 1977. Klondikers, including John McCormack, descended this river from Pelly Banks, 1898. My daughter Kris in foreground. (GSA #6292)

89: Pouce Coupe, BC, September 1977. Old BC Provincial Police barracks, now a motel. (GSA #6299)

90: Vic Peavine Lake, BC, September 1977. View north on "Heritage Highway", formerly Jim Young's "rum trail". (GSA #6300)

91: Vic Kelly Lake, BC, September 1977. View north along Alberta-BC Boundary (120th Meridian), on road from Goodfare, Alta. (GSA #6303)

92: Kelly Lake School, BC, September 1977. Large structure on right is the "gym". (GSA #6305).

93: Kelly Lake, BC, August 1981. View west from site of Jim Young's Store. Firewood was cut and hauled from bush, right background. (Courtesy Mike Robinson)

94: Kelly Lake, BC, August 1981. After 56 years I meet Mrs. Eva Calliou again (nee Campbell) with some of her grandchildren. (Courtesy Mike Robinson)

APPENDIX 3

ARCHIVAL MATERIAL (correspondence, etc.)

-- Index --

Editing has been minimal. Sequence generally chronological. Comment in brackets.

---

1. Flyingshot Lake, Grande Prairie. <u>18th July 1906</u> (to)
Hon F Oliver, <u>Minister of the Interior</u>, Ottawa.

We, the undersigned make a request that our respective claims of land be surveyed as a settlement and at as early a date as possible:-

       his
Culestan X Gladirn
      mark
       his
Baptiste X Besson
      mark
       his
St Pierre X Gochie
      mark
       his
William X Calleho
      mark
       his
Warsi X Bellecourt
      mark

Pierre Bellecourt

       his
Izaore X Calleho
      mark
       his
Joe X Bellecourt
      mark

Henry Callio

       his
Francois X Hamlin
      mark

his
Melton X Campbell
    mark

JI Brooks

    his
Peter X Calleho
    mark

Alexander Sinclair

    his
Peter X Calleho
    mark
    his
Adam X Calleho
    mark

CG Mead

W Grant

    his
Louis X Callehoo
    mark

(Note spelling vagaries for Gladu, Gauthier, Calliou, Belcourt, Hamelin, Celestin, Narcisse, Isidore and Milton. Only six of nineteen petitioners were literate.)

2. <u>Field Notes</u>, <u>Flyingshot Lake Settlement</u>, Tp71 R6 W of 6th Mer. Surveyed by <u>J.B. Saint Cyr</u>, <u>DLS</u> – 2nd to 20th August, 1907. Names and duties of party employed:

Eudore Germain, flagman; Ernest Saint Cyr, 1st chainman; Thomas Deschatelet, 2nd chainman; Dolphis Letentre, Ernest Constantin, Henry Calleho, Chs Joachim, Jos Fergusson, Mellon Campbell - laborers; Eugene Clairmont, cook.

(Items 1 and 2 above were obtained from Director, Land Survey Branch, Alberta Bureau of Surveying & Mapping, Edmonton, Alta.)

3. <u>J.S. Young</u>, 8 September, 1923, Leighmore, Alta to <u>GSA</u> c/o Education Office, Victoria, BC:

I wired the Teachers' Bureau accepting you to teach the Kelly Lake School if you wished to take it. I want to let you know what kind of a place and school this is. In the first place, this school will be all "Breeds", starting to school for the first time and not many can talk English. The people around here are mostly all "Breeds" and trappers. It is about 60 miles from Grande Prairie railroad station. You would have to batch. I stay there most of the winter buying fur. So if you would care to live in a place of this kind, it would be alright to come. I could meet you at Grande Prairie if you write me when you will be there, or wire to Beaverlodge. I had a friend here that wanted to get the school, but he didnt have a teacher's certificate for BC, and couldnt get a permit to teach it*. Yours truly, Jim Young [* Fred Barber, see Chapter 2].

4. <u>J.L. Watson</u>, 11 September, 1923, Education Office, Victoria, BC to <u>GSA</u> c/o F.W. Haggman, New Westminster, BC:

Dear Sir: I beg to advise you that confirmation of your appointment to the Kelly Lake School has just been received from J.S. Young, Secretary of the School Board.

Mr. Young advises that school will not be opened until October 1st. Will you kindly make the necessary arrangements to report for duty on that date.

It would be advisable for you to notify Mr. Young by telegram, addressed to Beaverlodge, Alberta, the time of your arrival.

Kindly acknowledge receipt of this letter. Yours very truly, J.L. Watson, Registrar.

5. <u>GSA</u>, 13 September, 1923, New Westminster, BC, to <u>J.S. Young</u>, Beaverlodge, Alta., (telegram):

Leaving New Westminster for Edmonton/Will arrive Grande
Prairie 21 September 4:45 pm/Thence will proceed to Pouce
Coupe/Wire me here if not correct route for Kelly Lake
School. Gerald S. Andrews.

6. S.J. Willis, 17 November, 1923, Education Office, Victoria,
   BC to GSA, c/o J. Young, Leighmore PO, Alta:

Dear Sir: I beg to acknowledge receipt of your letter of
the 31st ultimo. I am pleased to note that satisfactory
progress is being made at Kelly Lake School and I hope
that you will be able to maintain at least the minimum
attendance required under the School Act. Your salary
cheque for October has already been forwarded to you.
Yours very truly, S.J. Willis, Superintendent of Education.

7. A.T. Andrews (Druggist), Elgin, Man, 8 December, 1923 to
   GSA, Kelly Lake, BC (quite heavily abridged):

It has been great to receive your ... letters ...

First: Your snaps [photos] are going forward ... by parcel
post today. This has been a busy week getting our Xmas
displays ready. Have kept 7 negatives and 3 or 4 prints,
but will make them up to you. Am getting 3 of them enlarged [and] will have two of them mounted for Mrs.
Andrews for Xmas. They will hang in our rooms to enjoy.
You have a wonderful collection of snaps — those mountains
and valleys make me a little homesick for BC and my old
trips across — 4 times yearly.

Second: I'm sorry that one of your parcels did not arrive
— and hoping it will have reached you ere this...

Third: I am replacing the missing articles. I missed your
birthday, old top. The missing sox will have to do for
your birthday, and these two for your Xmas. Wish you could
help eat our Xmas turkey. We'll be thinking of all our
dear children that day ...

Fourth: I'm sending the "Deccaphone" [small portable
gramophone] by Xpress ... Most of the records we are
sending are old numbers. The Indians may be so taken with
the machine that the tribe will buy it. Mr. Burdex, Pres
of the Hockey & Baseball Clubs, suggests that you say
nothing to the children about it. Then get it all ready —
hide it behind your desk and start the 'bally' thing going
and watch their faces — I'd like to be peeking...

Ger, I'm so glad you are helping those fellows apart from
your school work. That's 'playing the game'. As we serve
so shall we score in the great 'tally' of Life's Game.

Say, Ger, what is the climate like? What time daylight and
dark, say, the day you answer this so I can compare. Also

what kind of country is it where you are? Where is your nearest Dr and Preacher? and Druggist? Do you use coal-oil lamps or candles? soap or brick to wash with — who makes your bread. Where do you go Saturdays & Sundays? What's her name? Perhaps she is dark-skinned? Your Loving Father, A.T. Andrews. PS: ... Send me a snap of your rabbit skin sleeping robe.

8. G.H. Gower, 12 March, 1924 — School Inspector's Report:

EDUCATION DEPARTMENT	BRITISH COLUMBIA	INSPECTION OF SCHOOLS

School Kelly Lake Div. Teacher Gerald S. Andrews

Training Normal, Vancouver Certificate Sec. Class Experience 1 year

Enrolled 13; Boys 9; Girls 4; Present 13

Grade I 11; II 2; III ; IV   Tone Good   Control Good

(Good, fair, etc.) (Good, fair, etc.)

V ; VI ; VII ; VIII   Character of teaching Satisfactory

(Satisfactory, unsatisfactory, etc.)

If character of teaching not satisfactory, state reasons here

Sanitary condition The school in this district occupies a portion of a large log building.

Janitor work

Desks The classroom is neither well lighted nor ventilated,

Maps   Standing of School The children in this district are "half breeds".

If teacher now in charge not responsible for present standing of school, explain here

and there is but a small area of slated canvas blackboard. When the school opened last

Blackboards

Water-closets There are no regular school closets. Home-made desks are

Water-supply

Grounds in use. Water is available.

October, for the first time, hardly a child had any knowledge of the English Language. Under Mr. Andrews

The regular set of maps, supplied by the Department, is in the school.

Progress of pupils

(Satisfactory, unsatisfactory, etc.)

Subjects of special merit the children are acquiring a knowledge of the Language and are progressing favourably

Buildings

Subjects of special defect

along other lines. Mr. Andrews is well adapted to work of this

Special remarks type. He has an abundance of

patience and shows skill in the teaching and management of non-English speaking pupils. His work in this district is very

Special remarks commendable.

March 12, 1924. , 19

G H Gower

Inspector of Schools.

8M-923-3007

246

9. G.H. Gower, 22 March, 1924, Prince George, BC to GSA, Leighmore, Alta:

> Dear Mr. Andrews: Will you kindly fill in your name and age on the enclosed application form for the examination. In remarks state the subjects you are writing on. With best wishes, G.H. Gower.

10. Registrar, 17 June, 1924, Victoria, BC to GSA c/o J.S. Young, Leighmore, via Beaverlodge, Alta (telegram):

> Application and fee received. Letter containing instructions and receipt forwarded May seventh. Arrangements made for you to take your examination at Rolla. You should be present at Rolla not later than nine on Monday, June twenty third. Registrar.

11. S.J. Willis, 18 September, 1924, Education office, Victoria, BC to GSA, Leighmore, Alta:

> Dear Sir: I beg to acknowledge receipt of your letter of the 2nd instant, enclosing the minutes of the Kelly Lake School meeting. Yours very truly, S.J. Willis, Superintendent of Education.

> Editorial Note: The above "report" could have been a "prize" item. Attempts to recover it from departmental records have been futile.

12. GSA, 10 October, 1924, Kelly Lake, BC, to Nora E. Andrews (sister, probably teaching at Bow Island, Alta):

> Dear Nora: I have just dismissed my 'evening class' consisting of four lusty dusky fellows of 18, 19, 23 [Johnny Calliou] and 28 [Isidore Gladu] years. The last two married and raising families. It is about 10:30 pm. You see we have a night class once a week for these four ambitious fellows who want to learn to read, write and figure. Perhaps I can get them started anyway.

> School is going nicely and I am in hopes of sticking it out for another year ... There are 17 enrolled now and they keep me quite occupied, quite a bunch of beginners — who cant speak anything but Cree. My last year's bunch are doing nicely though. The Inspector was due out last month but hasnt shown up yet. I hope he is blind in one eye and cross-eyed in the other.

> Last month slipped by pretty quickly, but it gets a bit lonely, as Jim Young hasnt come back yet. Expect him soon now and he'll be welcome believe me! He has some land near Empress [Red Deer, Alta] and took a trip down to see it, or sell it.

I wrote five exams for the Senior Matric last June and got by in each, but pretty low in two (just a 'pass'), however I made my average. Next year I will have four — Geometry, Chemistry, Algebra and History. With the same luck I'll get my full Senior Matric and a First Class Teacher's licence for BC, also full entrance to any science faculty at Varsity, or 2nd year 'Arts'. It will mean a lot of work this winter but its worth it. ...

Spent a lot of money, which should have been earning interest, on that trip to Vancouver by car with Jim Young. If I had only had the sense to come back here when he arrived at Vanderhoof with the horses, I would have had a swell summer and an economical one. But — the second lap to Vancouver by 'Tin Lizzie' — Wow! it cost money. Things are better this year tho'. Last year I taught nine months getting $1,188. This year is scheduled for 10 months for $1,320. I should save a thousand bucks of that.

Guess you think I went to Vancouver just to see a girl ...

Well — me for bed. Tomorrow (Saturday) must get a cord of wood sawn up. Its been almost winter since 21st September. Over half of the crops are still uncut and the recent snow I'm afraid will flatten them beyond redemption. It looks horrible to see a stretch of 60 to 100 acres of swell green oats standing with snow around and patches lying flat, beaten down. Its been so wet they simply couldnt get it cut. Best love Nora — Gerry. PS: 15 October '24: Jim arrived last night and returns to Leighmore tomorrow, so will get this ready to go. He brought yours of the 29th [September] and your parcel — pickles, jelly, the shirt and anchovy. They are slick, haven't eaten all of it yet. Say what is this — Xmas or birthday? Now, Nora, you must quit sending shirts to me! I have lots of money and can buy my own — and some for you if you need them. ... Best love, Gerry.

13. <u>GSA</u>, 10 January, 1925, Kelly Lake, BC to <u>Nora E. Andrews</u> (as above), Bow Island, Alta:

If I dont acknowledge my Xmas mail now, will have to frame an apology for each letter for being so slow — and my Xmas mail was no small one! Yours from Gull Lake [Sask] was a treat ... You are lucky to be close enough to spend Xmas with the family there [our oldest sister, Mrs Leila Rennie] ... when time and money are so hard to get. Last summer's escapades cost me over 300 bucks, and hadn't planned to spend more than 100. In the long run it was worth it ...

Your book and Bill's [our brother] ... were fine ... A book is a great solace when so far removed from civilization. My [Xmas] holiday was spent on the run, all over the country here, but now in settled solitude I can turn the pages and with them many a lonely hour.

The day before Christmas I hiked to Peavine Lake — 15 miles north, where Alec Anderson lives. Xmas Eve in a trapper's cabin, listening to his stories of youthful pranks in good auld Scotland — between these and smokes, my mind travelled far in time and space — to you and Ed [Rennie, brother-in-law] fixing up in good style for the kids next morning [our sister, Leila had just had her 3rd son on 21 December 1924], then to Elgin [Manitoba, where our father was living] and to 80 Balmoral Place [Winnipeg, our childhood home] — I was very happy!

Christmas morning, before daylight, Alec, the trapper and I started off to Swan Lake, 9 miles farther north. It was a good walk, and we got to Frank Ward's just in time for our 'trappers' Xmas Dinner — a goose, nuts and candy — and bushels of jollity. Our nine-mile appetite didn't leave much of the goose. Alec, Ward and Miller, all bachelors & trappers, are fine men. In the afternoon we took turns running down to the lake to catch fish through the ice. I got three dandies. About 6 o'clock all four of us tramped over to "Boone" Taylor's. His good wife had invited us for the evening meal. Here — more goose, turkey, plum pudding, Xmas cake — such a feed! They have five girls (the youngest, less than a year old) and it was really home-like. Their radio brought in Carols from everywhere, including Winnipeg. At midnight we staggered back to Ward's cabin to hit the hay till daylight. It was a great Xmas! On Xmas Day a year ago, Jim Young and I drove 40 miles from Grande Prairie to Leighmore in a bitterly cold wind — but were rewarded by having a good dinner with the Beadle family.

My school is nicely under way again but the old building is rather chilly on coldest days. Am alone tonight [Saturday]. Jim was due last Wednesday but has been delayed, I guess. Did a little exploring today — out to Crooked Lake on snowshoes — six miles from here. Had not been there before. Took about four hours there and back. I enjoy getting out into the air and snow after a week shut up in the school room. We had our "Xmas Celebration" for the school after New Year, because when we closed school for the holiday, none of the fathers and big brothers had returned from their trap lines. Am learning some Cree, but very slowly. It is hard to learn unless one lives right in their homes with them. It is inflected, like Latin, for plurals, prepositions etc, eg: kootsoowaguns = match; kootsoowagunsa matches; napayo = man; napayoic = men.

Last Fall I didn't do much studying, but now must brace up and work — work — work! Will write three papers next June — History, Algebra and Geometry. The last two a bit hard to plug alone, but it must be done. I must have the Senior Matric for entrance to Medicine or any scientific course ... Write soon ... with Love, Gerry.

14. G.H. Gower, 5 May, 1925, Prince George, BC to GSA, Teacher, Kelly Lake School, Leighmore, Alta:

Dear Mr. Andrews: Mr. Hull of Rolla has advised me that you desire to write the Algebra and History Examinations of the Senior Matriculation Course, in June at Rolla. I have notified the Sup't of Education to that effect. Kindest regards, Yours very truly, G.H. Gower, Inspector of Schools.

15. Clarence I. Cover, 18 May, 1925, Jesmond, BC to GSA, Leighmore, Alta:

Dear Gerry: Yours of recent date at hand and very glad to hear from you once more. Guess you didnt get my last epistle. You can get your old job back again and we will be glad to have you. We were all glad to hear you would come back. I will look for you here any time you can make it and will be glad to shake your old fist once more. I will register this so you will be sure to get it.

Everybody is busy as the typical cat. Those that are not working are fighting mosquitoes. By golly the skeeters are to thick they are like a dust storm. I am afraid it is going to be a dry year, and I am dry-farming again this year. We ought to have a good garden, as I have one that I can irrigate now. Will feed you on dutch cheese greens and young turkey when you get here, maybe a bean or two also. Living mostly on eggs now. Mrs. Coldwell went to the Coast to get her teeth fixed and Harry has to stay home, so I am carrying the mail for him this week. Well, so long Gerry. Will tell you the rest when you get here. Drop me a line now and again if you can. Yours, Clarence Cover. PS Glad you got such a good report, but you didnt need to send me no report, dogone you, I know you can teach, C-C. P.P.S. Millie and the kids send best regards.

Editorial Note: A previous letter from Cover, now lost, advised that they were planning to re-activate the Big Bar Creek School, and urged me to apply for the job as teacher. My reply in the affirmative is also lost.

16. GSA, 22 May, 1925, Kelly Lake, BC (via Leighmore PO, Alta) to Sup't Education, Victoria, BC:

Dear Sir: I have today received word from Mr. G.H. Gower, Inspector of Schools at Prince George, that I should be able to write the Algebra and History Examinations of the Senior Matriculation Course, in June at Rolla.

I enclose a Bank Money Order for the amount of Five Dollars in payment of fees.

Work on the subjects on which I wish to write has been by private study, while active in the teaching profession.

17. <u>Clarence I. Cover</u>, 14 June, 1925, Jesmond, BC to <u>GSA</u>, Jasper, Alta (?):

Dear Gerry: Yours of recent date at hand, was sure glad to hear you would be drifting along. I have been working on the road for the gov't for a while, and just got home.

The crops are almost a failure on the Mountain this year. I may not have any. This is one awful dry year here. No rain all summer. If you want to sell your horses up there, Bernice has a good colt that is 3, coming 4, that she said you could have for $25. He is bright sorrel with a white face, weight 1000 lbs. Of course there are plenty of others around here you can get, but they vary in price from $10 up. I think you will have plenty of kids for the school, as the Big Bar Mountain school will be closed this year, and some of them will be coming down here. Millie (that is my worst half) says she is going to board you, and do your washing for $25 per month. You can batch tho' if you want to. We can fix you up a cabin that I have got started.

Hope you have a great trip and we will look for you when we see you. With kind regards I remain your, in haste, Clarence Cover. Will give you all the news when you arrive. CC.

18. <u>Jim Young</u>, 19 October, 1925 Leighmore, Alta to <u>GSA</u>, at Jesmond, BC:

I just returned and got your letter. Glad to see you got over that trail alive and like your place there. McCormack sent all your stuff to Clinton, and the shipping bill, I think he said was $9.20, but I expect you got it by now. John Third didnt take the Kelly Lake School, they have a woman there, Mrs. Easton. I think it is the woman that taught the North Swan Lake School last year. She is living in the Calliou house and teaching there. I am going up to Maggie's to get the sorrel horse and will call at Kelly Lake to see how everything is going.

I got a letter and some pictures from Homer Wright. He is at Corvan, Montana. He is waiting for you to write him where you are. I will write again soon when I get back from Kelly Lake, Maggie's and Swan Lake. Your Friend Jim.

19. <u>Ed Johnston</u>, 4 November, 1925, Dewey, BC to <u>GSA</u>, at Jesmond, BC:

Dear Friend: I suppose by this time you will think me dead or worse. I went to Nazko & several other places. Have also been out to Burns Lake. I seen lots of lakes but as a fact, every place looked so dismal, so far away from home I have practically given up the idea of Fur Ranching. Was on my way to Chilliwack valley in hopes of starting a poultry ranch, when I met a man who wanted me to run an engine in a sawmill. I took the job, and am here now and expect to be for some time. I hope you made Big Bar OK and found everything as you expected. This is a hurried scrape, but if you answer I will give you more particulars. Perhaps you will send me a few photos, and would you kindly send me Mr. McClements' address. I may go back to Peace River. I sold all the horses. Ed.

20. <u>Alec Anderson</u>, 27 November, 1925, Peavine Lake (Tupper, BC) to <u>GSA</u>, Jesmond, BC:

I received your welcome letter a few weeks ago. Would have written you sooner, but have been waiting on Jim Young, but he has never arrived here yet. Frank Ward and Jim came from Edmonton together and had a big celebration. That was about 1st October. He told Frank not to take much grub up, as he was coming up next week with a load of grub for Frank Miller and myself. I have got my traps set but nothing yet. We have had such bad trapping weather. Frank got some $60 worth two weeks ago. He was on his trap line before me. [Jim had waited for the muskegs to freeze, see No 22 below.]

Now to tell you about my summer's work. Boon Taylor was foreman for Jack Fynn at Swan Lake, haying, so I worked for him there for 5 weeks, then I went on the road work 13 miles west of Rolla, toward Fort St. John, then I came to Pouce Coupe. Bob Baxter wanted me to go haying for him for two weeks. So you see I had lots of work, but have not all my money yet. Boon was foreman at Gundy's after he left Jack's for the harvest. He is not into his new house yet. He has got the doors and windows in. It was not all plastered when I was out two weeks ago. He might get into it soon. Mrs. Taylor says to tell you that she sure wished you were here to eat some of her Christmas dinner. Frank wished to be remembered to you. I forgot to tell Mrs. Fynn you were asking kindly for her. I cant tell you much about the Kelly Lake School. All I know is that "Ma" Easton went there, but whether she stayed, unable to tell you. From your old friend, A Anderson. PS Ed Miller was not come when I was in.

21. <u>Homer E. Wright</u>, 8 December, 1925, Springfield, Oregon, to <u>GSA</u>, Jesmond, BC:

Dear Gerry: I had better make my promise good now, as you have yours. You will think I've been a long time answering your letter, but I just received it the other day. It has been chasing me all over the continent. I heard from J.S. Young twice. He said he hadnt heard from you yet. If I had known where you were I would have come up to see you, as I was in Seattle for six weeks and doing nothing. I am working in Eugene now as a carpenter's helper. Have a better job in sight. Eugene is three miles from Springfield, so I drive to and from my work. Eugene is a pretty little town with quite a nice population. I would like to have been with you on the rest of the trip, and I might as well have gone as I have lost a lot of time anyway. Yes, I am in the land of cheap tobacco and expensive booze, but if Jimmy comes down to see me I will have a little whisky for him just the same.

Those snaps were good. You will have to wait until I write again for the snaps I promised, as I just sent all I had printed to Jim Young. I have three rolls to develop yet. How is Mike, my old dog? You didnt mention him in your letter. Wish I had brought him with me. I suppose you have lots of snow. We dont have any here. The people are planting their gardens already. Write soon. As ever, your old friend, H.E. Wright.

22. <u>Jim Young</u>, 9 December, 1925, Kelly Lake to <u>GSA</u>, Jesmond, BC:

Dear Gerry: I wrote you a note some time ago telling you I would write later. I am buying fur again, have put in a few days here. Mrs. Easton the woman that taught at North Swan Lake last year, has the school. She seems to like it here alright. She is living and teaching in the Calliou house you used last year. She is a pretty good old girl. She bakes bread for me when I am here. Miss Ryan got the Pouce Coupe School. John Third didnt want the Kelly Lake School. He is still at Grande Prairie. I havent seen Alec Anderson. I heard he got your letter. The muskegs are not frozen enough to travel that way yet. We havent much winter here so far. Frank Ward is back trapping at Swan Lake. Sarah and Zen [?] Gauthier got married. Did you ever hear from Homer. He was wondering why you never wrote him. He is in Oregon now. I am driving that horse of his I sent back, and the little sorrel we left at Maggie's. If you still have that key would you mail it to me. I gave a key to John Third before we left here and he lost it. I never heard from Ed Johnston. How did you like him to travel with? You fellows must have had some trip through there.

I would like to be down in that country with you and try those fellows' good moonshine. Could you buy me a cheap farm and get me a good woman there, and I'd be right down. I might leave here after New Years. Everything is the same in Red Willow, and no news. Wishing you a Merry Christmas, Your Friend, Jim. PS I asked the kids how they liked this teacher and they all said we like Gerry better!

23. George Emmila (Hamelin), 10 December, 1925, Kelly Lake to GSA, Jesmond, BC:

Mr. Andrews, Jesmond, BC. Dear Teacher: Just a few lines to let you know we going to school again. The teacher is Mrs. Easton. I beleav you know her. I am in grad 3 now. We start school in October I think. This teacher is good to me. I did not get wepping yet. I get three weppings from you but it makes no defrence, I like you all saim, teacher.

I like this teacher too. Teacher will go away about next week to Edmonton. I did not kill any weasles this winter. I diden trap very will this winter, ther is no snow in Kelly Lake. The snow is all milts. I bean sent you letter but you did not get it. I think this one I would like it if you get this letter. Send me letter Pleace soon as you get the letter. I killed 37 rats, that is all of I kill. The rats is not so good price as last winter. big rats cost 85 sentce, small ones is 60 sentce. That is all of I could send you today, so good bye. Your boy, George Emmila.

24. Leo Allgeier, 22 December, 1925, Dunster, BC to GSA, Jesmond, BC:

Dear Friend: I will write a few lines to you. I had a very fine trip last Fall hunting. We had very good luck. Plenty of rain, but one fine outfit to work with an good horses. I have not heard from Johnston. I guess he has forgotten me. I hope not. That was one fine colt I got from him, it weighs one 12-hundred weight. Thanks very much for the pictures. I have some of you taken at my place. Will send you some at a later date, as I am going to the coast for a trip. I think I will have a very interesting trip to write you about on my return. I have traded my big horse, the one I was looking for when I went part of the way with you on the trail. I got a fine saddle horse weighs about eleven eighty. The trail isnt too long for him. I expect to have a bear party of my own next Spring. I sure got some fine pictures of the grizzly last Spring. Well, so long. I will write more next time, have been so busy since coming home. Leo Allgeier. Merry Xmas.

25. George White, (January) 1926, Rio Grande, Alberta to GSA, Jesmond, BC:

Dear Gerry: I write you a few lines in answer to your letter Thank you ever so much for the snapshot. I wish you a Happy Christmas and a Prosperous New Year, and all kinds of good luck for the coming new year. I came back to Rio Grande about the 1st October from Jasper. I did not do too badly for the time I was there at Jasper. I might go back again next summer. Wright never sent me any of his snapshots. I never heard from him. Wright's dog followed me all the time this summer, and when I left Jasper, the darn dog got on the train. The conductor was going to put him off, so I took pity on him and bought a ticket to ride. I have him yet on the homestead, he is only an ornament but has a home etc.

I have only seen Jim Young once since he came back, and that was when he got his horse. I say, Gerry, they have got a lady teacher up at Kelly lake this winter, so Jim stays up there most of his time! Did you keep your promise not to take any more beer? I suppose you forgot all about that day — such is Life in the Far West! Have you ever heard from Johnston? I wonder what he is doing — I suppose drinking beer as long as the money lasts. I hope these lines will find you in the best of health, as it leaves me at present. Believe me, Yours truly, George White.

26. <u>Pete Stuart</u>, 30 January, 1926, Brainard to <u>GSA</u>, Jesmond, BC:

Dear Friend: Glad to get your card. I was at Brainard Christmas so was Maggie and H. Fielding. Mac and Jack were at Kelly Lake. The Breeds are putting a road to that lake up in the Monkman pass for fish. You might write a piece for a Vancouver Paper about the resources and trade they could get if they built the PGE through to the Peace. You can do it if you try. We have no snow this winter. They have a lady teacher in your place. Jim is looking after her. He says he is going to leave here. Silvertip Campbell was here going over to Kelly Lake. McKenzie King is a wash-out. I voted for the Conservative. Have you got any girls over there? Brainards have a radio, works good. Trappers are doing well this winter. Harry DeGrott has just started to skate to Hythe, down the creek — some trip! The SSB [Soldier Settlement Board] knocked 40% of any loan for stock. I am going to try to make a stake next summer, to go to the Old Country. This is no life for a young fellow, so think I would like a trip. Not much new — going over to Jim one of these days. Well, best of luck, Yours truly, Pete Stuart.

27. <u>Alec Anderson</u>, 21 February, 1926 Peavine Lake, BC to <u>GSA</u>, at Jesmond, BC:

Mr. Andrews: I received your welcome Christmas Card alright, but sure missed you at Christmas. We had no

Christmas dinner this year, we was so poor. Frank Ward was out on his trap line, but he got in that night, and I was at Peavine. Taylors are into the new house at Christmas. He is trapping rats at Fynn's place now. He gave Jack a horse and colt to trap. Al Miller did not come up this year. Only Frank.

Well Gerry, trapping was poor this year, sometimes a lot of snow and went away and bared our traps. That was in the Fall, but still we made good. Frank got 31 coyotes, some mink and about 40 weasels. I got 23 coyotes, 12 weasels, 5 rats and 1 lynx just last week. Alfred, Urbain and other three went to Pouce Coupe, a week today, and came back on Wednesday forenoon to my place, and got the lynx in one of my traps and brought it in to me, skinned it and cooked it and had a big feed and 2 or 3 bottles with them — had a great time. Alfred Gladu said he liked Ma Easton fine, but the children told Jim they liked Gerry best. Well, that is about all the news I have to tell you this time. Mrs Fynn wished to be remembered to you. I think I will have a big catch of rats in the spring. This leaves me in the best of health, hoping to find you the same. I am your aff. A Anderson.

28. <u>Herbert E. Drake</u>, 2 October, 1926 at Tupper Creek, BC to <u>GSA</u>, at Toronto (U of T):

Dear Gerry: Well here I am away up in the backwoods trying to earn my daily bread by imparting knowledge to several of the Swan Lake dumbells. Everything has been going shipshape so far although I thought for a while I might have to close the school down owing to lack of pupils. However I have 9 going now, so that everything is OK for the present.

I received the swell thermometer this week and certainly appreciate your thoughtfulness, Gerry. It is a thing that was most certainly needed. I hope the mercury doesnt get "bawled up" according to the way Coldwell described it. Rather cold weather then isnt it?

We've been having both good and bad weather to date. We've had a couple of snowfalls but it has all gone now. I have three of Boone Taylor's youngsters (one is 15), for pupils. Then another girl by the name of Reid is 17 — a regular high school, eh? Mrs. Fynn is sure some old girl isn't she? She treated me very kindly while I was there, but just the same she is one in a thousand, n'est ce pas? A fellow from Rolla by the name of Denny Cornock wishes to be remembered to you.

I havent seen Jim Young, but I met one of his sidekicks on the train. I dont remember his name, but he knew you, and paid you a rare compliment. Hold your hat on now old top.

Ive been to almost every place around here except Kelly Lake. Mrs. Easton is over there again this year.

I'm staying with Paynters at present. They have a cute little daughter of 17 and of course, we take a row on the lake now and again. Well Gerry, write soon. Kindest regards, Bert.

29. Tim Finn, 19 January, 1927, Leighmore, Alta to GSA, (U of T): Toronto:

To Friend Gerrie: I just thought I would drop you a line to find out how you are getting along down in that civilized country. Dont you get lonesome for the howl of the coyotes? We are having a very mild winter, no snow of any account and hardly ever below zero, but the thermometer has dropped pretty low this last few days. I was kind of surprised when I got your card — thanks for thinking of us. I see Jim Young quite often, every week or two. He is buying lots of fur. All the farmers around here have been making quite a killing on coyotes this winter. They have been very plentiful. I suppose you have been reading about the boost the Peace River is getting this year. There has been a bumper crop. The road is always lined with teams hauling grain. They keep the elevators at Wembley plugged up all the time. When do you think you will be coming west? I know you will be back sometime. If ever you come around this way, dont forget the number.

I should go down there this winter, but cant get away as Bill is on the road, and we are not near done hauling yet. I have a sister living in Toronto that I have not seen for years and years. She is thinking of coming out here next summer. Her name is Mrs. John Barrett, address 37 Bloor Street East. I thought sometime if you are not busy you might drop in and let her know you seen us and what kind of country this is. Well, guess I will ring off, so Goodbye — Drop a line sometime. Yours truly, Tim Finn.

30. George Emmila (Hamelin), 3 March, 1927 at Kelly Lake, BC (Goodfare PO, Alta) to GSA, at Toronto (U of T):

Mr. G.S. Andrews, Big Bear Kreek, BC. Dear Theacher: you donte know wow happy as I am when I get your letter come. My Father he sick bad, But he getten better. he is gone to the mountains. they kill lots of fur But fur diden worth nothing. A big coyot cost $4 and rats 90¢. That is good prise and mink is good prise to. My Grande Father is not hom now. he will com sune I think teacher. he kill not very much fur. That is all for my Grande Father.

The ice is not very strong. It is not frozen hard this winter. But we have skating all winter. It is very good to skate now at Kelly Lake. I have a good pair of skates Teacher gave me and she gave hus knifes. She gave ten boys. Mr. Young is not home to he go to the grande Prairie he will come back last of this week. I ask for a suite of clothes for me. It is no snow in here. It is gone be summer soon. We will play ball soons. now that you left Adolphus lost the ball. I like this teacher. Adolphus get about six whipings. I get one times strap. Theacher hit me both hands about five times each hand. That is all for today Theacher so good bye. send me a letter soon as you get my letter Please. Your loving boy George Emmila.

Editorial Note: George's unedited letters are interesting in that they demonstrate his command of written English, after little more than 3 years' schooling, starting with Cree only – his mother tongue – and no literate home influence whatever. He was probably 15 years of age at this time, and may have already begun to go trapping, with his elders. The scrawled date on his letter might have been interpreted as 1929, but by that time, Jim Young had given up his store at Kelly Lake, and Mrs. Easton did not stay there after midsummer, 1927, so I have decided on the earlier date, 1927. George was one of the brighter pupils, and I became very fond of him. His address for me at "Big Bear Kreek" instead of Big Bar Creek is interesting. The letter must have been forwarded to me in Toronto. George's phonetics are perhaps better than his spelling.

31. Alec Anderson, 26 January, 1928 at Peavine Lake (Tupper Creek, BC) to GSA, Toronto:

Peavine Castle, BC, Jan 26 1928/ Dear Gerry: I received your most welcome letter some time, but never got to answer it, but here goes. I have got no teacher coming to see me now. The teacher at Kelly lake has only [one] leg and crutches. He is a Frenchman [Joseph Lionel Marion]. Jim Young is still on the go, but he has no store at Kelly Lake this year. He went up to Kelly Lake before he came to me, and stopped two days there. He took some mail to the teacher but he never asked him to eat nor stay all night, so he went over to Milton Campbell and eat and sleep, so that was a change for Jim. He bought about $600 fur then he came to me, but he found Peavine Castle the same.

Mrs. Fynn is away from the Ranch now. It is a Mr and Mrs. Dow that is for the winter, but they are different to Mrs. Fynn. They just came in last summer. I was out there to a dance last week. They told me Jack Fynn said he had an offer for the ranch he thought he would take, but he had to the first of May to think it over. I think it is Jim Young, but dont say anything to let you know. Bert Drake was at the dance and Girlie Taylor and Ruth, but not their Mother. I was surprised. Frank Ward did not come up this winter. I think he went out the last time for good. If Jim gets the ranch, Frank would come and run the store for him. I only think it is Jim. Well, we had some winter, the last two months was a Devil. Now it had milded up, I hope for the rest of the winter.

Trapping has been bum so far, too cold, too much snow, but there was very little fur, more linx than anything else. I am feeling alright again. I will be able to go out in the spring as good as ever. I will draw to a close this time, as this leaves me in the best of health, hoping to find you the same. From your old Friend A. Anderson, Tupper Creek, BC. Write soon before I go to work and I will let you know if it is Jim, for he will not write — ha ha!.

32. <u>Herbert E. Drake</u>, 24 November, 1928 at Tupper Creek, BC to <u>GSA</u>, Toronto:

Dear Gerry: Hello there old chap. I'll bet you've been thinking that yours truly has side-tracked you, but far be it. As you see I'm back at Swan Lake expounding and impounding knowledge to my old set of habitual knot-heads. Such are the vagaries of Life, eh?

Suppose you are back at Varsity soaking up more knowledge about trees etc. Well, I wish I were there to give you a hand at it. It is a good thing you didn't take up the show proposition, because financially it was a pure flop. However, we all had a wonderful trip of it and learned a lot in the bargain. By gosh, Gerry but it sure is fun fooling the public with those tricks. My stage experience gave me a lot more confidence in myself than I could ever get any other way. Our show went over well in every town we played, even in places the size of Grande Prairie. However, the way things panned out, I'll be about ready for Varsity when you're through it a couple of years.

I didn't get home this summer at all. We went as far east as Wainwright and as far south as Red Deer — all of it by car. Say, Gerry if you ever come back up here, you should come by car. It is sure a great trip. We shipped from McLennan to Smith.

I haven't heard from Big Bar for a long time. If I get home next summer I think I'll try and motor up there from Penticton. It wouldn't be so much that way. My folks are still there, but Dad is running the Arena now instead of the orchard.

Alec is back from harvesting and is busy on his trap line. We both went up to Pouce Coupe last Sat morning and we had to hoof it almost all the way, almost there when we got a lift with a truck.

Myself and another chap are trapping weasels on the side, and I get a great kick out of it. Alec is going to sell the fur for us. The country is just lousy with the little rats. We are trapping them from the bridge down to the lake.

Jimmy Young is up North around Fort St. John I believe. I haven't seen him since we staged our show at Fort St. John Sports. He saw it while there.

We have had almost a month of skating on the lake. I've been skating up and back every morning. It sure is great exercise. Mrs. Paynter died the other day in Vancouver. Also Mr. Strong, Mrs. Fynn's father died about a month ago, and on the day of the funeral their house was destroyed by fire. They sure had bad luck all at once. Boone is still the same old fellow, getting bigger around, if anything. I have Girlie in grade VIII.

Well now Gerry I trust this will make up a bit for lost time. I know you are busy but drop me a line the first chance you get. Your sincere chum, Bert. PS: Alec has just come in, 10:30 am. He says for Christ sake to write him. He lost your address. Alec says he has a son-of-a-bitch of a cold, whatever that is. Excuse the language, but that's the way he put it.

33. <u>George Emmilia (Hamelin)</u>, no date (probably early 1928) to <u>GSA</u>, Toronto:

Dear Teacher, Mr. G.S. Andrews: Just a few lines to let you know I am going to mountains tomorrow morning. I have been at mountains twice with my brother so I dinent go to school not very good this winter. But I am going to school when other teacher comes, so I and not good writer yet. I am excuse with my writing I am sorry I cannot write good, mabe you will trow away my letter. That is all for that. My dade dinit kill much fur this winter because my little sister was sick. She is juss a bow two months old. She isn't very strong yet so goodby. If you write me I will tell you lots of things about Kelly Lake now. Please send me letter soon as you get my letter. I am very loonsome with you. Your strolly Mr George Emmila.

34. <u>Alec Anderson</u>, 28 January, 1929, Tupper Creek, BC to <u>GSA</u>, Toronto:

Peavine Castle Jan 28 1929 Dear Gerry: I received your letter some time ago and pleased to see you are in good health. You may think I have been slow in writing but I was waiting till I got the school teachers lined up, so I could let you know. First Bert Drake went to Dawson Creek.

Second the Kelly Lake one-legged fellow took Bert's school. They have not got to Kelly Lake yet. They have started the school at the South end of Swan Lake. It is a Miss Pearl Flint a hard name, but think she is a nice girl, only 20, but big. It is a Miss Grimmett that went to Rolla for head teacher. I saw the teacher for Fort St. John, a Miss Richard. She had long legs and her skirts was 4 inches above her knees.

Now Gerry, I was down at Clarmont last summer working with Al Miller. He has half a section now. I put in about 5 months with him, but must say he was the hardest man I ever worked for. I stooked 180 acres, daylight to sundown. I never did that before. I left in Sept and went to Pouce Coupe to get my winter grub, so I met Jim Young there. He just come Hudson Hope. He took up a homestead there. Grimmet and son, C Third from Goodfare was here hunting for 5 days, only got 3 moose. Third told me that Kelly Lake was dead to what it used to be. Half of the breeds has left last summer. They had smallpox. But lot of children yet for a teacher. Bert Drake asked me to have Christmas dinner with him, but with him going away, it fell threw, so I will just wait till Gerry comes back. Bill Cundiff sold out to a Mr. Cowell Colleson, sold over the Lake, I dont know who to. Jack Fynn sold the Borden ranch to Austin. He keeps a store 6 miles northeast of Pouce Coupe. Boone Taylor is still in the same place. Austin takes the place over first April, so we will have a store. Jack Fynn's wife is looking [after?] the place for the last 12 months. Old Mrs. Fynn is keeping house for Jack at Pouce Coupe. Trapping has been poor, only 70 weasels, 10 rats, as yet, up to New Year, no snow and little frost, but we have got the snow now. This is all the news, leaves me in the best of health, hopes to find you the same. From your old trapper A Anderson. Tupper Creek, BC.

35. Alec Anderson, 22 January, 1930, Tupper Creek, BC to GSA, Toronto:

Mr. Andrews: I received your welcome Card on Christmas Day and pleased to see from it you were in good health, and getting finished with your course this year and perhaps get up to the Peace River this summer and see us all. I saw Bert [Drake] when I came down from Rolla after finishing harvest and thrashing and he told me how near he was to you, and did not see you. He said he had a good trip. He seems to get along good at Dawson [Creek], the people like him well. I am still at Peavine Lake. We have had some very cold weather. I haven't been out at Tupper Creek this year. I spent a good Christmas cutting my wood. I went out to get Boone Taylor to come and haul it. It got so cold it took him 10 days before he came. But I had lots of wood over from last year. Gerry you would not know Swan Lake now, lots of new settlers around. Austin has a good store. Boone Taylor and myself about the only old-timers. Bill Cundiff took another place over beside Pat LaFarge. The school is going strong at the South end. It is Miss Gething. The one-legged fellow (Marion) is still at the North end. Girlie Taylor got married on the 15th November to Ernie Beattie. He is at Hythe. I worked at Pouce Coupe for a month after I left Rolla. I saw Jim Young. He has a store 25 miles northeast of Fort St. John, also the Post Office. He did not have the Post Office when I saw him. Cowell was up to see him, and he told me. Now Gerry, trapping is very poor this year, no fur around and rabbits either. I got weasel and will get a few rats, but not till March. I think we will get [the] Railroad to Swan Lake this summer. Some word of the Spirit River branch coming and join about Gundy's. That's [what] Boone told me. That is all the news this time. This leaves me in the best of health, and hope to find you the same. I will be pleased to hear from you again. I am your affec Friend, A. Anderson, Tupper Creek, BC.

36. Herbert E Drake, 4 February, 1930 at Dawson Creek, BC, to GSA at Toronto:

Dear Gerry: Here we are again, old man. What do you say to a trip up to Big Bar Mountain or else come on up and see Jim Riley? Do these words make you think of anything? I haven't been back since we took that last wild ride down the Cariboo Road with Jim. I suppose things are most likely about the same as before though.

Well, Gerry you will soon be a full fledged Forestry Engineer eh? I hope you can get by all OK. However, all the hope in the world wont help so much without the effort behind, will it? I've put in my application for a job to the J.S. Gordon at Vancouver and from his reply I think I stand a a pretty fair chance, although I'll have to bide my time.

I'm doing well up here, and seem to have won the confidence of most of the people. I've been elected Secretary of the Loyal Orange Lodge and to a chairmanship on the Dawson Creek Board of Trade. If I stay with it, I'll be an MP yet!!? I don't think. We've got another new Inspector which is the second since Gower left us. Plenty of changes. I haven't seen Alec for two or three months now. I think he vamoosed back to Peavine Castle. Jim Young is somewhere up north of Fort St. John but I haven't seen him for almost two years now.

Say, you know that girl I asked you to look up at Winnipeg, on Cathedral Ave? Well I met her up at Grande Prairie last Fall and say, but she is a peach. By the way the surveyors are laying out trial lines for the steel, at present they are working around Canyon Creek. Well Gerry, lets hear from you soon. Au revoir & good luck to you. As B4, Bert. PS: Dont forget that "Go West" feeling of yours when it comes time for shifting camp. That trip this summer was a humdinger. I'm enclosing one of the results of it.

37. <u>Jim Young</u>, 23 January, 1931 at Rose Prairie, <u>BC</u> to <u>GSA</u> c/o BC Forest Service, Victoria, BC:

Dear Gerry: I was surprised but very glad to get your letter. I had been often thinking of you and wondering if you were still going to college in Toronto. You would have a good summer on that survey. You better try and get up here in the BC Block for that work this summer. I am home-steading again here. I haven't bought any fur for two years, but am going out on a try about 200 miles north of here with some grub for some trappers.

Our Maggie McClements got married 2 years ago to Mr. Keeping and is living at Ocean Falls. Mrs. McClements died last Spring and Mr. McClements is in the Customs Department at Vancouver. Jack is still on the farm. Frank Gizler didn't get Maggie, so is still single and trapping. Lars and the Finn boys are on their farms. Finns have another brother and their sister with them. Old St. Pierre Gauthier, Mrs. Alfred Gladu and Francis Hamelin's wife died. The school is still running there [Kelly Lake]. We have a school here opposite from my place. The teacher is Mr. Holland and [he] stays with me.

Do you ever hear from Mr. Drake? I think he is teaching at Dawson Creek. Boone Taylor has a townsite on his place and is selling lots. Girlie, Boone's oldest girl is married. Old Alex Anderson is still at Peavine. I hope you are having a good time there this winter, Gerry. Try and get out this way for your survey work this summer. I got the Rose Prairie Post Office and am Postmaster here. Yours truly, Jim Young."

38. <u>Herbert E. Drake</u>, 25 January, 1931 at Dawson Creek, BC to <u>GSA</u> c/o BC Forest Branch, Victoria, BC:

Dear Gerry: Well old timer it sure did me good to hear from you once more and a pleasant surprise as well. No doubt Travis has given you most of the news from up in this country. Things have certainly made a marvelous change since I came to the country.

As you probably know we now have the train service up here
with this flourishing city as the terminal. I am enclosing
a snap of the town so you will see how things have changed
much better than I am able to tell you. School teaching is
coming along fine with me. I've been getting good reports
and as a result have practically made up my mind to stay
with it. We have two divisions now in the school with
myself Div I and a Miss Buchanan in Div II. Most likely it
will develop into a Superior School in a year or so, and
if it does I'm going to try hard for the principalship.
The Inspector Mr. T. Hall said he would pull hard for me
so that will help some wont it? The salary is $1,600 with
a raise once a year to a maximum, probably $1,800, and
most likely I'll be able to knock off my degree by that
time.

I intend going to summer school in Victoria this year.
Will you be down there then? I had the bum luck to get
Scarlet Fever in Dec so as a result I was in the Pouce
Coupe Hospital for a month Christmas included. I was there
when I received your card stating that you had met Travis.
By the way tell Travis that I saw his daughter Jean at New
Years when she was at the Convention in Pouce Coupe. It
was the first to be held in the Block. We call it the
Peace River District Teachers' Association. Long enough
name! Well now Gerry drop a line to "old stick in the mud"
some time. I haven't forgotten you. Good luck and kindest
regards, Bert.

39. Denny L. Cornock, 21 February, 1931, at Tupper BC to GSA,
c/o BC Forest Service, Victoria, BC:

Mr. G.S. Andrews: Well how are things driving along these
days? I was out by Alex Anderson's place last week went to
Kelly Lake, so stopped at Alex's for lunch and there I
received your address. I have not been working for the
Forestry Dept now for 2 years but am trying to get on
again this year. I have already made my application to the
District Forester at Prince George. Well Gerry I was
pleased to hear you are getting along OK. They have built
a nice little school at Kelly Lake. Teacher's name Mr.
Ward. I stayed all night with him Thurs night. I am now
working for the Public Works Dept, but prefer the Forestry
if I can get back. Will close, hoping to hear from you,
Yours truly, D.L. Cornock."

40. Alec Anderson, March 1931, Tupper Creek, BC to GSA c/o
BC Forest Service, Victoria, BC:

Mr. Andrews: I received your welcome letter some time ago,
and glad to see by it you got to the top of the tree at
last. I often think of you coming to the Castle on your

snowshoes. I had one of the old timers some time ago, D. Cornock. I gave him your address. He was to write you. I had Mr. Ward from Kelly Lake. He is the school teacher. He came there the time Bert [Drake] went to Dawson. He is a married man about 40. He took a homestead at Kelly Lake and one in Alberta. He put up a nice house and got a new school up last year. Now I must tell you something near Peavine. There is a school 3 miles from me. The youngest Paynter girl is teacher, 12 children and another 7 soon. It is on the Township Line between 26 and 27, ½ mile west of the Creek. The quarter next to me on 21 is taken; the ½ of 20 is taken west of me; ½ of 29 is taken. I took the NE of 17. My ¼ is NW 16 so the other one is west of that. The road is cut out to Kelly Lake. The road goes between 16 and 17. It is not graded, might be this summer. I am still living at the same place. If you come through, call for the Castle. The train comes three times a week. The station is at Boone's. Austin has his store and Post Office in the same place yet. I dont think there will be much of a town at Swan Lake, for while they have a pumping station, they get the best water there. Miss Gething is teacher at Swan Lake. The same man is still at the North end school and Bert [Drake] is still at Dawson [Creek]. I have not seen him for 4 months. I have not seem Jim Young for a Dog's age but he is still at Fort St. John. Well Gerry, I got 3 fox, 1 coyote, 30 weasel. I have not started on the rats yet. The price is low this year. I think that is all the news this time. I have a lot more to tell you if I only saw you, but am not very good at the pen. This leaves me in the best of health, hope to find you the same and will be glad to hear from you again. I am still Aff Friend, A. Anderson, Tupper Creek PO, BC.

41. <u>Denny L. Cornock</u>, 16 June, 1936, Tupper Creek, BC to <u>GSA</u>, Victoria, BC.

Mr. G.S. Andrews/Dear Friend: You will be surprised to hear from me. I was out and paid a visit to Alex and he gave me your address, and note you are with the Forest Service. Do you remember the day I showed you and Jimmy Young how to put the diamond hitch on, at Kelly Lake? Now you can guess who is writing. But things have changed a lot since those days. I am married now with children, 2 boys and 2 girls, the latter twins. I am living at the lake here at Tupper, half section trying to farm some, the the last few years have been lean ones. Am now working as a road foreman, and that aint much. I wish I could get back in the Forest Branch. And how are you getting along? I remember the time you told me you were going to take up a Forestry Course because you thought you would like it. I note you are now with that Branch, so you must have succeeded. I will close now, hoping to hear from you. Yours truly, D.L. Cornock.

Editorial Note: My reply to this letter advised that work was still very scarce at the Coast.

42. Jules H. Semans, 18 June, 1953, at Kelly Lake, BC to GSA, Victoria, BC:

Dear Mr. Andrews: Thank you so much for your kind compliment and your letter of June 8. Yes, we did appreciate greatly the fine map. The children in school and older pupils, especially your former pupils, expressed a keen appreciation, and a desire to meet you if and when you drive into Kelly Lake in August.

I can understand that in 1923 things were quite primitive here. Now we do have a two-roomed school. The one building is completely modern with residence attached. The other is the old log school renovated and remodelled. It proves to be a satisfactory classroom. There is also a new RC Church with a priest who is a part time resident. You will no doubt realize that the children here have not progressed to any great degree since 1925. Many of the children still do not understand English and their home life is still communicated completely in Cree. None of the new beginners understand a single English word. The emphasis in school therefore still remains RRR. However with varied degrees of success, we teach Health, Art, Music, Social Studies and give all these regular space on the daily study programmes. The names you mention in your letter are still in the foreground here. Although, the old timers are nearly all gone. Alfred Gladu [site of Jim Young's store] died in February 1953. Narcis Belcourt, original and first settler died of Frost Bite in January. He was 87, and wandered into the forest, lost his way, and was practically gone when found after 48 hours of exposure. I took him to Hospital in Beaverlodge where he died a short time later. Sid Gladu, Mrs. Louise Gray and others too are still around. Sid is now 59 and remembers you well. Mrs. Gray is past 70.

The road into this district is still very crude. The school board recently granted me $30.00 to fix a few culverts and thus make part of the trail passable. They are also dealing with Public Works to get the main road graded etc. so far only two of the original homesteaders have received title to their lands. The rest concentrate on trapping only. Some do well.

Mrs. Semans and I both teach here and our children, Grant 11, and Betty Lew 8 love the wilderness and its people. As for me I like the quietness of it here after quite a few years on the road. If it wasnt for the children's education we would probably stay here to see it through. But as is, Sonny will reach junior high by June 1954 and hence we will have to prepare to look elsewhere for a homestead. We spent four weeks in Victoria last summer and liked it there. It must be quite satisfying to have a permanent place there.

I regret very much that I am going away for a holiday on August 1, or I should have the personal pleasure of meeting you when you appear here in August. I trust that the information in this letter will be satisfying to you and that you are enjoying health and happiness. Thank you, I am Yours truly, sir, J.H. Semans. Kelly Lake School.

43. Justin E. McIntyre, 8 August, 1953, McLeod Lake, BC to GSA, Victoria, BC:

Dear Jerry: Last mail received a book on trees, shrubs and flowers from you. Many thanks Jerry. Shall be an expert on the plants by spring of next year. I note you have number of handles to your name, which I appreciate very much. But to me you are just old time Jerry. Mr. Campbell [Alan J, BCLS] and Ross [AD, BCLS] were in to see me, also George New and Art Swannell. Campbell informs me that they had a trailer also refrigeration. This country is getting too civilized. In our time we were d-m lucky to have beans. However we have to keep up with the times.

Have been kept quite busy. There has not been the travel this year that there was last year. Monday shall be another busy day for this young fellow, being Deputy Returning Officer. Have to see to it that people vote (right or wrong). BC went Social Credit for the Province. How it shall be for the Dominion, that is anybody's guess. To me it makes no difference so long as we have a government. The very best, Jerry, thanking you again, I remain Always your Pal, Mac.

44. Denny L. Cornock, Christmas, 1962, at Tupper, BC to GSA, Victoria, BC:

Well Jerry, I sold the farm, all but that lying south of the highway on Lot 249, 40 acres more or less. Now I have to start all over again, build house, barn etc. I believe that should keep a fellow active for a while, 75 on the 31st of Jan, next month. Best of Luck to all yours, Denny (and Anna) Cornock.

45. Lucille & Jules Semans, Christmas, 1962, Mile 6 Alaska Highway, to GSA, Victoria, BC:

After 11 years at Kelly Lake we are now teaching a new school [here]. [Card, Xmas 1963 from Beaverlodge, Alta.]

46. Guy H. Blanchet, DLS, BCLS, c1964 Memo "Lynx Paw Robe" (to accompany the subject robe given to GSA in Victoria, BC. In 1972, it was donated to the BC Provincial Museum, Victoria, and catalogued No 13576, Ethnology Division).

This is probably a museum piece for it is doubtful if any were made since about 1906 and if any others have been preserved. 1906 was a good rabbit year and consequently good for lynx. Many were killed along the Smoky [River] and it was from these that this robe was made by Celestin Gladu's wife. I bought this from Celestin in 1909 when he was attached to my party as guide on surveys south of Grande Prairie ... the 16th and 17th Base Lines from the 6th Meridian to the BC Boundary.

There were two trails to Grande Prairie then, one from Lesser Slave Lake west, and the other crossing Peace River at Peace River Crossing and following the North shore to Dunvegan, crossing the river again and proceeding South by Spirit River and Saddle Mountain. Both trails were bad. We travelled by Dunvegan and it took us nearly three months to reach Grande Prairie. At that time Bredin and Gunn had a ranch at Spirit River. There was a Hudson's Bay Co. post at Saskatoon Lake, a Red River half-breed at Bear Lake, an Indian village at Flyingshot near the Wapiti (River) and Bezanson at the Smoky Crossing where the railway now crosses. There were three hills, Beaverlodge at the West, Kleskun in the centre and Naitnaw at the East, where there were many wild horses. The prairie was very dry and had been reported by McConnell to be unfit for agriculture. This report in 1905 was immediately suppressed.

That year the prairie was subdivided by McFarlane brothers and in the Autumn I inspected this. During the summer the "Bull Gang" arrived, some 60 families from Ontario who settled in the Beaverlodge country.

I did not see Grande Prairie again till 1942 whe I flew back to the airport there and saw the changes, farms, railroads, roads and villages. Lack of transport had handicapped it and still does, but it had changed vastly in the 33 years.

Perhaps this robe is one of the few souvenirs of Grande Prairie prior to settlement.

Editorial Notes for No 46: Gladu, Celestin: In 1909, he lived at Flyingshot Lake. His wife was Marguerite Calliou. Gunn, Peter (?): See A33p218. McConnell, R.G., senior geologist with the GSC 1880 et seq (see A7p186, p 483). McFarlane Bros: Walter Graham McF., DLS No 300, 1905; John Baird McF, DLS No 358, 1908. Blanchet (1884-1966): repatriated from army service overseas. (1942) to make the location for the Canol Pipeline.

47. <u>Martin B. ("Boone") Taylor</u>, undated "memoir", Tupper Creek, BC (transcribed from the original manuscript with permission of his daughter, Bessie (Mrs. N. Albert), September, 1982):

> In 1918 the wife and 3 children and I were living on what now is the Tupper townsite in BC on Swan Lake. Times were very hard. I was in debt for our last year's grub-stake. The only thing in sight was trapping and it was not so good. A neighbour of the name Graham [?] came over and asked me to drive him to Grande Prairie to look for work and bring the team back, so I did this. It took only about on week's time for the trip, stopping at Hythe Alta for dinner. The next day I went to the Post Office for something or other and noticed a Notice for tenders for the mail contract from Beaverlodge Alta to Pouce Coupe, BC, 65 miles more or less. So I got a form from the Postmistress, carried it to Grande Prairie and back before I could make up my mind and what to bid. By this time, the time had run out. I would have to send the bid by some one to catch the train at Grande Prairie. If sent by mail stage it would not make Ottawa in time, so I left it with the storekeeper at Hythe to try and catch the train. I never heard from the PO dept so thought no more of it.
>
> Now in the meantime Revillon Freres Trading Co sent for me to come to Saskatoon Lake. And I hired out to them to buy fur for the season. They sent me $500.00 to buy a travelling outfit, team, sleigh, harness, pack saddles and robes. Now Mary, my wife says we've got to have clothes for these kids, of which there were 3, Leona Frances and Ruth. So we commenced to figure. (Mutt and Jeff says "figures don't lie, but liers will figure".) I said "Tell you what — we will sell them our team". But we did not like to sell them as they had come over the Edson Trail with us.
>
> But I had a job now for $100.00 per month and (all) found. I says "Look, I could buy them back in the Spring". So I booked the team in the expense account at $300.00. Now we had money and still had the team. Now the kids and Mary had clothes and I had a job. I had a home-made cutter that would do for buying fur. I booked the sleigh at $40.00. Now I am getting a small amount of capital. I had forgot all about the main contract since I had heard the storekeeper at Hythe had not got my tender for the same on the train, but mailed it on the stage one week later, so it could not get to Ottawa until 5 days after the tenders had closed. So we are going along fine, when, bang!, here comes a telegram from the PO department "START WITH MAIL WEDNESDAY NEXT". And I have neither horses, harness or sleigh or bondsmen.

I saw a notice in the PO at Pouce Coupe "Sleigh for sale, Frank Dewetter" so I bid for the sleigh with neck-yoke and doubletrees. This was bad business, for it left me wide open for a raise in price, but when I got there Dewetter was away, but his sister was there. I have found women more or less honest. If it had been the man he would have noticed the neck-yoke and double-trees, and up would have gone the price. I asked about the sleigh. She said, "Yes we have one for sale $40.00". OK I had a sleigh. Now this sleigh was automatically changed with my home-made cutter and became [property of] Revillon Freres.

Now in the meantime I had wired a friend at Rio Grande Alta [J.S. Young], "I have mail contract, no team or harness." The next stage brought a team and harness, and when I came back with the sleigh it was in the livery barn. I walked in the barn and noticed the strange team, asked the barn-man, "Who's team is that?". He kind of grinned and says, "You dont know about your own team? The stage brought them just a while ago". The harness was good so it [was] charged to Revillon's to replace my old harness. So the mail pulled out on time Wednesday next, with Revillon's sleigh and harness, my friend's team and the same stage driver that was driving the old contract.

One of the horses I had sold to Revillons had been sick for some time. Now it died. I reported to Edmonton the death of this horse and that I had borrowed another for the winter. I had thought the sale of the team to Revillons had been kept "at home" but it had leaked out as all secrets do when more than one know them, and as the saying is "If you want to find out about anyone, go to his neighbour". I had not got along any too well with my closest neighbour, so it got around that Taylor had sold the old team to Revillons, one was sick before the sale and now was dead.

Come Spring and Revillons' Inspector comes along to settle up and stops overnight at my neighbour's who ran a stopping place. Next morning he calls on me. First thing was count the cash on hand, now the books — everything checks on paper. I could see that the Inspector was loaded for bear. The sleigh was at Brainard, Alta where the snow went off and the mail had changed to a wagon. The harness was still on the mail team which was due in at noon. "Now," says Inspector Cowan (I think that was his name but am not sure as we had so many inspectors, and I had never seen him before). "Where did you get this team? You know we expect a pretty good team for $300.00." He was fairly shooting sparks. I could plainly see he had already passed sentence on me. The neighbour had filled him full. Now my father had always told me that if you tell the truth the hardest lawyer cant do anything with you. But lie once and you have to keep on lying to back up the first one, and you're lost. So I said "Now there is no use of us lying to each other, cause we are bound to find out. I bought the team from myself, really they were swipes, but that is the same. And why? You see the wife and them kids. We had no money. They needed clothes and food. I thought I could buy them back out of my wages because we did not want to part with the team. This way we could have our cake and eat it too. Now I made this deal all by myself — you had nothing to do with it at all, and I intended to buy them back, and now that one of them has died makes no difference. I have the money and am ready to buy them, but I think you should let me have them for the $300.00 that they cost you. Now I bought nothing with your money that I will not take off your hands at the price I paid for it". Well, he just sat there for a time and looked at me. The sparks passed away. He said "No, I wont do that at all. The company is more able to stand the loss of the horse than you are. But if you want the other horse for $150.00, alright. Now the articles we expect to lose 10% on them, and you can have them at 10% discount, and I don't suppose you will be any better off next Fall than you were last". I said, "No, I dont suppose I will". He said "Well, we will take your note for it and you can pay it out of your wages next season." Sometimes when a person throws a stone in the road for you, it is only a stepping stone. The next season I had $150.00 per month. The Post Manager at Saskatoon Lake fixed up my bonds. ...".

48. <u>BC PROVINCIAL VOTERS' LISTS</u>: Swan Lake, 1920; Kelly Lake 1924, 1928 & 1933:

1920

Swan Lake Polling Division.

2827. Adams, Simmion W., Tate's Creek, rancher.
2828. Adams, Nina, Tate's Creek, married woman.
2829. Anderson, Alex., Plavine Lake, farmer.
2830. Bell, Minnie Margrette, Tate's Creek, married woman.
2831. Bell, Angus Ross, Tate's Creek, rancher.
2832. Borden, Ellis P., Tupper Creek, rancher.
2833. Borden, Mary Elizabeth, Tupper Creek, married woman
2834. Callison, Frederic Charles, Tupper Creek, rancher.
2835. Callison, Dora Elton, Tupper Creek, married woman.
2836. Charls, William E., Swan Lake, farmer.
2837. Cundiff, William Harman, Pouce Coupe, farmer.
2838. Dickson, Walter Charles, Swan Lake, rancher.
2839. Dickson, Verna L., Swan Lake, married woman.
2840. Edgeworth, Albert, Tate's Creek, rancher.
2841. Groleau, Fred, Swan Lake, rancher.
2842. Reid, Edward, Swan Lake, rancher.
2843. Reid, Effie, Swan Lake, married woman.
2844. Robertson, Hugh G., Tupper Creek, farmer.
2845. Scott, Mathiew Clark, Swan Lake, rancher.
2846. Scott, Alice Mabel, Swan Lake, married woman.
2847. Taylor, Mary, Tupper Creek, married woman.
2848. Thomas, George John, Swan Lake, farmer.
2849. Taylor, Martin Batterton, Tupper Creek, farmer.

1924

KELLY LAKE POLLING DIVISION.

681 Belcort, Narce, Tupper Creek, trapper.
682 Burlay, Francis, Tupper Creek, trapper.
683 Callion, Kathrene, Tupper Creek, spinster.
684 Callion, Mary, Tupper Creek, housewife.
685 Callion, William, Tupper Creek, trapper.
686 Callion, Asleas, Tupper Creek, housewife.
687 Callion, John, Tupper Creek, trapper.
688 Callion, Pet, Tupper Creek, trapper.
689 Callion, Joe, Tupper Creek, farmer.
690 Callion, Sam, Tupper Creek, trapper.
691 Campbell, Pet, Tupper Creek, farmer.
692 Campbell, Milton, Tupper Creek, trapper.
693 Campbell, Leo, Tupper Creek, trapper.
694 Cameron, Pat, Tupper Creek, farmer.
695 Campbell, Lecoff, Tupper Creek, trapper.
696 Campbell, Maggie, Tupper Creek, housewife.
697 Campbell, Edward, Tupper Creek, trapper.
698 Campbell, Louise, Tupper Creek, housewife.
699 Gladue, Alfred, Tupper Creek, trapper.
700 Gladue, Ubain, Tupper Creek, trapper.
701 Gladue, Annie, Tupper Creek, housewife.
702 Gladue, Madalen, Tupper Creek, housewife.
703 Gladue, Isdoar, Tupper Creek, trapper.
704 Gladue, Selistene, Tupper Creek, trapper.
705 Gladue, Marguerite, Tupper Creek, housewife.
706 Gladue, John, Tupper Creek, trapper.
707 Gladue, Marcellene, Tupper Creek, housewife.
708 Gouchie, St. Pierre, Tupper Creek, trapper.
709 Gouchie, Zen, Tupper Creek, trapper.
710 Gouchie, Million, Tupper Creek, housewife.
711 Hambler, Francis, Tupper Creek, farmer.
712 Lattent, Zen, Tupper Creek, trapper.

1924 (cont)

713 Lattent, Liza, Tupper Creek, spinster.
714 Napoleon, Edward, Tupper Creek, trapper.
715 St. Arnoult, Floristine, trapper.
716 Supermint, John, Tupper Creek, farmer.
717 Taylor, William, Tupper Creek, farmer.
718 Ward, Carlun, Tupper Creek, spinster.

1928

16 VOTERS' LIST—FORT GEORGE DISTRICT 1928

KELLY LAKE POLLING DIVISION

963 Belcourt, Narce, Tupper Creek, trapper.
964 Burlay, Francis, Tupper Creek, trapper.
965 Callion, William, Tupper Creek, trapper.
966 Callion Asleas, Tupper Creek, housewife.
967 Callion, John, Tupper Creek, trapper.
968 Campbell, Milton, Tupper Creek, farmer.
969 Cameron Pat, Tupper Creek, farmer.
970 Dashersky, Hyman Eckar, Tupper Creek, farmer.
971 Gladue, Ubain, Tupper Creek, trapper.
972 Gladue, Isdoar, Tupper Creek, trapper.
973 Gladue, Selistene, Tupper Creek, trapper.
974 Gouchie, St. Pierre, Tupper Creek, trapper.
975 Gouchie, Zen, Tupper Creek, trapper.
976 Lattent, Zen, Tupper Creek, trapper.
977 Supermint, John, Tupper Creek, trapper.
978 Taylor, William, Tupper Creek, farmer.

1933

25 VOTERS LIST—PEACE RIVER DISTRICT 1933.

KELLY LAKE POLLING DIVISION

1535.	Belcourt, George	Goodfare, Alta.	Farmer
1536.	Belcourt, Henry	Goodfare, Alta.	Labourer
1537.	Belcourt, Narcisse	Goodfare, Alta.	Farmer, Trapper
1538.	Berland, Francois	Goodfare, Alta.	Farmer
1539.	Callieou, Adolphus	Goodfare, Alta.	Farmer
1540.	Campbell, Annie	Goodfare, Alta.	Housewife
1541.	Campbell, Caroline	Goodfare, Alta.	Housewife
1542.	Campbell, Harry	Goodfare, Alta.	Farmer
1543.	Campbell, Louis	Goodfare, Alta.	Farmer, Trapper
1544.	Dashevsky, Esther	Brainard, Alta	Housewife
1545.	Dashevsky, Jacob	Brainard, Alta	Farmer
1546.	Gladu, Alfred	Goodfare, Alta.	Farmer, Trapper
1547.	Gladu, Alvina	Goodfare, Alta.	Housewife
1548.	Gladu, Annie	Goodfare, Alta.	Housewife
1549.	Gladu, Celestin, M.	Goodfare, Alta.	Retired
1550.	Gladu, Isidore	Goodfare, Alta.	Farmer
1551.	Gladu, Louisa	Goodfare, Alta.	Housewife
1552.	Gladu, Pascal	Goodfare, Alta.	Farmer
1553.	Gladu, Urbain	Goodfare, Alta.	Trapper
1554.	Gladu, William	Goodfare, Alta.	Trapper
1555.	Gouchier, Eugene	Goodfare, Alta.	Farmer
1556.	Hambler, Francois	Goodfare, Alta.	Farmer, Trapper
1557.	Hambler, George	Goodfare, Alta.	Trapper
1558.	Hambler, Joseph	Goodfare, Alta.	Farmer
1559.	Lee, William	Goodfare, Alta.	Trapper
1560.	LeTendre, Eliza	Goodfare, Alta.	Housewife
1561.	LeTendre, Jean	Goodfare, Alta.	Farmer
1562.	L'Hirondelle, Julia	Goodfare, Alta.	Housewife
1563.	L'Hirondelle, Thomas	Goodfare, Alta.	Farmer
1564.	Neufeld, Peter	Brainard, Alta.	Farmer
1565.	Savard, William	Goodfare, Alta.	Farmer
1566.	Suprenant, John	Goodfare, Alta.	Farmer
1567.	Ward, Cephas Arthur	Goodfare, Alta.	Teacher
1568.	Ward, Lillian B.	Goodfare, Alta.	Housewife

Editorial Notes: The 1920 List for Swan Lake includes Alec Anderson, Mr & Mrs. E.P. Borden, Mr. & Mrs. Fred Callison and "Boone" and Mary Taylor. The Fynns, Jack and his mother do not appear. There was no poll at Kelly Lake, confirming that most people settled there after 1920.

The 1924 list for Kelly Lake shows 38 voters. This election, Friday, 20 June, 1924, was the one I witnessed, being then too young to vote, as mentioned in Chapter 1. Most names are familiar despite vagaries in spelling. I do not remember Burlay, Cameron, Taylor or Ward. Baptiste Besson, brother-in-law of C143Adam Calliou and mentioned in Chapter 1 does not appear but he could have been eligible by affidavit.

The 1928 list with only 16 names reflects a low ebb in the vitality of the Kelly Lake community. Jim Young had already closed his store and departed. The 1933 list with 33 names indicates a revival. It shows several of my older pupils – Henry Belcourt, Billy Gladu and George Hamelin (Hambler). The teacher C.A. Ward and his wife are identified. St. Pierre Gauthier and Mrs. Alfred Gladu (nee Madeline Gauthier) on the 1924 list do not appear in 1933, having died in 1930.

In many cases these lists show full names – rarely given otherwise. The 1933 Kelly Lake list may be unique in that all addresses are in Alberta!

95: At Kelly Lake School, August 1981. Eva Calliou sees cartridge belt she made for me in 1925. (Courtesy Mike Robinson)

96: Kelly Lake, BC, August 1981. First Kelly Lake teacher showing today's pupils the site of their grandparents' original school. (Courtesy Mike Robinson)

97: Kelly Lake, BC, August 1981. Mrs. Annie Gladu (nee Thomas) and I. Annie made my moosehide jacket, 1925. (Courtesy Mike Robinson)

98: Kelly Lake, BC, August 1981. Alfred Campbell welcomes his old schoolmaster. (Courtesy Mike Robinson)

99: Kelly Lake, BC, 1981. Cemetery: note spelling of HAMELIN for Delphine (nee Gladu) and Joseph. (Courtesy Mike Robinson)

100: Dawson Creek, BC, August 1981. George Hamelin with his old schoolmaster.
(Courtesy Mike Robinson)

101: Peavine Lake, BC, August 1981. View east near site of Alec
Anderson's cabin. (Courtesy Mike Robinson)

102: Lac Ste Anne Mission, Alta, July 1983. Founded by Father J-B
Thibault about 1842, it still is the site of the Metis pilgrimages
in late July each year. They camp on the surrounding fields. The
lake is less than a mile to the right. (GSA #7297)

APPENDIX 4

GENEALOGIES

General:

Full and true genealogies exist only in Saint Peter's Sacred Register — forever closed to mortal scrutiny.

Good breeding in livestock, particularly horses, and its like importance in human ancestry first engendered my interest in genealogy, such that I have now traced my Andrews forbears back through eight generations to 1704, in Suffolk, and hope to pursue them further when opportune. The study is onerous, but rewarding. Recorded data are usually fragmentary and can be faulty. Sources, like Church records, the census, legal documents, voters' lists, school registers, surveyors' notes and cemetery epitaphs are seldom conveniently accessible. Spelling may be corrupt, especially if informants are illiterate and recorders are of mediocre scholarship. Large families compound the task. Orphans adopted by relatives may be confused with their proper children. Many did not survive to adulthood. The Church's aversion to marriage between blood relatives favored keeping such records, but in early communities, isolation and propinquity caused some inbreeding, the effect of which may be to accentuate both good and bad heritable characteristics.

Tabulations for 10 Kelly Lake Metis families with comment and summaries make up the bulk of this Appendix. Also, for the record and with permission, I include two quite unrelated families — the "Boone Taylors" of Swan Lake and the "Jim Youngs" of Rose Prairie. Both have generously supplied me with data. I should like to have attempted others for friends like Denny Cornock, Sam Wilson and "Big Johnny" Supernat, but must observe limits to what my readers and myself can endure.

Roots of Kelly Lake genealogies go deep into the earliest strata of Canadian history, drawing substance from aboriginal Indians, explorers, fur traders, voyageurs, hunters, guides and interpreters. Marriage to local Indian women gave contentment far from home and encouraged alliances with local tribes — valuable for trade and security. These unions, often sanctioned only by tribal custom, were mostly permanent, happy, faithful and prolific. When missionaries arrived, the Metis offspring were baptized, mostly into the Roman faith, and marriages were solemnized.

Patriarchs of the Calliou, L'Hirondelle, Thomas and some other families were Iroquois. In 1982, I compiled "preliminary" Kelly Lake genealogies with information from Jarvis Gray, my old pupils and Ray Irwin. They identified about 360 individuals through nine generations back to c1750. Now, after study of additional references (qv), including Sprague & Frye's Red River genealogies (A50), I have revised and amplified them for which, now the head-count is nearly doubled. If Sprague & Frye's work had not appeared in 1983, this book could have been on the press several months earlier!

I have attempted to consolidate a considerable amount of data from a variety of sources, with some discrete speculation, into reasonable family structures. Basic biology has helped. Women may marry as early as 15, but have few if any children after age 45. Fathers do their part mostly between ages 25 and 55. I inserted a generation between the patriarch "C Louis Calliou (c1750-c1840)" and "C14Thomas Calliou (c1810-?)". Jarvis Gray showed them as father and son. I date all approximate births after their parents' marriage, but adhere to my private belief that in Saint Peter's Divine Register, there is no such category as "illegitimate".

Psychology also can help. Children are often named for parents, grandparents, favorite aunts and uncles. When I found that C143Adam Calliou had a daughter, C1433Marceline, I realized that she could well be the mother of my pupils Billy and Adolphus Gladu, being in the appropriate generation. In this case Billy was named for his uncle C1431William Calliou. Marceline, presumably a widow when I knew her (1923-25), was Mrs. Johnny Supernat, a near neighbor. She was friendly, spoke some English and helped with my aspirations in Cree. No 710 on the 1924 Kelly Lake Voters' List is "Million Gouchie [sic], housewife". She could be Madeline Gauthier, the blind wife of G.11St Pierre Gauthier. Mrs. Alfred Gladu was Madeline, nee Gauthier, possibly named for her mother. She, in turn had a daughter Madeline whose older brother, Joe, and sisters were my pupils (1924-25). A pleasing photo of this fine family is reproduced herein with permission. Alfred Campbell's first son is Alex, probably named for his great grandfather Alex C Campbell who married a Gauthier at Lac Ste Anne c1880. She could have been St Pierre's sister. Most Metis children seem to have only one given name. The second given name of non-Metis children often identifies their mother's family. This is how I was given the glamorous second name "Smedley" – which I appreciate now, but hated as a child.

Individuals must be allocated to their proper generation, on the basis of their known or assumed birthdate. Thirty years is accepted as the average interval between successive generations. My data for the Kelly Lake people was analyzed for time-incidence of generations as shown on a following page. With a "life-expectancy" of 70 years, "middle age" would be 35. On this basis, some "orphans" are placed in their probable generation and given a generalized code, eg, C14..xAdolphus Calliou (c1910-?) in the "n+6" generation. Late members of one generation may take a spouse in the next. Where do their children belong? "C..x9Lective Campbell (1914-)" in the "n+5" Campbell generation married "C14471 Caroline Gladu (c1921KL-)" in the "n+6" Calliou generation. Lective's mother was a Gauthier from Lac Ste Anne.

Mechanics of Tabulation:

The mysterious code prefixes for several names above will now be explained. A method developed for my "Andrews Genealogy – 1982" is used for lack of a better one. The task is to organize a large and complex mass of information systematically, comprehensively and without ambiguity, in minimal space. This calls for some austerity in spacing, punctuation and abbreviations. The result may seem bewildering at first glance, but with a little study and familiarity it should become logical and clear. My system does have merit.

Reference should be made now to the first page of the CALLIOU TABULATION. Generations n+1, etc are arranged left to right across the page and are spaced only one digit apart, viz "0....5....". The value of "n" is the same for all tabulations. It might approach 133 if we could go back to the biblical Adam. Children of each family are numbered in sequence of birth, known or assumed, below their parents, and aligned in the next generation. In (such) large families the 10th, 11th, 12th, etc children are designated "0", "1", "2" etc, to keep within the single digit column allowed for their generation. An example is C143310Vera Gladu (1959KL-), the 10th child of C14331Wm Gladu (1909FL-) and his wife C14424Mary Belcourt (1916KL-). For the initial "n+1" generation, instead of a numeral, the symbol "C" for Calliou is used. For other families an appropriate letter symbol is likewise used "B" for Belcourt, "C" for Campbell, "G" for Gladu, "H" for Hamelin, etc.

Each individual has a unique code prefix, the number of digits of which including the initial symbol (say, "C") indicates his or her appropriate generation. To avoid clutter, these codes are shown in full only at suitable intervals.

After the heading "CALLIOU", some variations in spelling appear in brackets. Some preliminary remarks may follow before the tabulation begins. The extreme left column is reserved for references or sources. "B6" in the first item refers to correspondence with Jarvis Gray, 1979. For the second item "*" indicates the conjecture of an inserted generation as mentioned previously. I assume that Marie Patenaude was old Louis Calliou's daughter-in-law, not his wife, because of their difference in age. In the third line, "A50" refers to Sprague & Frye's Red River genealogy as detailed in the References. All "ID" numbers are also from that source.

Refer now to the first individual "Louis Calliou". His code is simply "C" placed in the n+1 generation. We dont know his birth sequence among his siblings if any or whoever, so "C" identifies him. He was born c1750 at Caughnawaga, the old Iroquois Mission near Montreal. He died c1840 in the NW Territories. He married c1775 an unidentified wife. His presumed grandson "C14Thomas Calliou," is said to be the fourth child of his parents. Thomas's wife, Marie Finlay, was the centenarian at whose burial I officiated at Kelly Lake (1925). Each succession is followed directly through to the latest generation. This keeps recent families more or less together but members of earlier families may be dispersed through several pages. However, their codes preserve their identity, family connections and proper generation.

If "C141Wm Calliou" and "C142Esau Calliou" were as prolific as their brother, "C143Adam Calliou", and their sister "C144Marguerite Calliou", and if their progeny were known, this Calliou tabulation would be three times as large. Also, when we realize that each new arrival in the "n+9" generation has, in the "n+1" generation, no fewer than 256 different ancestors, the potential size of a full genealogy is colossal. Ignorance may be a blessing in disguise. Saint Peter's data-processing hardware and software make our latest human sophistications seem elementary in the extreme.

103: Edson, Alta, July 1983. The plaque is self-explanatory. (GSA #7298)

CALLIOU (Calahoo, Calleho, Callehoo, Callihoo, Callot, Galliou, Kwarakwante)

Code symbol: "C" (as distinct from "C" for Campbell)

From data in hand, this family permeates the Kelly Lake genealogies more than any other, so its tabulation is completed through to the latest births reported, in Generation "n+9". Other families are tabulated only as far as they fuse with the Callious.

The patriarchal Louis Calliou(c1750-c1840) alias Kwarakwante was Iroquois from the Caughnawaga Mission (1676+) near Montreal. The early Callious evidently by-passed the Red River Settlements as none is identified in the Sprague & Frye Genealogy (A50) nor is any noted in the DCB, 1983 (A15). No telephone listings east of Alberta were noted (1981).

Sources:	0....5....0.. (n+ generations)
B6	CLouis Calliou(c1750Cg-c1840NWT) +c1775 wife nee?(c1760-?). Ch inc
*,B6	1son Calliou(c1780NWT?-?)+c1805 Marie Patenaude(c1790-?) ? sister of ID3854
A50	Michel Patenaude(1784Cda-?); 9 ch inc
B6 B9	4Thos Calliou(c1810-?)+c1835 Marie Finlay(c1820-1925KL). the "Widow Callot"?
A5p505	1Wm Calliou(c1835-?)
do	2Esau Calliou(c1840-?)
do D26,27	3Adam Calliou(1854LSA?-1948RG)+c1878 Veronique nee?(1863-1956RG)
B5 A52	1Wm Calliou(c1879LSA?-?)+c1910 Mary? nee?(c1885-?) /(c1885-1980KL)
A3p159	2Gibney Calliou(c1887LSA?-?)+c1912 Asleas? nee?(c1890-?)/John Supernat /
* A3p159 A52	3Marceline Calliou(c1890LSA?-?)+(1)c1905 husband Gladu(c1885-?)+(2)"Big /
C9	C14331Wm Gladu(1909FL-)+c1935 C14424Mary Belcourt(1916KL-)
	1Betty Gladu(1936KL-)+c1957KL Janus Pastovik(c1931-)
	1Daryl Pastovik(1958-)+c1980 Josephine Belcourt(c1960-)
	1daughter Pastovik(1981-)
	2Redney Pastovik(1959-)+c1978 wife nee?(?-?)
	1Child Pastovik(c1979-)
	2Child Pastovik(c1980-)
	3Child Pastovik(c1981-) /Meck, below ?)
	3Audrey Pastovik(1962-)+c1980 husband Meck(c1961-)(nephew of Harold/
	1Neil Meck(1980-)
	C1433114Fay "Cindy" Pastovik(1963-)+c1978 husband nee?(
	1Greg surname?(1979-)
	5Dennis Pastovik(1966-)
	6Calvin Pastovik(1971-)
	C143312Frank Gladu(c1940KL-)
A47p112,3	3Bernice Gladu(1942KL-)+c1958 Harold Meck(1932Gf-)
	1Viola Meck(1959-)
	2Linda Meck(1964-)
	3Bryan Meck(1966-)
	C1433134David Meck(1968-)
	C143314Lloyd Gladu(1944KL-)+c1961KL C144712Jean Campbell(c1944KL-)
	1Cindy Gladu(1962-)
	2Charlotte Gladu(1964-)
	3Kevin Gladu(1965-)
	4Chaline Gladu(1967-)
	C143315Stanley Gladu(1946KL-)+c1968 Ruth Horsman(c1947-)
	1Cynthia Gladu(1969-)
	2Michelle Gladu(1975-)
	3son Gladu(1979-)
	C143316Jennie Gladu(1948KL-)+c1965 Arnold Volden(c1945-)
	1Arlene Volden(1966-)
	2Pamela Volden(1968-)
	C143317Melvin Gladu(1950KL-)
	8Arnold Gladu(1952KL-)
	9Glen Gladu(1955KL-)
C9	OVera Gladu(1959KL-)
C19 A47p431	C14332Adolphus Gladu(c1914FL-)+c1940 Adeline LaGlace(c1920HL-) 12 children
	names, sequence and dates unknown. /served in World War I)
A47p70 A5p505	4David Calliou(1894LSA-1981DC)+c1915(1) wife nee? +(2)Mrs Gladu (David /
	1Archie Calliou(c1915-)┐(both in World War II)
	2Edward Calliou(c1916-)┘ /DC) qv
C12	3step-daughter Mabel Gladu(c1920-)+c1937KL C14462Geo Hamelin(1912FL-1983/
A3p159	C1435Lillian Calliou(c1895-?) (If Mrs Lawrence her birth c1890 or earlier).
do	6Victoria Calliou(1897Gr-1981+)+ 1920FL Geo Laplante(c1895LSA-?)
do	1Lena Laplante(1923-)+c1940 husband Longson(c1920-)
	1son Longson)
	2son Longson)- names, sequence & dates unknown
	3son Longson _____)
	C143614daughter Longson_)
	0....5....0.. (n+ generations) ...... See next page

```
(GSA 050384)          CALLIOU TABULATION (cont)

Sources:         0....5....0.. (n+ generations)
                                                        /mother C1435Lillian Calliou?
A6p211         C143x1Geo Lawrence(1905FL-)+1934GP Sarah Peters(1918Sask-) Was George's /
(See con-)          1Robt Lawrence(1936RG-)+c1960 Alvina Lindbloom(?-?) Children?
(cluding )          2Ken Lawrence(c1938-)+c1963 Madelyn Toloway(?-?) Children?
(comment )          3Irene Lawrence(c1940-)+c1960 Ed Schanuel(?-?) Children?
                    4Keith Lawrence(c1942-)  wife? children? /see Margaret's photo A44p47.
B6 B9 A51    ↘ C144Marguerite Calliou(1856LSA-?KL)+c1880 G.x1Celestin Gladu(1859LSA-c1945KL) /
                    1Louise Gladu(c1878LSA-?)+(1)c1898 Jos Gray(c1875-?)+(2)Ernie Horsman(?-?)
B6 C11              1David Gray(1916FL-)+c1940 G...x4Jean Gladu(c1917FL-)
                       1Della Gray(c1941KL-) Husband? children?
                       2Jarvis Gray(c1943KL-) Wife? children?
C11                 2Joe Horsman(c1920-)+c1945 Wife, nee?
                       1Joe Horsman Jr(c1947-)
B6 B5 B11      C1442Emily Gladu(c1883LSA-?KL)+c1900 B1111Narcisse Belcourt(1866LSA-1953KL)
B6 A52              1Geo Belcourt(c1902FL-?) Wife children?
C9 C19 A52          2Henry Belcourt(c1909FL-1978KL) did not marry
                    3Patrick Belcourt(c1911KL-) wife? children?
C9                  4Mary Belcourt(1916KL-)+c1935KL C14331Wm Gladu(1909FL-) qv above
                    5Annie Belcourt(c1917KL-) Husband? children?
C2 A47p100          6Francis Belcourt(c1919KL-)+c1943 B....1Ida Belcourt(c1925-) Children?
C9                  7Wm Belcourt(c1921KL-) wife? children?
B6             C1443Celestin Gladu Jr(c1885LSA-?) Wife? children?
B6                  4MargaretGladu(c1887LSA-?)+c1910 C..x4Harry Campbell(c1887-?) Children?
B6 C4               5Annie Gladu(c1890LSA-?KL)+c1905 C..x1Milton Campbell(c1881-c1950KL)
B8 C9 C19              1Eva Campbell(c1906FL-)+c1922 C14.xJohnny Calliou(1901FL -?)
                          1Galena Calliou(1929KL-)+c1949 L....xJim Letendre(c1917-)
                             1Howard Letendre(c1950-) Wife? Children?
                             2Ron Letendre(c1951-)         do       ?
                             3Robt Letendre(c1952-)         do       ?
                             4Evelyn Letendre(1953-)        do       ?
                             5Henry Letendre(1954-)         do       ?
                             6Marlene Letendre(1959-)
                       C144512Joe Calliou(c1930KL-)+c1952 G.....xIsabel Gladu(c1932-)
                             1Brenda Calliou(1954-)
                             2Sidney Calliou(1957-)
                             3Bernardine Calliou(1958-)
                             4Beverley Calliou(1960-)
                             5Betty Calliou(1963-)
                             6Patsy Calliou(1966-)
                             7Ruth Calliou(1969-)
                       C144513Florence Calliou(1934KL-)+c1952 husband Davidson(c1930-)
                             1Jeanette Davidson(1954-)
                             2Faron Davidson(1955-)
                             3Robin Davidson(1957-)
                             4Daniel Davidson(1961-)
                       C144514Charlie Calliou(1935KL-)+c1956 L.....xElsie Letendre(c1937-)
                             1Laura Calliou(1957-)
                             2Judy Calliou(1958-)
                             3Gloria Calliou(1960KL-)+c1981 Ray Irwin(c1958-) Children?
                             4Chas Calliou(1961-)
                             5Robt Calliou(1962-)
                             6Rodney Calliou(1963-)
                             7Norman Calliou(1964-)
                             8Terry Calliou(1966-)
                       C144515Lawrence Calliou(1940KL-) wife? children?
                             6Irene Calliou(1942KL-)+c1960 Greg Duke(c1940-)
                             1Timothy Duke(1961-)
                             2Lois Duke(c1963-)
                             7Elizabeth Calliou(1944KL-)+c1961 husband? etc?
                             1Rebecca nee?(1962-)
                             2Gary nee?(1966-)
                             3Pricilla nee?(1972-)
                       C144518Geo Calliou(1948KL-)+c1966 Margaret Whitford(c1950-)
                             1Deana Calliou(1967-)
                             2Derwin Calliou(1968-)
                             3Derek Calliou(1970-)
                       C144519Clifford Calliou(1950KL-)+c1967 G.....xMargaret Gladu(c1952-)
                             1Lynette Calliou(1968-)
                             2Laurian Calliou(1970-)
                             3Shelley Calliou(1972-)
B8             C1445194Brent Calliou(1973-)
                 0....5....0.. (n+ generations)              (.... continued next page)
```

CALLIOU TABULATION (cont)

```
Sources:    0....5....0... (n+ Generations)

C4 B12      C14452Sarah Campbell(c1909FL-c1940KL)+1925KL G.1111Eugene GauthierJr(c1905-)
C4 C12      │    1Archie Gauthier(c1926KL-)+c1955 C144622Gladys Hamelin(c1940KL-)
C12         │      1Darlene Gauthier(1957-)+c1978 husband?
            │       1Allen nee?(1979-)
            │       2son nee?(1981-)
            │    C1445212Dianne Gauthier(1958-)+c1975 husband nee?
            │      1Clayton nee?(1978-)
            │      3Donna Gauthier(1960-)+c1975 husband nee?
            │      1son nee?(1978-)
            │      4Dolores Gauthier(1962-)
            │      5Archie Gauthier Jr(1964-)
C12         │      6Doris Gauthier(1967-)
            │    C144522Florence Gauthier(c1928KL-)
            │      3Lorne Gauthier(c1930KL-)
            │      4Lillian Gauthier(c1932-)
            │      5Margaret Gauthier(c1934KL
            │      6Lloyd Gauthier(c1936KL-)
C4          │    C14453Alfred Campbell(1914FL-)+c1935 B...x1Virginia Belcourt(c1916-)
            │      1Alex Campbell(1936KL-)+c1958 Beatrice Supernat(c1940-)
            │       1Kenney Campbell(1959KL-)
            │       2Philip Campbell(1960KL-)+c1980 Ruby Knott(c1961-)
            │        1Sonia Campbell(1981-)
            │       3Lester Campbell(1962-)
            │       4Veronica Campbell(1964-)
            │       5Joan Campbell(1965-)
            │       6Jerry Campbell(1972-)
            │       7Charlotte Campbell(1978-)
            │    C144532Jeanette Campbell(1938KL-)+c1953 Geo Davis(?-?) Children?
            │      3John Campbell(1941KL-)+c1965 Barbara Cardinal(?-?) Children?
            │      4Marcel Campbell(1944KL-)
            │      5Linda Campbell(1954KL-)+c1974 Robt Laufman(c1950-)
            │       1Robt Laufman Jr(1974KL-)
            │       2Jennifer Laufman(1976KL-)
            │       3Kelly Laufman(1979KL-)
            │      6Irene Campbell(1959KL-)
C4          C14454Leo Campbell(c1918KL?-?)
B6 C12      C1446Caroline Gladu(c1891LSA-1930KL)+c1906 H...xFrancis Hamelin(c1885-?)
C12 D6,7 A52 │    1Joe Hamelin(1906FL-1980KL)+c1929 G...x2Delphine Gladu(1913FL_1980KL)
            │      1Lena Hamelin(c1930KL-)+c1952 C145121Vern Knott(c1930-)
            │       1Keith Knott(1957-)
            │       2Kurt Knott(1962-)
C12 A52     │    C14462Geo Hamelin(1912FL-1983DC)+c1937KL G.... xMabel Gladu(1920Gr?-)
            │      1Patrick Hamelin(1938KL-)+c1960 Annette Vanderik(c1940-)
            │       3daughters Hamelin(c1961-) (c1963-) (c1965-)          /above.
            │      2Gladys Hamelin(1940KL-)+c1955 C144521 Archie Gauthier(c1926KL-) qv /
            │      3Gardner Hamelin(1942KL-)+c1972 Marie Vanderik(c1942-)
            │       1Patricia Hamelin(1973-)
            │       2Shaman Hamelin(1975-)
            │       3daughter Hamelin(1981-)
            │    C144624Gilbert Hamelin(1943KL-1968KL)
            │      5Rose Hamelin(1945KL-)+c1963 C144121Joc Horsman Jr(c1945-)
            │       1Calvin Horsman(1964-)
            │       2Victor Horsman(1965-)
            │       3Joanne Horsman(1967-)
            │       4Noreen Horsman(1971-)
            │       5June Horsman(1974-)
            │      6Georgina Hamelin(1947KL-)+c1962 Elmer Desjarlais(c1945-)
            │       1Wesley Desjarlais(1964-)
            │       2Reg Desjarlais(1972-)
            │       3Sharon Desjarlais(1974-)
            │    C144627Alvina Hamelin(1949KL-)+c1967 T.....xKenny Napoleon(c1945-)
            │       1Claudette Napoleon(1968-)
            │       2Roxan Napoleon(1970-)
            │       3Floyd Napoleon(1972-)
            │       4Leila Napoleon(1974-)
            │       5Everett Napoleon(1976-)
            │    C144628Doreen Hamelin(1951KL-)+c1970 Peter Joachim(c1950-)
            │       1Brest Joachim(1972-)
            │       2Trudy May Joachim(1973-)
            │       3Joy Joachim(1975-)
            │    C144629Richard Hamelin(1953KL-)+c1972 Evelyn Potts(c1955-)
            │ │    1Rachel Hamelin(1973-)
C12         C1446292Billy Joe Hamelin(1975-)

            0....5... (n+ generations)                    (... continued)
```

CALLIOU TABULATION (continued)

Sources: 0....5....0.. (n+ generations)

```
C12         C144620Alvin Hamelin(1955KL-)+c1977 Sheri Martin(c1957-) Children?
                1Lester Hamelin(1957KL-)+c1977 Rose Kay(c1960-)
                 1Jesse Paul Hamelin(1978-)
                 2Jonathin Hamelin(1981-)
            C144622Gloria Hamelin(1958KL-)+c1975 Michael Lambert(c1955-)
                 1Shawn Lambert(1976-)
                 2Jodie Lambert(1977-)
                 3Amanda Lambert(1981-)
            C144623Catherine "Babe" Hamelin(1959KL-)+c1978 husband nee?(?-?)
                 1Jordan surname?(1979-)
C12              2Laura Lee surname?(1981-)
A46 C19     C14463Albert Hamelin(c1915FL-) Wife and Children?)
B7              4Daughter Hamelin(1928KL-?)
B6 C8 B3 A52 C1447Isidore Gladu(1896LSA-1974KL)+c1917 T..x3Annie Thomas(1902DC-)
C5              1Caroline Gladu(c1921KL-)+c1940 C..x9Lective Campbell(1914-)    /dren?
                 1Shirley Campbell(c1942KL-)+c1962 L.....xWalter Letendre(c1940-) Chil- /
                 2Jean Campbell(c1944KL-)+c1962 C143314Lloyd Gladu(1944KL-) 4 ch see above.
                 3Betty Campbell(c1946KL-)+c1964 Malcolm Supernat(c1944-) Children?
                 4Dennis Campbell(1953KL-)+c1973 Lottie Paul(c1955-) Children?
                 5Geraldine Campbell(1955KL-) marriage & children?
                 6Glenda Campbell(1956KL-)         ditto          ?
                 7Dezmar Campbell(1961KL-)
C8          C14472Lillian Gladu(c1922KL-dec infant?)         /Horsman(c1920-)? qv above.
                3Fred Gladu(c1924KL-)+c1950 Jean Horsman(c1930-) sister of C14412 Joe /
C8 A42p476 * 4Nora Gladu(c1926KL-)+c1950 C14517John Calliou(1924-) see below
                5Lydia Gladu(c1927KL-)+c1947 Riley Whitford(c1925-)
D9               1Randy Whitford(c1948-?KL)
                 2Margaret Whitford(c1950-)+c1966 C144518Geo Calliou(1948KL-)qv above
                 3Barbara Whitford(c1952-)+c1975 B.....xCurtis Belcourt(c1950-) ch?
            C14476Francis Gladu(c1929KL-)+c1955 B....xLillian Belcourt(c1930-) Children?
                7Kathleen Gladu(c1932KL-)+c1955 L....xEd Letendre(c1930-) Children?
            C1448Patrick Gladu(c1897LSA-?)+c1922 Eva Horsman(c1905-?)
C8          C14481Philomene Gladu(c1923-)+c1940 Stan Smith(c1920-)
B6               1Ronald Smith(c1941-)
            C144812Pauline Smith(c1943-)
B5 A14pix   C145Louis Calliou(c1860LSA?-?)+1878 B..xVictoria Belcourt(1861LSA-1966SA)
A42p476          1Henry Calliou(c1885Ed-?)+c1912 Lucy Testawich(c1897-?)
                 1Louise Calliou(c1913-)
                 2Julia Calliou(c1914-)+c1929 Ted Knott(c1905-)
                  1Vern Knott(c1930-)+c1952 C144611Lena Hamelin(c1930KL-) qv above (2 ch)
                 3Mary Calliou(c1916-)+c1931 G.1112Dan Gauthier Jr(c1910-)
                  1daughter Gauthier(c1932-)
                  2  do   Gauthier(c1934-)
                 4Virginia Calliou(c1918-)+c1933 John Testawich(c1915-) Children?
                 5Malcolm Calliou(c1920-)
                 6Alberta Calliou(c1922-)
A42p476     C14517John Calliou(c1924-)+c1950 C14474Nora Gladu(c1926KL-) qv above
B5 A3p130   C146Peter Calliou Sr(c1862LSA?-?)  Wife, children etc?
                7Isidore Calliou(c1864LSA?-?) Wife etc?           /1954RG)
A6p257-8        8Melanie Calliou(1865LSA-1959HL)+c1885LLB Jean Baptiste Besson(1860LSA- /
                 1Marie Besson(c1886LLB-c1906)+c1905 John LaRondelle(c1880-?) Children etc?
            C14811Florence LaRondelle(c1906-)+c1938 Joe Cowpar(c1900-?) Children etc?
            C1482Caroline Besson(c1887-?)+c1910 husband Horsman(c1880-?) Children etc ?
                 (Seven other Besson children, all deceased)

    "Orphans" for adoption:

B5 A52      C14.xPeterCalliou Jr(c1890-?)
A52         C14.xJoseph Calliou(c1892-?)
A52         C14.xSamuel Calliou(c1894-?)
A52.        C14.xKatherin Calliou(c1896-?)
A52.        C14.xJohn Calliou(1901 -?) (Husband of C14451Eva nee Campbell? qv.)
A52.        C14..xAdolphus Calliou(c1910-)
C19         C14..xDelphine Calliou(c1917-)
C19         C1445.xGordon Belcourt(c1945-) (grandson of C..x1Milton Campbell)
C19         C14477xShirley Letendre(c1955-) (granddaughter of C1447Isidore Gladu?)
                 0....5....0.. (n+ generations)
```

Comment: Eight children of C144Marguerite Calliou and G.x1Celestin Gladu were tabulated from data supplied by Jarvis Gray (B6), which were not 100% legible. In the 1973 taped interview (B3). C1447Isidore Gladu said his father, Celestin, deceased c1945KL, was survived by three sons, of whom Isidore claimed to be the eldest, and four daughters. Revision of my tabulation must await more authentic information if and when available. The same interview identifies Isidore's daughter, Mrs Leo Ferguson, who is not included in my tabulation above. Her husband could be grandson of Leon Ferguson, HBC trader at Dunvegan c1897 and at Lake Saskatoon (Beaverlodge) c1911, (see A3p16,17 and A5p168 in "References").

L'HIRONDELLE: Code Symbol: "L" (as distinct from "L" for Letendre)

 This family, with Iroquois roots, like Calliou, is a primary source of Kelly Lake ancestry. In early generations, probably at Lac Ste Anne, it introduces such prolific families as Belcourt and Gladu, but unlike these, few L'Hirondelles seem to persist in the Kelly Lake picture now. The 1933 Kelly Lake Voters' List identifies L...xThomas L'Hirondelle and (his wife?) Julia, nee? A "Mrs L'Hirondelle" sold her land southwest of Goodfare to A Bricker, c1940 (A47p69). Possibly she was Julia, by that time a widow? No L'Hirondelle appears in the DCB (1983). In Sprague & Frye (A50) are ID2954 Joseph L'Hirondelle and two sons ID2953 Joseph and ID 2952 Alex, as tabulated below. The original Iroquois name could have had an ornithological connotation "swallow". The following tabulation is carried only as far as it fuses with other more numerous Kelly Lake families.

Sources:	0....5.... (n+ generations) (Note: ID3935 Antoine Pilon(1789-?) (A50) could) (have been a brother of Josette, below.)
B6	LJacques L'Hirondelle(1759Cg-1854LSA)+c1800 Josette Pilon(1782-?) 8 ch incl
	1Catherine L'Hirondelle(1802-?)+c1820 B1Joseph Belcourt(c1795-?) 8 ch incl
	1son Belcourt(c1820-?)+c1840 wife nee?(c1822-?) ch incl
	1son Belcourt(c1840-?)+c1865 wife nee?(c1842-?) ch incl
B6 B11	L1111Narcise Belcourt(1866LSA-1953KL)+c1900 C1442Emily Gladu(c1883LSA-?KL)qv
B6	L14Marie A Belcourt(c1835-?)+c1855 G.xJoseph Gladu(c1830-?) 9 ch incl
B6	1Celestin Gladu(1859LSA-c1945KL)+c1880LSA C144Marguerite Calliou(1856LSA-?)
A47p69 A52	L...xThomas L'Hirondelle(c1885-?)+c1910 Julia nee?(c1890-?) (Ap 3 No 48 - 1933)
ID2954	L.xJoseph L'Hirondelle(1820-?)+c1845 Marguerite Nepissing(1824-?)
ID2953	1Joseph L'Hirondelle Jr(1844-?)+c1870 Elise Thorn(1850-?)
ID2952	L.x2Alex L'Hirondelle(1849NWT-?)+c1875 Philomene Fosseneuve(1852RR-?)
	0....5.... (n+ generations)

BELCOURT (Belcort, Belcour, Belcours, Bellecours, Bellecourt)   Code Symbol: "B"

 With the marriage of L1Catherine L'Hirondelle c1820 to B1Joseph Belcourt, this family follows Calliou and L'Hirondelle in the line of "Kelly Lake" antiquity. Belcourt origins were evidently in France and in French Canada. Jean Francois Pouteret de Bellecourt was among the first to go to "le pays d'en haut", 1660, after Radisson (DCB I). Jacques Lafontaine de Belcour(1704-63) came from France 1726, was prominent and had fifteen children in New France (DCB III p 338). The Rev Georges-Antoine Belcourt(1803LC-1874NB) was the celebrated missionary and champion of the Metis in the RR Settlements 1832-53 (A38, A15 X). A contemporary and possible relative was B1Joseph Belcourt who c1820 married L1Catherine L'Hirondelle. No Belcourt identities appear in Sprague & Frye (A50). Several "orphan" Belcourts "for adoption" appear in the Tabulation. In most cases, the "Sources" quoted give interesting background.

Sources:	0....5... (n+ generations)
B6	B1Joseph Belcourt(c1795-?)+c1820 L1Catherine L'Hirondelle(1802-?) children inc
*	1son Belcourt(c1820-?)+c1840 wife nee?(c1822-?) children include
*	1son Belcourt(c1840-?)+c1865 wife nee?(c1850-?) ditto
B6 B11 A52	B1111Narcisse Belcourt(1866LSA-1953KL)+c1900 C1442Emily Gladu(c1883LSA-?KL)qv
B6	B12Marie (Emma?) Belcourt(c1835-?)-c1855G.xJoseph Gladu(c1830RR?-?) children inc
B6 C10	1Celestin Gladu(1859LSA-c1945KL)+c1885LSA C144Margaret Calliou(1856LSA-?KL)
	(for other children etc see Gladu & Calliou Tabulations)
A15 X, A38	BxGeorges-Antoine Belcourt(1803LC-1874NB) Missionary priest, no children.
A15 XI p354	B..xAdelaide Belcourt(c1850SA-c1920Cy)+1873SA John Glenn(1833Ir-1886Cy) 6 ch
B9	B..x"Widow" Belcourt(c1850-?)
B9	B..xBenjamin Belcourt(c1850-?)
B9	B..xJean-Baptiste Belcourt(c1850-?)
A61p145	B..xVictoria Belcourt(1861LSA-1966SA)+1878 C145Louis Calliou(c1860-?) qv.
C2	B...xJohn Belcourt(c1880-?)+c1905 wife nee?(c1890-?)
C2	1Ida Belcourt(c1925-)+c1943 C14426Francis Belcourt(c1919KL-) see Calliou
B5	B...xJoe Belcourt(c1875-?)
B5 A3p130	B...xPierre Belcourt(c1875-?)
C4	B...xMike Belcourt(c1890-?)+c1915 Clare Bezant(c1895-?)
	1Virginia Belcourt(c1916-)+c1935 C14453Alfred Campbell(1914FL-) qv
B3	B...xFrancis Belcourt(c1885Cda-c1940Gr)+c1910Gr "Cree" wife nee?(c1895-c1920Gr)
B3	1"Rick" Belcourt(c1915Gr-) reputed interviewer Cree, Beaver etc
A5p391	B....xEvelyn Belcourt(c1915-)+c1930RG L....xFrank Letendre(c1910FL-)
	(see Letendre Tabulation for 9 children)
	B....xLillian Belcourt(c1930-)+c1955 C14476Francis Gladu(c1929KL-) qv
A6p332	B....x"Mugler" Belcourt(c1910-) at Stony L & Redwillow R c1950
A44p27	B....xAdolphus Belcourt(c1910-)
ditto	B....xClarence Belcourt(c1910-)
A5p524	B.....xMadeline Belcourt(c1940-)+c1960 Leslie Leonard(c1933BL-)
	B.....xCurtis Belcourt(c1950-)+c1975 C144753Barbara Whitford(c1952-) qv
A47p431 D23	B.....xArchie Belcourt(1924-1945RG) drowned upper Wapiti R, buried RG
	B......xJosephine Belcourt(c1960-)_c1980 C1433111Daryl Pastovik(c1958-) qv
D24	B......xEdward Chas Belcourt(1957-1974RG)
D25	B......xRoger Geo Belcourt(1960-1974RG)
A44p22	B....xJohn Belcourt(c1910-)
A52-1933	B....xGeo Belcourt(c1910-)
D4	B.....xAlbert Belcourt(1930-1980KL)
	0....5... (n+ generations)

CAMPBELL   Code symbol for Campbell is "C" as distinct

Sources: 0....5....0... (n+ generations)   from "C" for Calliou.

Source	Entry
A5p90 C4,5	C..xAlex C Campbell (c1855Cda–c1950RG)+c1880LSA wife nee Gauthier (c1861LSA–?)
A3p208	reputed 17 ch inc /Calliou
B5 A52 C4	1Milton Campbell (c1881–c1950KL)+c1905 C1445Annie Gladu (c1890LSA–?) see /
A52	2Leo Campbell (c1883–?)
A52	3Lecoff Campbell (c1885–?)
B6	4Harry Campbell (c1887–?)+c1910 C1444Marguerite Gladu (1887LSA–?) see Calliou
A52	5Edward Campbell (c1890–?)
A3p261*	6Lester Campbell (c1900–1931?)
A3p256	7Ray Campbell (c1902–?) /d of Walter E Eaton, CE
A5p90 A52	8Peter Campbell (1903SR–)+c1928 Christine Eaton (widow of Frank Aldridge /
C4,5	9Lective Campbell (1914FL–)+c1939 C14471 CarolineGladu (c1921KL–) see Calliou
A33	CxColin Campbell (c1787–1853) see also HBRS Vol XXX. Joined NWCo 1804, later Chief Trader with HBC. At Dunvegan c1828 et seq.
A52–1933	C..xxxLouis Campbell (c1910–)

         0....5.... (n+ generations)

GAUTHIER (Gochie, Goosi, Goshie, Gouchie, Gautier)   Code symbol for Gauthier is "G" as distinct from "G" for Gladu.

    The DCB (1983) identifies eight Gauthiers in French Canada between c1627 and 1815+ including Louise, nee Gauthier, wife of the celebrated artist Cornelius Krieghoff (1815–72). Sprague & Frye (A46) lists only one Gauthier family in the RR settlements, all French Canadian, not Metis, as below:

Sources: 0....5.... (n+ generations)

Source	Entry
ID1816	G.1Jean-Baptiste Gauthier (1831LC–?)+c1855 Rosalie Germain (1836LC–?)
	1Eliza Gauthier (1855RR–?)
	2Paul Gauthier (1857RR–?)
	3Alphonsine Gauthier (1859RR–?)
	4Leonard Gauthier (1861RR–?)
	5Pierre Gauthier (1863RR–?)
	6Jos Gauthier (1866RR–?)
	7Leonide Gauthier (1868RR–?) /Hector Tremblay Pouce Coupe pioneer.
A32p12+	G..xPaul Gauthier (c1860–1942DC)+c1920 Melena Tremblay (c1870–1939DC) widow of /
A32 p416	G...xWayne Gauthier (c1895–?) son of Paul above by earlier marriage?

    Question: Are the two contemporary Pauls in the 4th generation above one and the same? No evidence has been found to relate the above to the Metis Gauthiers of Lac Ste Anne, Flyingshot Lake and Kelly Lake as below. It is assumed that St Pierre and Louis were brothers and that a sister was Mrs Alex C Campbell. Million Gouchie (sic) on the 1924 Kelly Lake Voters' List is assumed to be Madeline, the blind wife of St Pierre. She could have been a sister of Celestin Gladu – all in the same generation. St Pierre had at least one daughter, assumed to be Madeline, wife of Alfred Gladu, and two sons, Eugene ("Zen"?) Sr and Dan. Lorne Gauthier (c1930KL–) son of Eugene Gauthier Jr and Sarah Campbell claims St Pierre was his great grandfather which places Lorne in the 7th generation. The following tabulation incorporates these assumptions.

         0....5....0.. (n+ generations)

Source	Entry
A3p130 B5	G.1Father Gauthier (c1830_?)+c1855 wife nee?(c1835–?) /(c1860–?KL) (blind)
A5p505 A52 B12	1St Pierre Gauthier (c1855–1930KL)+c1880 Madeline nee Gladu? or Calliou? /
A52	1Eugene Gauthier Sr?(c1880LSA–?)+c1905 wife nee?(c1885–?)
C4 B12 B10	1Eugene Gauthier Jr?(c1905FL–)+1925 C14452Sarah Campbell (c1909FL–c1940KL)
	(see Calliou for 6 children, inc C144523Lorne Gauthier (c1930KL–)
A42p476	2Dan Gauthier Jr (c1910–)+c1931 C14513Mary Calliou (c1916–) qv
B10	2Daughter Gauthier (c1882–?)
	3Dan Gauthier (c1890–?) /1953KL)
A5p505 B11,12	4Madeline Gauthier (c1895LSA?–1930KL)+c1912 G...xAlfred Gladu (c1890LSA– /
A44p45	(see Gladu Tabulation for chidren etc)
A5p505 A3p130 B5	2Louis Gauthier (c1858LSA?–?) brother of St Pierre above?
A5p90 C4 C5	G.13Daughter Gauthier (c1861LSA–?)+c1880LSA C..xAlex C Campbell (c1855Cda–c1950RG)
	(see Campbell Tabulation for 9 children etc)

         0....5....0... (n+ generations)

GRAY:

    This family joins the Kelly Lake Callious with the marriage, sometime after 1900, of C1441Louise Gladu, in the n+5th Generation, to Joseph Gray. Their progeny includes C14411 David, C144111Della and C144112 Jarvis Gray, all with Calliou ancestry.   Jarvis Gray, who generously supplied so much genealogical data for the Kelly Lake families, and his father, David, who also helped, have given no information about their paternal Gray ancestry. The fault is mine. In sources like the DCB (A15) and Sprague & Frye (A50) there are too many Grays for selection of possible Kelly Lake connotations.

GLADU (Gladieux, Gladue)   Code Symbol: "G" (as distinct from "G" for
                                                                              Gauthier)
Sources: 0....5....0.. (n+ generations)

A21p231,2 | G(male) Gladu(c1770Cda?-?) with David Thompson, Rocky Mts 1801
ID1969 | G.Chas Gladu(1776Cda-?)+c1800RR? Elsie nee?(1785-?)
ID1975 | G.1Louis Gladu Sr(1815RR-?)+c1838 Susanne Desjarlais(1810NWT-?) (A12p580)
* | G.11Esau Gladu(c1839-?)
ID1967 | 2Pierre Gladu Jr(1840-?)+c1865 Isabelle Moosette(1849-?)
ID1976 | 3Louis Gladu Jr(1842RR-?)+c1867RR Philomene Morrisette(1848RR-?)
           | 1Chas Gladu(1868RR-?)
           | 4Paschal Gladu(1846RR-?)
ID1977 | 5Francois Gladu(1847RR-?)+c1873 Marguerite Welsh(1850-)
           | 6Cuthbert Gladu(1849RR-?)
           | 7Justin Gladu(1851RR-?)
           | 8Joseph Gladu(1852RR-?)
           | 9Andre Gladu(1854RR-?)
           | 0Madeline Gladu(1857RR-?)   /Bourassa(1825NWY-?)
ID1964 | G.2Antoine Gladu(1817NWT-?)+(1)c1842 Josephte Desjarlais(1823-?) +(2) Marie /
           | 1Joseph Gladu(1852RR-?)
           | 2Eliza Gladu(1858RR-?)
           | 3Isabelle Gladu(1862RR-?)
ID2473 | G.Chas Gladu Jr(1799-?)+c1825RR? Madeline Laurin(1804-?)
ID1979 | G.1Pierre Gladu(1815RR-?)+c1840RR? Nancy Dease(1824RR-?)
ID1978 | G.11Jos Gladu(1849RR-?)+c1874RR? Adele Lafournais(1850RR-?)
           | G..2Wm Gladu(1857RR-?)
           | G..3Alexandre Gladu(1859RR-?)
           | G..4Elise Gladu(1861RR-?)
           | G..5Pierre Gladu Jr(1864RR-?)
           | G..6Alfred Gladu(1867RR-?)
ID1966 | 'G.2Chas Gladu(c1820-?)+c1845 Madeline Poitras(c1830-)
(Note: All "ID" Gladus and their progeny are from source A50 (Sprague & Frye, Tables 1,2,4 &5)

B6 | G.xJoseph Gladu(c1830-?)+c1855 B12Emma (Marie) Belcourt(1835RR?-?)   / qv
           | 1Celestin Gladu(1859LSA-c1945KL)+c1880LSA C144 Marguerite Calliou(1856LSA-?KL)/
           | 2Jas Gladu(1862Ed-?)
           | 3Honore Gladu(1864LSA-1875LSA)   /Vermilion, Alta.
           | 4Annie Gladu(1865LSA-?)+c1890 Albert Ducharme(c1860-?)Descendants at Ft /
           | 5Lucille Gladu(?-?)+   John Leone(?-?)
           | 6Marguerite Gladu(1868LSA-?)
A38p242]_[GxLisette Gladu(1792-1907Ed)+c1807 husband Quinn(c1770-?)
A16p133] [Gxher bro Gladu(1797-?) baptized by Rev J-B Thibault LSA 1845
A35p72,144 | Gxhusband Gladu(c1780-?)+c1805 Marie Rose Besson(1788Gr-1899+Calling L) ½sister
           | of| Catherine Besson(1793Gr-1899+Gr) (?d's of J-B Bisson see A38p26 ?)
B9 A52 | G..xBenoit Gladu(c1860LSA-?)
B9 | G..xJohn Felix Gladu(c1860LSA-?)   /also A52 A44p45
A5p505 B12 | G...xAlfred Gladu(c1890LSA-1953KL)+c1912 Madeline Gauthier(c1895LSA-1930KL)see/
A44p45 | G...x1Joe Gladu(c1912-)+c1935 Tootsie Halpenner(c1915-) divorced
           | 1Donald Gladu(c1941KL-)   /see Calliou for ch
D6,7 | 2Delphine Gladu(1913FL_1980KL)+c1930 C14461 Joe Hamelin(1906FL-1980KL) /
           | 3Florence Gladu(c1915FL-)+c1935 David Capot(c1912-)
           | 1son Capot(c1936-)
           | 2daughter Capot(c1937-)
           | 4Jean Gladu(c1917FL-)+c1940 C14411David Gray(1916FL-) for ch see Calliou
           | 5Madeline Gladu(c1922FL?-)   /was uncle of Dan St Arnaud
C19 A3p9 C11| G...xUrbain Gladu(c1890LSA-?KL)+c1910FL? wife nee Breland(c1895LSA?-?) Urbain /
           | 1Colin Gladu(c1912FL-c1940)+c1935 wife nee?(c1915-?)one or more ch
           | 2Alec Gladu(c1915FL-?)
           | 3Josephine Gladu(c1917FL-?)   Note:-(Breland a prominent RR family, see
           | 4Dewdney Gladu(c1920FL-?)   (A50. See also "Berland" in Morice A35.
A5p166 | G...xJohn Gladu(c1895?-) met "Bull Gang" vic Lake Saskatoon, c1909.
           | G...xhusband Gladu(c1885-?)+c1910 C1433Marceline Calliou(c1890LSA-?) see Calliou
           | G...xhusband Gladu(c1890-?)+c1915 wife nee?(1899-) m-in-law of C14462Geo Hamelin
A47p432 | G....xCharley Gladu(c1910?-) moved from Horse Lake to Kelly Lake c1920?
C12 | G....xMabel Gladu(1920Gr?-)+c1937KL C14462Geo Hamelin(1912FL-1983DC) qv
A47p147 | G....xJennie Gladu(c1935Gf-)+c1950 Peter Volden(c1932Gf-)
   (| G....x1Leonard Gladu(c1940Gf-)   )
A47p346(| 2Ronnie Gladu(c1944Gf-)   )- children at Lambert School, vic Lymburn
   (| 3Sidney Gladu(c1946Gf-)   ) 1952
B8 | G.....xIsabel Gladu(c1932-)+c1952 C144512Joe Calliou(c1930KL-) see Calliou
B8 | G.....xMargaret Gladu(c1952-)+c1967 C144519Clifford Calliou(1950KL-) ditto
A3p130 | G...xPierre Gladu(c1890LSA?-?)
A52-1933 | G....xPascal Gladu(c1910-)
           | 0....5...(n+ generations)

No Gladus appear in the DCB (1983) but many occur in the Red River Settlements (A50).
The "Kelly Lake" patriarch, G.xJoseph Gladu, who married B12Emma Belcourt, could have
been uncle of the three Josephs (Gladu) in the n+4 generation above.

HAMELIN (Amlin, Amlyn, Emlin, Emlyn, Emmila, Hambler, Hamlin, Hemlin, Omlin)

Early Canadian Identities: (from Dictionary of Canadian Biography, 1983)
Vol I: Jaques Francois Hamelin(1664Fr-1696Fr) in Canada 1687-95.
Vol III: Louis Hamelin: with Pierre de LaVerendrye at Nipigon c 1727; in Quebec 1729.
Angelique Hamelin:married Arnold Balthazar Pollet at Quebec 1729.
Vol IV: Nicholas Hamelin: creditor of Capt Antoine Rodrigue, Louisbourg, c1752.

Sources: 0....5....0... (n+ generations) HAMELIN Code Symbol: "H"

A38 HLouis Hamelin(c1730-?) (comrade of Chas-Michel de Langlade L Michigan, c1750.
ID2114 HxJacque Hamelin(1771Cda-?)+c1800 Angelique Tourangeau(1770-?)
ID2110 1J-B Hamelin(1805RR-?)+c1840 Marianne Comtois(1826RR-?)
ID2105 A15 XI 1Jos Hamelin(1840RR-?)+c1865 Louise Laurence(1844-?)
2Francois Hamelin(1851RR-?)
3Domitilde Hamelin(1854RR-?)
4Paul Hamelin(1859RR-?)
5Louis Hamelin(1862RR-?)
6Louisa Hamelin(1864RR-?)
7Wm Hamelin(1867RR-?)
ID2112 * 2Francois Hamelin(1809-?)+c1830 Marguerite (Indian)(1814-?)
ID1785 A38 1J-B Hamelin(c1830?-?)+(1)c1850 Houle(1825-?)+(2)c Piwanook(1814-?)
ID2104 * 3Louis Hamelin(1809NWT-?)+c1834 Cecile Bruyere(1814-?)
ID1780 1Augustin Hamelin(1840-?)+c1865 Marie Bouvette(1845-?)
ID2113 A15 XI 4(Hon)Salomon Hamelin(1810RR-1893RR)+c1833 Isabelle Vandal(1809RR-?) /-?)
ID1779 1Jos Hamelin(1833RR-?)+(1)c1858 Julie Laurance(1826-?)+(2)Josephte Sayer(1834/
1Napoleon Hamelin(1855RR-?)
2Rose Hamelin(1857RR-?)
3Eleanor Hamelin(1864RR-?)
4Jos Hamelin(1869RR-?)
2Josephte Hamelin(1837RR-?)+c1852 Baptiste Laurence(1836-?)
1David Laurance(c1852-?) /Pinaud(1841-?)
ID2111 Hx43Alex Hamelin(1841RR-?)+(1)c1861 Marguerite Houle(1844RR-?)+(2)Marguerite /
1Eulalie Hamelin(1861RR-?)
2Eliza Hamelin(1863RR-?)
3Ste Anne Hamelin(1866RR-?)
4Louis Hamelin(1868RR-?)
ID1776 4Antoine Hamelin(1842RR-?)+c1861 Philomene Perreault(1843RR-?)
1Leon Hamelin(1861RR-?)
2Eleanore Hamelin(1863RR-?)
3Angele Hamelin(1865RR-?)
4Adeleine Hamelin(1868RR-?)
5Antoine Hamelin(1875 -?))
6Antoine Hamelin(1877-?) (sic))settled at File Hills, NE of Qu'Appelle
7Albert Hamelin(1879-?))
5Sara Hamelin(1845RR-?)
ID1777 6Firmin Hamelin(1847RR-?)+c1872 Clemence Breland(1849RR-?)
1Eleanore Hamelin(1869RR-?)
ID2115 H.xJos Hamelin(1811-?)+c1836 Therese Ducharme(1812-?)
ID2106 H.xJ-B Hamelin(1814-?)+c1840 Francoise McKay(1819-?)
ID1788 H.xNarcisse Hamelin Sr(1818-?)+c1843 Marguerite Racette(1823-?)
ID2108 1Narcisse Hamelin Jr(1843RR-?)+c1868 Marguerite Gaudreau(1847RR-?)
1Marguerite Hamelin(1866RR-?)
2Alexandre Hamelin(1867RR-?)
3Jos Hamelin(1869RR-?)
ID1778 H.xJ-B Hamelin(1822-?)+c1847 Josephte Larocque(1827RR-?)
1J-B Hamelin(1848RR-?)
ID2095 H.xJonas Hamelin(1829-?)+c1854 Marie Daigneault(1834-?)
ID1781 H.xJos Hamelin(1831-?)+c1856 Anabelle Comtois(1836-?)
ID1430 H.xLouis Hamelin(Emlyn)(c1810RR-?)
ID1787 H..xJos Hamelin(1838-?)+c1863 Zoe Pelerin(1842-?)
ID1783 H..xGaspard Hamelin(1841-?)+c1866 Louise Landry(1846-?)
ID2109 H..xBernard Hamelin(1849-?)+c1874 Angelique Parisien(1852RR-?)
B3 H...xWillie Hamelin(c1890Gr-1973+Gr)
A52 B5 C12 H...xFrancis Hamelin(c1885-?)+c1906 C1446Caroline Gladu(c1890LSA-1931KL))
A52 C12 D6,7 1Joe Hamelin(1906FL-1980KL)+c1929 G...x2Delphine Gladu(1913FL-1980KL)) Kelly Lake Hamelins
C12 A44p48 A52 2Geo Hamelin(1912FL-1983DC)+c1937 G....xMabel Gladu(1920-))
C11 3Albert Hamelin(c1915FL-) (Note: for progeny of Kelly Lake Hamelins
B7 H...x4daughter Hamelin(1928KL-?) see CALLIOU tabulation)
0....5....0..(n+ generations)

The numerous Hamelins in Sprague & Frye (A50) are listed above in full to facilitate recognition of likely connections to the Kelly Lake Hamelins.

LETENDRE (La Tendre, LaTente, Lattent) Code Symbol: "L"

Early Identity (from DCB Vol II p655): Genevieve nee Letendre, widow of Jean Francois
Xavier Pelletier married Etienne Volant de Radisson 1693 at Sorel (now) PQ.

Sources:	0....5... (n+ generations)
A38 p 186	L1Jean-Baptiste Letendre(c1780Cda-?) Interpreter NWCo vic Edmonton 1804, later free-trader & hunter NWT +(1) c1808NWT Cree wife(c1790NWT-1809NWT) +(2) c1810RR Cree wife(c1795RR-?)
A38 ID2945	L11Louis Letendre(c1810NWT-?)+c1833 Marie Hallet(1810-?)He was celebrated buffalo hunter vic Pembina c1850.
A38 ID2943	1Louis Letendre(1833RR-?)+c1853 Champagne Beaugrand(1835-?)
ID2898 *	2A Letendre(1839-?)+c1864 Catherine Godon(1841-?)
A38 ID2942	3Xavier Letendre(alias Batoche)(c1840RR-?NWT)+c1865RR Margaret Parenteau (1844RR-?) He was prominent merchant etc at Batoche & vic c1870 et seq.
A50 Tab 4	1Helene Letendre(1867RR-?)
	2Alexandre Letendre(1869RR-?)
	3Xavier Letendre(1871NWT-?)
	4John L Letendre(1876NWT-?) Fish Creek 1900
	5Flor Letendre(1877NWT-?) Batoche 1900
A50 Tab 6	6Josephte Letendre(1880NWT-?) Fish Creek
	7Marie Letendre(1882NWT-?) Batoche
	8Emanuel Letendre(1884NWT-?)Batoche
	L1139Jos A Letendre(1885NWY-?) Batoche
ID2939 *	2Baptiste Letendre(1819-?)+c1845 Marguerite Lyonnais(1822-?)
B9 *	1Jean Baptiste Letendre(c1855-?) Occupant Lot 7 LSA Settlement 1890
A50 Tab 3 *	3Jos Letendre(c1820-?) "middleman" HBC 1853-57
ditto *	4Pierre Letendre(c1830-?) do do 1860-66
A15 XIp193*	5Oiseau Letendre(c1835RR-?) convicted of sedition, Manitoba 1871
HBRS Vol X	LxJos Letendre(c1790-?) Employee HBC McLeod Lake Post, BC, 1828.
A52 1924	L...xZen Letendre(c1890-?)
A52 1924,33	xLiza Letendre(c1890-?)
A52 1933	xJean Letendre(c1905-?)
A5p391	xFrank Letendre(c1910FL-)+c1935 Evelyn Belcourt(c1915-)
	1Norma Letendre(c1936-) (These Ch as listed- in correct time sequence?)
	2 to 9 inc Harriette, Gladys, Margaret, Edna, Dinah, Linda, Mavis & Robt.
A47p431 D29	L....xJosie Letendre(1915-1945RG) Drowned upper Wapiti R buried RG(A5p338)
A6p338 D30	xNoel Letendre(1917-1945RG) (Note: Letendre ch attended Cariboo Sch
do D28	xDorothy Letendre(1923-1941RG) (vic RG c1928.)
B8	L....xJas Letendre(c1917-)+c1949 C144511Galena Calliou(1929KL-) qv
A44p27	L....xRoland Letendre(c1910-)
C8	L....xEd Letendre(c1930-)+c1955 C14477Kathleen Gladu(c1932KL-) qv
C5	L.....xWalter Letendre(c1940-)+c1962 C144711Shirley Campbell(c1942KL-)
B8	L.....xElsie Letendre(c1937-)+c1956 C144514Chas Calliou(1935KL-) qv
A6p141	L.....xRobt Letendre(c1950-)+c1975 Ginny Van Erve(c1953-)
	0....5... (n+ generations)

Comment: The conjectural items (*) are biologically and chronologically feasible. The birth
year for ID2942 L113Xavier Letendre is given as 1841 by Morice (A38) and 1838 by Sprague &
Frye (A50). It is highly probable that the Red River and Batoche Letendres are related to
those at Lac Ste Anne, Rio Grande and Kelly Lake. Hopefully the structure tabulated above
may be amended, confirmed and expanded by further research.

St ARNAUD (St Amand, St Arnaude, St Arnault, St Arnoult) Code Symbol: "S"

Early St Arnaud connotations in the DCB are scant. Damase St Arnaud was artist in wood
carving etc, Lower Canada 1832, (Vol XIp506). Several Arnaud identities between 1692 and
c1850 appear to be irrelevant.

Sources:	0....5... (n+ generations)
ID4579	S1Bonaventure St Arnaud(1798Cda-?)HBC middleman & fisherman 1828-46 +c1832 Genevieve Contre(1817-?) (Metis)
*	1Louis St Arnaud(c1833RR-?) HBC middleman 1853-56
ID4468	2Chas St Arnaud(1840RR-?)+c1860 Genevieve Rainville(1843-?)
	1Genevieve St Arnaud(1861RR-?)
	2Chas St Arnaud(1863RR-?)
	3Geo St Arnaud(1864RR-?)
	4Julie St Arnaud(1866RR-?)
	5Annie St Arnaud(1869RR-?) / Ladouceur(1845RR-?)
ID4470	S.3Alexander St Arnaud(1841RR-?) HBC middleman 1861-64 +c1866 Philomene /
ID4469	4Jean-Baptiste St Arnaud(1847RR-?)+c1872 Marguerite Laderoute(1843RR-?)
A3 p9,10	S...1Dan St Arnaud(1889LSA-1954S Wapiti) to FL c1906 with uncle Urbain Gladu
A3p16	+c1910 Florence Ferguson(1893LS-1970LS) d of Leon Ferguson? (A6p168)
	1John St Arnaud(c1912-)
	2Jean St Arnaud(c1914-)+c1930 Theodore Seward(c1910-) ch?
	3Madeline St Arnaud(c1916-)+c1931 Adolphus Beaulieu(c1910-)
A3 p10	4Jimmie St Arnaud(c1918FL-1937Ed) pupil at KL Sch 1924-25
A3p257	5Josephine St Arnaud(c1920-)+c1935 Marshall Chenoweth(c1915-) 4 ch
	6Dorothy St Arnaud(c1922-)+c1940 Don Johnson(c1920-)
	7Mary St Arnaud(c1924-)+c1940 Sandy Creighton(c1920-)
A52	S...2Floristine St Arnaud(c1890-?) on KL Voters' List 1924
	0....5... (n+ generations)

THOMAS (Napoleon, Thoma, Toma):   Code Symbol: "T"

This family enters the Kelly Lake ancestral complex primarily by T..x3Annie Thomas (1902DC-) who c1917 married C1447Isidore Gladu(1896LSA-1974KL). Their numerous progeny appear in the Calliou Tabulation, qv. Like Calliou and L'Hirondelle, this Thomas family has Iroquois paternal roots. The name Thomas is not very selective in references like the DCB (A15) or Sprague & Frye (A50). The latter lists many Thomas's with mostly HBC connections and European ancestry - not Iroquois. David Thompson's guide through the Athabasca Pass 1810-11 was the "Iroquois Indian" Thomas (A21p280).

One of Sir George Simpson's "best voyageurs" was an Iroquois, Toma, whom he seconded to Lord Southesk as personal attendant at Fort Garry in 1859. Southesk referred to Toma as "a most faithful and excellent fellow" (A18p58-62).

In the Sekani community at Finlay Forks on the historic furtrade highroad to New Caledonia, in the 1950's was Isidore Toma. I have color-photo copies of portraits of him and his wife Julia painted by the late Mrs Marge McDougall who with her husband Roy lived there many years operating the store, post office and a trapline. Possibly Isidore was another of the Iroquois Tomas.

The Tabulation below is derived mostly from Mrs D Calverley's excellent article about "The Napoleon Thomas Family", original and respected pioneers on the "Pouce Coupe Prairie" c1897 (A32p9-10). T..xNapoleon Thomas was guide etc for Inspector John Douglas Moodie, NWMP on his expedition via Sifton Pass to the Klondike 1897-8. Evidently he was with Moodie as far as Lower Post, late August 1898.

Sources: 0....5... (n+ generations)

A21p280	T'Iroquois Indian" Thomas(c1770-?) with David Thompson, Athabasca Pass 1810-11
A18p58-64	T.x"Voyageur" Toma(c1820-?) with Sir Geo Simpson & Lord Southesk 1859.
A32p9-10	T.xAntoine Thomas(c1830-?) at Sturgeon Lake c 1890.
A32p202	T..xRomeo Napoleon(c1850-1920Arras)
A32p9,10	T..xFrancois Thomas(c1860-?) from Sturgeon Lake.
ditto	T..xDuncan Thomas(c1862-?) brother of Napoleon (below).
ditto	T..xNapoleon Thomas(c1864-?) with Moodie 1897-98.
A32p651	T..x1Felix Napoleon(c1894-1978Chetwynd)
A32p9,10	T..x2Johnny Thomas(c1897-?)"rodeo champion" son of Napoleon Thomas above.
A46p32,39	T..x3Annie Thomas(1902DC-)+c1917 C1447Isidore Gladu(1896LSA-1974KL) see Calliou.
A46p32	T..x4Maggie Thomas(c1903-1915Callazon Flats)
C12	T.....xKenny Napoleon(c1945-)+c1967 C144627Alvina Hamelin(1949KL-)
C19	T....xNora Napoleon(c1918-)

0....5... (n+ generations)

T..xNapoleon Thomas had more children than the four listed above. Some settled in the Moberly Lake vicinity and use the surname Napoleon.

* ** *** ** *

SELECTED PERSONAL TELEPHONE LISTINGS - 1981

	Names (include some spelling variations) / Areas:	BELCOURT[1,2]	CALLIOU[1,2]	CHATELAINE	DESJARLAIS	DUCHARME[2]	GAUTHIER[1,2]	GLADU[1,2]	HAMELIN[1]	HORSMAN[1,2]	LEIFNDRE	L'HIRONDELLE[2]	PATENAUDE[2]	PILON[2]	Totals
YT	Whitehorse									3			1		4
BC	Chetwynd	2	1		1	1	1	4			1				11
	Creston					2	3		1						6
	Dawson Creek	2	3		3			3		2	1				14
	Mackenzie	1			1		1	1	1						5
	Prince George	4	1		4	6	10	1	8		6		6	5	51
Alberta	Beaverlodge		2	4		2				1	2		5	13	11
	Calgary	8	2		11	16		3	6	5	9	3	5	13	81
	Edmonton	50	36		25	23	60	18	8	5	45	29	10	20	329
	Grande Prairie	4	1			1		1			1	5	1	1	15
	Grouard		7		1		10	2	1		6	1			28
	Lac Ste Anne	2	3						1		9	1			16
	Valleyview	5	1			3						1			10
Sask	North Battleford				2		1								3
	Prince Albert	1		4	1	1			1	3	3			9	20
	Regina	3			25	2			8	3	2		2	2	47
	Saskatoon	3		1	6	3		1		2			6	10	32
Man	Brandon				3	6		1		1			1	1	13
	Flin Flon				1	13	7						3	1	25
	Portage la Prairie					25		7			2			1	35
	Winnipeg	6		5	52	104	100	19	17	10	5		16	23	357
	Totals:	91	57	14	136	208	193	61	52	32	86	45	52	86	1113

1 = Prominent at Kelly Lake 1923-25. 2 = Significant in"Kelly Lake" ancestry. Larger tallies are approximate.

"Kelly Lake" Genealogies: HEAD-COUNT by Surnames

Surnames:-	n+ generations									Totals
	1	2	3	4	5	6	7	8	9	
Beaugrand				1						1
Beaulieu					1					1
Belcourt		2	2	5	6	17	4	3		39
Besson		1			2	3				6
Bezant						1				1
Bourassa		1								1
Bouvette					1					1
Breland				1	1					2
Bruyere			1							1
Calliou	1	1	1	9	11	12	9	24		68
Campbell		1		1	9	5	13	7	1	37
Capot						1	2			3
Cardinal							1			1
Chenoweth						1				1
Comtois			2							2
Contre	1									1
Cowpar						1				1
"Cree" (wives)		2								2
Creighton						1				1
Daigneault			1							1
Davidson							1	4		5
Davis							1			1
Dease			1							1
Desjarlais			2				1	3		6
Ducharme			1	1						2
Duke							1	2		3
Eaton				1	1					2
Ferguson				1	1					2
Finlay			1							1
Fosseneuve			1							1
Gaudreau			1							1
Gauthier			2	11	5	2	8	6		34
Germain			1							1
Gladu	1	5	5	26	15	22	18	6		98
Glenn			1							1
Godon			1							1
Gray					1	1	2			4
Hallet			1							1
Halpenner					1					1
Hamelin	1	1	11	19	22	4	14	9		81
Horsman					3	2	2	5		12
Houle			2							2
"Indian" (wife)			1							1
Irwin								1		1
Joachim						1	3			4
Johnson						1				1
Kay							1			1
Knott						1	1	3		5
Laderoute			1							1
Ladoucer			1							1
Lafournaise				1						1
LaGlace					1					1
Lambert							1	3		4
Landry				1						1
Laplante					1	1				2

Surnames:	n+ generations									Totals
	1	2	3	4	5	6	7	8	9	
LaRondelle				1		1				2
Laroque			1							1
Laufman						1	3			4
Laurence				3	1					4
Laurin	1									1
Lawrence							1	4		5
Leonard							1			1
Leone				1						1
Letendre	1	2	5	4	11	8	12	6		49
L'Hirondelle	1	1	1	2	1					6
Lindbloom							1			1
Longson							1	4		5
Lyonnais			1							1
Martin							1			1
McKay			1							1
Meck							1	5	1	7
Modsette				1						1
Morrisette				1						1
Napoleon				2			2	5		9
Nepissing			1							1
Parenteau				1						1
Parisien				1						1
Pastovik							1	9	2	12
Patenaude		2								2
Paul							1			1
Pelerin				1						1
Perreault				1						1
Peters					1					1
Pilon	2									2
Pinaud				1						1
Pinawook				1						1
Poitras			1							1
Potts							1			1
Quinn	1									1
Racette			1							1
Radisson	1									1
Rainville			1							1
St Arnaud		1	4	5	2	5	2			19
Sayer				1						1
Schanuel						1				1
Seward						1				1
Smith						1	2			3
Supernat					1		2			3
Testawich					1	1				2
Thomas	1		1	3	3					8
Thorn				1						1
Toloway							1			1
Toma			1							1
Tourangeau	1									1
Vandal		1								1
Vanderik							2			2
VanErve							1			1
Volden						1	1	2		4
Welsh				1						1
Whitford						1	3			4
Surnames (?)	1	1	2	5	6	1	2	10	5	33
Totals:	11	24	57	120	107	106	129	113	9	676

Comment:

    High counts for Gauthier, Gladu, Hamelin, Letendre and St Arnaud, derive partly from identities in the Red River Settlements (A50). Their relationship to Kelly Lake families, while very probable, remain to be clarified. No Calliou's or Belcourts are from that source, but most of these do have numerous Kelly Lake connections.

    Comparatively low totals for the 5th and 6th generations confirm that basic data are incomplete.

    Members of the 7th, 8th and 9th generations share the predominant ancestral bloodlines, such as Calliou, Campbell, Gauthier, Gladu, Hamelin and Letendre. A healthy infusion of new blood is also evident in these later generations.

    The identities "Leonard" and "Leone" were inadvertently omitted from the "Nominal Index" (see following pages). Details for them are inserted under "Concluding Remarks".

TIME INCIDENCE OF GENERATIONS ("Kelly Lake" Genealogies):

Generations:	n	n+1	n+2	n+3	n+4	n+5	n+6	n+7	n+8	n+9
No of births	1	8	20	56	118	103	95	126	113	11
Earliest)	1730	1750	1770	1805	1814	1852	1898	1917	1950	1978
Average)	1730	1766	1790	1823	1851	1884	1916	1943	1966	1980
Latest)	1730	1782	1817	1847	1870	1914	1935	1960	1981	1981
"Adjusted") Average)	1733	1763	1793	1823	1853	1883	1913	1943	1973	2003

Some birth dates were estimated on the assumption that fathers average 25 and mothers 18 years' age when their first child was born and that successive children average two years apart. Thirty years is generally accepted as the interval between generations. Without a better clue, "middle age" for adults is assumed to be 35 years.

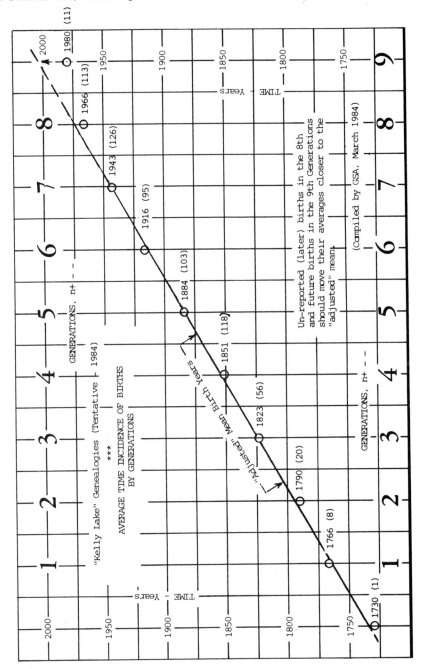

Nominal Index: "Kelly Lake" Genealogies: (Some names simplified).

Surnames, given names:	Code	Spouse
BEAUGRAND, Champagne		L111 (Louis Letendre)
BEAULIEU, Adolphus		S...13 (Madeline StArnaud)
BELCOURT, Adelaide		GLEN, John
" , Adolphus	B..x	
" , Albert	B.....x	
" , Annie	C14425	
" , Archie	B..x	
" , Benjamin	B..x	
" , Clarence	B.....x	
" , Curtis	B.....x	C144753 (Barbara Whitford)
" , Edward Charles	B......x	
" , Evelyn	B.....x	L....x (Frank Letendre)
" , Francis	B...x	"Cree"
" , Francis	C14426	B...x1 (Ida Belcourt)
" , George	C14421	
" , George	B....x	
" , Georges Antoine	Bx	(Priest)
" , Henry	C14422	
" , Ida	B...x1	C14426 (Francis Belcourt)
" , Jean-Paptiste	B..x	
" , Joe	B...x	
" , John	B...x	nee?
" , John	B....x	
" , Joseph	B1	L1 (Catherine L'Hirondelle)
" , Josephine	B.....x	C1433111 (Daryl Pastovik)
" , Lillian	B...x	C14476 (Francis Gladu)
" , Madeline	B.....x	
" , Marie Emma	B12	
" , Mary	C14424	C14331 (William Gladu)
" , Mike	B....x	BEZANT, Claire
" , Mugler	B....x	
" , Narcisse	B1111	C1442 (Emily Gladu)
" , Patrick	C14423	
" , Pierre	B..x	
" , Rick	B...x1	
" , Roger George	B.....x	
" , (son)	B11	(wife, nee?)
" , (son)	B111	(wife, nee?)
" , (son)	B..x	"widow" Belcourt
" , Virginia	B...x1	C14453 (Alfred Campbell)
" , William	C14427	
BESSON, Caroline	C1482	HORSMAN
" , Catherine		(sister of Marie Rose)
" , Jean-Baptiste		(father of above)
" , Jean Baptiste		C148 (Melanie Calliou)
" , Marie	C1481	LaRONDELLE, John
" , Marie Rose		Gx (Gladu)
BEZANT, Clare		B...x (Mike Belcourt)
BOURASSA, Marie		G.2 (Antoine Gladu)
BOUVETTE, Marie		Hx31 (Augustine Hamelin)
BRELAND, Clemence		Hx46 (Firmin Hamelin)
BRELAND, (wife)		G...x (Urbain Gladu)
BRUYERE, Cecile		Hx3 (Louis Hamelin)
CALLIOU, Adam	C143	Veronique nee?
" , Adolphus	C14..x	
" , Alberta	C14516	
" , Archie	C14341	
" , Bernardine	C1445123	
" , Betty	C1445125	
" , Beverley	C1445124	
" , Brenda	C1445121	
" , Brent	C1445194	
" , Charles, Sr	C14514	L.....x (Elsie Letendre)
" , Charles, Jr	C1445144	
CALLIOU, Clifford	C144519	G.....x (Margaret Gladu)
" , Darwin	C1445182	
" , David	C1434	Mrs Gladu (widow?)
" , Deana	C1445181	
" , Delphine	C14..x	
" , Derek	C1445183	
" , Edward	C14342	
" , Elizabeth	C144517	(Name?)
" , Esau	C142	
" , Florence	C144513	DAVIDSON
" , Gary	C1445172	
CALLIOU, George	C144518	C144752 (Margaret Whitford)
" , Gibney	C1432	(nee?) Asleas
" , Gloria	C1445143	IRWIN, Ray
" , Henry	C1451	TESTAWICH, Lucy
" , Irene	C14516	DUKE, Greg
" , Isidore	C147	
" , John	C14.x	C1445 (Eva Campbell (?)
" , John	C14517	C14474 (Nora Gladu)
" , John	C14..x	
" , Joe	C144512	G.....x (Isabelle Gladu)
" , Joseph	C14.x	
" , Judy	C1445142	
" , Julia	C14512	KNOTT, Ted
" , Katherine	C14.x	
" , Laura	C144514	
" , Laurian	C1445192	
" , Lawrence	C1445115	
" , Lillian	C1435	(Lawrence?)
" , Louis	C	(wife, nee?)
" , Louis	C145	(nee?) Victoria
" , Louise	C14511	
" , Lynette	C1445191	
" , Malcolm	C14515	
" , Marceline	C1433	(1)G...x (2) SUPERNAT, J
" , Marguerite	C144	G.x1 (Celestin Gladu)
" , Mary	C14513	G.1112 (Dan Gauthier)
" , Melanie	C148	BESSON, Jean-Baptiste
" , Norman	C1445147	
" , Patsy	C1445126	
" , Peter	C146	
" , Peter	C14.x	
" , Pricilla	C1445173	
" , Rebecca	C1445171	
" , Robert	C1445145	
" , Rodney	C1445146	
" , Ruth	C1445127	
" , Samuel	C14.x	
" , Shelley	C1445193	
" , Sidney	C1445122	
" , (son)	C1	PATENAUDE, Marie
" , Terry	C1445148	
" , Thomas	C14	FINLAY, Marie
" , Victoria	C1436	LAPLANTE, George
" , Virginia	C14514	TESTAWICH, John
" , William	C141	
" , William	C1431	(nee?) Mary

Surnames, given names:	Code	Spouse
CAMPBELL, Alex	C144531	SUPERNAT, Beatrice
" , Alex C	C..x	GAUTHIER, (Madeline?)
" , Alfred	C1453	B...x1 (Virginia Belcourt)
" , Betty	C144713	SUPERNAT, Malcolm
" , Charlotte	C1445317	
" , Colin	Cx	
" , Dennis	C144714	PAUL, Lottie
" , Dezmar	C144717	
" , Edward	C..x5	
" , Eva	C14451	C14.x (?) (Johnny Calliou)
" , Geraldine	C144715	
" , Glenda	C144716	
" , Harry	C..x4	C1444 (Margaret Gladu)
" , Irene	C144536	
" , Jean	C144712	C143314 (Lloyd Gladu)
" , Jeanette	C144532	DAVIS, George
" , Jerry	C1445316	CARDINAL, Barbara
" , Joan	C1445315	
" , John	C144533	
" , Kenny	C1445311	
" , Lecoff	C..x3	
" , Lective	C..x9	C14471 (Caroline Gladu)
" , Leo	C..x2	
" , Leo	C14454	
" , Lester	C..x6	
" , Lester	C1445313	
" , Linda	C144535	LAUFMAN, Robert
" , Louis	C....x	
" , Marcel	C144534	
CAMPBELL, Milton	C..x1	C1445 (Annie Gladu)
" , Peter	C..x8	EATON, Christine
" , Phillip	C1445312	KNOTT, Ruby
" , Ray	C..x7	
" , Sarah	C14452	G.1111 (Eugene Gauthier)
" , Shirley	C144711	L.....x (Walter Letendre)
" , Sonia	C14453121	
" , Veronica	C1445314	
CAPOT, (daughter)	G...x32	G...x3 (Florence Gladu)
" , David		G...x31
" , (son)	G...x31	
CARDINAL, Barbara		C144533 (John Campbell)
CHENOWETH, Marshall		S...15 (Josephine St Arnaud)
COMTOIS, Annabelle		H.x (Joseph Hamelin)
" , Marianne		Hx1 (Jean-Baptiste Hamelin)
CONTRE, Genevieve		S1 (Bonaventure St Arnaud)
COWPAR, Joe		C14811 (Florence La Rondelle)
CREE, (wife) (1)		L1) Jean-Baptiste
" , " (2)		L1) Letendre
CREIGHTON, Sandy		S...17 (Mary St Arnaud)
DAIGNEAULT, Marie		H.x (Jonas Hamelin)
DAVIDSON, Daniel	C1445134	
" , Faron	C1445132	
" , (husband)		C144513 (Florence Calliou)
" , Jeanette	C1445131	
" , Robin	C1445133	
DAVIS, George		C144532 (Jeanette Campbell)
DEASE, Nancy		Gx1 (Pierre Gladu)
DESJARLAIS, Elmer		C144626 (Georgina Hamelin)
" , Josephte		G.2 (Antoine Gladu)
" , Reg	C1446262	
" , Sharon	C1446263	
" , Susanne		G.1 (Louis Gladu)
" , Wesley	C1446261	
DUCHARME, Albert		G.x4 (Annie Gladu)
" , Therese		H.x (Joseph Hamelin)
DUKE, Greg		C144516 (Irene Calliou)
", Lois	C1445162	
", Timothy	C1445161	
EATON, Christine		C..x8 (Peter Campbell)
" , Walter E (her father)		
FERGUSON, Florence		S...1 (Dan St Arnaud)
" , Leon (her father)		
FINLAY, Marie		C14 (Thomas Calliou)
FOSSENEUVE, Philomene		L..x2 (Alex L'Hirondelle)
GAUDREAU, Marguerite		H.x1 (Narcisse Hamelin)
GAUTHIER, Alphonsine	G.13	
" , Archie, Sr	C144521	C144622 (Gladys Hamelin)
" , Archie, Jr	C1445215	
" , Dan, Sr	G.113	
" , Dan, Jr	G.1112	C14513 (Mary Calliou)
" , Darlene	C1445211	(Husband?)
" , (daughter)	G.112	
" , (daughter)	C145131	
" , (daughter)	C145132	
" , Dianne	C1445212	(Husband?)
" , Dolores	C1445214	
" , Donna	C1445213	(Husband?)
" , Doris	C1445216	
" , Eliza	G.11	
" , Eugene, Sr	G.111	(wife?)
" , Eugene, Jr	G.1111	C14452 (Sarah Campbell)
" , Florence	C144522	
" , Jean-Baptiste	G.1	GERMAIN, Rosalie
" , Joe	G.16	
" , Leonard	G.14	
" , Leonide	G.17	
" , Lillian	C144524	
" , Lloyd	C144524	
" , Lorne	C144523	
" , Louis	G.114	
" , Madeline	G.114	
" , Margaret	C144525	
" , Paul	G.12	
" , Paul	G..15	TREMBLAY, (Mrs) Melena
GAUTHIER, Pierre	G.15	
" , St Pierre	G.11	(nee?) Madeline
" , Wayne	G...x	
" , (daughter)	G.13	C..x (Alex C Campbell)
" , (father)	G.1	(wife?)
GERMAIN, Rosalie		G.1 (Jean-Baptiste Gauthier)
GLADU, Adolphus	C14332	LaPLACE, Adeline
" , Alec	G...x2	
" , Alexandre	Gx13	
" , Alfred	Gx16	
" , Alfred	G...x	G.114 (Madeline Gauthier)
" , Andre	G.19	
" , Annie	G.x4	
" , Annie	C1445	C..x1/(2) BOURASSA, Marie
" , Antoine	G.2	(1) DESJARLAIS, Josephte /
" , Arnold	C143318	

Nominal Index: "Kelly Lake" Genealogies (cont)

Surnames, given names	Code	Spouse
GLADU, Benoit	G..x	
" , Bernice	C143313	MECK, Harold
" , Bernice	G....x	
" , Betty	C143311	PASTOVIK, Janus
250 " , Caroline	C1446	H...x(Francis Hamelin)
" , Caroline	C14471	C...x9(Lective Campbell)
" , Celestin	G.xl	C144 (Marguerite Calliou)
" , Celestin	C1443	
" , Chaline	C1433144	
" , Charles	G.	(nee?) Elsie
" , Charles	Gx	LAURIN, Madeline
" , Charles	G.2	POITRAS, Madeline
" , Charles	G.131	
" , Charley	G...x	
" , Charlotte	C1433142	
" , Cindy	C1433141	
" , Colin	G...xl	(nee?)
260 " , Cuthbert	G.16	
" , Cynthia	C1433151	
" , Delphine	G...x2	C14461 (Joe Hamelin)
" , Dewdney	G...x4	
" , Donald	G...xl	
" , Elise	Gx14	
" , Eliza	G.22	
" , Emily	C1442	B1111(Narcisse Belcourt)
" , Esau	G.11	
" , Florence	G...x3	CAPOT, David
270 " , Francis	C14476	B....x(Lillian Belcourt)
" , Francois	G.15	WELSH, Marguerite
" , Frank	C143312	
" , Fred	C14473	HORSMAN, Jean
" , Glen	C143319	
" , Honore	G.x3	
" , (husband)	Gx	BESSON, Marie Rose
" , (husband)	G...x	C1433(Marceline Calliou(?)
" , (husband)	G...x	(Mrs David Calliou)
" , Isabelle	G.23	
280 " , Isabelle	G.....x	C144512(Joe Calliou)
" , Isidore	C1447	T..x5(Annie Thomas)
" , James	G.x2	
" , Jean	G...x4	C14411(David Gray)
GLADU, Jennie	G....x	VOLDEN, Peter
" , Jennie	C143316	VOLDEN, Arnold
" , John	G...x	
" , John Felix	G..x	
" , Joseph	G.x	B12(Marie (Emma) Belcourt)
" , Joseph	Gx11	LAFOURNAIS, Adele
290 " , Joseph	G.18	
" , Joseph	G.21	
" , Joseph	G...xl	HALPENNER, Tootsie
" , Josephine	G...x3	
" , Justin	G.17	
" , Kathleen	C14477	L....x(Ed Letendre)
" , Kevin	C1433143	
" , Leonard	G...xl	
" , Lillian	C14472	
" , Lisette	Gx	QUINN (husband)
" , Lisette's brother	Gx	
300 " , Lloyd	C143314	C144712(Jean Campbell)
" , Louis	G.1	DESJARLAIS, Susanne
" , Louis	G.13	MORRISETTE, Philomene/Ernie
" , Louise	C1441	(1) GRAY, Joseph (2)HORSMAN,/
" , Lucille	G.x5	LEONE, John
" , Lydia	C14475	WHITFORD, Riley
" , Mabel	G...x	C14462(George Hamelin)
" , Madeline	G.10	
" , Madeline	G...x5	
310 " , Margaret	C1444	C..x4(Harry Campbell)
" , Margaret	G.....x	C144519(Clifford Calliou)
" , Marguerite	G.x6	
" , Melvin	C143317	
" , (name?)	G	
" , Nora	C14474	C14517(John Calliou)
" , Pascal	G.14	
" , Pascal	G...x	
" , Patrick	C1448	HORSMAN, Eva
" , Philomene	C14481	SMITH, Stan
320 " , Pierre	Gxl	DEASE, Nancy
" , Pierre	Gx15	MOOSETTE, Isabelle
" , Pierre	G...x	
" , Ronnie	G...x2	
" , Sidney	G...x3	
" , (son)	C1433153	
" , Stanley	C143315	HORSMAN, Ruth
" , Urbain	G...x	BRELAND, name?)
" , Vera	C143310	
" , William	Gx12	
330 " , William	C14331	C14424(Mary Belcourt)
GLENN, John		B..x (Adelaide Belcourt)
GODON, Catherine		L112(A Letendre)
GRAY, David	C14411	G...x4(Jean Gladu)
" , Della	C144111	
" , Jarvis	C144112	
" , Joseph		C1441(Louise Gladu)
HALLET, Marie		L11(Louis Letendre)
HALPENNER, Tootsie		G...xl(Joe Gladu)
HAMELIN, Adeleine	Hx444	
340 " , Albert	Hx447	
" , Albert	C14463	/(2)PINAUD, Marguerite
" , Alexander	Hx43	(1)HOULE, Marguerite /
" , Alexandre	H.x12	
" , Alvin	C144620	MARTIN, Sherrie
" , Alvina	C144627	T.....x(Kenny Napoleon)
" , Angele	Hx443	
" , Antoine	Hx44	PERREAULT, Philomene
" , Antoine	Hx445	
" , Antoine	Hx446	
350 " , Augustine	Hx31	BOUVETTE, Marie
" , Bernard	H..x	PARISIEN, Angelique
" , Catherine	C14623	(husband, name?)
" , (daughter)	C14464	
" , (daughter)	C1446211	
" , (daughter)	C1446212	
" , (daughter)	C1446213	
" , (daughter)	C1446233	
" , David	Hx421	
" , Domitilde	Hx13	
360 " , Doreen	C144628	JOACHIM, Peter
" , Eleanore	Hx413	
" , Eleanore	Hx442	
" , Eleanore	Hx461	

Surnames, given names:	Code	Spouse
HAMELIN, Eliza	Hx432	
" , Eulalie	Hx431	
" , Firmin	Hx46	BRELAND, Clemence
" , Francis	H..x	C1446(Caroline Gladu)
" , Francis	Hx2	(Indian) Marguerite
" , Francois	Hx12	
370 " , Gardner	C144623	VANDERIK, Marie
" , Gaspard	H..x	LANDRY, Louise
" , George	C14462	G....x (Mabel Gladu)
" , Georgina	C144626	DESJARLAIS, Elmer
" , Gilbert	C144624	
" , Gladys	C144622	C144521 (Archie Gauthier)
" , Gloria	C144627	LAMBERT, Michael
" , Jacques	Hx	TOURANGEAU, Angelique
" , Jean-Baptiste	Hx1	COMTOIS, Marianne
" , Jean-Baptiste	Hx21	(1) HOULE, ?(2) PINAWOOK, ?
380 " , Jean-Baptiste	H.x	McKAY, Francoise
" , Jean-Baptiste	H.x	LAROQUE, Josephte
" , Jean-Baptiste	H.xl	
" , Jonas	H.x	DAIGNAULT, Marie
" , Jonathin	C1446212	
" , Joseph	H.x	DUCHARME, Therese
" , Joseph	H.x	COMTOIS, Anabelle
" , Joseph	Hx11	LAURENCE, Louise /Josephte
" , Joseph	Hx41	(1) Laurence, Julie (2) SAYER/
" , Joseph	Hx414	
390 " , Joseph	H.x13	
" , Joseph	H..x	PELERIN, Zoe
" , Joseph	C14461	G...x2 (Delphine Gladu)
" , Josephte	Hx42	LAURENCE, Baptiste
" , Lena	C144611	C145121 (Vern Knott)
" , Leon	Hx441	
" , Lester	C144621	KAY, Rose
" , Louis	Hx3	BRUYERE, Cecile
" , Louis	H.x	
" , Louis	Hx15	
400 " , Louis	Hx434	
" , Louis	H	
" , Marguerite	H.xl1	
" , Napoleon	Hx411	
" , Narcisse	H.x	RACETTE, Marguerite
" , Narcisse	H.xl	GAUDREAU, Marguerite
" , Patricia	C1446231	
" , Patrick	C144621	VANDERIK, Annette
" , Paul	Hx14	
" , Rachel	C1446291	
410 " , Richard	C144629	POTTS, Evelyn
" , Rose	Hx412	
" , Rose	C144625	C155121 (Joe Horsman Jr)
" , Ste Anne	Hx433	
" , Salomon (Hon)	Hx4	VANDEL, Isabelle
" , Sarah	Hx45	
" , Shaman	C1446232	
" , William	Hx17	
" , William	H..x	
" , William Joe	C1446292	
420 HORSMAN, Calvin	C1446251	
" , Ernest		C1441 (Louise Gladu)
" , Eva		C1448 (Patrick Gladu)
" , (husband)		C1482 (Caroline Besson)
" , Jean	C14413	C14473 (Fred Gladu)
" , Joanne	C1446253	
" , Joseph Sr	C14412	
" , Joseph Jr	C144121	C144625 (Rose Hamelin)
" , June	C1446255	
" , Noreen	C1446254	
430 " , Ruth		C143315 (Stanley Gladu)
" , Victor	C1446252	
HOULE, Marguerite		Hx43 (Alex Hamelin)
" , (name?)		Hx21 (Jean-Baptiste Hamelin)
(Indian), Marguerite		Hx2 (Francois Hamelin)
IRWIN, Ray		C1445143 (Gloria Calliou)
JOACHIM, Brent	C1446281	
" , Joy	C1446283	
" , Peter		C144628 (Doreen Hamelin)
" , Trudy May	C1446282	
440 JOHNSON, Don		S...16 (Dorothy St Arnaud)
KAY, Rose		C144621 (Lester Hamelin)
KNOTT, Keith	C1446111	
" , Kurt	C1446112	
" , Ruby		C1445312 (Phillip Campbell)
" , Ted		C14512 (Julia Calliou)
" , Vern	C145121	C144611 (Lena Hamelin)
LADEROUTE, Marguerite		S.4 (J-B St Arnaud)
LADOUCER, Philomene		S.3 (Alex St Arnaud)
LAFOURNAISE, Adele		Gx11 (Joseph Gladu)
450 LaGLACE, Adeline	C1446223	C14332 (Adolphus Gladu)
LAMBERT, Amanda	C1446222	
" , Jodie	C1446222	
" , Michael		C144622 (Gloria Hamelin)
" , Shawn	C1446221	
LANDRY, Louise		H..1 (Gaspard Hamelin)
LAPLANTE, George		C1436 (Victoria Calliou)
" , Lena	C14361	
LaRONDELLE, Florence	C14811	COMPAR, Joe
" , John		C1481 (Marie Besson)
460 LAROQUE, Josephte		H.x (J-B Hamelin)
LAUFMAN, Jennifer	C1445352	
" , Kelly	C1445353	
" , Robert Sr		C144535 (Linda Campbell)
" , Robert Jr	C1445351	
LAURENCE, Baptiste		Hx42 (Josephte Hamelin)
" , Julie		Hx41 (Joseph Hamelin)
" , Louise		Hx11 (Joseph Hamelin)
" , David	Hx421	
LAURIN, Madeline		Gx (Chas Gladu, Jr)
470 LAWRENCE, George	C143x1	PETERS, Sarah
" , Irene	C143x13	SCHANUEL, Ed
" , Keith	C143x14	
" , Ken	C143x12	TOLOWAY, Madeline
" , Robert	C143x11	LINDBLOOM, Alvine
LETENDRE, A	L112	GODON, Catherine
" , Alexandre	L1132	
" , Baptiste	L12	LYONNAIS, Marguerite
" , Dinah	L....x6	
" , Dorothy	L....x	
480 " , Edna	L....x5	
" , Edward	L....x	C14477 (Kathleen Gladu)
" , Elsie	L.....x	C144514 (Charlie Calliou)
" , Emanuel	L1138	
" , Evelyn	C1445114	

Nominal Index: "Kelly Lake" Genealogies (cont)

Surnames, given names	Code	Spouse
LETENDRE, Flor	L1135	
" , Frank	L....x	B....x(Evelyn Belcourt)
" , Genevieve	L	RADISSON, EV
" , Gladys	L....x3	
" , Harriette	L...x2	
490 " , Helene	L1131	
" , Henry	C1445115	
" , Howard	C1445111	
" , James	L....x	C144511(Galena Calliou)
" , Jean	L....x	
" , Jean-Baptiste	L1	(1) Cree wife (2) Cree wife
" , Jean-Baptiste	L121	
" , John L	L1134	
" , Joseph	Lx	
" , Joseph	L13	
500 " , Joseph A	L1139	
. , Josephte	L1136	
" , Josie	L....x	
" , Linda	L....x7	
" , Liza	L...x	
" , Louis	L11	HALLET, Marie
" , Louis	L111	BEAUGRAND, Champagne
" , Margaret	L....x4	
" , Marie	L1137	
" , Marlene	C1445116	
510 " , Mavis	L....xx8	
" , Noel	L....x	
" , Norma	L....x1	
" , Oiseau	L15	
" , Pierre	L14	
" , Robert	L.....x	Van ERVE, Ginny
" , Robert	L....x9	
" , Robert	C1445113	
" , Roland	L....x	
" , Ron	C1445112	
520 " , Walter	L....x	C144711(Shirley Campbell)
" , Xavier	L113	PARENTEAU, Margaret
" , Xavier	L1133	
" , Zen	L...x	
L'HIRONDELLE, Alex	L.x2	FOSSENEUVE, Philomene
" , Catherine	L1	B1(Joseph Belcourt)
" Jacques	L	PILON, Josette
" , Joseph Sr	L.x	NEPISSING, Marguerite
" , Joseph Jr	L.x1	THORN, Elsie
" , Thomas	L...x	(nee?) Julia?
530 LINDBLOOM, Alvina		C143x11(Robt Lawrence)
LONGSON, (daughter)	C143614	
" , (husband)		C14361(Lena Laplante)
" , (son)	C143611	
" , (son)	C143612	
" , (son)	C143613	
LYONNAIS, Marguerite		L12(Baptiste Letendre)
MARTIN, Sherrie		C144620(Alvin Hamelin)
McKAY, Francoise		H.x(J-B Hamelin)
MECK, Bryan	C1433133	
540 " , David	C1433134	
" , Harold		C143313(Bernice Gladu)
" , (husband)		C1433113(Audrey Pastovik)
" , Linda	C1433132	
" , Neil	C14331131	
" , Viola	C1433131	
MOOSETTE, Isabelle		G.12(Pierre Gladu)
MORRISETTE, Philomene		G.13(Louis Gladu)
NAPOLEON, Claudette	C1446271	
" , Everette	C1446275	
550 " , Felix	T..x	
" , Floyd	C1446273	
" , Kenny	T.....x	C144627(Alvina Hamelin)
" , Leila	C1446274	
" , Nora	T.....x	
" , Romeo	T..x	
" , Roxan	C1446272	
NEPISSING, Marguerite		L.x(Joseph L'Hirondelle)
PARENTEAU, Margaret	L113	(Xavier Letendre)
PARISIEN, Agelique		H..x(Bernard Hamelin)
560 PASTOVIK, Audrey	C1433113	MECK (husband)
" , Calvin	C1433116	
" , (child)	C1433121	
" , (child)	C1433122	
" , (child)	C1433123	
" , Daryl	C1433111	B.....x(Josephine Belcourt)
" , (daughter)	C14331111	
" , Dennis	C1433115	
" , Fay Cindy	C1433114	(Husband, nee?)
" , Janus		C143311(Betty Gladu)
570 " , Neil	C14331131	
" , Rodney	C1433112	(wife, nee?)
PATENAUDE, Mary		C1(Louis Calliou)
" , Michel (bro of Marie		
PAUL, Lottie		C144714(Dennis Campbell)
PELERIN, Zoe		H..x(Joseph Hamelin)
PERREAULT, Philomene		Hx44(Antoine Hamelin)
PETERS, Sarah		C143x(George Lawrence)
PILON, Antoine (bro of Josette		
" , Josette		L(Jaques L'Hirondelle)
580 PINAUD, Marguerite		Hx43(Alex Hamelin)
PINAWOOK, (wife)		Hx21(Jean-Baptiste Hamelin)
POITRAS, Madeline		G.2(Charles Gladu)
POTTS, Evelyn		C144629(Richard Hamelin)
QUINN, (husband)		Gx(Lisette Gladu)
RACETTE, Marguerite		H.x(Narcisse Hamelin Sr)
RADISSON, EV		L(Genevieve Letendre)
RAINVILLE, Genevieve		S12(Charles St Arnaud)
ST ARNAUD, Annie	S125	
" , Alexander	S.3	LADOUCER, Philomene
590 " , Bonaventure	S1	CONTRE, Genevieve
" , Charles Sr	S12	RAINVILLE, Genevieve
" , Charles Jr	S122	
" , Dan	S...1	
" , Dorothy	S...16	JOHNSON, Don
" , Floristine	S...2	
" , Genevieve	S121	
" , George	S123	
" , James	S...14	
" , Jean	S...12	SEWARD, Theodore
600 " , Jean-Baptiste	S.4	LADEROUTE, Marguerite

Surnames, given names	Code	Spouse
ST ARNAUD, John	S...11	
" , Josephine	S...15	CHENOWETH, Marshall
" , Julie	S124	
" , Louis	S11	
" , Madeline	S...13	BEAULIEU, Adolphus
" , Mary	S...17	CREIGHTON, Sandy
SAYER, Josephte		Hx41(Joseph Hamelin)
SCHANUEL, Ed		C143x3(Irene Lawrence)
SEWARD, Theodore		S...12(Jean St Arnaud)
610 SMITH, Pauline	C144812	
" , Ronald	C144811	
" , Stanley		C14481(Philomene Gladu)
SUPERNAT, Beatrice		C144531(Alex Campbell)
" , Johnny		C1433(Marceline Calliou)
" , Malcolm		C144713(Betty Campbell)
TESTAWICH, John		C14514(Virginia Calliou)
" , Lucy		C1451(Henry Calliou)
THOMAS, Annie		C1447(Isidore Gladu)
" , Antoine	T.x	
620 " , Duncan	T..x	
" , Francois	T..x	
" , "Indian"	T	
" , Johnny	T..x2	
" , Maggie	T.x4	
" , Napoleon	T..x	
THORN, Elsie		L.x1(Joseph L'Hirondelle Jr)
TOLOWAY, Madelyn		C143x12(Ken Lawrence)
TOMA, :Voyageur"	T.x	
TOURANGEAU, Angelique		Hx(Jacque Hamelin)
630 VANDAL, Isabelle		Hx4(Hon) Salomon Hamelin)
VANDERIK, Annette		C144621(Patrick Hamelin)
" , Marie		C144623(Gardner Hamelin)
VAN ERVE, Ginny		L.....x(Robert Letendre)
VOLDEN, Arlene	C1433161	
" , Arnold		C143316(Jennie Gladu)
" , Pamela	C1433162	
" , Peter		G....x(Jennie Gladu)
WELSH, Marguerite		G.15(Francois Gladu)
WHITFORD, Barbara	C144753	B.....x(Curtis Belcourt)
640 " , Margaret	C144752	C144518(George Calliou)
" , Randy	C144751	
" , Riley		C14475(Lydia Gladu)
SURNAME?, Allen	C14452111	(mother Darlene Gauthier)
" , Clayton	C14452121	(" Dianne Gauthier)
" , Gary	C1445172	(" Elizabeth Calliou)
" , Greg	C14331141	(" Fay Cindy Pastovik)
" , Jordan	C1446231	(" Catherine Hamelin)
" , Laura Lee	C1446232	(" " ")
" , Priscilla	C1445173	(" Elizabeth Calliou)
650 " , Rebecca	C1445171	(" " ")
" , (son)	C14452112	(" Darlene Gauthier)
" , (son)	C14452131	(" Donna Gauthier)
" , (husband)		C144623(Catherine Hamelin)
" , (husband)		C144517(Elizabeth Calliou)
" , (husband)		C1433114(Fay Cindy Pastovik)
" , (husband)		C1445211(Darlene Gauthier)
" , (husband)		C1445212(Dianne Gauthier)
" , (husband)		C1445213(Donna Gauthier)
" , "Widow"		B...x(Belcourt)
660 " , (wife) Asleas	nee?	C1432(Gibney Calliou)
" , (wife) Elsie	nee?	G.(Charles Gladu)
" , (wife) Julia	nee?	L....x(Thomas L'Hirondelle)
" , (wife) Madeline	nee?	G.11(St Pierre Gauthier)
" , (wife) Mary	nee?	C1431(William Calliou)
" , (wife) Melena	nee?	G..x(Paul Gauthier)
" , (wife) Veronique	nee?	C143(Adam Calliou)
" , (wife) Victoria	nee?	C145(Louis Calliou)
" , (wife)	nee?	C(Louis Calliou)
" , (wife)	nee?	E11(Belcourt)
670 " , (wife)	nee?	G.1(Gauthier)
" , (wife)	nee?	B111(Belcourt)
" , (wife)	nee?	B...x(John Belcourt)
" , (wife)	nee?	G.111(Eugene Gauthier Sr)
" , (wife)	nee?	G...x1(Colin Gladu)
" , (wife)	nee?	C1433112(Rodney Pastovik)
Addenda (to be inserted above, alphabetically)		
*BELCOURT, Gordon	C1445.x	
*LETENDRE, Shirley	C1447x	
*LEONARD, Leslie		B.....x(Madeline Belcourt)
*LEONE, John		G.x5(Lucille Gladu)

Concluding Remarks for the Kelly Lake genealogies:

"Personal Telephone Listings – 1981" show the incidence of some Kelly Lake surnames across Western Canada. These tallies vary somewhat from the proportions shown in the "Kelly Lake Head-count".

Families of historical interest but not prominent numerically include Besson (Bisson), Breland (Berland) Cardinal, Desjarlais, Horsman, Joachim, Supernat, and Whitford. Of the last-mentioned, many are prominent in the Red River lists (A 50), the earliest being ID 5168 Peter Whitford (1771-?) from England who married an Indian, "Sarah" (1776NWT-?). Families connected with Sam Wilson, our companion on the Nose Mountain trail, 1925 (Chapter 4) are Chatelaine, Nease and Wanyandie. These interesting people were located mostly along and south of the Wapiti River (A3p9, p11, p12; A6p238-42), with less prominence at Kelly Lake, where Alfred Chatelaine and his daughter Lena trapped c1930 (A6p241).

More than 75 per cent of the total "Head-count" (676 individuals) have code indices and about half of these are Callious ("C"), practically all of whom have Kelly Lake relationships, close or distant. The Gladus ("G") are next in number; many of them are from the Red River lists (A50), probably but not clearly related to the Kelly Lake families. Only seven of the Calliou codes (about 2 per cent) are not fully specific. For these, the device of "." or "x" is used to place them in their probable "n+" generation.

The code indices show both close and distant relationships. For example, C143311 to C143310 inclusive, are 10 brothers and sisters, all children of C14331Billy Gladu and C14424Mary (nee Belcourt). Mary's mother, C1442Emily (nee Gladu), and C1451 Henry Calliou, are cousins of each other and of the Besson sisters, C1481Marie and C1482Caroline, all in the "n+5" generation. All four are grandchildren of C14Thomas Calliou and his wife Marie Finlay, in the "n+3" generation. As previously remarked, a member of the "n+9" generation has 256 different ancestors in the "n+1" generation! If all these are unrelated, it implies that same number of different genetic codes for a complete genealogy. Obviously, the system used here would be quite inadequate. There is logic in the maxim "Let well enough alone".

I must emphasize that these "Kelly Lake" genealogical tabulations are incomplete and partly speculative. Some residual errors, both editorial and typographical are inevitable, but I hope minimal. Only those who have attempted similar compilations can appreciate the colossal amount of detail which must be assembled from various sources, analyzed, correlated, organized, transcribed, checked and double-checked. The job has taxed human capability almost beyond its limits. On the other hand, these tabulations are likely the fullest and most comprehensive yet attempted for the

Kelly Lake families. Hopefully they will stimulate interest, corrections and amplification – which should not be delayed. Old-timers still with us, whose memories are vital, will, all too soon, be forever silent. These austere skeletal lists support and correlate the warm flesh and blood of a rich human heritage – from real people in their true family perspectives, with their loyalties, aspirations, tragedies and triumphs – and with much color and humour implied. This should afford pride and pleasure to their living heirs.

104: Indian cemetery at Pipestone Park, July 1983. Duff Wight, BCLS, was my companion on this trip. (GSA #7302)

The "BOONE" TAYLOR FAMILY   Code Symbol: "T"

Martin Batterton "Boone" Taylor and wife Mary, nee Hoffman came to the Peace River country by wagon on the Edson Trail from Lake Lenore, Sask, in 1914, with "Girlie" age four and Frances one. They wintered 1914-15 in the Red Willow vicinity living mostly on rabbits and beans. A kind neighbour, "Diamond Dick" lent them a milch cow and gave them turnips. The next winter was spent west of the Cutbank River where Boone and Van Wartenbe put up wild hay. In summer 1916 Boone with his family located at Swan Lake (Tupper) on his pre-emption Fractional S24 Tp26 W6 (PRB) fronting the west shore of the lake. This was their home for 50 years. At first, Boone bought fur for Revillon Freres. Later, c1921 he won the mail hauling contract between Beaverlodge and Pouce Coupe. Crops and livestock on their rich land augmented the family larder and income. Both Boone and Mary were expert hunters and game was plentiful. The children, five girls at first helped to maintain the minimum enrolment at the Tupper School. For Christmas 1925 they moved into their new 9-room house overlooking the lake. In the 1930's Boone operated a sawmill, with a good market to settlers arriving on the new railroad from Grande Prairie. Rheumatism and heart troubles preceded Boone's death in May, 1953 in his 66th year. Mary "carried on", progressively subdividing the homestead into Lots for the Tupper Townsite till 1966 when she moved to Dawson Creek closer to son Jerry and daughter Iris. She died there, April 1977 in her 90th year. (Abridged from articles by Ruth and Leona Taylor in "Lure of the South Peace" (A32p157 et seq).

In response to my request for family statistics, remarkably full data were supplied by Bessie Taylor (Mrs N Albert), as tabulated below. Mrs Mary Taylor, nee Hoffman was 7th of 11 children all born in Millerville, MN. Her mother nee Gaetz was from Regensburg, Germany. "Boone"'s mother was an accomplished concert pianist. Her grandchildren were thrilled to hear her play on the early KOMO Broadcasts, c1924.

```
0....5.... (n+ generations)
|
|T.1Samuel Columbus Taylor(c1830-?)+c1854 Josephine Outten(c1832-?)
|    1Benjamin Franklin Taylor(1855USA-1922)+c1880 Ida May Duffy(c1856Du-1938Ta)
|    1Arthur Taylor(c1881-c1885)
|    2Maude Ray Taylor(1883-1922)+c1905 Orvil Melvin Bristo(?-?)
|    3Martin Batterton "Boone" Taylor(1887Bn-1953DC)+1908LL Mary Hoffman(1887Mv-1977DC)
|    !1Anna Leona "Girlie" Taylor(1910LL-)+1929GP Ernest Beatty(?-) s of Alex B & Sarah Gray
|     1Verna Vera Beatty(1933GP-)+1952Ont Wm Jas MacDonald)?-)
|     |  1Sandra Lee MacD(1954Acton Ont-)
|     |  2Wm Bradley MacD(1955Acton Ont-)
|     |  3Barry Richard MacD(1956Acton Ont-)
|     |  4Theresa Lynn MacD(1958Acton Ont-)
|T.11312Rose Mary Beatty(1936Hy-)+1953Ont Ross Culp(?-)
|     |  1Donna Marie Culp(1954Acton Ont-)
|     |  2Wanda Jean Culp(1955Guelph-)+1973    Frank Fuller(?-)
|     |   1Terrance Ross Fuller(1974Ont-)
|     |   2Franklin Frederick Fuller(1975Ont-)
|     |   3David Roy Fuller(1977Ont-)
|     |  3Brian Wilbert Ross Culp(1962Georgetown Ont-)
|T.11313Claudia Wanda Beatty(1938Hythe Alta-)+1959Ont James Gibson(?-)
|     |  1Paul Gibson(1960Guelph Ont-)
|     |  2Michael Gibson(1961  do   -)
|     |  3Mark Gibson(1965     do   -)
|T.1132Frances Rose Taylor(1913LL-1968Vr)+1937Ro Frederick Wm Levey(?-)
|     |  1Lawrence Michael Duff Levey(1940DC-)+1960Ed Katharine June Stich(?-)
|     |   1Kim Michelle Levey(1961      -)
|     |   2Michael Wm Levey(1962       -)
|     |   3Sandra Faye Levey(1964       -)
|T.11322Rae Lynn Levey(1944DC-)+1967Ed Ron Stevenson(?-)
|     |   1Andrea Dell Stevenston(c1968      -)
|     |   2Jason Grant Bryan Stevenson(1971     -)
|     |   3Gregory Ron Stevenson(1973        -)
|     |   4Elizabeth Rose Stevenson(1977      -)
|T.11323Christopher Leonard Levey(1953DC-)+           Gail nee?(?-)
|     |   1Jodi LynnLevey(1977Vr-)
|     |   2Jenni Lynn Levey(   Vr-)
|     |  4Thomas Frederick Levey(1956DC-)
|T.1133Ruth Taylor(1917Tu-)+1938 Frank Irwin Gardner(1917De-)s of Wm & Christine nee?
|     |   1Jeanette Ellen Gardner(1939PC-)+1958Ed Jack Garfield Kelly(?-)
|     |   1Jo Anne Kelly(1959Ed-)+              ?
|     |    1Taran nee?(      -)
|     |    2Jessica nee?(      -)
|     |   2Judy May Kelly(1961        -)
|     |   3Jack Kelly(1967          -)
|T.11332Ruth Cora Gardner(1941PC-)+1964    Jack Thompson(?-) (Address 1981:        )
| |   1Robt Thompson(1965      -)               (RR2 Box 7 New Glasgow NS)
| !   2Douglas Thompson(1966      -)
| !   3Lisa Thompson(1967      -)
|T.113324Andrew Thompson(1968      -)
0....5.... (n+ generations)                      ... (Continued next page)
```

0....5.... (n+ generations) (The "BOONE" TAYLOR Family, Cont.)

```
|T.1134Bessie Louise Taylor(1921Tu-)+1942DC Nick Albert(1918Nc-) s of Samuel A & Mary (nee Moses)
|    | 1Nicki Mary Albert(1943Nc-)+1974Ed Clive Fred Pettifer(1943Ln-)     Walter & Violet /
|    |   1Michelle Suzanne Pettifer(1965Ed-)                           /nee Cornes    /
|    |   2Ian Nicholas Walter Pettifer(1977Ed -)               /Eliz Darroch(1950-) /
|T.11342Jack Paul Albert(1944Ed-)+(1)1965Ed Judith Ann Laviolette(1946Ed-)+(2)1974 Gloria /
|    |   1Colleen Marie Albert(1968Ed-)    _(insert)T.113423Chad Taylor Nicholas Albert(1982Ed-)
|    |   2John Paul Albert(1969Ed-)___/
|    | 3David Michael Albert(1948Ed-)+1966Ed Sandra Lorraine King(1948-) d of John Arthur /
|    |   1Laurel Ann Albert(1967Ed-)                          & Marjorie nee Heyes  /
|    | 4Janice Elaine Albert(1952Ed-)
|    | 5Tony Miles Albert(1955Ed-)                          / Elizabeth nee Lamont /
|T.1135Beatrice Olive Taylor(1924Tu-)+1947Ed Robt Shield McConnell(1920On-)s of RS McC & /
|    | 1Sharon Beatrice McConnell(1949Ed-)+1967Ed Gordon Wallace Arndt(1946Sask-) s of
|    |   1Gordon Wallace Arndt(1969Sask-)             Adolph A & Amelia nee Simon
|    |   2Paul Ray Arndt(1972       -)
|T.1136Gerald Jas Taylor(1928Tu-)+1952Tu Irene Stredulinsky(1936     -) d of Frank & wife nee?
|    | 1Theresa Taylor(1953Hy-)+1975DC Helmut Johanssen(1952     -) (living Vancouver 1981)
|    | 2Rockney Taylor(1954Hy-)+1974DC Louise Steinke(1956     -) (living Dawson Creek 1981)
|T.1137Iris June Taylor(1932Tu-)+1948TC Johann Scholz(1922Cz-1984DC) s of Eduard & Marie
|    | 1Marie Ann Scholz(1949Tu-)+1968DC Nolan Alderson(1941      -)          nee Lorenz
|    |   1Becky Alderson(1967By-)
|    |   2Evelyn Alderson(1971MB-)
|    | 2Martin Edward Scholz(1952Tu-)+1974DC Laverne Neiman(          -)
|    |   1Jarrid Scholz(1977 -)       -)
|T.113722Robt Edward Scholz(1979      -)
|T.114Imogene Taylor(1889       -1931)+              Propst
|    5Fay Edward Taylor(1895       -1954)
|T.116Grace Philo Taylor(1899       -)+1914 Edward Dixon Damero(          )
```

0....5.... (n+ generations)

"TAYLOR" HEAD-COUNT (by generations):

Generations (n+):	3	4	5	6	7	8	9	Totals
Adj Av Birth Years: 1810	1825 1840	1855 1870	1885 1900	1915 1930	1945 1960	1975 1990	2005 2020	
Surnames								
Albert				1	5	4		10
Alderson					1	2		3
Arndt					1	2		3
Beatty				1	3			4
Bristo			1					1
Culp					1	3		4
Damero			1					1
Duffy		1						1
Fuller						1	3	4
Gardner				1	2			3
Gibson					1	3		4
Hoffman			1					1
Johansson					1			1
Kelly					1	3		4
King					1			1
Laviolette					1			1
Levey				1	4	5		10
MacDonald					1	4		5
McConnell				1	1			2
Neiman					1			1
Outten	1							1
Pettifer					1	2		3
Propst			1					1
Scholz				1	2	2		5
Steinke					1			1
Stevenson					1	4		5
Stich					1			1
Stredulinsky				1				1
Taylor	1	1	6	7	2			17
Thompson					1	4		5
* Darroch					1			1
Un-identified					1	1	2	4
Totals	2	2	10	14	36	40	5	109

Insert as) below *)

The assumed average interval between generations is 30 years. The 7th and prior generations above are now stabilized for births. Un-reported recent births in the 8th and future births in the 9th generations should bring their averages close to the "adjusted" values shown above.

(... see following page)

THE "JIM YOUNG" FAMILY: Code Symbol: "Y"

I have already remarked that if my Kelly Lake story needs a hero, Jim Young is "it". He and or his family feature all parts of the narrative. The Youngs' praiseworthy presence at Rose Prairie has been well told by Cora Ventress in "Peacemakers of the North Peace", (A43p243-5). Jim and Mrs Young have passed on, but their benevolence remains and proliferates in ever-widening scope in their viable progeny as tabulated below. Son Rob's family carries on valiantly at Rose Prairie. Mary's family (the Mickeys) are reputably established in the Yukon at Whitehorse, and Dorothy's (the Snippas) likewise at Fort St John, and indeed far afield. Vital data of all three families have been kindly supplied, with permission for inclusion. The Tabulation begins with Jim's father in the n+4 generation. The value for "n" is the same for all others in this Appendix.

```
0....5.... (n+ generations)
Y..1James Young(1838Ont-1922Ont)+c1870 Jane Sutherland(1847Ont-1909Ont) 4 ch incl
   2James Sutherland Young(1883Sa-1976Ww)+1931Ed Angharad Meirion Roberts(1895Rd-1973FSJ)
     1Robt Benson Young(1932RP-1980FSJ)+1958RP Gerry-Ann Taylor(1936Tr-)
      1Kevin Sandford Young(1960RP-)+1980 Theresa Sorenson(1961-)
        1Tory Ann Young(1981RP?-)
Y..1212Darla Rae Young(1962RP-)+1983RP John McAleney(1959-)
        1Jason Robert McAleney(1984RP-)
      3Sheri-Lynn Young(1964RP-)
      4Tracy-Lee Young(1973RP-)
Y..122Mary Sydney Young(1933RP-)+1957RP Thomas Oliver Mickey(1934Ry-)
       1James Wm Mickey(1958PC-)+1983Wh Rilla Bjork(
       2Glen Weston Mickey(1961FN-)
       3Michael Thomas Mickey(1964Ed-)
Y..123Dorothy Anne Young(1936RP-)+1953Ed Roy Douglas Snippa(1932PR-)
       1Rocky Lee Snippa(1954FSJ-)+1983Ed Marie Marshall(1960Nfd-)
       2Randall Douglas Snippa(1955FSJ-)
Y..1233Shane Roy Snippa(1961FSJ-)
0....5.... (n+ generations)
```

NOTES:

Y..1James Young was farmer, vic Sarnia Ont. A relative James Dougal was a Mayor of Ottawa.
Y..12Jim Young was first Postmaster at Rose Prairie and Justice of Peace for many years.
    Mrs Young was first Registered Nurse in the North Peace at the Outpost Hospital,
    Grand Haven, having arrived from England early 1930.
Y..121 Gerry-Ann's parents are Sandford Taylor and Mary nee Ryder. Her grandfather was
    Donald H Taylor, pioneer at Taylor (Flat), BC.
Y..122 Tom Mickey's parents are Wm & Celia Mickey of Rimbey, Alta.
Y..1222 Glen Mickey is an undergraduate at UBC, Vancouver.
Y..123 Roy Snippa pioneered in petroleum exploration in NE BC. and now owns R.D. Sales &
    Rentals Ltd, Fort St John.
Y..1231Rocky Snippa graduated in Engineering, U of A, 1980 and now is engaged in petroleum
    exploration from Newfoundland.
Y..1232Randall Snippa is engaged in petroleum exploration overseas.
Y..1233Shane Snippa anticipates a degree in Engineering from UBC, Vancouver, 1985.

"YOUNG" HEAD-COUNT (by Generations): (Parents etc in "Notes" may be added)

Generations (n+):	4	5	6	7	8	Totals
Av Birth Years:	1842	1889	1934	1961	1982	
*Adj " " " :	1859	1893	1927	1961	1995	
Surnames:						
Bjork				1		1
Marshall				1		1
McAleney				1	1	2
Mickey			1	3		4
Roberts		1				1
Snippa			1	3		4
Sorenson				1		1
Sutherland	1					1
Taylor			1			1
Young	1	1	3	4	1	10
Totals:	2	2	6	14	2	26

(* Average interval 34 years, somewhat abnormal due to small data base. Larger families with several hundred births average close to a 30-year interval.)

* ** *** ** *

To conclude this Appendix, I quote from my "Andrews Genealogy - 1982"

"Each individual blessed with posterity by marriage and procreative offspring is the focal point of an infinite number of convergent ancestral rays from the Past - and a like number of divergent rays to countless descendants in the Future. What a legacy to inherit, to enhance - and to bequeath!"

* ** *** ** *

APPENDIX 5

CREE COMMENTARY AND VOCABULARY

My failure to acquire fluency in Cree during the two years at Kelly Lake has been a matter of regret. It can be explained if not excused. I lived among but not with the Cree-speaking people there. My stay was not "total immersion". Jim Young and I were the only White residents and lived quite to ourselves in his store. The men, who spoke adequate English, came freely to the store to trade with relaxed sociability but they never imposed on our privacy nor did we on theirs. Jim never dispensed liquor at Kelly Lake. He, as trader, and I, as teacher, had to maintain a degree of respectability in the community. My visits to the homes were only for a specific purpose, never casual. My time and energies were fully committed to the school, to Jim's store when he was away, house-keeping, the woodpile, care of my saddle horse, my own academic studies and our voluntary program of adult education. Local help to learn Cree was always generous but never programmed. A serious handicap was utter lack of literary aids such as a dictionary or a grammer. Had I acted on initial advice that the best way to learn Cree was with a "bed-teacher" this book – and, indeed, my whole life – might have been very different!

Cree belongs to the Algonkian linguistic family, one of the largest and most widespread in North America. The eminent authority, Dr. Diamond Jenness,[122] whose nomenclature and spelling I use, identifies a dozen tribal dialects of this group in Canada including Blackfoot, Blood and Piegan near the Rocky Mountains; Plains and Woodland Cree; Ojibwa, Algonkin, Montagnais, Naskapi progressively eastward to Labrador; and Malecite and Micmac in New Brunswick and Nova Scotia. Some of these and others extended south into the USA. Unrelated neighbors of this Algonkian family were Kootenayan west of the Rockies, Athapaskan (Sarcee, Beaver and Chipewyan) to the north, and west of Hudson Bay, Eskimoan (Inuit) north and east to Labrador, and Iroquoian south along the St Lawrence River to Georgian Bay. In the central prairie and south into the USA were the Siouan family (Assiniboine, Crow, Sioux and Stony).

The vast east-west extent of this Algonkian family was a distinct advantage to early explorers and traders as they probed westward from the Atlantic shores. Having learned the eastern dialects they were able to communicate in "basic" Cree with those progressively encountered farther west. Similarly, the eastern dialects were first to receive attention from philologists. John Eliot (1604-90) produced the first Bible in the Natick dialect (Massachusetts) in 1663 and a grammar in 1666.[123] Henry Kelsey (c1670-c1725), first to see the prairies travelling with native Crees from

Hudson Bay (1690-92), later compiled a Cree dictionary (c1720) which has not survived.[124] James Evans (1801-46), a Wesleyan missionary invented the Cree Syllabic script at Norway House c1841.[125] This has had wide application to Cree and other tongues including Inuit. My Kelly Lake friends affirmed that with reasonable diligence they could become literate in this script in a matter of days. (My step-grandmother, Mrs. Alfred Andrews, nee Caroline Matilda Jones (1844-c1935), told me that James Evans was her uncle.)

Joseph Howse (1774-1852) of the HBC published "A Grammar of the Cree Language", 1844, a scholarly work widely used and acknowledged by later students[126] including E.A. Watkins, who published his Cree dictionary in 1865.[127] Father A. Lacombe, OMI, (1827-1916) produced his excellent French-Cree dictionary and grammar in two volumes 1874.[128] (This was particularly for the Plains Cree dialect.) The Rev. J. Horden produced his Cree grammar 1881.[129] A revision of Watkins' dictionary was published in 1938, and a Cree grammar by H.E. Hives in 1948.[130] Since my time at Kelly Lake I have had the good fortune to acquire some of the aforementioned works, but too late for practical benefit.

Land surveyors, like fur traders and missionaries, found it expedient to communicate in Algonkian dialects. My treasured volumes of Lacombe's dictionary were well-thumbed when given me by Guy H Blanchet, DLS, BCLS, FRGS (1884-1966). One of Blanchet's many admiring colleagues, Colonel Robert A. Logan, DLS (1892-) has published several in-depth treatises on Cree,[131] copies of which he has kindly given me and which I shall try to interpret for lay readers like myself. He quotes several well-known Algonkian place names such as Chesapeake, Illinois, Michigan, Mississippi, Saskatchewan, and Winnipeg, to which I may add Assiniboine and Mistassini (the lake in northern Quebec). Algonkian dialects are still in domestic use by thousands of Canadians in wilderness country from Labrador to the Rocky Mountains, many of whom read publications in the Cree syllabic script. Earliest encounters by Europeans were Algonkian dialects corrupted by proximity to alien neighbors along the eastern and southern limits of Algonkian territory. Logan emphasizes that the purest form of Algonkian was the Plains Cree in the far West, and that it was the mother tongue of all related dialects, like Latin was of the Romance languages. (French, Italian, Spanish, Portugese and Roumanian). This gives special significance to Father Lacombe's work which was specifically for Plains Cree.

Elements of Cree vocabulary, grammar and syntax seem strange, especially to monolingual anglophones. Particles, gender, number, tense and mood are often inflected with the verb root such that a single, rather complicated word (verb) in Cree often is equivalent to a whole sentence in English. Inflections for gender are governed more by whether an object is animate or inanimate, than masculine, feminine or neuter. Cree syntax is somewhat like Gaelic (Irish), and the second person takes precedence over the first person. Ambiguities possible in English are avoided in Cree. Logan's examples include:

English (syntax):	Cree (syntax):
I am walking	It is walking I am
I see you	You are seen by me
He is walking	Walking that doing is he
We saw Sam hunting (ambiguity)	It was Sam hunting that we saw
	It was Sam we saw when hunting we were

Knox F. McCusker, DLS, ALS, (1890-1955), late of Fort St John, BC, in reminiscences of surveying east of Lake Winnipeg [132] gives some quaint examples of how the Crees there expressed themselves in English; eg, "That's the stuff [rolled oats] he like to eat mouses"; "Wake it up; it have to clean its teeth" (referring to G.W. Malaher, McCusker's "junior" on the party); "Oh these pups, he'll drive me crazy!" and "right away she'll put it in the oven some bannock".

My phonetic interpretation of "teacher" was "okiskanhamagao". Lacombe gave "kisk" as the root for: to show, to inform, to know, to remember, to mark, etc., and listed more than a dozen derivatives. Some examples from him and from Watkins follow:

English:	Watkins: (1938 edition)	Lacombe:
teacher	okiskino humakao	okiskino hamakew
pupil, student	kiskino humowakum	?
school	kiskino humatoo wikunik	kiskino ikamik hamakew
lesson, instruction	kiskino huma kowin	kiskino hama kewin
knowledge	Kiska yetum oowin	kiske yittam owin

A related example from Logan is "kiskay itumun" for "to be knowing it you are". The breaks in the Cree equivalents are mine, to facilitate comparison.

Logan remarks that, in the opinion of experts, pure Cree, among the known languages, is unsurpassed for wealth of vocabulary, orderly grammar, logical syntax and freedom from ambiguity.

The vocabulary of some 200 words which follows is tabulated in four columns (1) English in alphabetic sequence (2) "Kelly Lake Cree" as phonetically interpreted by me 60 years ago (3) Watkins (1938 edition) and (4) Lacombe (1874). In most cases differences are minor. My Kelly Lake versions may reflect local peculiarities or imperfections in my phonetic interpretation. I believe Watkins favors the "Woodland Cree" and Lacombe the "Plains Cree". Major peculiarities in my Kelly Lake list may be errors. The Kelly Lake versions show a tendency to favor the gutteral value "g" where Watkins and Lacombe use "k". Other vocal subtleties not indicated are the aspirative "k" and "p". Unfortunately, circumstances have not allowed the checking of these with a Kelly Lake expert like Mrs. Caroline Campbell.

105: Flyingshot Lake, near Grande Prairie, Alta, July 1983. The Lac Ste Anne Metis settled here about 1900-1920 before moving again to Kelly Lake, BC. (GSA #7300)

106: Kelly Lake, BC, July 1983. Billy Gladu at his home on the old Belcourt homesite. (GSA #7308)

ENGLISH-CREE VOCABULARY

Compiled by the author (as in Column 2) entirely by ear and haphazardly without aid
of references during his 2-year sojourn at Kelly Lake, 1923-25. Equivalents from
sources   indicated are   in Columns 3 and 4.

(1)		(2)	(3)	(4)
English: Phonetics:		GSA, Kelly Lake 1923-1925	Watkins 1865 et al 1938	Lacombe 1874 (from French-Cree)
a	as in	bat, far	far	
ā	" "	hate	hate	
e	" "	bed	me	
ē	" "	me		Phonetics
ew	" "		few	
i	" "	pin	pin	not
ī	" "	time	time	
o	" "	Bob	note	
ō	" "	note		tabulated
oi	" "	boil		
oo	" "	soon	soon	
ou	" "	bound		
ow	" "		now	
u	" "	bud	bud	

	English	GSA, Kelly Lake 1923-1925	Watkins 1865 et al 1938	Lacombe 1874 (from French-Cree)
A	after	moistus	mwastus	ekusi?
	afternoon	pōnapēta gēsigou	pooneapita kesikaw	ekiabbittawi kijikak
	air (wind)	yōatin	yootin	yotin
	arm (limb)	mispitun	mispiton	misputin
	axe	shēkahigan	chekuhikun	tchikahigan
B	bad	namōa mēosin, muche	muche, muchatisew	matchi
	badger	nestānus	wēnisk, mistunusk	mistanask
	bad (man)	muche napāo		
	bannock	pakwāsigun	pukwasikunikan	pakkwejigan
	bear	muskwa	muskwa	maskwa
	beaver	amisk	umisk	amisk
	beer	skwāsis apoē	iskwasisapoo	tchipayiwat
	before	myawās	amoyas	mayowes
	believe (I ____ it)	dapooktin	tapwatum	tapwetan
	birch	wuskwoi	wuskwiatik	waskway
	blizzard	kewādin	pewun	?
	blood	amikwoo	miko	mikkow
	boat	ōseō	osis	osi
	book	musnahigan	mussinuhikan	masinahigan
	boy	napāsis	napasis	nabesis
	broom	wepahigan	wapuhikun	webahigan
	bush (forest)	sagou	piskokopaw	sakow
C	camera	musnahipaechikun	chikastapichikun	?
	caribou	atik	utik	?
	cat	manosē	minoos	kasakes
	cellar	watichan	watekan	watikkan
	cent (one ___, 1¢)	pāek pēopskwus	?	?
	cents, 25 (25¢ piece)	pāek sōnias	?	?
	chest (anatomy)	waskun	maskikun	maskigan
	chief	hogēmou	okimaw	okimau
	chimney (stove etc)	atsēou	iskutākan	kutawanabisk
	cloud	eguskwun	wusko	waskow
	coal oil (kerosine)	wasakatāmigun pēmē	uskewe pime	?
	cold (day)	kasin	kissin	kissin
	colt	mestatimāsis	mistutimosis	?
	come (here!)	astum	?	?
	cousin (kin)	nēstou	nesta	nistou
	cow	mustūs	noosamostos	onitjaniw
	coyote	mistachōguns	mastuchakunis	?
	crack (fracture)	ataskou	tatopuyewin	?
	creek (stream)	sēpēsus	sepesis	?
D	dark	ōnetipscou	tipiskaw	wanitibiskaw
	day	gēsigou	kesikaw	kijikau
	day after tomorrow	wosawipaki	?	?
	day, (a) fine ___	meōgēsigou	meyo kesikow	miwasin kijikaw
	deer	absimāsis	upitstamoosos	ayabewawskesiw

	(1) English	(2) Kelly Lake 1923-25	(3) Watkins 1865 et al 1938	(4) Lacombe 1874
	difference (not much)	moinsta pechatos	numoweyu petus	nanawiya pitus
	difference (little)	absis patos	upi petos	?
	difference (big)	mista patos	mistuhe petos (?)	?
	dipper (ladle)	kwopahigan	kwapuhikan	emikkwan
	direction	nota	oyayetunoowın	oyeyıttamowın
	doctor (medical)	muskeke aweno	muskikeweyinew	maskikiwiyiniw
	dog	atim	utim	atim
	door	skwatihim	iskwatam	iskwatem
	down	chupesis	neche	tabasis, nete
E	ear	mitoo-ogawa	mitowuki	mittawekay
	East	Sagastanota	wapunotak	sakastonok
	egg	wawa	wawe	wawa
	eight, eighteen, eleven (see "Numerals")			
	eye	muskesig	miskesik	miskijik
F	fire	eskootaoo	iskotao	iskutew
	five (see numerals)			
	flour	pakwasigun	pukwasikun	pakkwejigan
	foot	misit	misit	misit
	forest	sagou	sukow	sakaw
	four, fourteen (see "Numerals")			
	fox	mokases	mukasew	makkesis
	Friday (see "week, days of")			
	frost (on window)	akwatin	akwutin	akwatin
	fur	atay	uti	attay
G	get (lots of --)	ataskou	?	ottisiw
	girl	skwasis	iskwasis	iskwesis
	goat	waputik	waputik	?
	go (home)	keway	kewao	kiwawin
	good	meosin	meyo, meyuwasin	miwasin
	good day!	" gesigou	?	miwasin kijikaw
	grass	muskwasea	muskoseu	maskusiy
	grease	peme	pime	pemiy
	gun	pasahigan	paskisikun	paskisigan
H	hair	mistagaso	mastuki	mestakay
	half	apata	apeytoo	abittaw
	hand	michuche	michiche	mitchitch'y
	hard (work)	atoaskeo soke	ayimesew utoskawin	atiskewin meskawisiw
	head (anatomy)	oostagwan	mistikwan	mistikwan
	hill	spetanou	wuchi	ispatinaw
	holiday	getsi-gesigou	uyapewe kesikaw	kitchi kijikaw
	horse	mestatim	mistutim	mistatim
	hot	sitaoo	kisisoo kesikaw	kisastew
	house	waskagan	waskuhikun	waskahigan
K	know (I ___)	ungskatin	kiskayetak	kiskayimew
L	lake	sagahigan	sakuhikun	sakahigan
	lamp	wasakatanigan	wastahumakun	wasaskutenigan
	light	washaoo	wastawin	wasseyaw
	little (few)	namoia mechat	chukuwasis	apisis, tchikawasis
	log	mistik	mistik	kiskatahigan
	lots (of)	mechat	mistuhe	mistaha
	lynx	pesu	pisew	pisew
M	man	napao	napao	iyiniw
	man, old	eksaeno	kisayinew, kisanapao	kiseyiniw
	man, young	eskinakwoo	oskinekew	oskinikiw
	mare	kiskisis	kiskisis	kiskisis
	marten	wapschans	wapistan	wapistan
	match (to ignite)	kootswaguns	kotowakunis	kutawagan
	milk	totosapue	totoosapoo	totosabuy
	mink	sangwish	sakuwasew	wapistan (?)
	moccasin	muskasin	muskisin	?
	Monday (see week, days of)			
	money	soniou	sooneyaw	soniyaw
	month	pesum	pesim	pisim
	moon	tipskou pesum	tipskawe pesim	tibiskawipisim
	moose	mooswa	mooswu	moswa
	morning	keksapa	kakesapayan	kikisebaw

English	(1) Kelly Lake 1923-25	(2) Watkins 1865 et al 1938	(3) Lacombe 1874
moss	uskēwa	uske	askiya
mountain	oochē	wuchi	watjiy
much	mechāt	mistuhe, mechāt	mistahi
N neck (anatomy)	ogwāoo	mikwuyow	mikweyou
night	tipskou	tipiskaw	tibiskaw
nine, nineteen (see numerals)			
no	namoya	numuweyu	namawiya
none	mukekwa	numukakwi	namakekway
noon	apāta gēsigou	apetakesikaw	abittawikijikaw
North	kewādinōta	kewātinotak	kiwetinok
nose	miskūwan	misikwun	miskiwan
numerals:			
one	payek	payuk	peyak
two	nesō	nesoo	niso
three	enstō	nistoo	nisto
four	nayawō	nāo	newo
five	neanin	neyanun	niyanan
six	gutosik	nekotwasik	nikotwasik
seven	tāpagopf	tapukoop	tepakup
eight	ananāo	eananāo	ayaenanew
nine	kekametatakt	kākatmitatut	kekamitatat
ten	metatakt	mitatut	mitatat
eleven	payeksap	payukosap	payakosap
twelve	nesōsap	nesoosap	nisosap
etc	etc	etc	etc
nineteen	kekanēstanō	kākanesitanow	?
twenty	nēstanō	nesitunow	nistanou
O ocean	gichēgaumi	kichekume	kitchigamiy
one (see "numerals"			
P pack horse	mestatim nēachikwis	?	atuskewatin (?)
packrat	wēchig muskakē	?	?
paper	musnahigan	mussinuhikunakik	masinahiganegin
pencil	" achigoos	mussinuhikunatik	masinahiganattik
pig	kōkūs	kookoos	kokus
pine (tree)	wuskatuk, minahik	oskatik, minuhik	minahik
poplar (tree)	mētoos	metos	?
prairie	muskwatāoo	muskootāo	maskutew
priest	amahayawēno	uyumehāweyinew	ayamihewiyiniw
Q quickly	kēpa,	keyipu	kiyipi
R rabbit	wapoos	wapoos	?
railroad	pēwapistmaniskanou	pewapiskamaskunow	?
right, that is __ !	tapooē mēosin	meywasin	tapwe
river	sepē	sepē	sipiy
rock	asinē	mistasinne	assiniy
Rocky Mountains	Asinē Oochē	Usinne Wucheyu	Assini Watjiy
roof	pakwan	upukwan	apakkwan
run	permōtin, pimoktan	pimiputaw	pimitattaw
S sand	ēagou	yakow	yekaw
sap (of birch tree)	wuskwoi apuē	mastun uskatik	mestan
Saturday (see "week, days of")			
seven, seventeen (see "Numerals)			
sheep (mountain)	mīachikwus	mayutik	mayattik
side, the other __	kwaskīē	kwaskita	kweskayik
sit up (straight)!	kwoisapē	sumutupen	?
six, sixteen (see "Numerals")			
skunk	sigok	sikak	sikak
sky	wuskū. gēsik	kesik	kitchikejik
sleigh	wōtapanask	otapanask	otabanask
smoke	kuskapatāoo	kuskaputāo	kaskabasuw
snow (on ground)	kwona	koona	kona
snowing, it is	mispun	mispoon	mispun
South	apāta gesigou.ota	sowunok	sawan, sawanok
spade (tool)	peopskwapooē	pewapiskamukayipan	piwabiskwabuiy
spruce (tree)	minahik	minuhik	minahik
squirrel	antikwōchas	unikwuchas	anikwatchas
star	achoukwis	uchukoos	atchakus
stink	wētsigan	wechakisew	witjekisiwin

(1) English	(2) Kelly Lake 1923–25	(3) Watkins 1865 et al 1938	(4) Lacombe 1874
stomach	wametā	mutak	matay
stone	asinē	usinne	assiniy
stove	kootoowanapsk	kootuwanapisk	piwabiskokutawanabisk
sugar	sēspaskwut	sesepaskwut	sisibaskwat
sun	pēsum	pesim	kijikawipisim
Sunday (see " week, days of)			
sunrise	sagastānou	sakastāo	sakastew
sunset	poksmō	pukisimoon	pakissimow
T tamarack (tree)	waganoqan	wakinakun	?
teacher	ōkiskanhamagāoo	okiskinohumakāo	okiskinohamakew
ten (see "numerals')			
think (I __ so!)	daktin	ōkwane (?)	?
do (I dont __ so)	namoya daktin		
thirteen, three (see "Numerals")			⟨≂⟩
Thursday (see week, days of)			
tobacco (trade)	stāmou	chistamow	tchistemaw
tobacco (Red Willow)	mikwapemigwa	uspakosawan	atchakasipak
today	anōts	anochkakesikak	anotch
tomorrow	wapakē	wapukā	wabaki
tonight	anotskatipscou	anoochtapiskak	tibiskaw
trader (fur buyer)	otatawoo, ashta-hogemou	otutawāo	atawewiyiniw
trail, road	meniskanou	maskinow	meskanaw
Tuesday (see week, days of)			
twelve, twenty, two (see "Numerals")			
U uncle	nokōmis	okomismaw	nokkomis
up	spēmē	ispimik	ispimik
V valley	wyachou	wayutinaw	wayatchaw
visitor	keōkwis	keokakun	kiyutamawew (?)
W water	nēpē	nipe	nipiy
do (dirty)	ēpatamago nēpē	wenakumin	sewittaganabuy
weasel	sēkwis, chākus	sekosiw	?
Wednesday (see week, days of)			
week, days of			
Monday	payek gēsigou	nestum kesikaw	nistam kijikaw
Tuesday	neso "	neso "	nejo "
Wednesday	ensto "	nisto "	nisto "
Thursday	nayawō "	nāo "	newo "
Friday	neanin "	neyanuno "	?
Saturday	gutosik "	nekotwaso "	?
Sunday	Amahō "	Uyumea "	Ayamihew "
West	pouksnota	nakapahunok	?
where?	tandē	tanta	tandē
whiskey (or rum)	eskootaoo apue	iskotawapoo	iskutewabuy
whistler (marmot)	oogwāsēs	?	kweskusiw
willow	nipshēa	nēpise	?
window	wasānamcun	wasanumawin	wassenamawin
wolverine	kēkwaseagō	kwekwuhakāo	?
woman	skwāoo	iskwāo	iskwew
woman (old)	nōtakwō	nootokāo	notukew
work (hard)	atōaskeo sōkē	utoskāo	atuskew
Y yes!	aha	?	euh euh
yesterday	ōktoksē	otakosak	otakusik
English (1)	GSA 1923–25 (2)	Watkins 1865 et al 1938 (3)	Lacombe 1874 (4)

APPENDIX 6

GEOGRAPHICS

Only a small selection of more than 400 geographic features, named or implied, in the foregoing text can be shown on the maps provided. This list is to clarify what and where each is in relation to what is shown, or if beyond, to a well-known place. Geographic co-ordinates, to the nearest minute of arc, serve to locate any item within about a mile on any map having the grid for Latitude and Longitude. For this remarkable facility we thank especially Eratosthenese, the old scholar and librarian at Alexandria (c200 BC), who was aware of the Earth's shape and made the first close approximation of its size. He also originated the idea of parallels of Latitude and meridians of Longitude for a co-ordinate reference system.

A minute of Latitude closely equals one nautical mile (6,076 ft), anywhere between the Equator and the Poles. A minute of Longitude is about the same, only on the Equator, and diminishes north or south to zero at the Poles. For this list, values in degrees and minutes, are ocular estimates from available maps, including the Canadian "National Topographic Series" (NTS) at 1/250,000 scale (1"=4 mi, approx), which now covers all of Canada with remarkable accuracy and detail, thanks to early and modern surveyors and to air photography. For large features like lakes and cities, co-ordinates quoted should be within their boundaries. For streams they locate the mouth. For trails, railways and such, terminals and/or routings are given. Many well-known places are omitted. Where applicable, nomenclature and spelling are those as adopted by the Canadian Permanent Committee on Geographical Names. Elevations quoted may be approximate.

It is gratifying that six new names for mountains southwest of Kelly Lake, selected from the manuscript of this book to commemorate pioneer individuals and families, have been officially adopted. These are marked with "**". Other names with Kelly Lake connotations are shown with "*". Interesting historical derivations for many names in Alberta, British Columbia and Yukon Territory, may be found in my Bibliography & References. [133]

Alaska Highway: Original mileages: Dawson Creek, BC 0; Fort Nelson 300; Lower
   Post, BC 620; Watson Lake, YT 635; Whitehorse 918; Fairbanks AL 1527.
Alkali Lake, BC: 51°47-122°17; 30 mi S of Williams Lake; Map 1.
Anderson Lake, BC: 50°40-122°25; 100 mi N of Vancouver; Map 1.
**Anderson, Mount, 5876ft, BC: 54°43-120°42; 46 mi SW of Kelly Lake; Map 2.
Anzac River, BC: 54°48-122°37; 60 mi N of Prince George; Map 2, 6.

Arras (Loc), BC: 55°45-120°33; 16 mi W of Pouce Coupe; Map 1.
Ashcroft (Loc), BC: 50°43- 121°17; 40 Mi W of Kamloops; Map 1.
Assiniboia Settlement, 1812-1870: 50 mi radius from Fort Garry; Map 1.
Assiniboine River: 49°50-97°10; Joins Red River at Fort Garry; Map 1
Athabasca Landing, Alta: 54°43-113°16; 80 mi N of Edmonton; Map 1, 2.

Athabasca Pass, 5730ft, Alta-BC: 52°23-118°10; 40 mi S of Jasper; Map 1, 2.
Athabasca River, Alta: 58°40-110°50; Flows NE to Lake Athabasca; Map 1, 2.
Atlin, BC: 59°34-133°42; 100 mi SE of Whitehorse, YT; Map 1.
Atunatche Creek, BC: 55°20-122°35; Drains Azouzetta Lake S to Misinchinka R; Map 2, 6.
Azouzetta Lake, BC: 55°23-122°37; In Pine Pass; Map 2, 6.

Barkerville, BC: 53°04-121°31; 40 mi E of Quesnel; Map 2.
Batoche, Sask: 52°40-106°02; 43 mi NNE of Saskatoon; Map 1.
Battleford, Sask: 52°44-108°19; 225 mi NW of Regina; Map 1.
Bear Lake, Alta: 55°15-119°00; 1 mi NW of Grande Prairie; Map 2.
Bear Lake, BC (now Bowron Lake, qv).

Bearhole Lake, BC: 55°03-120°41; Source of Kiskatinaw R, 30 mi SW of Kelly Lake; Map 2.
Beatton River, BC: 56°06-120°22; Flows SE to Peace R, 20 mi SE of Fort St John; Map 2.
Beaverlodge, Alta: 55°12-119°25; 24 mi W of Grande Prairie; Map 1, 2, 3.
Beaverlodge Hill, Alta: 55°13-119°24; Near Beaverlodge town; Map 2, 3.
Beaverlodge Lake, BC: 55°21-120°02;Source Beaverlodge R, 6 mi N of Kelly Lake; Map 2, 3.

Beaverlodge River, BC-Alta: 55°02-119°19; Flows SE to Wapiti R; Map 2, 3.
Beaver Pass House, BC: 53°04-121°50; 28 mi E of Quesnel; Map 2.
Beavertail Creek, BC-Alta: 55°20-119°37; Flows NE to Beaverlodge R; Map 2, 3.
Bedson Ridge, Alta: 53°15-117°55; 30 mi N of Jasper; Map 2.
*Belcourt Creek, BC: 54°41- 120°07; flows NE to Wapiti R, 40 mi S of Kelly Lake; Map 2.

*Belcourt Lake, BC: 54°25-120°24; 60 mi SSW of Kelly Lake; Map 2.
*Belcourt, Mount, 7000+ft, BC:54°26-120°26; 60 mi SSW of Kelly Lake; Map 2.
Bella Coola, BC: 52°23-126°45; midway between Vancouver & Prince Rupert; Map 1.
Bennett Dam (see WAC Bennett Dam)
Berens River, Man: 52°20-97°00; flows W to Lake Winnipeg, 170 mi N of Fort Garry; Map 1.

*Berland River, Alta: 54°03-116°50; flows NE to Athabasca R, 55 mi NE of Hinton; Map 2.
Bezanson, Alta: 55°14-118°21; 17 mi E of Grande Prairie; Map 2.
Big Bar (Loc), BC: 51°11- 122°07; on Fraser R, 125 mi S of Quesnel; Map 1.
Big Bar Creek, BC: 51°11-122°07; flows SW to Fraser R, near above; Map 1.
Big Bar Mountain, BC: 51°14-122°07; N of Big Bar Creek; Map 1.

Bijoux Falls Park, BC: 55°17-122°40; on Misinchinka R, 10 mi S of Pine Pass; Map 2, 6.
Blackwater River (see West Road River)
Blackwater Trail, BC: from Quesnel NW to Vanderhoof; Map 2.   /Map 1.
Blanchard Creek, BC: 57°07-125°14; flows SW to Finlay R, 200 mi N of Fort St James; /
Blanchard Mountain, 5573ft, BC: 57°08-125°09; near above; Map 1.

Bloomington (city), IL: 40°29-88°57; 120 mi SW of Chicago.
Blueberry River, BC: 56°44-120°49; flow E to Beatton R, 35 mi N of Fort St John; Map 2.
Bone, Mount, 7466ft, BC: 54°40-120°51; 50 mi SW of Kelly Lake; Map 2.
**Boone Taylor Peak, 7500ft, BC: 54°51-121°17; 64 mi SW of Kelly Lake; Map 2.
Bounding Creek, BC: 53°28-120°39; flows NW to Goat R, 23 mi NW of McBride; Map 2.

Bow Island, Alta: 49°52-111°22; 100 mi N of Fort Benton, MT; Map 1.
Bowron Lake, BC: 53°14-121°25; 13 mi NE of Barkerville; Map 2.
Brainard,Alta: 55°23-119°44; 14 mi NW of Beaverlodge; Map 2, 3.
Brandon, Man: 49°50-99°57; 135 mi W of Fort Garry; Map 1.
Brule Lake, Alta: 53°17-117°51; expansion Athabasca R, 30 mi N of Jasper; Map 2.

Burnaby, BC: 49°15-122°55; 12 mi E of Vancouver; Map 1.
Burns Lake, BC: 54°12-125°45; 125 mi W of Prince George; Map 1.
Cache Creek, BC: 50°48-121°18; 60 mi S of Quesnel; Map 1.
Cairns Creek, BC: 55°30-122°31; flows S to Pine R, 10 mi NE of Pine Pass; Map 2, 6.
*Calahoo Creek,Alta: 54°55-119°41; 22 mi SW of Beaverlodge; Map 2, 3.

*Calahoo Lake, Alta: 54°51- 119°58; 27 mi S of Kelly Lake; Map 2, 3.
 Callazon Creek, BC:55°32-122°43; flows SE to Pine R, 10 mi NW of Pine Pass; Map 2, 6.
 Callazon Flats (loc), BC: 54°56-120°45; 36 mi SW of Kelly Lake, Map 2.
*Calliou Creek, BC: 54°44-120°27; flows S to Wapiti R, 40 mi SW of Kelly Lake; Map 2
*Calliou Lake, BC: 54°47-120°28; source of Calliou Cr, as above.   / Map 2.

*Campbell Creek, Alta: 54°53-118°49; flows SE to Bald Mt Cr, 20 mi S of Grande Prairie;/
 Campbell Highway (see Robert Campbell Highway)
*Campbell Lake, BC: 55°10-120°08; 8 mi SW of Kelly Lake; Map 2, 3.
 Canada East (1841-1867) now Quebec Province.
 Canada West (1841-1867) now Ontario.

 Canoe Creek, BC: 51°26-122°15; flows W to Fraser R, 112 mi S of Quesnel; Map 1.
 Canol Road, YT: from Johnsons Crossing NE to Ross River & Macmillan Pass, YT.
 Canyon Creek, BC (see John Bennett Creek).
 Cariboo (Land) District, BC: East Central BC to Rocky Mts.
 Cariboo Road, BC: (hist) Lillooet, Clinton, Soda Creek, Quesnel, Barkerville; Map 1, 2.

 Carp Lake (and Park), BC: 54°45-123°20; 20 mi SW of McLeod Lake; Map 2.
 Carrier Lake, BC: 54°32-123°54; 17 mi E of Fort St James; Map 2.
 Cassiar (Land) District, BC: NW BC; Map 1.
 Cathay: medieval name for China.
 Caughnawaga, PQ: 45°25-73°42; Iroquois mission after c1676; 10 mi S of Montreal.

 Centurion Creek, BC: 55°40-121°39; flows SW to Pine R, 60 mi W of Pouce Coupe; Map 2.
 Chesapeake Bay, USA: on Atlantic coast vic Virginia.
 Chetwynd, BC: 55°42-121°37; 57 mi W of Pouce Coupe; Map 2.
 Chicken Creek, Alta: 54°15-119°29; flows SW to Kakwa R, 85 mi NW of Hinton; Map 2./Map 1.
 Chilcotin River (& region), BC: 51°45-122°24; Flows E to Fraser R, 80 mi S of Quesnel;/

 Chilliwack River, BC: 49°06-121°58; flows W to Fraser R via Vedder & Sumas Rs; Map 1.
 Chingee, Mount, 4220ft, BC: 55°02-122°54; 6 mi NE of McLeod L Post; Map 2.
 Clairmont, Alta: 55°15-118°47; 6 mi N of Grande Prairie; Map 2.
 Clinton, BC: 51°06-121°36; on Cariboo Road, 60 mi N of Lytton; Map 1.
 Colbourne Creek, BC: 55°04-122°53; flows SW to Parsnip R, 10 mi NE of McLeod Post; Map 2.

 Coppermine River, NWT: 67°47-115°04; flows NW to Coronation Gulf, Arctic Coast.
**Cornock, Mount, 6483ft, BC: 54°41-121°01; 57 mi SW of Kelly Lake; Map 2.
 Coventry, England: 52°24-01°31W; 85 mi NW of London.
 Creston, BC: 49°07-116°30; c300 mi E of Vancouver.
 Crooked Lake (see Beaverlodge Lake, BC).

 Crooked River, BC: 54°50-122°53; flows N from Summit L to McLeod L; Map 2.
 Cutbank (Loc), BC, see Arras). Cutbank River (see Kiskatinaw R).
 Cutpick Hill, 6068ft, Alta: 54°05-119°09; 6 mi NW of Smoky R; Map 2.
 Cypress Hills, Alta-Sask: 49°40-110°00; Map 1.
 Dakota Territory, USA, 1861-1889; now N Dakota, S Dakota, Montana & Wyoming; Map 1

 Dawson City, YT: 64°04-139°25; former capital of Yukon Territory.
 Dawson Creek, BC: 55°45-120°15; 6 Mi NW of Pouce Coupe; Map 1, 2.
 Demmitt, (Loc), Alta: 55°27-119°55; 25 mi NW of Beaverlodge; Map 2, 3.
 Dewey, (loc), BC: 54°05-121°50; 40 mi E of Prince George; Map 2.
 Diggins Creek, BC: 53°27-120°44; flows W to Goat R; Map 2.

 Doe River, (Loc), BC: 56°00-120°05; 20 mi N of Pouce Coupe; Map 2.
 Dog Creek, BC: 51°35-122°14; 95 mi S of Quesnel; Map 1.
 Doig River, BC:56°25-120°39; flows SW to Beatton R, 14 mi NE of Fort St John; Map 1.
 Dokie, (Loc), BC:55°39-121°43; 61 mi W of Pouce Coupe; Map 2.
 Dresden, (East) Germany: 50°59-13°47E; 107 mi S of Berlin.

 Dunster, (Loc), BC:53°07-119°50; 20 mi SE of McBride; Map 2.
 Dunvegan, Alta: 55°55-118°35; Fur Depot 1805 et seq; 65 mi E of Pouce Coupe; Map 2.
 East Murray Creek, BC:54°03-124°04; 3 mi NW of Vanderhoof; Map 2.
 East Pine, (Loc), BC:55°43-121°13; at confluence Murray & Pine Rivers; Map 2.
 Edmonton, Alta: 53°33-113°28; Map 2.

Lethbridge, Alta: 49°40-112°50; SW corner Alberta; Map 1.
*L'Hirondelle (loc), Alta: 56°26-116°06; 70 mi NE of Kelly Lake; Map 2.
Liard River, BC, NWT, YT: 63°00-122°00; flows NE to Mackenzie R; Map 1.
Lillooet, BC: 50°42-121°56; on Fraser R, 36 mi N of Lytton; Map 1.
Little Valley Mine, BC: 53°08-121°32; 5 mi N of Barkerville; Map 2.

Lower Canada (1791-1841) now Quebec Province.
Lower Post (loc), BC: 59°56-128°29; confluence Liard & Dease Rivers; Map 1.
Mackenzie River, NWT: 69°15-134°08; flows NW from Great Slave L to Arctic Ocean.
MacLeod Creek, BC: 53°23-120°51; flows SE to Goat R, 31 mi W of McBride; Map 2.
McBride, BC: 53°18-120°10; on Fraser R, 110 mi SE of Prince George; Map 2.

McGregor River, BC: 54°11-122°02; flows W to Fraser R, 35 mi NE of Prince George; Map 2.
McLennan, Alta: 55°42-116°55; 80 mi NE of Grande Prairie; Map 2.
McLeod Lake (PO), BC: 54°59-123°02; N end McLeod L, 78 mi N of Prince George; Map 2.
McLeod River, BC: 55°00-123°02; drains Carp L to Pack R near above; Map 2.
Meason Creek (& Ranch), BC: 51°41-122°21; on Fraser R, 90 mi S of Quesnel; Map 1.

Milk River, BC: 53°26-120°44; flows NW to Goat R, 24 mi NW of McBride; Map2.
Minaki, Ont: 49°58-94°40; on Winnipeg R, 18 mi E of Manitoba Bdy; Map 1   / 6.
Misinchinka River, BC: 55°06-122°57; flows NW & SW to Parsnip R, S of Pine Pass; Map 2/
*Moberly Lake, BC: 55°49-121°45; 18 mi SE of Hudson Hope; Map 2.
*Monkman Cabins (loc), BC: 54°48-120°44; 42 mi SW of Kelly Lake; Map 2.

*Monkman Lake, BC: 54°37-121°12; 65 mi SW of Kelly Lake; Map 2.
*Monkman Pass, c3450ft, BC: 54°32-121°14; 65 mi SW of Kelly Lake; Map 2.
Moose Lake, BC: 52°57-118°55; expansion Fraser R, 35 mi W of Jasper; Map 2.
Moosomin, Sask: 50°09-101°40; 119 mi E of Regina; Map 1.
Murray Range, BC: 55°20-122°35; E of Pine Pass; Map 2, 6.

Murray River, BC: 55°43-121°14; flows N to Pine R at East Pine; Map 2.
Muskeg River, Alta: 54°02-119°03; flows NW to Smoky R, 87 mi NW of Jasper; Map 2.
Muskeg River, BC: 54°24-123°11; flows S to Salmon R, 38 mi NW of Prince George; Map 2.
Nazko River, BC: 53°08-123°34; flows N to West Road R, 44 mi W of Quesnel; Map 2.
Nechako River, BC: 53°55-122°43; flows E to Fraser R at Prince George; Map 2.

New Caledonia (hist, c1805-1858; Territory W of Rocky Mts & N of "Oregon Territory".
Newcastle, PN: 40°55-80°20; 190 mi S of Toronto.
New Westminster, BC: 49°14-122°55; 12 mi E of Vancouver; Map 1.
Nipigon (Fur depot), Ont: 49°30-89°00; N of Lake Superior; Map 1.
Norway House, Man: 54°00=97°50; 24 mi N of Lake Winnipeg; Map 1.

Nose Creek, Alta: 54°52-119°38; flows N to Wapiti R, 16 mi S of Rio Grande; Map 2, 3.
Nose Mountain, 5000ft, Alta: 54°30-119°32; 60 mi S of Grande Prairie; Map 2.
Ocean Falls, BC: 52°21-127°42; 225 mi W of Quesnel; Map 1.
OK Ranch, BC: 51°18-121°59; upper Big Bar Cr, 120 mi S of Quesnel; Map 1.
Okanagan Lake & Valley, BC: 49°50-119°30; between Fraser & Columbia R's; Map 1

Old Friend Creek, BC: 55°15-122°41; 9 mi SW of Pine Pass; Map 2, 6.
Old Friend Mountain, 6133ft, BC: 55°15-122°37; 10 Mi S of Pine Pass; Map 2, 6.
Olds, Alta: 51°47-114°05; 120 mi S of Edmonton; Map 1.
Oliver, BC: 49°11-119°34; 165 mi E of Vancouver; Map 1.
120th Meridian, W Long: Bdy between Alta & BC, Intersection Mt N to 60°N Lat.

Onoway, Alta: 53°42=114°11; 1 mi E of Lac Ste Anne; Map 2.
Oregon Territory (hist); W of Rocky Mts, later Washington, Idaho & Oregon States.
Oroville WA: 48°56- 119°25; 125 mi S of Kamloops; Map 1.
Osoyoos, BC: 49°03-119°28; 120 mi S of Kamloops; Map 1.
Oxford, England: 51°46-01°16W; 54 mi NW of London.
                                                                    / Map 1, 2.
PGE Ry (now BCR): Originally Squamish, Lillooet, Clinton, Williams Lake, Quesnel; /
Pack River, BC: 55°09-123°08; flows N from McLeod L to Parsnip R & Williston L; Map 2.
Paddle Prairie, Alta: 57°55-117°20; 200 mi N of Grande Prairie; Map 1.
Parsnip River, BC: 55°59-123°50; flowed NW to Finlay R (now to Williston L); Map 2.
Peace River, BC, Alta: 59°00-111°24; drains Williston L NE to Slave R; Map 1.

Peace River Block, BC: (72x76) sq mi N&S of Peace R, Fed'l admin, 1907-30; Map 1.
Peace River (Land) District, BC: E of Rocky Mts & 126th Meridian; Map 1.
Peavine Creek, BC: 55°27-120°07; drains Peavine L to Tupper Cr; Map 2, 3.
Peavine Lake, BC: 55°25-120°05; 12 mi N of Kelly Lake; Map 3.
Peever, Mount, 7100ft, BC: 53°16-121°07; 40 mi W of McBride; Map 2.

Pelly Banks (loc), YT: 61°45-131°08; 150 mi NE of Whitehorse on Pelly R.
Pelly River, YT: 62°47-137°20; flows W to Yukon R at site Ft Selkirk.
Pemberton, BC: 50°19-122°48; 75 mi N of Vancouver; Map 1.
Penbina (hist), ND: 48°58-97°17; 65 mi S of Fort Garry; Map 1.
Penticton, BC: 49°30-119°35; 75 mi E of VAncouver; Map 1.

Perth, Scotland: 56°22-03°29W; 32 mi N of Edinburgh.
Peterson's Crossing (loc), BC: 56°34-120°42; Beatton R, 23 mi N of Fort St John; Map 2.
Pincher Creek, Alta: 49°28-113°58; 105 mi S of Calgary; Map 1.
Pine Pass, 2850ft, BC: 55°24-122°37; 98 mi N of Prince George; Map 2, 6.
Pine River, BC: 56°08-120°42; flows NE to Peace R, 10 mi SE of Fort St John; Map 2.

Pine Valley (loc), BC: 55°38-122°07; 21 mi WSW of Chetwynd; Map 2
Pipestone Creek & Park, Alta: 55°03-119°06; Wapiti R, 11 mi SW of Grande Prairie; Map 2.
Placer County, CA: 38°50-121°10; 30 mi NE of Sacramento.
*Poona-tik-sipi Flats (loc), BC: 54°59-120°46; 34 mi SW of Kelly Lake; Map 2.
Pope, Mount, 4828ft, BC: 54°30-124°20; 5 mi NW of Fort St James; Map 2.

Poplar River, Man: 52°59-97°19; flows NW to L Winnipeg; Map 1.
Porcupine River (see Kakwa River)
Porcupine River, AL, YT: 66°32-145°05; flows NE & SW to Yukon R.
Portage la Prairie, Man: 49°58-98°18; 50 mi W of Fort Garry; Map 1.
Port Coquitlam, BC: 49°15-122°45; 15 mi E of VAncouver; Map 1.

Pouce Coupe, BC: 55°43-120°08; 45 mi NW of Beaverlodge, Alta; Map 2, 3.
Pouce Coupe River, Alta, BC: 56°08-119°53; loops into BC vic Pouce Coupe; Map 2.
Prairie Creek, Alta: 54°18-118°45; flows NE to Kakwa R 105 mi N of Jasper; Map 2.
Prince Albert, Sask: 53°12-105°46; 37 mi NNE of Batoche; Map 1.
Prince George, BC: 53°55-122°45; 67 mi N of Quesnel; Map 2.

Puntzi Airfield, BC: 52°07-124°09; 100 mi SW of Quesnel; Map 2.
Qu'Appelle, Sask: 50°45-103°38; 40 mi NE of Regina; Map 1.
Quesnel, BC: 52°58-122°39; 67 mi S of Prince George; Map 2.
Raush River, BC: 53°12-120°01; flows N to Fraser R, 10 mi SE of McBride; Map 2
Red Deer, Alta: 52°16-113°49; midway, Calgary - Edmonton; Map 1.

Red Pass Junction, BC: 52°59-119°00; W end Moose L, 40 mi W of Jasper; Map 2.
*Red River & Valley, Man: 50°23-96°49; flows N to L Winnipeg; Map 1   Map 2.
*Redwillow River, BC, Alta: 55°02-119°18; flows E to Wapiti R, 23 mi S of Grande Prairie; /
Regensburg, West Germany: 48°56-12°06E; 140 mi E of Stuttgart.
*Rhubarb Flats (see Poona-tik-sipi)

Rimbey, Alta: 52°38-114°14; 70 mi SSW of Edmonton; Map 2.
*Rio Grande (loc), Alta: 55°06-119°42; 13 mi SW of Beaverlodge; Map 2, 3.
Rochdale, England: 53°37-02°12W; 10 mi NE of Manchester.
Robert Campbell Highway, YT: Carmacks ESE to Watson L on Alaska Highway.
Rocky Mountain Trench, BC: W flank Rocky Mts from Montana to Liard R; Map 1.

Rolla (PO), BC: 55°54-120°09; 13 mi N of Pouce Coupe; Map 2.
Rose Prairie (PO), BC: 56°31-120°48; 20 mi N of Fort St John; Map 2.
Ross River (& loc) YT: 61°59-132°25; flows SW to Pelly R, 124 mi NE of Whitehorse.
St Albert (loc), Alta: 53°38-113°37; 12 mi N of Edmonton; Map 2.
St Boniface, Man: 49°53-97°07; E side Red R at Ft Garry (Winnipeg); Map 1.

St Joseph (hist), ND: 48°57-97°53; 30 mi W of Pembina; Map 1.
St Norbert (loc), Man: 49°47-97°09; 9 mi S of Ft Garry (Winnipeg); Map 1.
St Vital (loc), Man: 49°51-97°07; NE suburb Winnipeg; Map 1.
Sarnia, Ont: 42°58-82°23; outlet L Huron, 162 mi W of Toronto.
Saskatchewan River, Alta, Sask, Man: 53°11-99°16; flows E to L Winnipeg; Map 1.

Saskatoon, Sask: 52°08-106°38; 147 mi NW of Regina; Map 1.
Sault Ste Marie, Ont: 46°31-84°21; Between Lakes Huron & Superior.
Sea Island, BC: 49°12-123°10; in Fraser River Delta, s of Vancouver; Map 1.
Sekani Bay, BC: 54°47-123°25; NW shore Carp L, 22 mi SW of McLeod L Post; Map 2.
Sentinel Peak, 8000ft, BC: 54°54-121°58; 44 mi E of McLeod Lake; Map 2, 3.

17th Baseline (DLS), Alta: 54°35-118° to 120°; Tp 65, 40 mi S of Grande Prairie; Map 2.
Sheep Creek, BC, Alta: 54°04-119°00; flows E from Rocky Mts to Smoky R; Map 2.
Shetler Flats (loc), Alta: 54°46-119°33; on Nose Cr, 30 mi S of Beaverlodge; Map 2.
Sidney, BC: 48°38-123°24; 16 mi N of Victoria; Map 1.
Sifton Pass, 3273ft, BC: 57°57-126°12; 250 mi NW of McLeod Lake; Map 1.

Sinclair Mills (loc), BC: 54°0--121°40; 42 mi E of Prince George; Map 2.
16th Base Line (DLS), Alta: 54°14-118° to 120°; Tp 61, 64 mi S of Grande Prairie; Map 2.
6th Meridian (DLS), Alta: 49° to 60° - 118°; 30 mi E of Grande Prairie; Map 2.
Skagway, AL: 59°27-135°20; near NW corner BC; Map 1.
Slave River, Alta, NWT: 61°19-113°38; drains Athabasca L N to Great Slave L; Map 1.

Smith, Alta: 55°10-114°04; 185 mi N of Grande Prairie; Map 1.   / Map 2.
Smoky River, Alta: 56°10-117°19; from Rocky Mts to Peace R, 30 mi NW of McLennan;/
"Smoky River Pass" (Robson Pass), Alta, BC: 53°09-119°07; 48 mi NW of Jasper; Map 2.
Snake Indian River, Alta; 53°11-117°59; flows SE to Athabasca R, 21 mi N of Jasper; Map 2.
Snake River, NW USA: 46°12-119°04; flows NW to Columbia R from SE Idaho; Map 1.

Soda Creek (loc), BC: 52°20-122°17; on Fraser R, 41 mi S of Quesnel; Map 1.
Sorel, PQ: 46°02-73°06; on St Lawrence R, 50 mi NE of Montreal.
Spirit River, Alta: 55°45-118°47; 47 mi N of Grande Prairie; Map 2.
Springfield, OR: 44°02-123°01; 300 mi S of Victoria, Map 1.
Springhouse (loc), BC: 51°55-122°06; 75 mi S of Quesnel; Map 1.   / 3.
*Steeprock Creek, BC, Alta: 55°18-119°44; flows E via Kelly Lake to Beavertail Cr; Map/
*Stony Lake, BC: 54°50-120°34; source of Redwillow R; Map 2, 3.
"Stuart Flats" (loc), BC: see Groundbirch)
Stuart Lake, BC: 54°35-124°40; source Stuart R, 38 mi NW of Vanderhoof; Map 2.
Stuart River, BC: 53°59-123°32; flows SE to Nechako R from Stuart L; Map 2.

Sturgeon Lake, Alta: 55°05-117°31; 50 mi E of Grande Prairie; Map 2.
Suffolk County, England: on North Sea between Essex & Norfolk.
Sukunka River, BC: 55°36-121°35; flows N to Pine R, 15 mi SW of East Pine; Map 2.
"Sulphur Creek, Springs", BC:(see Cairns Creek).
Summit Lake, BC: 54°17-122°40; 27 mi N of Prince George, source of Crooked R; Map 2.

"Summit Lake" (now Azouzetta).
*Sundance Lakes, BC: 55°43-121°23; 7 mi W of East Pine; Map 2.
*Swan Lake, Alta, BC: 55°32-120°01; on Alta-BC Bdy, 16 mi N of Kelly Lake; Map 3.
Tacoma, WA: 47°15-122°25; 90 mi SSE of Victoria; Map 1.   / 3.
Tate Creek, BC: 55°33-120°04; flows E to Tupper Creek, 6 mi N of Tupper (PO); Map 2,/

Taylor (loc), BC: 56°10-120°42; on Peace R, 9 mi SE of Fort St John; Map 2.
Teslin, YT: 60°12-132°42; 90 mi ESE of Whitehorse; Map 1.
Tete Jaune (loc, BC: 52°58-119°25; on Fraser R, 41 mi SE of McBride; Map 2.
Thompson River, BC: 50°14-121°36; flows W & S to Fraser R, at Lytton; Map 1.
"Tillicum Creek" (now Atunatche Cr).

Tonasket, WA: 48°43-119°26; 180 mi E of Victoria, BC; Map 1.   / 2.
Trappers Creek, BC: 55°08-122°48; flows S to Misinchinka R, 14 mi NE of McLeod L; Map/
Tumbler Ridge, BC: 55°08-121°00; 40 mi SW of Kelly Lake; Map 2.
Tupper Creek, BC: 55°30-120°02; enters Swan L near Tupper PO; Map 2, 3.
*Tupper (PO), BC: 55°31-120°02; 15 mi S of Pouce Coupe; Map 2, 3.

Twidwell Bend (loc), BC:55°37-121°34; 16 mi SW of East Pine; Map 2.
Upper Canada (hist, 1791-1841) now Ontario.
Valleyview, Alta: 56°04-117°17; 60 mi E of Grande Prairie; Map 2.
Vanderhoof, BC: 54°01-124°01; on Nechako R 53 mi W of Prince George; Map 2.
Victoria, BC: 48°26-123°22; S end Vancouver Island; Map 1.

Wabi (loc), BC:55°43-121°24; 7 mi W of East Pine; Map 2
WAC Bennett Dam, BC:56°01-122°12; on Peace R, 11 mi W of Hudson Hope; Map 2.
Wainwright, Alta: 52°50-110°51; 118 mi SE of Edmonton; Map 1.   / Map 2.
Wanyandie Creek, Alta: 54°04-118°52; flows N to Smoky R, 75 mi S of Grande Prairie; /
*Wapiti River, BC, Alta: 55°08-118°18; flows E to Smoky R, E of Grande Prairie; Map 2.

Ware (loc), BC: 57°25-125°38; 190 mi N of McLeod L, on Finlay R; Map 1.
War Lake, BC: 54°51-123°17; on McLeod R, 16 mi SW of McLeod L PO; Map 2.
Wartenbe, Mount, 4003ft, BC: 55°39-121°23; 9 mi SW of East Pine; Map 2.
Watson Lake, YT: 60°04-128°42; 222 mi E of Whitehorse; Map 1.
Wembley, Alta: 55°10-119°08; 14 mi W of Grande Prairie; Map 2.

Wenatchee, WA: 47°25-120°19; 156 mi SE of Victoria, BC; Map 1.
West Road River, BC: 53°18-122°52; flows E to Fraser R 28 mi NW of Quesnel; Map 2.
Whitecourt, Alta: 54°08-115°41; 60 mi NW of Lac Ste Anne; Map 2.
Whitehorse, YT: 60°43-135°02; beyond NW BC; Map 1.
Whitelaw, Alta: 56°07-118°05; 70 mi NNE of Grande Prairie; Map 2.

Williams Creek, BC: 53°05-121°33; flows W to Willow R vic Barkerville; Map 2.
Williams Lake, BC: 52°08122°09; 61 mi S of Quesnel; Map 1.
Willow Creek, BC: 55°37-122°15; flows N to Pine R, 42 mi W of East Pine; Map 2.
Wolf Creek, BC: 55°27-122°43; flows N to Pine R, 5 mi NW of Pine Pass; Map 2, 6.
Wolverine Mountain, 6747ft, BC: 53°20-121°04; 39 mi W of McBride; Map 2.

Wolverine River, BC: 53°19-121°07; flows SW to Isaac L, 40 mi W of McBride; Map 2.
Yellowhead Lake, BC: 52°51-118°32; 19 mi W of Jasper; Map 2.
Yellowhead Pass, 3717ft, Alta, BC:52°54-118°28; 16 mi W of Jasper; Map 2.   /Map 1.
Yoho River (&Valley), BC: 51°26-116°25; flows S to Kicking Horse R, 100 mi W of Calgary;/

107: Kelly Lake, BC, July
1983. Gerry Andrews with
his friend Lective Camp-
bell. (GSA #7307)

FOOTNOTES

(References are identified by code to conserve space)

1. A49p139; A51p164
2. A23p337
3. A13
4. A13 Vol 2 p65 et seq
5. or "traineaux" as in A62
6. A25
7. A24 Vol XXX p167-8
8. A40p4
9. A23p299 et seq
10. A24 Vol XIII
11. A13 Vol I p72
12. A58
13. A16p133
14. A33p222
15. A5p505
16. B5
17. A41p367
18. Appendix 3 No 46
19. A2p146-7
20. Appendix 3 No 48
21. A44; A45; A46
22. A5p161-4, 168
23. A47p347, 353, 404
24. A47p31, 40
25. A47p180
26. A32p176
27. A32p698
28. A3p369
29. Appendix 3 No 46
30. = "ustivwan" or "ustise" in Cree
31. A32p21
32. A32p856
33. A32p261
34. A5p504
35. A3p222; A5p531
36. A6p204
37. A5p525
38. A5p504-5
39. Appendix 3 No 37
40. Appendix 3 No 8
41. Appendix 5
42. Appendix 3 No 48
43. Baptiste Besson? A6p257
44. A2p190-1
45. A8
46. A3p225, 334, 386
47. A7p125
48. A7p129; A54p132
49. A7p183
50. A32p11
51. A11p8
52. A5p551
53. BC Hist News Vol 7 No 1 p24
54. A32p194
55. A59 1875-6 p59
56. A32p353
57. A32p124
58. Named for Lt E.K. Colbourne, MC, BCLS, died of wounds, France, 1915
59. See BC Land Surveyor's "Roll of Honour, 1919"
60. A34p303
61. Appendix 3 No 43
62. A28p16-18
63. A24 Vol X pxxvii
64. A32p202-4
65. A47p68
66. A3p171-2, 348; A5p307
67. Dr. Sproule? see A3p105; A6p106
68. A5p143, 5
69. A32p 35-6
70. A5p542-3
71. A3p915; A6p239
72. A6p238
73. A2
74. A17p145-161
75. A17p154
76. A45p44; A46p30, 32, 39
77. A3p9
78. A5p276
79. A20p141
80. Appendix 3 No 24
81. A26
82. Appendix 3 No 19
83. A43p31
84. A43pH2, H63
85. A32p151
86. Appendix 3 No 42
87. C3
88. Appendix 3 No's 3, 18, 22 37
89. A43p293-5
90. A37
91. B3
92. B10
93. A44p51
94. Appendix 3 No 48
95. D4-9
96. D23-32
97. A5p504
98. see Appendix 4
99. A44, A45, A46
100. A32
101. A5, A6
102. A3p179-180
103. Appendix 3 No 1
104. A3p130
105. D10-22
106. A3p208; A5p90
107. A3p9-15; A5p217; A47p75
108. A43pH9
109. A50
110. B3
111. B12
112. C4
113. B10
114. A47p431
115. B12
116. B11
117. B8
118. A3
119. A3p225, 334, 386
120. A32p35-6
121. A5p504
122. A25
123. A30p2
124. A57
125. A30p3
126. A30p2
127. A53
128. A27
129. A22
130. A19
131. A29, A30, A31
132. A37
133. A1, A20, A60

BIBLIOGRAPHY & REFERENCES

(Frequently cited by number to save space)

A. PUBLICATIONS

1. Akrigg, G.P.V. & Helen B.; 1001 British Columbia Place Names, Vancouver, 1981.
2. Alberta-British Columbia Boundary Commission Report (Part III) & Atlas (Part III), Ottawa, 1925.
3. Along the Wapiti, Grande Prairie, 1981.
4. Andrews, G.S. "British Columbia's Air Survey Story", BC Historical News, Vol 7, No's 1, 2 & 3, 1973-74.
5. Beaverlodge to the Rockies, E.C. Stacey, Ed, Beaverlodge, 1974.
6. Supplement, E.C. Stacey, Ed, Beaverlodge, 1976.
7. Bowes, Gordon E., Ed, Peace River Chronicles, Vancouver, 1963.
8. BC Dept Education, Annual Reports, 1924-62.
9. BC Dept Lands, etc., Annual Reports, 1946-67.
10. BC Geographical Gazetteer, Victoria, 1930; Gazetteer of Canada (BC) Ottawa, 1953, 1956; Gazetteer of Canada (BC): Supplement, Ottawa, 1975.
11. BC Land Surveyors' Reports on Peace River & Cassiar Districts, BC Dept Lands, Victoria, 1929.
12. Canadian North-West: Pub No 9, Canada Archives, Ottawa, 1914.
13. Catlin, Geo, North American Indians, 2 vols, 1841, reprint Edinburgh, 1926.
14. Chinook Arch, Edmonton, 1967.
15. Dictionary of Canadian Biography, Vols. I, II, III, IV, V, IX, X, XI, Toronto (as cited).
16. Duchaussois, Pierre, OMI, Aux Glaces Polaires, Lyon, 1921.
17. Fleming, Sandford, Report on Surveys ... CPR ... to Jan 1877, Ottawa, 1877.
18. Fraser, Esther, The Canadian Rockies, Edmonton, 1969.
19. Hives, H.E., A Cree Grammar, Toronto, 1948.
20. Holmgren, E.J. & P.M., Over 2000 Place Names of Alberta, 3rd Ed, Saskatoon, 1976.
21. Hopwood, Victor G., David Thompson Travels ..., Toronto, 1971.
22. Horden, J., A Grammar of the Cree Language, London, 1904.
23. Howard, Joseph, Strange Empire, Toronto, 1974.
24. Hudson's Bay Record Society, Vols I to XXXIII (as cited).
25. Jenness, Diamond, Indians of Canada, 3rd Ed, Ottawa, 1955.
26. Kopas, C., Packhorses to the Pacific, Sidney, BC, 1976.
27. Lacombe, Albert, OMI, Dictionnaire de la Langue Cris, 2 vols, Montreal, 1874.

28. Lamb, W. Kaye, Ed, Simon Fraser ... 1806-1808, Toronto, 1960.
29. Logan, Robt A., DLS, "Notes on the Cree Language", Canadian Surveyor, Vol 8, No 3, January, 1941.
30. Logan, Robt. A., DLS, Cree Language Notes, Lake Charlotte, NS, 1958.
31. Logan, Robt.A., DLS, The Cree Language As It Appears to Me, Lake Charlotte, N.S., 1958.
32. Lure of the South Peace, Lillian York, Ed, Dawson Creek, 1981.
33. MacGregor, J.G., Land of Twelve-Foot Davis, 2nd Edn, Edmonton, 1952.
34. Mackenzie, Alexander (Sir), Voyages...1789, 1793... , London, 1801; reprint Toronto, 1927.
35. Mair, Charles, Through the Mackenzie Basin, 1899, Toronto, 1908.
36. Map: "Jasper Park — North Sheet" (Scale: 1/190,080); Ottawa, 1934.
37. McCusker, K.F., "All in a Day's Work", Canadian Surveyor, Vol 3, No 5, July, 1929.
38. Morice, A.G., OMI, Dictionnaire Historique des Canadiens et des Metis français de l'Ouest, Winnipeg, 1912.
39. Native Trees of Canada, 4th Edn (Bul 61), Ottawa, 1949.
40. Osler, E.B., ... Louis Riel, Toronto, 1961.
41. Palliser Papers, Irene M. Spry, Ed, Toronto, 1968.
42. Patterson, A.B. Smoky River to Grande Prairie, 1978.
43. Peacemakers of the North Peace, Fort St John, 1973.
44. Petro-Canada, Monkman Pass & Trail, Michael Robinson, Ed, Calgary, 1982.
45. Petro-Canada, Monkman Coal Project ..., Michael Robinson, Ed, Calgary, 1982.
46. Petro-Canada, Monkman Coal Project ..., Michael Robinson, Ed, Calgary, 1983.
47. Pioneer Roundup, Hythe, Alta, 1972.
48. Ross, Eric, Beyond the River and the Bay, reprint, Toronto, 1973.
49. Sealey, D.B. & Lussier, A.S., The Metis ..., 5th printing, Winnipeg, 1981.
50. Sprague, D.N. & Frye, R.P. Genealogy ... First Metis Nation, Winnipeg, 1983.
51. Stanley, G.F.G., Louis Riel, Toronto, 1972.
52. Voters' Lists, British Columbia: Swan Lake, 1920; Kelly Lake, 1924, 1928, 1933.
53. Watkins, E.A., Dictionary of the Cree Language, London, 1865, Toronto, 1938.
54. Winslow-Spragge, Lois, ... George Mercer Dawson ..., 1962.
55. The Columbia Encyclopedia, 2nd Edn, New York, 1950.
56. Colombo, J.R., Colombo's Canadian References, Toronto, 1976.

57. The Kelsey Papers, Public Archives of Canada, Ottawa, 1929.
58. Parsons, John E., West on the 49th Parallel, New York, 1963.
59. Geological Survey of Canada, Annual Reports (as cited).
60. Coutts, R.C., Yukon Places & Names, Sidney, BC, 1980.
61. MacEwan, Grant, Metis Makers of History, Saskatoon, 1981.
62. Parkman, Francis, The Oregon Trail, 1849.
63. Taylor, R. Leslie, The Native Link, Victoria, 1984.

B. MANUSCRIPT MATERIAL (Selected items are in Appendix 3):

1. Barrow, A.R.M., BCLS Field Notes, 1921 Surveyor General's Office, Victoria, BC.
2. "Bennett, John N.P., Inquest into Death of", Prince George, BC, 1 June, 1931, PABC, Victoria.
3. Calverley Archives: "History is Where You Stand", Public Library, Dawson Creek, BC. (Incl five transcribed tape interviews, 1973, with Isidore Gladu and Mary Gladu at Kelly Lake, and Willie Hamelin at Grouard, Alta).
4. Calverley, Mrs. Dorthea H., Dawson Creek, BC – personal correspondence.
5. Flyingshot Lake Settlement: Petition for Survey, 1906 & Field Notes by J.B. Saint Cyr, DLS, 1907. From Land Survey Branch, Edmonton.
6. Gray, Jarvis: Correspondence, Edmonton, 1979.
7. Hamelin (Hambler, Emmila), George: Correspondence, 1925 et seq.
8. Irwin, Ray: Correspondence, Kelly Lake, 1982.
9. Lac Ste Anne Settlement – Survey Notes by P.R.A. Belanger, DLS, 1890. From Land Survey Branch, Edmonton.
10. Robinson, Michael: Correspondence, notes, etc, Calgary, 1981 et seq.
11. Semans, Jules H. & Lucille: Correspondence, Kelly Lake, 1953 et seq.
12. Young, J.S.: Correspondence Kelly Lake, Rose Prairie, 1925 et seq.

C. VERBAL INTERVIEWS

1. Beck, Mrs. Lucille (formerly Mrs. Jules H. Semans), Beaverlodge, 1981, 1983.
2. Belcourt, Francis, Kelly Lake, 1982.
3. Calverley, Mrs Dorthea H., Dawson Creek, 1981, 1982, 1983.
4. Campbell, Alfred & Virginia, Kelly Lake, 1981 et seq.
5. Campbell, Lective & Family, Kelly Lake, 1978, 1983.
6. Cornock: Denny, Tupper & Kelly Lake, 1953; Bruce & Joan, Tupper, 1983.

7. Dumont, Mrs Augustus (Odila, nee Marion), Sidney, BC, 1982.
8. Gladu, Mrs Isidore (Annie, nee Thomas), Kelly Lake, 1981 et seq.
9. Gladu: Billy & Mrs. (Mary, nee Belcourt), Kelly Lake, 1981 et seq.
10. Gladu, Isidore, Kelly Lake, 1973.
11. Gray, David, Dawson Creek, 1978; Kelly Lake, 1981 et seq.
12. Hamelin (Hambler): George & Mabel, Dawson Creek, 1978, 1981, 1982, 1983.
13. McFarlane: N. Douglas & Doris, Beaverlodge, 1983.
14. McNaught, Euphemia & (sister) Mrs. Isabel Perry, vic Beaverlodge, 1983.
15. Nawican Friendship Centre, Dawson Creek, 1982, 1983.
16. Taylor Family: Mrs. Mary, Iris & Marie Scholz, Tupper, 1960; Mrs. Mary, Dawson Creek, 1967; Leona (Mrs. Beatty), Bessie (Mrs. N. Albert), Jerry Taylor, Iris & Hans Scholz, Dawson Creek & vic Tupper 1982, 1983.
17. Truax: Albert & Madelon, vic Beaverlodge, 1982.
18. Young, Jim & Family, Rose Prairie, 1947 et seq.
19. Personal knowledge, G.S. Andrews.

D. CEMETERIES (Selected names):

Halcourt (1983)
1. Geo J. Beadle 1887-1957
2. Sarah E Beadle 1899-1931
3. Geo Samuel Cox White
   18 August 1892 -
   29 January, 1980

Kelly Lake (1925, 1981, 1983)
(most identities now illegible)
4. Albert Belcourt 1930-1980
5. Marie Calliou c1820-1925
6. Delphine Hamelin c1914-1980
7. Joe Hamelin 1906-1980
8. Johnny Supernat ? - 1980
9. Randy Whitford c1948-?

Pipestone Creek (1983)
10. Alice Chatelaine
11. Francois Chatelaine
12. Louis Chatelaine
13. Pete Chatelaine
14. Henry Kenny
15. Baptiste Kenny
16. Henry Stoney
17. Marie Stoney

Pipestone Creek (cont)
"Children"
18. Chatelaine
19. Kenny
20. Stoney
21. White
22. Wilson

Rio Grande (1981) (many identities now illegible)
23. Archie Belcourt 1924-1945
24. Edward Chas Belcourt 1957-1974
25. Roger Geo Belcourt 1960-1974
26. Adam Calliou 1854-1948
27. Veronique Calliou 1863-1956
28. Dorothy Letendre 1923-1941
29. Josie Letendre 1915-1945
30. Noel Letendre 1915-1945
31. James Finn 30 November, 1931
32. William Finn 1872-1931

R.I.P.

ABBREVIATIONS

(Many are to save space in Appendix 4: Genealogies)

ac	=	acre(s)	E	=	East
Admin	=	administration	Ed	=	Edited, Edition, Editor(s)
AL	=	Alaska	Ed	=	Edmonton, Alta & vic
ALS	=	Alberta Land Surveyor	ED & BC =		Ed, Dunvegan & BC Ry
Alta	=	Alberta (province)			(now NAR)
An	=	Acton, Ont	eg	=	exempli gratia (for example)
Ap	=	Appendix	Eliz	=	Elizabeth
app	=	approximate(ly)	et al	=	and others
Assoc	=	Association	etc	=	et cetera, & so forth
av	=	average	et seq	=	et sequential, following
b	=	born	ex	=	former (ly); from; out of
B	=	Belcourt (family)	f	=	father (of)
Ba	=	Batoche, Sask	F	=	Fahrenheit
BC	=	British Columbia (province)	Fed	=	Federal (gov't)
BCHQ	=	BC Hist Quarterly	FJ	=	Fort St James, BC & vic
BCLS	=	BC Land Surveyor	FL	=	Flyingshot Lake, BC & vic
BCR	=	BC Railway	FN	=	Fort Nelson, BC & vic
Bdy	=	Boundary	For	=	Forestry
biog	=	biographical, biography	fr	=	from
BL	=	Beaverlodge, Alta & vic	FRGS	=	Fellow, Royal Geographical Society
Bn	=	Bloomington, IL	FSJ	=	Fort St John, BC & vic
br	=	branch	G	=	Gladu (family)
bro(s)	=	brother(s)	G	=	Gauthier (family)
Bul	=	Bulletin	Ḡeo	=	George
By	=	Burnaby, BC & vic	Geog	=	Geographic(al)
c	=	circa, about, app	Gf	=	Goodfare, Alta & vic
C	=	Calliou (family)	GP	=	Grande Prairie, Alta & vic
C̲	=	Campbell (family)	Gr	=	Grouard, Alta & vic
C̄A	=	California (state)	GSA	=	GS Andrews
Capt	=	Captain	GTP	=	Grand Trunk Pacific (Ry)
Cda	=	Canada	Gt	=	Georgetown, Ont
Cdn	=	Canadian	Gu	=	Guelph, Ont
CE	=	Canada East (now PQ)	H	=	Hamelin (family)
CE	=	Civil Engineer	HBC	=	Hudson's Bay Company
Cg	=	Caughnawaga, PQ & vic	hist	=	history, historical
CW	=	Canada West (now Ont)	HL	=	Horse Lake, Alta & vic
ch	=	chapter, church	Hon	=	(the) Honorable, Honorary
Chron	=	Chronicle	hus	=	husband (of)
CIS	=	Cdn Inst Surveying	Hy	=	Hythe, Alta & vic
CNR	=	Cdn Nat Ry	ID	=	Idaho (state), Identity No (see A50)
Co	=	Company	IL	=	Illinois (state)
Com'n	=	Commission	IN	=	Indiana (state)
Conf	=	conference	Insp	=	Inspector
Const	=	Constable	Inst	=	Institute
Cpl	=	Corporal	Int	=	International
Cr	=	Creek	Intr	=	Introduction
Cy	=	Calgary, Alta & vic	IR	=	Indian Reserve
Cz	=	Czechoslovakia	Ir	=	Ireland
d	=	daughter	Jas	=	James
DC	=	Dawson Creek, BC & vic	J-B	=	Jean-Baptiste
DCB	=	Dictionary Cdn Biog (A15)	Jos	=	Joseph
De	=	Demmitt, Alta & vic	Jour	=	Journal
Dept	=	Department	Jr	=	Junior
desc	=	descendant(s)	juv	=	juvenile
Dist	=	District (BC Land Act)	KL	=	Kelly Lake, BC & vic
div	=	division, divorce(d)	L	=	Lake, left
DL	=	Dist Lot (BC Land Act)	L	=	Letendre (family)
DLS	=	Dom Land Surveyor, System	L	=	L'Hirondelle (family)
Dn	=	Dublin, Ireland	L̄at	=	Latitude
Dom	=	Dominion	LC	=	Lower Canada (later PQ)

LD	=	Land Dist (BC Land Act)	Ref	=	Reference(s)
Lieut	=	Lieutenant	Res	=	Reservation (Indian), Resources
LL	=	Lake Lenore, Sask	RG	=	Rio Grande, Alta & vic
LLB	=	Lac la Biche, Alta & vic	Ro	=	Rolla, BC & vic
Ln	=	London, England	Robt	=	Robert
loc	=	location, locality	RP	=	Rose Prairie, BC & vic
Long	=	Longitude	RPF	=	Registered Professional Forester
LS	=	Lake Saskatoon, Alta & vic	Ry	=	Railway
LS	=	Land Surveyor	S	=	Section (DLS System)
LSA	=	Lac Ste Anne, Alta & vic	s	=	son(s)
m	=	married (to), mother (of)	S	=	South
Man	=	Manitoba (province)	S	=	St Arnaud (family)
Matric	=	Matriculation	SA	=	St Albert, Alta & vic
MB	=	McBride, BC & vic	Sa	=	Sarnia, Ont & vic
MBE	=	Member, Order of the British Empire	Sask	=	Saskatchewan (province)
MC	=	Military Cross (decoration)	Sch	=	School
Mgr	=	Manager	SD	=	School District
MI	=	Michigan (state)	SE	=	Southeast
MN	=	Minnesota (state)	Sec'y	=	Secretary
Mon	=	Monument (marker)	set	=	settler(s) settlement(s)
ms	=	manuscript	sic	=	as originally written
MT	=	Montana (state)	SL	=	Sturgeon Lake, Alta
Mt	=	Mount, Mountain(s)	Soc	=	Society
Mv	=	Millerville, MN	sp	=	spelling
N	=	North	spec	=	speculative
NAR	=	Northern Alberta Ry	Sr	=	Senior
Nat	=	National	Sr	=	Spirit River, Alta & Vic
NB	=	New Brunswick (province)	SSB	=	Soldiers Settlement Board
Nc	=	Newcastle, PN	sta	=	station
ND	=	North Dakota (state)	St(e)	=	Saint(e), Street
NE	=	Northeast	Supt	=	Superintendent
NF	=	New France (later PQ)	Svy(or)	=	Survey(or)
No	=	Number	SW	=	Southwest
nr	=	near	T	=	Thomas (family)
NS	=	Nova Scotia (province)	T	=	Taylor (family)
NTS	=	Nat Topo System (Series) Maps	Ta	=	Tacoma, WA & vic
NW	=	Northwest	Tab	=	Table, Tabulation
NWCo	=	North West Company	TC	=	Tate Creek, BC & vic
		(1783-1821)	Thos	=	Thomas
NWT	=	NW Territories	Topo	=	Topographic
obit	=	obituary	Tp	=	Township (DLS System)
obs	=	obsolescent, obsolete	Tr	=	Taylor, BC & vic
OLS	=	Ontario Land Surveyor	Tu	=	Tupper, BC & vic
OMI	=	Order Mary Immaculate	TX	=	Texas (state)
On	=	Onoway, Alta & vic	UBC	=	University of BC
Ont	=	Ontario (province)	UC	=	Upper Canada (now Ontario)
OR	=	Oregon (state)	U of A	=	University of Alberta
p(p)	=	page(s)	U of T	=	University of Toronto
PABC	=	Prov Archives of BC	US, USA	=	United States of America
PC	=	Pouce Coupe, BC & vic	vic	=	vicinity, near
P Eng	=	Professional Engineer	viz	=	videlicet, namely
PG	=	Prince George, BC & vic	vol	=	volume(s)
PGE	=	Pacific Great Eastern (Ry)	Vr	=	Vancouver, BC & vic
Pk	=	Peak (mountain)	W	=	West
PN	=	Pennsylvania (state)	WA	=	Washington (state)
PO	=	Post Office	Wh	=	Whitehorse, YT & vic
PQ	=	Province of Quebec	WI	=	Wisconsin (state)
PR	=	Peace River, Alta (town)	Wm	=	William
PRB	=	Peace River Block (c1907-30)	Wpg	=	Winnipeg, Man & vic
Prof	=	Professional, Professor	Ww	=	Whitelaw, Alta
Prov	=	Province, Provincial	Xg	=	Crossing (river, etc.)
Pub	=	Publication, Published	Y	=	Young (family)
PWD	=	Public Works Dept	YMCA	=	Young Men's Christian Assoc
Que	=	Quebec (province)	YT	=	Yukon Territory
qv	=	quod vide (which see)	+	=	and later, married (to),
R	=	Range (in DLS System)			plus, with
R	=	Right, River	?	=	unknown, uncertain; possibly
Rd	=	Road, Rochdale, England	*	=	conjecture; footnote

ACKNOWLEDGEMENTS

Grateful thanks are directed to:

My family and friends for abject neglect during many months. My wife has cheerfully excused me of all domestic chores and has tactfully tried to keep me clean, tidy, overfed and spiritually healthy. She has served as guinea-pig for segments of the manuscript. I tell her that if she understands, anybody can! Her advice certainly has been valid.

Friends who patiently read preliminary manuscripts with warm encouragement. Mrs. Madge Hamilton surely smartened up my English and editorial discipline, but with great kindness!

Individuals and agencies responsible for the "Bibliography and References". Mrs. Dorthea Calverley arranged access to her own archives, "History is Where You Stand", and directed me to other valuable material. Mike Robinson reactivated serious embrace of my theme. He won warm cooperation at Kelly Lake and generously shared his notes, photos and reports. Through his good offices, just prior to press time, the enigmatic message in Cree Syllabics taken on the Smoky River, 1925, was translated by Mr. Adolphus Ghostkeeper, age 92, of Paddle Prairie, Alta, to whom I and no doubt others are grateful.

Old and new friends encountered on my field trips described in Chapter 5. Their hospitality has been traditional and their response to tiresome queries has been generous. This includes families identified in the Genealogies (Appendix 4).

Robert F. Baker, ALS, at Edmonton, who supplied the historic survey data for Lac Ste Anne and Flyingshot Lake settlements. At the Provincial Archives of BC, Fran Gundry who reviewed the manuscript and Peter Westoby who made superb prints from my ancient Kelly Lake negatives. Former colleagues in the Environment Ministry who supplied air photos, maps and other data with cheerful promptness. Don Pearson of the Toponymy Division who processed several names commemorating early Kelly Lake and related pioneers which he selected from the manuscript. The cartographic skill of Sam Vanderjagt is evident in the better maps.

Dr. W. Kaye Lamb, OC, FRSC, the eminent historian and a friend of long standing, was the ideal choice for the "Foreword". His response speaks for itself. It was a stroke of rare good fortune that two renowned artists, Elizabeth Goward and Euphemia McNaught, generously contributed to the decor of front and back covers. Another good friend, Gray Campbell shared his vast knowledge in the publishing field. John Stuart was generous with editing and agreed to help with marketing.

Finally, tribute is certainly due those whose art, skills, technology and diligence have transformed my untidy manuscript into a product of which all concerned may be gratified. This vital service has centred around Mrs. Judy Brownoff, Effective Information Processing Ltd, and Mr. John Young of Amity Press, with whom it has been a pleasure to work.

108: Tumbler Ridge, BC, July 1983. (GSA #7309)

CORRIGENDA

The following have been detected too late to remedy. The author would appreciate advice of others.

Map 3: for Demmit read Demmitt/p 45 line 11: for just read yust/ p 56 line 9: for Flynn's read Fynn's/p 70 line 9: for east Pine read East Pine/p 110 line 20: for Marceline read Madeline/p 141 Annie Belcourt attended 1924-25, not 1923-24/p 153 line 27: for supples read supplies/p 162 line 18: after led over deleted to/ p 164 and Photo 51: for Diggins read Diggings/p 169: for Snaring River read Snake Indian River/p 190 line 13: for Petersen's read Peterson's/p 191 line 32: for McKusker read McCusker/p 212 line 24: for LeGlace read LaGlace/p 213 line 4: for Photo 32 read Photo 33/p 278 line 3: for discrete read discreet/pp 312, 315, 316, 323: AL should read AK.

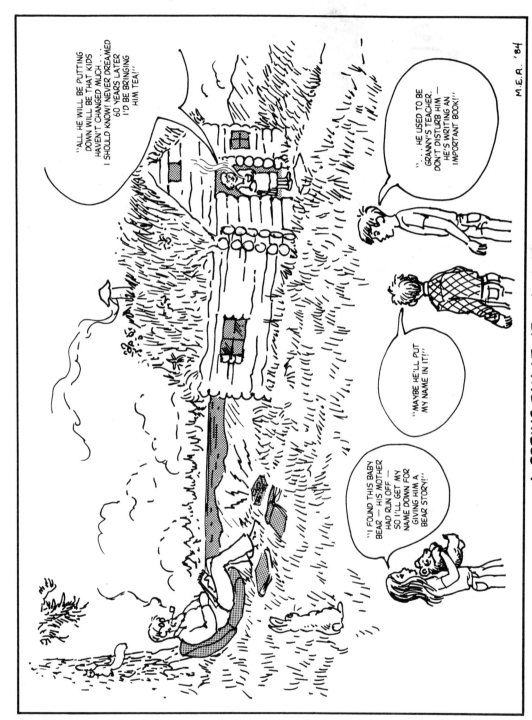

A SPRING DAY AT KELLY LAKE

48,010

SMEDLEY ANDREWS
M.   BScF, P Eng, RPF, BCLS

Born: Winnipeg, Manitoba,   1903.

Educated: Winnipeg, Calg   ncouver, Toronto, Oxford, Dresden (1910-1934).

Messenger, office boy, pap   rier, farm and ranch hand, waiter, bullcook, horse-
    wrangler, packer, fron'   schoolmaster, timber cruiser, deck-hand (1916-1933).

Officer i/c surveys of F   ead, Tranquille, Niskonlith and Shuswap provincial
    forests, British Columbi   1930-1932).

Commissioned in the Royal   ngineers and the Royal Canadian Engineers (1940-1946).

Pioneered airphoto intellig   e in War and in Peace (1931-1973).

Surveyor General and D   or Surveys & Mapping for British Columbia (1951-1968).
    Boundaries Commission.   (1952-1968). Member Fraser River Board (1955-1964).

President Canadian Inst of   urveying 1952 and of Com IV, Int Soc of Photogram-
    metry, Washington 1952, R me 1954 and Stockholm 1956.

Survey consultant Mekong River, Southeast Asia, 1958.

Guest professor Universidade Federal da Paraiba, Escola Politecnica, Campina Grande,
    Brazil 1972-1973.

Hon President BC Hist Federation 1983-1986.

Married Jean E. Bergtholdt from California 1938; prewar daughter Mary, a librarian;
    postwar daughter Kristan, a biologist.

Selected publications by the author:

"Air Survey and Forestry Developments in Germany" For Chron, June 1934.

"Tree Heights from Air Photographs" Assoc Prof Engineers, BC, 1936.

"Alaska Highway Survey in British Columbia" Geog Jour Vol C No 1, July 1942.

"Wave Velocity Soundings from Air Photos (for Normandy Landings)" Cdn Army
    Overseas Oct 1944.

"Survey & Mapping in Various War Theatres" GSGS, Dept Nat Defence, Ottawa 1946.

"Air Survey & Photogrammetry in British Columbia" Photogrammetric Engineering Mar
    1948.

"The Land Surveying Profession in BC" BCLS, AGM, 1955.

"Surveys & Mapping, Lower Mekong River," Ottawa 1958.

"British Columbia's Major River Basins" 14 BC Nat Res Conf, 1962.

"Administration of Surveys & Mapping in Canada" Ottawa, 1970.

"Sir Joseph William Trutch," Victoria, 1972.

"British Columbia's Air Survey Story" BC Hist News, Vol 7, 1973-74.

"East Kootenays' Survey History" BC Hist News, Vol 8 #2, 1974.

"BC Land Surveyors - Cumulative Nominal Roll", Victoria 1978.

"The Bell-Irving Land Surveyors in British Columbia" BC Hist News, Vol 12, No 4,
    1979.

"Impressions of A.G. Morice, OMI" BC Hist News, Vol 14, No 4, 1982.